VULTURES
OF THE VOID

THE LEGACY

CW01496696

OTHER BOOKS BY PHILIP J. HARBOTTLE

Novels (all posthumous collaborations with John Russell Fearn)
OUTLAW'S REVENGE (as Conrad G. Holt)
DYNAMITE'S DAUGHTER
DEAD MAN'S LEGACY
VALLEY SHADOW (as Jack R. Phillips)
THE AVENGING RANGER (as Conrad G. Holt)
UNDERCOVER MARSHAL (as Russell James)
PALEFACE KILLER
ARIZONA LAW (as Conrad G. Holt)
SNAKE VENGEANCE
MEREDITH'S JUSTICE
MEREDITH'S GOLD
MEREDITH'S TREASURE
CHAMELEON PLANET

Non-Fiction
THE MULTI-MAN
VULTURES OF THE VOID
BRITISH SF PAPERBACKS AND MAGAZINES (1949-1956) (with Stephen Holland)
THE TALL ADVENTURER (with Sean Wallace)

Books edited by Philip Harbottle
THE BEST OF E. E. 'DOC' SMITH
THE BEST OF SYDNEY J. BOUNDS Volume 1 and 2
THE BEST OF JOHN RUSSELL FEARN Volume 1 and 2
THE BEST OF PHILIP E. HIGH
A STEP TO THE STARS
LIQUID DEATH AND OTHER STORIES
MIRROR OF THE NIGHT
FANTASY QUARTERLY
FANTASY ADVENTURES Volumes 1 through 13
THE COMPLETE ADVENTURES OF
THE GOLDEN AMAZON Volumes 1 through 3
THE GOLDEN AMAZON OF VENUS
SCIENTIFIC DETECTIVE STORIES OF JOHN RUSSELL FEARN
THE STAR WEEKLY THRILLERS OF JOHN RUSSELL FEARN
A CASE FOR BRUTUS LLOYD
THE HAUNTED GALLERY
SPIDER MORGAN'S SECRET
EXPERIMENT IN MURDER
MOTIVE FOR MURDER
BURY THE HATCHET
DEPARTMENT OF SPOOKS
THE WAGER

Books edited by Philip Harbottle and Sean Wallace
FANTASY ANNUAL Volumes 1 through 5

VULTURES
OF THE VOID

THE LEGACY

PHILIP J. HARBOTTLE

COSMOS BOOKS

VULTURES OF THE VOID

Copyright © 2011 by Philip J. Harbottle.
Cover art by David A. Hardy.
Cover design by Garry Nurrish.

Cosmos Books
www.cosmos-books.com

Publisher's Note: No portion of this book may be reproduced by any means, mechanical, electronic, or otherwise, without first obtaining the permission of the copyright holder.

For more information, contact Cosmos Books.

ISBN: 978-1-60701-149-1

TABLE OF CONTENTS

DEDICATION

For my daughter, Claire Jane King, and my grandchildren
Eleanor Rose King and Arthur Philip King

Also in memoriam for: Maureen

ACKNOWLEDGMENTS

The author wishes to thank the many writers, editors, friends, and correspondents who have furnished help and encouragement together with information and confirmation of many of the literary and biographical facts presented in this volume.

Especial thanks are due to my late wife Maureen, and my parents, Agnes and James Harbottle—sadly all now gone, but never forgotten. Thanks also to the late Sydney J. Bounds, John Carnell, G. Ken Chapman, A. Vincent Clarke, Ian Dick, Carrie and John Russell Fearn, Walter Gillings, John Glasby, Ron Graham, Philip E. High, Nini Japp, Leslie J. Johnson, Gordon Landsborough, Norman Lazenby, Rick Minter, Ken Slater, Joseph Storm, E. C. Tubb, Ron Turner and Iris Weigh, and to Tony Glynn, Lee Harding, Matt Japp, John Lawrence, Gary Lovisi, Derek Thomson, Morgan Wallace, Sean Wallace, David Ward, Peter Weston—and to them, and to dozens of others (simply too many to list) my sincere thanks:

Unless otherwise stated, all quotations and memoirs used in this book are taken from personal letters, or recorded and written interviews undertaken by myself with the principals during their lifetimes, and all books and magazines described and dated are from the collection of the author.

The following reference books were also consulted:

Ashley, Michael: *A Complete Index and Annotated Commentary to the John Spencer Fantasy Publications, 1950-1966*, Wallsend: Cosmos Literary Agency, 1979.

Ashley, Michael: *The History of the Science Fiction Magazine*, 4 volumes, London: New English Library, 1974-1978.

Gillings, Walter: *Science Fantasy Review,* Gillings, Ilford, 1947-1949

Stone, Graham: *Index to the British Science Fiction Magazines,* 5 volumes, Canberra: Australian SF Association, 1968-1971,

Tuck, Donald H.: *The Encyclopaedia of Science Fiction and Fantasy,* 3 volumes: Chicago: Advent, 1974-1982.

Whitaker's Cumulative Book List (annual compilations). London, Whitaker, 1947-1955.

INTRODUCTION: MUSHROOM LEGACIES

That there are a wealth of collectable British generic science fiction books and magazines from the decade following the Second World War is a demonstrable fact, with the choicest examples now selling for hundreds of pounds from dealers or on eBay, and even thousands of pounds at auction, as witness Sotherby's in New York sale of *Creature From the Black Lagoon* by Vargo Statten (John Russell Fearn). And yet their history is something that has frequently been glossed over in historical texts in favour of more 'literate' SF (or something that will shed a better light on science fiction). Nevertheless, it remains a fact that in this decade British science fiction hit an all-time low in academic esteem, while sales of the books produced a sudden 'boom' period. Why this happened is the main subject of this book—the product of a lifetime's research.

An earlier, very much shorter version (less than a third) of this book was published as *Vultures of the Void* in 1992 by Borgo Press, along with a companion bibliographic volume, *British Science Fiction Paperbacks and Magazines 1949-1956*. And whilst there have been a few books by others since, somewhat related, they had a different focus that did not greatly *add* to a proper understanding and appreciation of this intriguing period in British science fiction history.

More recently, however, an admirably detailed and authoritative study of the British science fiction magazines in the decade following the Second World War *has* appeared—Mike Ashley's landmark study of the history of *all* science fiction magazines worldwide from 1950 to 1970, *Transformations* (Liverpool University Press, 2005). This volume, (and the earlier and later titles in the series) is thoroughly recommended to anyone interested in magazine science fiction history.

But I still feel that the SF *book* publishing side has not yet been properly addressed, so now—having bought back from Borgo the copyrights to both earlier books—I feel the time is right to present this new and greatly expanded version of my earlier and ongoing researches, including coverage of the generic hardcover titles that briefly flourished alongside the paperbacks. *Vultures of the Void: The Legacy* also deals with related shaping events before and after the notorious postwar 'mushroom-period', in particular their legacy for myself and some of the authors.

—Philip Harbottle.
Wallsend,
Tyne and Wear, England
2011

FOREWORD:
A PERSONAL VIEW

by E. C. Tubb

Looking back, none of us knew it at the time, but we were on the threshold of something that grew like a weed in the garden. In the 1930s, SF was restricted to a few, by way of imported American magazines. The war came, fans got scattered, and when they got back together, they had a Great Dream. "Let's produce our own SF magazine, let's get a British magazine going." But it wasn't easy to do this. First you had to find a lot of money!

The breakthrough came when, Britain being starved of magazines because of the paper shortage, business restrictions started to be lifted, and your wide boys got in on the act. The pocket book—the paperback—was born. Now it wasn't born in the sense of it never having been known before, but it took off after the war. People were eager to make money, printers wanted to print, publishers wanted to publish, shops wanted to sell. But there was a sudden dearth of writers who could produce all this stuff. The only real source for science fiction writing was science fiction fandom, because they knew it all, didn't they? They were steeped in the background. So there was a scurrying round by publishers wanting people who could write this stuff.

Some people could; John Russell Fearn, for example, was a past master. Others, who were established writers. A lot of new writers came in on the wave, myself amongst them. And what had been a hobby became a business. I'm not saying that was a good thing, but it happened.

And it just grew; publishers flowered, they proliferated. Scion, Panther, Curtis Warren, Paladin, Milestone . . . They were all there. Most of them (at least initially) paid low rates. So in order to survive you had to be prolific. Turning out work quickly meant of course that some of it was poor quality. But one quality they did have was an enthusiasm—a zest. I mean, 90% of all writing is poor, even today's writing is poor. But at least then there was more excuse for it.

The publishers set certain limits; the story was so long, you were paid so much for it, and let's go to town! And this kind of publishing expanded and grew, until the collapse came, with the scandal of Hank Janson and sado-masochistic detective stories.

For fear of being prosecuted for selling obscene material, the sellers simply refused to accept anything from these publishers. So your gangsters and your SF and westerns wouldn't sell: end of boom!

And that hit me very hard at the time, because I'd just bought a house. I was left with a mortgage and no job and no publishers, which meant I had to scurry around like the proverbial blue-arsed fly to get a job, and keep the wolf from the door. So that's what happened to me, and to others.

But I have happy memories of that boom: of the exuberance of it. I was a chap who was asked by publishing houses to produce books—or sometimes I went to them. They'd tell me that they'd pay so much, and some of them would offer a little more than the other chap. So you sat down, and did whatever you did as quickly as you could. Now, because publishers were nasty, and grasping and mean (they still are!) the advent of the house name came in. If someone became very popular, the publisher owned the house name, and that's where the nom de plumes started.

With Curtis Warren you were 'King Lang', you were 'Karl Marx' or whatever—half a dozen authors all using the same name! These bylines were distinct from the nom de plume you deliberately chose because you had two stories in one issue of the magazine, so in that case you became 'Charles Grey' or somebody else. But the novels started that way, and then of course by the laws of the market place, you became that publisher's author, until somebody else wanted to use you and invented a different name. It became a kind of merry-go-round.

More importantly though, whilst you learned the trade, you learned it in the worst possible way, and some authors will back me up on this. You learned to write in a certain way: it was fast, it was interesting, it was entertaining. It had to be, because that audience wanted that style of writing. No deep introspection, no social criticism, no political things—it was bang, bang, and where's the next piece of action? A lot of the logic went out of the window.

I was fortunate in having been well grounded in science fiction. I knew about space . . . I knew you couldn't breathe on the moon without a helmet. So I had an edge—I was up on the rest of the crowd. I knew how a rocket worked. I knew there was a little bit of a difference between a solar system, and an intergalactic system. This is something that even a lot of modern writers, such as the writers of *Star Trek*, still haven't learned. To them, it's not another planet, it's another galaxy, it's another dimension, another universe. Christ knows where they come from, but they do. So I had an edge over a lot of people in the market. I knew my stuff, so I became quite popular in the science fiction pocket book field, writing for Milestone, Scion, and others. I sort of proliferated, and that was it—until the boom busted. And that's another story.

Publishers wouldn't take anything for fear of prosecution, frightened that in the pile there was some sado-masochistic stuff. Tame by our present day standards, but it was there. So the bubble burst. The cycle of trust, of credit, borrowing, paying for the last one after you'd done the six . . . it was like a bank collapsing. There was a hell of a flap, which was rather disastrous for authors in on the scheme at the time.

Looking back on my early days now, I can see that in the beginning, I was the pawn of the publisher. They said they would give you X pounds, and you took it or you left it.

There was an amusing incident about the naivety of a young would-be author, namely me! I used to go to a pub with other writers and fans, to the *White Horse* in London. One chap there, Dave Griffiths, told me: "Don't worry, boy, I'm a reader for Curtis Warren. You just let me have your novel. I'll put it in under my own name, they're bound to take it, and I'll pay you." Well, we've all been this route, haven't we? I actually got paid for the first one—still waiting for the other two!

That should have warned me! So that's where the old King Lang and Gill Hunt came in—that's what went on at that time. You couldn't trust anyone! When publishers accepted a manuscript, they said here's your cheque—nothing else! When you asked about rights, they said they'd just bought the story. "Don't worry about that, boy, don't worry about that." So, if you wanted the money you took the terms. And by the time you'd thought about it, the mss was usually in print anyway.

But it wasn't all that bad, in some ways. For my early novels to Curtis Warren the rate was 27 pounds 10 shillings—so Curtis Warren still owe me 55 pounds for two novels! But in 1951 the average wage was only 7 pounds a week. And by 1953, I'd progressed to the magnificent sum of 90 pounds a month, by writing one for Scion and one for Milestone, at 45 pounds a book—their upper rates. So I quit work and decided to become a full-time writer. I succumbed to this glittering prize, this lure of money! 90 pounds a month then, if you take inflation into account, is worth a lot more than the average monthly wage nowadays, as it was then.

But to earn this money I had to write two novels a month, and this didn't give you a great deal of time to be too specific. So you sat down at the typewriter:

'She screamed as a hand ripped her dress.' You've got a beginning, so you go on. Or: 'He fell back, one hand clamped to his eye', or the classical one: 'the flare gun thundered its song of doom', and you were off, weren't you? That's all the writer in those days needed to know, how to get the hell off the ground.

You never worked out a plot. Characters? You had your characters. Three or four—don't go mad. There was a gorgeous blonde, and a gorgeous brunette; a lean, tough hero, a big engineer, and an old scientist. I well remember that at one time I had two books out with the hero called Brett, the same bloody name! Inevitably, there was a certain amount of recycling ideas. *The Living World* and *The Metal Eater* were two books using the same plot. And sometimes, the publishers would give you ideas.

I well remember *Planetoid Disposals Ltd.* I was told: 'We want a faster than light drive, but we want another one, used by different groups. And the hero has to die, but at the same time survive!' And I did it, and earned my 45 pounds!

Before then, I had been working, and the writing was a nice little bonus. This was England in 1950. Things were rough at that time. I was living in a flat with my wife and kid. We lived in one room. Now, all these people who whine and beat their gums about the underprivileged living in tough housing . . . they don't know what they're talking about. When I was in America and saw the slave quarters, they lived a bloody sight better than I did, and that's true! One room, shared toilet, all those things the people nowadays scream about. So I'd made up my mind to make the classical sacrifice: I was going to Australia on the ten pounds passage! In those days you could do it, if you had a bit of labouring skill, which I had. So I was to help build a tram shed. Sign up for six months on the tram shed construction, and then once out there, I'd send for the wife and child. That was my plan.

Just when I was all ready to go (there was no future for me in England. I mean, what the hell, they talk about the classless society and the land of opportunity and all that—but we won't go into that!) I sold a short story. 'No Short Cuts', to Ted Carnell, 1950. And this fired me!

This was a way to earn money, something I could do. I couldn't play stocks and bonds and all that, but I could write stories. And this was the worst thing that could have happened to me! I'll never know what would have happened to me out in Australia. I could have married some Sheila whose old man owned a million sheep, or fallen down an opal mine! One thing's certain: the wife wouldn't have come out; she told me that afterwards!

In those early days, my method was to write one chapter a day, 12 pages on the typewriter, foolscap, double line . . . this was a chapter. I finished a book in 12 days, and got paid. I remember one novel I sent in, this plaintive letter came back: 'Your novel is 3,000 words short!'

That is why, on *City of No Return*, the beginning is not the beginning! It was something I wrote to stick on the front. That entire beautiful tavern scene, the hissing alien begging for tobacco, and your snarling drugged villains shooting everybody, the hero's intervention . . . the story is sheer padding, just to fill the novel out. It really starts of with that beautiful line: 'From the foothills of the Blue Mountains the city of Klaglan seemed to rest like a shimmering jewel in the cup of a mighty palm.' That's where the story really starts!

I've used this theme a couple of times—the concept of a hidden place, which can give you everything. I used it in my Dumarest novel *Jack of Swords* . . . but I did it better in the Dumarest, as I'd had more practice!

Let me say this: we may have been driven by necessity, but everyone who wrote those old pocket books had a genuine passion for writing!

PREFACE:
HOW IT ALL STARTED

My interest in things fantastical began when I was four years old. My Mother took me to the cinema for the first time, to see a compendium of Walt Disney technicolor cartoons. These were several short films linked by a musical theme, but the *only* one I can remember was about 'Willie the Whale'—a whale that could sing! His subsequent exploitation—giving operatic performances—struck a responsive chord in an impressionable four year old. A taste for the outré and the fantastic was born. I was also fascinated by the colourful artwork, showing animated quavers and crotchets coming from the whale's mouth, and I began to draw these images myself. Thus was born an obsessive interest in fantasy and graphic art. For more than fifty years I tried unsuccessfully to trace the title and date of the remembered film, and I am grateful to my bookseller friend and film buff Bob Cook for recently providing the answer. The film was a compendium of 10 short cartoons released by RKO in England in August 1946, under the title *Make Mine Music*.

The segment I remembered as 'Willie the Whale' was the tenth and last cartoon, *The Whale Who Wanted to Sing at the Met* and the singing voice had been provided by Nelson Eddy.

Six months later, like all children in those days, I was admitted to hospital for an operation to have my tonsils removed. I was kept in for two days, and found relief from the monotony by looking at what I later realized were some American newspaper comic sections, which were lying around in my ward. I distinctly remember being fascinated by a full-page strip of *Superman*, in which the Man of Steel could be seen flying through an open window carrying a mermaid! Although I could not read, I was fascinated by the images and knew that this was something that required subsequent investigation and exploration.

Beginning school at age five, I soon discovered the world of comic books from my friends and classmates. In Britain in the late 1940s, there were many British and Australian reprints of American SF and fantasy superheroes, including *Superman* and *Captain Marvel*, and I soon became an avid comics reader. There were also lots of cowboy and adventure comics around, but I had no interest whatsoever in these—my taste was entirely for science fiction and fantasy, *although I had no conception that it existed as a distinct genre.* The phrase 'science fiction' remained completely unknown to me. I simply recognized what I liked when I saw it.

I did not read my first science fiction *novel* until September 1954. It served to introduce me to the pleasures of SF reading and collecting, which has remained a lifelong interest ever since. I can still remember how it came about as if it were yesterday.

My best childhood friend was Ian Dick, a boy who lived a few doors away from me in David Street, Wallsend, on Tyneside. Ian was some months older than me, and became my comics mentor. We swapped titles and discussed the stories endlessly, and with other friends we attended the childrens' Saturday morning cinema matinees to watch the old SF serials, In 1950, we both became avid readers of a new weekly comic, *Eagle*, because it featured the famous Frank Hampson SF strip, *Dan Dare*. We were also both followers of Steve Dowling's *Garth*, the legendary newspaper strip cartoon hero then appearing in the *Daily Mirror,* whose daily continuities by 1950 had settled into a distinctly science fiction streak with an interplanetary story called *Journey to Jason.*

Throughout the early 1950s, I continued to devour all the strip cartoon science fiction I could find, whilst remaining completely oblivious to its manifestation in books. I *had* discovered written science fiction to some degree, but these were only the occasional written SF serials appearing in D. C. Thomson's weekly comic story papers, such as *Adventure, Hotspur* and *Wizard.* I used to stay for weekends at my grandmother's in order to read vast piles of back issues of these story papers, which had belonged to my uncles. I was also enthralled by a B.B.C. Sunday afternoon radio serialization of H. G. Wells' *The First Men in the Moon* in 1953, which I adapted (as it ran) into my own hand-drawn, then inked and colour-crayoned strip cartoon version, complete in 270 panels, plus painted covers (which I still have). However, I simply was not aware of paperback books, and of science fiction as a distinct genre.

Then came one glorious Saturday in 1954 when my friend Ian excitedly told me of his previous night's stay at the home of his Grandfather. He had shown him, and let him read, a 'science fiction pocket book'. He described the plot to me, waxing enthusiastic over the book, which had been about 'a man who saw into the future, and knew when he was going to die'. (I would later identify this as *Zero Hour* by Vargo Statten [J. R. Fearn]).

At first, I couldn't believe that such things existed. It seemed too good to be true. But Ian evidently knew whereof he spoke, and described to me the location of a local 'second-hand bookshop' about half a mile away "on Benton Road, just off Carville Road", where his Grandfather had told him these fabulous items could be purchased. The previous year I had actually been passing very close to it on my way to and from my former school each day, without being aware it existed.

Following his directions, I hurried off to Benton Road, one of the older, run-down areas of Wallsend, and cautiously entered the dingy premises of 'Joseph Storm: Book Seller'.

Behind a counter was Joseph Storm himself, a shabbily dressed, unhealthy-looking morose individual, cigarette dangling from a corner of his mouth. Lining the wall behind him were wooden cupboard shelves, with small piles of indistinguishable paperbacks. "Do you have any 'science fiction' books please?" I asked hopefully.

A small pile of paperbacks was placed on the counter for my inspection. "One shilling each, sixpence trade-in when you bring them back," wheezed Joe.

One shilling was quite expensive to an unemployed schoolboy in 1954, particularly as the price of comic books was only half this sum, and weekly comics were even cheaper. Fortunately, I had just received my pocket money for the week—all of three shillings.

I looked at the books, and made my fateful choice of three titles. They were all published by Scion Ltd., and bore the legend 'science fiction' prominently on the cover, which probably influenced my choice. I handed over my entire week's pocket money, and left the shop clutching copies of *A Thing of the Past* by Volsted Gridban, *The Dust Destroyer* by Vargo Statten, and *The Resurrected Man* by E. C. Tubb.

When I got home I studied the covers of my reckless purchases. *A*

Thing of the Past had the most splendidly lurid picture: it showed a man and a scantily clad girl confronting a fearsome dinosaur. I immediately selected this for my initial reading. *The Dust Destroyer* showed two men in spacesuits standing on the outside of their spaceship, in orbit above the Earth. *The Resurrected Man* had the most restrained cover of the three, showing a group of tiny space-suited figures jetting through space towards a spaceship airlock. And that was the order in which I read the books, beginning with *A Thing of the Past*.

To say that I read the book is something of an understatement—I *devoured* it!

This was *real* science fiction, completely eclipsing all of the ersatz flimflam of the comic strips, which now seemed utterly childish in comparison. I was so elated at my discovery, that as soon as I had finished reading *A Thing of the Past* I passed it that same evening to my father, insisting that he read it too—enthusing that it was absolutely wonderful.

I remember being stunned the next morning when he handed it back, grudgingly admitting that it had been "all right, I suppose," but adding that I should try reading "real books, like Jules Verne and H. G. Wells." Later I would better appreciate his remarks, but at the time I was disappointed at his evident lack of literary perspicacity. *I* knew better, and my illusions were reinforced as I read and thoroughly enjoyed the other two books.

They made a tremendous and lasting impression. I was 'hooked' on SF, and needed regular fixes beyond the scope of my limited pocket money. I soon solved the problem by applying for, and getting, a job as a paperboy, hand-delivering morning and evening newspapers before and after school. By a happy coincidence, *Sawford's* news agency was only a hundred yards from my beloved second-hand bookshop, and so there was no danger of the money I received each week—the munificent sum of seven shillings and sixpence—wearing a hole in my pockets. Over the succeeding months and years I read any and every science fiction paperback I could find. I also introduced my comic reading friends to paperback SF, and they too 'graduated' to the new form, like ducks to water.

As I continued to read all 'new' SF books I could find, Statten, Gridban and Tubb remained my favourite authors, not least because there seemed to be more of their titles around than anyone else's.

By then I had also earned my father's approval by showing him a new 1955 Fontana paperback edition of Verne's *Twenty Thousand*

Leagues Under the Sea which I had also bought from Storm's bookshop (he kept a small front window display of new titles), and telling him that I had enjoyed it. Only then did he reveal to me his own hitherto secret predilection for science fiction by taking down from the loft and showing me his own childhood storypaper collection—a two year run of the earliest issues of *Modern Boy*, dating from 1928. They featured two long (and astonishingly well-written) serials by Alfred Edgar telling how Martians invaded the Earth.

Actually, although I was not to realize it until many years later, John Russell Fearn's own early inspiration came directly from the English boys' storypapers of the 1920s, which were a rich source of science fiction, pre-dating the American SF pulps, and owed almost nothing to American writers, with the notable exception of Edgar Rice Burroughs' many influential UK appearances.

In reading and enjoying Fearn's 1950s Scion books I was reliving much the same sense of discovery and excitement as my father must have done in the 1920s. Enthusiasm for science fiction, it seems, can be carried in the genes!

Then came the fateful day when I chanced to read in quick succession two other Scion epics, *Operation Venus* by John Russell Fearn and *Reverse Universe* by Volsted Gridban.

This was the first time I had came across Fearn's name on a book. And I thoroughly enjoyed it, and was electrified to see a house ad on the back page urging readers to *look out for the next title by John Russell Fearn—Annihilation!*

I already had a copy of *Annihilation*, and knew it to have been written as by Vargo Statten. The penny dropped immediately: Fearn and Statten were one and the same person, and his real name was probably Fearn, since I'd never met anyone called 'Vargo', but knew plenty of Johns and Russells! In my literary naivety, I had never thought of the use of pseudonyms (or even knew what the word meant).

After a few moments came another blinding realization: The tongue-twisting 'Volsted Gridban' must be another made-up name, and that was probably Fearn too, which was why I enjoyed his stories so much.

Delighted, I then settled into reading *Reverse Universe*, anticipating another Fearn epic, only to receive a profound shock.

The style was nothing like Fearn's at all—they were chalk and cheese.

If Fearn had not written this book—then who had? I finished the book, and in fact thoroughly enjoyed it, and by the time I came to the end, I knew who the author was—none other than my other great favourite: E. C. Tubb!

The hunt was on—the game was afoot!

I knew then that I would just have to read every other similar science fiction book I could find to see if I could find any other pen names of Fearn and Tubb, and also to unravel the profound mystery of why two different authors could write under the same name—and why so many of the SF books and magazines I had only recently discovered seemed to have abruptly ceased publication.

It took more than fifty years before I eventually discovered the answers—and this book is the direct result of my ongoing researches!

CHAPTER 1:
THE STORY BEGINS

Most followers of science fiction are aware that the first all-SF magazine appeared in America in April of 1926—Hugo Gernsback's *Amazing Stories*. But few people appreciate that it was another eleven years before Britain gained a comparable home-produced publication in the shape of Walter Gillings' *Tales of Wonder*, which appeared in the summer of 1937. In the interim, science fiction tales seldom appeared at all in British magazines, unless it was in the juvenile field. For British editors, science fiction began and ended with H. G. Wells as far as adult readers were concerned. The very few exceptions appeared in such magazines as *The Strand* or *Pearson's Magazine*, and then they were usually what we would today call borderline material.

The avid reader of science fiction, having exhausted the supply of Verne and Wells from his local library, was forced to prospect in the juvenile magazines, where there were occasionally rewarding discoveries to be made. George C. Wallis had presented *Union Jack* readers with a serial called 'In Trackless Space', dealing with Mars and Venus, as far back as 1902.

Never sufficiently recognized was the influence of Edgar Rice Burroughs on juvenile British science fiction. His *At the Earth's Core*, telling the story of how a newly invented 'iron mole' carried David Innes and Abner Perry deep down into the bowels of the Earth to emerge into a strange inner world teeming with prehistoric life influenced countless British writers for the boys' papers after it was serialized in 11 weekly parts in *Pluck*, simultaneously with its Methuen 1923 hardcover edition.

Lester Bidston authored *The Space Destroyer* in a 1924 issue of *Boys'*

Friend Library (No.723), telling the tale of a marvellous gravity-nullifying metal and a visit to Mars and Vulcan. Later it came out in book form as *A Voyage Into Space*, and there was a sequel, *Scund the Eternal* (*Boys Friend Library* No.727 (1924), in which Earth was bombarded by a huge cannon on Venus. Other ingredients were giant wasps, a heroine named Thensla, and a tough-guy hero named Scund who could not die. Naturally, three intrepid boys were mixed up in it somewhere. Bidston appeared again in *Boys' Friend Library* with *The Stolen Ocean*, a novel that told of a journey to Mars, super radio transmissions, and the theft of an ocean from Earth. Such random examples show how old some of these plots are, but they presented British readers with some of the earliest SF available in Britain.

1928 was a vintage year for juvenile science fiction, *The Modern Boy* running two exciting serials by the talented and prolific Alfred Edgar telling of the exploration of Mars, and of a subsequent Martian invasion of the Earth.

The *Modern Boy* later ran a long series by 'Murray Roberts' (Robert Murray Graydon) featuring the SF exploits of 'Captain Justice', who anticipated the much later 'Thunderbirds' concept of International Rescue. Brian Aldiss has written nostalgically of how these stories impacted on him as a boy. Most of the Captain Justice stories were later issued as paperbacks in the *Boys' Friend Library* between 1935 and 1939, when the war killed it off. During its long run (beginning in 1906!) the *Boys' Friend Library* published a great deal of juvenile SF by the likes of Lester Bidston, Alfred Edgar and others, that anticipated many of the iconic SF concepts that later became staples of the American pulps.

Of especial significance was the issue of *The Nelson Lee Library* for September 29th, 1928. At the head of the Readers' Letters column presided over by Edwy Searles Brooks (who edited the magazine and wrote the lead novella for it), was a photograph of a young man identified as "John Fearn." At the time, John Russell Fearn, later to become Britain's most prolific SF writer, was twenty years of age and had yet to publish his first work. It should come as no surprise that a 20-year old should have been a regular reader of a Boys' Paper, for Fearn was in good company. The fact was that most British SF fans, of all ages, regularly followed the juvenile papers, for the very good reason that it was their only regular source of new science fiction!

Nelson Lee readers were encouraged to write to Brooks, who occasionally made personal replies. It is almost certain that Fearn went on to establish a personal correspondence with Brooks, because twenty years later, when Fearn was at the height of his own literary career, he dedicated his fourth 'Black Maria' detective thriller *Thy Arm Alone* 'to Brooky". This could only have been E. S. Brooks. Strong evidence for this was given in June 1954, when Fearn was Guest of Honour at a science fiction convention in Manchester. Following his speech, during a question-and-answer session, Fearn was asked which author had been his greatest influence. Fearn unhesitatingly replied: "Edwy Searles Brooks."

Brooks leavened many of his novellas of Nelson Lee (a schoolmaster detective!) with all kinds of fantastic adventures that sometimes veered into full-blooded SF. One particular sequence of adventures evidently made a great impression on the youthful Fearn. The schoolboys of St, Franks School, accompanied by their Master Nelson Lee and a party of scientists, went on a round-the-world exploratory trip in a futuristic 'omniplane', equally at home on land, sea, and air.

In *The Secret World* they penetrate a hidden subterranean passage through the Antarctic ice pack, emerging to discover 'a verdant, gloriously green valley in the very midst of the Antarctic wastes'. Localised volcanic warmth has created a closed, tropical basin, complete with strange time-lost flora and fauna. The cover of the 1939 *Schoolboy's Own Library* reprint edition shows the emerging school party encountering a small dinosaur. They went on to discover cultivated fields with grazing cattle, and an entire medieval township, with buildings with mullioned windows straight out of the Middle Ages. Variations on this theme were popular between the wars, most notably S. Fowler Wright's *Beyond the Rim* (1932), in which explorers in the Antarctic find another warm valley, encountering the long-lost descendants of puritans who had sailed from England in the 17th century, only to be blown off course.

Fearn later wrote a novelette 'Arctic God' for *Amazing Stories* (May 1942), which seems to have been directly based on Brooks' story, notwithstanding that it was transposed to the North Pole. Later on he incorporated its plot into his 'Golden Amazon' novel *The Amazon Strikes Again* (1948), returning the action to the South Pole.

Chums was a famous weekly British boys' magazine, priced at tuppence, and printed entirely in black and white. It ran mainly fiction, with non-fiction features. The pages were numbered consecutively January through December: each year, and then the entire year's issues were bound by the publisher and issued as a large hardcover annual. However, each issue had a bound-in eight-page supplement, and the pages were separately numbered i to viii. This section contained serials, and these sections were later reissued, and published separately as a *Chums* monthly, priced one shilling, with a new colour cover. I suspect that the bound annuals did not contain these stories.

In 1931, the editor of the magazine tried a unique experiment to introduce American SF to Britain. Two stories were reprinted from a 1929 *Air Wonder Stories* and ran as two-part serials in consecutive issues: 'Beyond the Aurora' by A. Hyatt Verrill on 14 and 21 March, and 'The Second Shell' by Jack Williamson followed on 28 March and 4 April. Both stories were subsequently included in the monthly omnibus in May the following year, with Verrill's story featured on the colour cover. Possibly the editor might have continued in the same vein, but perhaps the reader reaction was insufficient to justify the experiment.

Amongst *Chums'* readers was a sixteen-year-old cub reporter named Walter H. Gillings. Born in Ilford, Essex on February 19, 1912, Gillings first discovered *Amazing* in 1928. The magazine at the time was presenting a regular diet of new and old 'scientifiction'; reprints of Wells and Verne rubbed shoulders with such new authors as A. Hyatt Verrill, Stanton A. Coblentz, Harl Vincent, and David Keller. In 1929, Gernsback lost control of *Amazing*, and his company was bought out. The magazine continued under the editorial guidance of T. O'Conor Sloane, and Gernsback was left to form his own company, Stellar Publishing, and introduce more magazines in the shape of *Science Wonder Stories* and *Air Wonder Stories*. With the new magazines, new authors were arriving: Jack Williamson, Raymond Z. Gallun, Edmond Hamilton (the star sf writer in America's premier weird magazine, *Weird Tales*) and others, and all the new talent was available to British readers at a penny a time.

By 1930, Britain had a small but dedicated band of followers of 'scientifiction' as it was then known, and it was not long before they began to discover each other. Walter Gillings had written to *Amazing* in its formative years; later, via leaflets slipped into second-hand SF magazines and an advertisement in the *Ilford Recorder* (where he worked as a reporter), he formed the 'Ilford Science Literary Circle', which became one of the earliest fan gatherings, meeting for the first time in October of

1930. It was not long before British authors began to appear in the United States—George C. Wallis, Benson Herbert, Festus Pragnell, John Beynon (Wyndham) Harris, and John Russell Fearn among them.

The formation of the British Interplanetary Society (B.I.S.) brought many of these early fans and authors together. An advertisement in the *Liverpool Echo* written by Philip Cleator, attracted the attention of local fan Leslie J. Johnson, and the B.I.S. held its first meeting on October 18, 1933. Other members were soon attracted, and the roster eventually included the late Norman Weedall, Walter Gillings, Ted Carnell, Ken Chapman, Eric Frank Russell, William F. Temple, and the illustrious Arthur C. Clarke.

The vital significance of the B.I.S. in establishing science fiction in Britain has rarely been properly acknowledged. *It was absolutely crucial.* One of the very few men to know and appreciate the catalytic role it played was the late Leslie J. Johnson.

I had been in correspondence with Les since before 1973, when I published for the first time his story 'Eternal Rediffusion', which he had co-authored with Eric Frank Russell in 1937. After I had published it in pamphlet form in my *Fantasy Booklet* series, it was quickly reprinted in *Weird Tales* in the U.S. and also anthologized, and we became friends. We arranged a meeting in Blackpool in 1978, where we discussed my arranging for publication of his other unpublished work, including a non-fiction book he was presently working on.

In 1979 he sent me his 45,000-word manuscript, *A History of the British Interplanetary Society, 1933-1945.* This was a minutely detailed documented history of the Society, from its beginnings in Liverpool, through its transfer to London in 1936 up to the end of the war in 1945. Although he intended to send a copy to the B.I.S. (and also to his friend Arthur C. Clarke) he was not entirely sanguine that they would use it, because of his 'feud' with Cleator.

It had been our intention that I would either publish it as a book myself, or agent it. Unfortunately, shortly thereafter, my wife fell seriously ill, which meant I had to look after our young daughter whilst holding down an increasingly demanding full-time job in local government. I was forced to abandon my plans, and suspend any SF publishing and agenting activities. Regrettably, then, I lost contact with Les, along with many other correspondents and agent clients. Les passed on a number of years ago, but I am sure he would have approved the publication of extracts from his memoir in this present book. Extracts that would show conclusively how closely intermingled were the early British SF fans and the British Interplanetary Society in sharing a common dream of space travel,

Just as I was about to re-read his mss in order to select suitable extracts for this book, Peter Weston sent me a sample copy of the February 2010 issue of his magazine *Relapse*. I discovered this to be an admirable publication dedicated to recording and preserving the history of British SF fandom.

I was astonished—and pleased—to open Peter's magazine and find that someone else had also read a copy of Les' memoir and had *precisely* anticipated my own intention. The magazine contained an article entitled 'A Tale of Two Fandoms: SF fans and the space enthusiasts', which had been written by Bob Parkinson, using selected extracts from the memoir!

I immediately contacted Peter, and asked if it might be possible for me to include some of Bob Parkinson's splendid piece in this present volume. Peter had no objection, and kindly put me in touch with the article's author.

Bob Parkinson turned out to be a long-time SF fan, and as Dr Bob Parkinson, M.B.E., he works as an Aerospace Consultant Engineer specialising in Spacecraft System Design and is President of the British Interplanetary Society, along with many other qualifications! On learning of my connections with Les Johnson and the present book, Bob has generously agreed to my using an extract from his article:

Before handing over to Bob Parkinson's excellent essay (which leads off the next chapter), I should first like to present a short extract myself from Les Johnson's original memoir that both sets out Johnson's own background in science fiction, and bears out much of my foregoing paragraphs:

> From an early age, I had shown an interest in the more imaginative types of literature, including stories concerning *Beowolf*, then fiction by A. Conan Doyle, Jules Verne and H. G. Wells. There had been stories of mechanical armies in *Comic Cuts*, while I used to look forward eagerly to reading *The Boys' Magazine* every Saturday morning, a publication which regularly featured stories of the kind we now know as Science Fiction. During the summer of 1930, when I had left St. Francis Xavier's College in Liverpool, I was unemployed, and had more time to look around the bookshops of Liverpool, I came across issues of the American Science Fiction magazines. I also became an ardent collector of secondhand books on Astronomy . . .

Looking back on my work for the British Interplanetary Society, I do so with the greatest satisfaction. I am staggered when I consider the vast amount I must have got through, first as Hon. Secretary, later as Hon. Treasurer then as Hon. General Secretary-Treasurer—not to mention having edited the *Bulletin*, *The New Columbus* and *The Journal* of the Society.

Over forty-five years have elapsed since the formation of the BIS in October 1933, and the names of the original Members of the Society (both in Liverpool and in London) are fading with the passage of time. It was with this thought in mind that I have written this account of the Society in its earliest years . . .

Amongst the original Members on Merseyside, every tribute must be paid to P. E. Cleator, Founder and the First President of the Society, as well as to Colin Askham, the first Vice-President. Mention must be made of the valuable contributions made by James A. Free, Jr. as Assistant Hon. Secretary and as Hon. Treasurer, as well as my late friend, Norman Weedall (1914-1978) as Hon. Librarian. Particular mention must be made of the advice, effort and contributions of Science Fiction writer, Eric Frank Russell (1905-1978) during the formative years of the Society and the early days of his successful writing career.

Amongst the early London Members during the period 1936 to 1939, the efforts and influence of J. Happian Edwards, Founder of the London Branch of the Society, must be recorded, together with the secretarial assistance of Miss Elizabeth Huggett (later to become Mrs. J. H. Edwards). Not the least of the London Members, and later to become President of the Society, was Professor A. M. Low, B.Sc. Following the transfer of Society Headquarters from Liverpool to London in February 1937, few could have worked harder to maintain and develop the Society than Edward John Carnell (1912-1972) and Arthur C. Clarke. Other names amongst the Londoners who gave invaluable assistance to the Pre-War Society were Walter H. Gillings, William F. Temple, Ralph A. Smith, H. E. Ross, Arthur Janser, H. Branhill and F. E. Day.

"The Space Destroyer"
by Lester Bidston (uncredited).
Boys' Friend Library # 723, 1924

"The War in Space" by Raymond Quiex
(uncredited). *Boys' Magazine* # 229, 1926

"The Secret World!" by Edwy Searles
Brooks (uncredited). *Schoolboys' Own
Library* # 387, 1939

"The World in Darkness" by Murray
Roberts (uncredited). *Boys' Friend
Library* # 505, 1935

"The Mechanical Monster" by W.B. Home-Gall (uncredited). *Boys' Friend Library* # 175, 1925

Photo: Leslie J. Johnson and Eric Frank Russell, 1937 (Courtesy Peter Weston)

Photo: Olaf Stapledon, ca. 1937

Photo: Walter H. Gillings, ca. 1937

CHAPTER 2:
SCIENCE FICTION
PIONEERS

The following essay has been extracted from an article that originally appeared in Peter Weston's magazine *Relapse*, with his kind permission. The article was edited by Bob Parkinson, from the memoir by Leslie Johnson. Bob's linking words appear without quotes.

A Tale of Two Fandoms: SF fans and the space enthusiasts

In 2008 I assembled a book for the British Interplanetary Society: *Interplanetary; A History of the British Interplanetary Society*. It was the 75th anniversary of the Society, and in that year the Society also hosted the annual International Astronautical Congress in Glasgow. I got the job by dint of having been around longer than most (I joined in 1957), but the origins of the BIS go back to pre-war days. Digging in the archives I came across a carbon copy of a 125-page typed manuscript by one Leslie Joseph Johnson, who was actually the first Secretary of the Society, back in the days when Philip E. Cleator founded it in Liverpool. The mss was written in 1979, but Johnson had obviously kept all his records.

Having run the manuscript through the copier to make sure we had a back-up copy, I started to read. My first shock came on page 5, when I read the roll-call of the first half dozen who met at Philip Cleator's house at Wallasey on 28th September 1933 to discuss forming the BIS;

'Apart from the host, Philip Cleator, those present included Leslie Joseph Johnson, Colin Henry Askham and Percival Norman Weedall . . . while Norman Weedall was a confirmed Science Fiction enthusiast.'

At that point I realized that I had met Norman Weedall when I was a very new fan at the time the Cheltenham Science Fiction Circle made a visit to the Liverpool Group back in 1960 or so. Johnson had already noted the link between science fiction and interplanetary flight in the early pages of his memoir:

'The ordinary members of the Society in those early days were practically one hundred percent science fiction readers. It is not surprising, therefore, to find that the Hon. Secretary, himself an ardent science fiction fan, apart from seeking publicity through reports of meetings sent monthly to *Practical Mechanics*, made a special point of obtaining members through the correspondence columns of the American science fiction magazines.'

The subsequent history and growth of the BIS in Johnson's memoir is contained in my *Interplanetary* book, and I do not intend to repeat more than is necessary here. But the memoir also keeps bringing up the parallel history of science fiction fandom in the UK and a number of names very familiar to me, and so I thought it worth extracting some of the relevant bits for the interest of others. All the quotes (but one) are taken directly from Johnson's document. One passage talks about how the American SF 'pulp' magazines came to the UK. (I had an uncle who had a pile of these pre-war pulps stacked in his garage when I was a boy—which probably set me off on a lifetime's reading of the genre.)

'The first of the Hon. Secretary's letters to the American Science Fiction magazines asking for members for the BIS was to appear in the April 1934 issue of *Amazing Stories*, followed by a similar letter in the November 1934 issue of *Astounding Stories*.
'Current issues of these magazines (dated two months ahead of their actual publication dates) were usually available from a limited number of bookstalls in Britain at prices ranging from 1/3d to 1/6d, but the vast majority of the science fiction readers of the time were introduced to the cult by picking up so-called 'remainder' magazines. These could be obtained from

branches of Messrs. F. W. Woolworths and from second-hand bookshops at 3d per copy.

' "Remainder" magazines were unsold copies sent over from America as ships' ballast. They sometimes bore a special mark rubber-stamped on the front cover. Other copies had the top right-hand corner of the magazine cut off; still others had the front covers ripped off. The covers were sent back to the publishers in order to get credit refunds. These unsold copies took some months to percolate through to the British market, usually arriving some six months or more after their publication in the U.S.A.

'One of the earliest results, obviously following from the letter that had appeared in the April 1934 issue of *Amazing Stories*, was a letter received from a sixteen-year-old lad named Arthur C. Clarke of Bishop's Lydeard in Somerset. His letter was dated July 30th, 1934.

'On August 25th 1934 an enquiry was received from one Eric Frank Russell (who said he had seen the letter published by Teck Publications)— *Amazing Stories*, and on September 14th of the same year a letter from Walter H. Gillings, with whom the Hon. Secretary had been in correspondence in 1931 on the subject of setting up Science Fiction Clubs throughout Britain.'

The fledgling Society had financial difficulties in maintaining a printed *Journal* (and Cleator objected to having a mimeographed *Bulletin*) but it is clear that Johnson as Secretary kept up a very active correspondence with certain members, in particular Arthur Clarke and Walter Gillings, and—by the end of 1934—Eric Frank Russell.

'Following receipt of the first letter by the Hon. Secretary from Eric Frank Russell and a personal visit to Mill Lane by all six-foot-three of Russell, correspondence commenced between them—although they lived only about ten miles apart. At first, this was centred mainly around the possibility of Russell's articles on 'Interplanetary Communications' appearing in a publication of the BIS, but rapidly developed into regular exchange visits and collaboration in numerous projects involving the writing of science fiction.'

It should be pointed out that at this time Johnson, while a senior officer of the BIS, was still just twenty.

Meetings of the Society were held at a room above McGhie's Café at 56 Whitechapel, Liverpool—a location Johnson observes was still in existence at the time of his memoir (in 1979). 'At street level, No. 56 is currently tenanted by 'Tape Electronics', and on the First Floor, at the top of the wide staircase up which trod pioneering member the BIS in the middle thirties, is 'Sukie's Unisex Hair Styles'. However, this location (and the early members of the Society) nearly did not survive. In February 1935, Willy Ley made a visit—on his way to become a refugee from Nazi Germany in the USA, and a few weeks later Johnson records:

> 'The Members were so engrossed in their deliberations one evening that in spite of the noise and commotion prevailing downstairs, it was not realised that the premises were on fire. While comments were being made by the Members with regard to the likelihood of a drunken brawl prevailing in the lower portion of the café, or perhaps even in the street outside, they did not immediately appreciate the reality or indeed the desperate nature of their situation.
>
> 'Not until the door burst open and a smoke-begrimed fireman appeared brandishing an axe, did they come to any understanding as to what was happening. And the fireman, himself, was as astonished as anybody else to find the members of the BIS oblivious to the fact that the downstairs portion of the café had been gutted—while they were debating as to how a rocket ship could reach the Moon!'

In late 1935 another contact was made of some importance to the Society and science fiction: 'About this time, a letter was received from Eric Frank Russell asking for a current issue of *The Journal* of the Society and any back numbers available, to be sent to one Dr. W. Olaf Stapledon, a Professor at Liverpool University, who was also the author in 1930 of *Last and First Men*—a science fiction epic. Unfortunately—or otherwise, as the case may be—Stapledon had never heard of science fiction (apart from H. G. Wells) until Eric Russell and L. J. Johnson visited him (and were royally entertained at his bungalow at Caldy Hill, Wirral, Cheshire.

> ' . . . At the close of the year, a letter dated December 30th 1935, was received by the Hon. Secretary from one Edward John Carnell, Science-Fiction League Member Number 1197—the Hon. Secretary himself being able to boast of having been SFL Member No. 383. Mr. Carnell was writing to the Hon. Secretary rather than to Mr. Cleator because he was familiar

with the name of the Hon. Secretary through the 'frequent' letters that had appeared in *Wonder Stories*.

'Mr. Carnell went on to explain that he was the London Correspondent of George Gordon Clark's *Brooklyn Reporter* (a science fiction 'fan' magazine), and it would be quicker for Carnell to communicate with the Hon. Secretary on behalf of George Gordon Clark than to have to endure the delays that would otherwise be involved in transatlantic mail.

'Carnell was endeavouring to find out the extent of science fiction enthusiasm in Britain (which he suggested was 'extremely low'), together with news of Rocketry and Esperanto.'

By 1936 a substantial group had begun to form in London:

'It was at this stage in the proceedings that Eric Frank Russell and Leslie J. Johnson decided that it would be an appropriate moment to visit London, both from the point of view of Interplanetary Travel and of science fiction . . . Amongst other destinations that they had in mind were the Editorial Offices of the proposed new British Science Fiction Magazine, where the prospective editor was Mr. T. Stanhope Sprigg of Newnes Publications. They were also to have what turned out to be a momentous first meeting with Edward John Carnell and Walter H Gillings, neither of whom up to that time had ever met, and in fact knew very little about each other or about each other's activities. . . . At the end of the visit, they (EFR & LJJ) left Paddington Station, London, at midnight, and after dropping newspapers and milk churns at every railway station in Wales, reached Lime Street Station, Liverpool at 8.15 am—with Johnson reporting for duty at the Liverpool Education Offices at 9.00 am.'

Carnell then went on to become an active member in the London Branch of the BIS. During the summer of 1936 he met with others at the Radio Show at Olympia:

'It was there that Carnell was able to meet [Jack Happian] Edwards in September when they were joined by Eric Frank Russell, as well as by Gillings and Clarke. Also visitors to Edwards at Radio Olympia were Maurice Hanson and Dennis Jacques of Leicester and Nuneaton respectively: the two last named were Joint Editors of *Novae Terrae* ('New Worlds') a science fiction fan magazine, which they produced on behalf of Chapter No.22 of the Science Fiction League.'

Tuesday, October 27th 1936 was chosen as the first official meeting in London for BIS members, held in the offices of 'Professor' A. M. Low. Low, an inventor and writer on popular science, was not actually a Professor of anything, although he seems to have adopted the title from a brief period as Associate Honorary Assistant Professor of Physics at the Royal Ordnance College between 1919 and 1922. A note on the dust jacket of his juvenile novel, *Adrift in the Stratosphere* describes him as one who 'during the War was Officer Commanding the Royal Flying Corps Experimental Works'.

A small committee was formed including Edwards, Arthur Clarke, Jim Strong, Ted Carnell and K. W. Chapman, who met in a little Italian restaurant off Piccadilly. Initially the group had been simply the 'London Branch' but increasing problems in running the Society from Liverpool meant that by November the London Group would become the headquarters of the Society.

'Accordingly, Mr. L. J. Johnson arranged that his fiancée (Miss Hilda Margaret Crossen) and himself would visit London on Sunday, November 15th 1936, in order to give London members an insight into BIS affairs. They would arrive at Euston Station at about 2 pm, meet the London Committee members in the afternoon, and then proceed to the 'Mason's Arms', Maddox Street, for 7 pm, where the Londoners in general would congregate.

'One of Johnson's most persistent memories after the meeting was of Miss Crossen and himself dashing to catch the later train back to Liverpool, accompanied by a very young and very attentive Arthur C. Clarke. Describing Miss Crossen as a 'Martyr to Science'; Clarke was so kind and considerate that it almost became embarrassing. This was especially so, as it was known that in seeing them to Euston Station, he was going in totally the wrong direction, and he seemed completely unconcerned as to how he was going to make his own way back to his lodgings. The two travellers arrived back in Liverpool at 4.45 am, while Clarke reached his bed at 2.00 am, no doubt pondering the fact that at the Meeting he had been confirmed as Hon. Treasurer at the London end of the BIS.'

If matters were progressing satisfactorily with the BIS, developments were less satisfactory on the SF front, as Johnson records:

'In the meantime, the news from London was that Messrs. Newnes had abandoned their proposal to publish a British science fiction magazine, and the manuscript of 'Seeker of Tomorrow' had been returned with thanks to Eric Frank Russell. However, three other publishers had been in communication with Walter Gillings, with a view to the publication of a British science fiction magazine, and he would be discussing the matter with them. In the meantime he was determined to bring out his science fiction fan magazine *Scientifiction* as soon as possible.

'Eric Frank Russell had some consolation for the return of the MS of 'Seeker of Tomorrow', inasmuch as his first story to be granted acceptance, 'The Saga of Pelican West', had been taken by *Astounding Stories*, and he had been paid eighteen dollars 'on the nail' and before publication.'

The transfer of power to London required the Society to draw up a new Constitution—something that appears to have been a perpetual problem with the early BIS. A Special General Meeting was called for 6th December 1936, which was held at Johnson's home in Liverpool, which prepared for the Annual General Meeting on Sunday 7th February 1937 at the 'Mason's Arms' in London.

'The hiatus that would otherwise have existed between the time of the Special General Meeting . . . and the Annual General Meeting . . . was to be a period to be gainfully employed by some of the BIS members in Leeds, Leicester, Liverpool and London who also professed an interest in the field of science fiction.

'The first-ever British Science Fiction Convention had been arranged by the Leeds Chapter of the Science Fiction League, to be held in Leeds on Sunday, January 7th, 1937. Other chapters of the Science Fiction League also existed at that time in Nuneaton (Leicester), Glasgow, Belfast and Burnley. Enthusiasts from all parts of the British Isles were cordially invited to attend. The Convention, which in many ways could hardly have been labelled as a great success, was nevertheless notable on two points:

1. It was the first British Science Fiction Convention ever to be held;

2. In spite of the fact that only six enthusiasts from outside the Leeds area attended, the Convention resulted in the formation of the pre-war *Science Fiction Association*.

'The six "outsiders" who were able to be present at the Leeds Convention were Carnell, Clarke and Gillings from London, Johnson and Russell from

Liverpool, and Maurice K. Hanson from Leicester. They were all destined to become closely associated . . . in the years to come.'

After the Annual General Meeting Johnson gave up his position as Hon Secretary to the Society, and that position was taken over by Miss Elizabeth Huggett. Johnson describes Miss Huggett as Jack Edwards 'fiancée'. This is not actually true—actually she was his mistress. Jack Happian Edwards was one of the stranger characters in the pre-war BIS. His dynamism was responsible for energising much of the Society's pre-war activities. Carnell thought him a 'mutant genius'. Val Cleaver's opinion was 'completely in the lunatic fringe'. Perhaps fortunately, with the outbreak of War he disappears from the annals of the BIS. Read the book if you want to know more.

Ted Carnell became 'Publicity Director', editing the Society's *Bulletin* until May 1938 when it was taken over, first by Maurice Hanson and then by Arthur Clarke, by this time residing at 88 Grays Inn Road, London.

'To the names of the three Londoners (Carnell, Clarke and Gillings) who had attended the Science Fiction Convention at Leeds, must be added the name of William F. Temple, as one who managed to reconcile the twin worlds of Science Fiction and Interplanetary Travel. Born in 1914, he had read most of the science fiction magazine since he had picked up a copy of *Amazing Stories* in 1927; he was a somewhat unenthusiastic employee of the Stock Exchange and confessed that he was not qualified in any particular branch of Science, but was anxious to do any general work that he could on behalf of the Society.

'W. F. Temple had contributed an exhilarating series of articles to *Novae Terrae* commencing with the April 1938 issue, entitled 'The British Fan in his natural haunt', his first subject having been Eric C. Williams, at one time a Council Member of the Science Fiction Association.

'Following the second British Science Fiction Convention held in London on April 10th, 1938 (and much better attended than the Leeds Convention), it was typical of the close association that existed between science fiction and Interplanetary Travel that the man elected as President of the SFA was none other than the ubiquitous and genial Professor A. M. Low. And it was not remarkable that at the Annual General Meeting of the SFA at the Convention that the members agreed to transfer the headquarters of the Science Fiction Association from Leeds to London—in the wake of the BIS.

'Others to be honoured by W. F. Temple's attention in his series of articles in *Novae Terrae* were Edward John Carnell, Arthur C. Clarke, Maurice K. Hanson, G. Ken Chapman and Walter H. Gillings. In a Supplement to the last issue of *Novae Terrae* dated January 1939 (after which Edward John Carnell took over the fanzine as *New Worlds*) Arthur C. Clarke retaliated by adding a seventh name to the series by featuring William F. Temple himself—in *his* natural haunt.

'And Clarke was well able to indulge in a verbal caricature of Temple, because in June 1938, Clarke had decided to move in with Temple and to share the flat at 88 Grays Inn Road, WC1. In September 1938, Maurice Hanson, who had previously shared a bed-sitter in Bernard Street (having wangled a Civil Service appointment in the metropolis) moved in with Clarke and Temple, who by that time had thrown open The Flat to SFA Members on Thursday evenings.

'It was not particularly surprising, therefore, to find that 88 Grays Inn Road became Combined Headquarters of both science fiction and of Interplanetary Travel. From this address was issued not only *Novae Terrae* but also *The Bulletin* of the BIS. Indeed, William F. Temple was to go on to become Publicity Director of the Society in succession to Edward John Carnell (who had become Hon. Treasurer of the SFA), and to succeed Carnell as Editor of the *Journal* of the BIS.

'Carnell had resigned as Publicity Director of the BIS in order to become the Editor of *New Worlds*, which was to feature science fiction stories rather than science fiction 'fan' activities that had been the highlight of Maurice Hanson's *Novae Terrae*.

'The transfer of the headquarters of the BIS having taken place, Mr. L. J. Johnson arranged for a combined meeting of science fiction enthusiasts and BIS members to take place in Liverpool on April 16th, 1937, but despite having sent out invitations to thirty individuals only six turned up, including Eric Frank Russell and Johnson himself. An appeal was made in *Novae Terrae* for any fans in the Liverpool area to contact Mr. Johnson with a view to enlivening (and re-populating) future meetings in the city.'

Johnson had a little more luck later in the year: On 19th August 1937 he invited local fans to a meeting, and

' . . . over eighteen persons attended, including Mr. P. E. Cleator and his wife, as well as Walter Gillings, who was on holiday with the Russells.

Gillings' visit was particularly opportune, as he had just realised his great ambition to edit a British science fiction magazine; Messrs. World's Work (1919) Ltd had agreed to the production of a trial issue of such a magazine, to be called *Tales of Wonder and Super-Science*. Following the relative success of the first issue, 16 issues in all were to appear between summer 1937 and spring 1942.

'When E. J. Carnell visited L. J. Johnson in Liverpool in August 1937, the two decided to form a partnership in a part-time mail-order science fiction book and magazine business, to be called 'Science-Fiction Service', with branches in Liverpool and London. In September 1938, the Service opened in an office in the centre of Liverpool at Room 7, at 15 Houghton Street, at a cost of 7s.6d. per week.

'In June 1938, a Liverpool Branch was formed of the Science Fiction Association. Early meetings were held at the old BIS rendezvous, 'The Hamilton Café', then at a famous Liverpool lunch-time eating house, Messrs. G. Petty's Café in Hackins Hay. Then, just as 'The Flat' had become the centre for BIS/SF fans in London, so 'The Office' became the focal point until the outbreak of War for fans in Liverpool and elsewhere.

'No.15 Houghton Street has long since been demolished; but it is perhaps significant that the former site of 'The Office' is now clearly visible for miles around Liverpool, and even out to sea. For rising right through the centre of what had been No.15 is The Radio City Tower, thrusting its umbrella-like shape 450 feet into space above the remains of Houghton Street, and looking for all the world like a giant H. G. Wells-type spaceship about to blast-off from the Earth.'

The outbreak of War brought an end to BIS activities, and in October 1939 its operation was formally suspended for the duration. A new Society would be reformed after the War as a joint merger between the old BIS and 'The Combined British Astronautical Society'. Johnson finishes his memoir by recording various members' activities in the War:

"Amongst the first to go was James A. Free Jr., who as a Sergeant in the Territorial Army was away even before War broke out. Clarke became a Flight Lieutenant in the RAF, working on the Ground Controlled Radar system. To the RAF also went L. J. Johnson and Eric Frank Russell, as Wireless Mechanics, with Norman Weedall as a Bomb Armourer. W. H. Gillings experienced but a brief Army career because of health considerations, but

E. J. Carnell and W. F. Temple found themselves eventually with the Army in the Mediterranean Zone. Also to the Army went Professor A. M. Low to undertake 'experimental work'."

Through the early 1930s, not content with American imports, the small (but vocal) fan groups made every effort to convince publishers that Britain had both talented writers and the market for a homegrown magazine. But all efforts seemed fruitless, with publishers believing that the adult readership would be too small, and that the 'Yank Mags' catered to them anyway. They did recognise that science fiction attracted a strong following, so they began including more SF stories in their general magazines, but still not enough to satisfy the enthusiasts.

Thus, when *Scoops*, Britain's first SF magazine, did arrive, the publishers were aiming at the juvenile market, trying to capture the audience that read such boys' magazines as *Boys' Friend* or *Boys' Magazine*.

The latter magazine, in particular, published by Allied Newspapers Ltd. had published a vast amount of SF in its weekly run between 1922 and 1934, much of it anticipating the ideas and concepts that would be popularised through the American pulp magazines in later years: interplanetary warfare, bug-eyed monsters, robots, matter transmitters. All the paraphernalia of what became known as 'space opera' was anticipated by such boys' writers as W. E. Home-Gall, who had numerous SF serials in *Boys' Magazine*, such as *The Mechanical Monster* (1925) and *The Coming Doom* (1925), billed as a 'Wonder Tale of Science and Invention . . . a Hundred Years from Now'. The prolific and versatile John Hunter penned *The Quest of the Leaping Death* (1926) billed as 'A dazzling searchlight on the primeval darkness of the past. A professor and two boys find themselves thrust behind the curtain of a mysterious land of prehistoric monsters—into a world of mad peril and thrills'. Perhaps the most iconic of the tales was *The War in Space* by Raymond Quiex (1926), billed as: 'A startling new serial of a mad astronomer's bid for world domination . . . the threat of the planet Ikon to collide with the world . . . Rival scientists—one on Earth, the other on a hurtling world in the heavens—fighting out their feud'.

When the magazine was discontinued in 1934 it left a definite gap in the market, which prompted Pearson's to issue their own weekly juvenile story paper, *Scoops*, devoted entirely to SF. (*Boys' Magazine* had featured the usual traditional detective, historical and sports stories as back-ups to their SF serials)

We are fortunate that Sean Wallace, a young American editor and publisher, was intrigued enough by the magazine when he learned of it, to have thoroughly researched its short life and death. His findings were published as 'Scoops: The Story Paper of Tomorrow' in the first issue of *Fantasy Annual* (1997), a semi-professional transatlantic magazine he and I jointly edited. He has kindly consented to its reprinting here:

Britain's first science fiction weekly newspaper was published by C. A. Pearson Ltd., a publishing house noted for its monthly *Pearson's Magazine* and *Pearson's Weekly* (after various title changes, titled *Tit-Bits*), both of which published works by H. G. Wells, M. P. Shiel, H. Rider Haggard, and many others. Much later, when it re-entered the science fiction field in the early 1950's, and with a better understanding of the market, it utilized the *Tit-Bits* title for two noted science fiction series, the *Tit-Bits Science Fiction Library* (19 issues, 1953-55) and the *Tit-Bits Science Fiction Comics* (6 issues, 1953-55) which were a success and are today, highly collected.

However, in the 1930's, science fiction had yet to gain a foothold in the United Kingdom, and for the most part, science fiction was only being printed in boy's papers such as *Nelson Lee* or *Boys' Friend Library*. No British writer could even make a living writing science fiction with the sole exception of John Russell Fearn, who had just begun to make an impact in America. For adult readers, however, there was only one place in which to escape from reality, as remembered by noted SF editor, Walter Gillings:

'F. W. Woolworth might seem a strange father-figure to choose, but the sense of wonder that Woolies instilled in young readers of the "Yank Mags" that they sold, brought over as ballast in cross-Atlantic ships, introduced many to the excitement and imagination proliferating in the pages of *Astounding Stories, Amazing Stories, Wonder Stories*, and the rest of the then-young American SF magazines.'

But with the introduction of the 'Yank Mags', there came a desperate need, a nagging itch in the minds of English sf fandom, that Britain as well should have a science fiction magazine. Dogged attempts by John Russell Fearn and Walter Gillings to create such a magazine failed during the early 1930's, and it was not until 1934, that *Scoops* suddenly burst onto the scene.

On February 10, 1934, the first issue of *Scoops* was released upon an unsuspecting public. Printed on newsprint in a bed-sheet format (9.25 by 12.5 inches), its closely set type and small columns allowed enough room for several novelette-length stories. The cover featured a robot striding amongst the streets of London, evoking a sense of menace while high above, the block letters shouted out *'No.1 of an Amazing New Wonder Weekly!'*

The editor, F(rederick) Haydn Dimmock (1895-1955), was a capable editor in his own right, though his own experiences in science fiction had been minimal at best. He had joined the staff of *The Scout* starting in 1913, and quickly worked through the ranks until World War I reared its ugly head. After war's end and demobilization, he soon resumed working at his old job, and continued doing so until 1954. A strong advocate of the Boy Scout movement, he himself wrote to some degree, with numerous books and dozens of scouting tales that were published by C.A. Pearsons throughout the 1930's and up to the early 1950's.

From the beginning, *Scoops* was intended to appeal to a younger audience, probably readers from between the ages of eight and fourteen, for the sole reason that Dimmock actually thought that science fiction would not appeal to adult readers. His editorial decision to market *Scoops* only to young readers then perhaps was a blunder, at least at a time when English science fiction fandom was growing strong and actively demanding a magazine.

And as for the contents . . .

No credit was ever given for the majority of short stories and novels for the first six issues, which perhaps was a blessing in disguise. With titles like 'When The Skull Men Swooped', 'Rebels of the Penal Planet', and 'Wimpole's Weight Reducer', a writer would have been shamed to tears if his byline was ever attached. The contents of the stories themselves were quite juvenile, but some harkened back to the future-war stories of the early 1880's and up to the late 1920's. But as Walter Gillings has written, when he discovered *Scoops*:

"There was no doubt of it—it was science fiction, however crude. Or some of it was . . . There were Rebel Robots, Terror Beasts of Space, a Penal Planet, a Human King Kong, a Time Traveller, a Devilman of the Deep, an Immortal Man and an Iron Woman, sixty foot tall and 'fair of face'. Fortunately she was kept well apart from The Striding Terror . . . "

Strangely enough, the only name that cropped up consistently for eleven issues was Professor A(rchibald) M(ontgomery) Low (1888-1956), a British writer, academic, and inventor with an eleven-part serial titled 'Space', which began in issue two, and ended after three months. It was then compiled and published as his first book, *Adrift in the Stratosphere* (1937). Well-known and respected, Low's name in *Scoops* served to assure parents that this was a respectable publication, as opposed to the juvenile boys' papers accompanying it at the stands.

Realizing his mistake soon after, (probably after a number of fans wrote and demanded change, or off with his head, most likely!) Dimmock's editorial policy did a quick turn-around. Perhaps the turning point was the May 5 issue, in which the serial *The Poison Belt* by Sir Arthur Conan Doyle was begun. This sequel to his classic *The Lost World* (UK 1912) was first serialised much earlier in *The Strand Magazine* (1913) and published in book form that same year by Hodder & Stoughton. At this time, he started introducing names that were somewhat recognizable to fandom. Later he even added a reader's letter column, 'The Reader's Platform', to the back page, to encourage criticism and discussion: "The Editor Thanks—All of the hundreds of readers who have sent congratulatory messages about *Scoops*. It is most encouraging to know that our efforts to popularise scientific fiction have met with such a splendid reception. I shall welcome letters from you. Tell me frankly what you like or dislike in the paper. Your opinions will be of special value."

All this and more officially marked the beginning of the 'Change'.

Other notable bylines began to appear with some regularity, especially P(hilip) E(llaby) Cleator (1908-1994), a British scientific researcher who contributed several small articles about the planets, and who, earlier, had founded the British Interplanetary Society (B.I.S.) in October 1933 at Liverpool. John Russell Fearn (1908-1960), the 'Blackpool Wonder', made his UK debut with a short story, 'Invaders from Time'. A prolific British writer in several genres, Fearn is now best known for his 'Golden Amazon' novels as well as many short stories and novels. His work and career has been well-covered by *The Multi-Man* (privately published, 1968) and in many subsequent features by Philip Harbottle.

Other British writers, less well known, also appeared, such as W(ilfred) P. Cockcroft (1913-) a British writer whose later stories were published in *New Worlds* and *Tales of Wonder*; Maurice G(aspard) Hugi (1904-1947) a British science fiction writer who later wrote short stories for *Tales of Wonder*, as well as for the first and third issues of *New Worlds*; Moore Raymond, a British film critic and writer associated with *The Scout* and *The Daily Express*; George Ernest Rochester (c1895-c1966), a prolific British writer of juvenile novels up to the 1950's, and who often appeared in *Boys' Friend Library* throughout the 1930's; C(hristopher) St. John Sprigg (1907-1937) a British novelist, poet, and aviation expert who edited the anthology *Uncanny Stories* (1936), a year before he was then killed in action in the Spanish Civil War.

The rest sadly remain untraced, although a few scant facts have surfaced: D. G. Turner was the compiler of *The Camp-fire Book* (C. A. Pearson 1932), and also author of *The Silver Greyhound Saunders* in C. A. Pearson's *Boy's Ace Library*, no. 16; and Stuart Martin (1882-?) a British writer who wrote a number of fiction and non-fiction books, including *Pirates of the Main* (C. A. Pearson 1924), and *Minto of the Movies* (*Boys' Ace Library*, no. 9).

The garish, grab-you-by-the-throat covers were painted by the Russian-born Serge R. Drigin, a noted commercial artist, who after *Scoops*, painted several covers for the adult British science fiction magazine *Fantasy*. He then became a successful illustrator for many children's books and annuals into the 1950's, working for Sampson Low, Blackie, and several other publishers. His colour covers for other publications were attractively painted, but his *Scoops* covers were printed in black and red in the beginning (#''s 1- 7) and later, in blue and red (#'s 8 - 20).

However, the interior illustrations for *Scoops* are more difficult to identify. Drigin did the majority of them, signing himself Drigin, or S.D., and with others under the pseudonym Shirley (the signatures of both are so similar as to suggest that they are indeed the same person). Drigin's black-and-white line drawings were impressive, despite his being used to mundane subjects, rather than spaceships and other science fiction concepts. An unidentified third artist has also been discovered, whose signature is probably 'Winter', who mostly drew technical artwork for the nonfiction department, Can it Be Done?

Reaction to *Scoops* was varied, as Gillings' account makes clear:

> 'At least, the publishers learned something about science fiction and its fans. It had never occurred to them that grown men like Len Kippin and myself would have to sneak, shame-faced, into a newsagents and ask for *Scoops*, as though we were buying a halfpenny gobstopper—or assume the air of one doing his young brother a good turn.'

For the most part, English fandom took *Scoops* in its stride and made the best with what they had. Had *Scoops* continued, it might have had a lasting impact on British sf, but unfortunately the day the serials ended, so did *Scoops*. And though *Scoops* itself would never be seen again, five short stories were later assembled along with eight new tales (not all SF) and all published in the annual-format anthology *The Boy's World of Adventure* (1937). Serge Drigin resurfaced once again with contributions of colour plates and line drawings to accompany the short stories of this juvenile anthology.

On reflection, there were many reasons why it failed, but Gillings says it best:

> 'Mainly because it started off on the wrong foot, in my view. Having been launched as a 'penny dreadful', it could not remove the stigma as far as discerning SF readers were concerned . . . Had it been started as a monthly, it might have been a different story.'

There could be a very good argument for actually having boy's SF papers, at least during the 1930's and earlier, but by 1934 they were probably beginning to decline, and lose their readership as paperbacks increased their hold upon the market. It was too late for them to change, and though there were various attempts, only a few succeeded for any length of time (notably *Modern Wonder*). *Scoops* and others of its ilk actually did serve a purpose: to introduce SF concepts to its young readers. In today's world, perhaps there is less need for a boy's paper, especially since science fiction has diversified and permeated the media.

'*Scoops* was a mistake, and remains unique as a juvenile science fiction magazine. Nothing quite like it has been tried since', wrote Graham Stone in his *Index to British Science Fiction Magazines* (ASFA, 1968). Nothing ever has come even close to resembling *Scoops* to this day, though there have been other juvenile science fiction magazines, most notably *Thrills Incorporated*, an Australian magazine.

But at the very least, *Scoops* today can amuse collectors with its wonderfully garish covers and naive stories, and remind them that science fiction can come in many forms, indeed.

Very much unjustly overlooked in most reference books and histories of British science fiction was *Modern Wonder*, a 2d juvenile weekly, which was launched in May 1937. It was published by the giant Odhams Press, and was very different and superior in format to *Scoops*. It was printed in glossy photogravure, with full colour in the middle, and on the front and back pages. Edited by a young science graduate, H. T. Cauldwell, it contained mainly science fact articles, and features on modern transport, engineering, etc—but also had a small but significant amount of science fiction, which it ran in serial form.

The most notable serialization was that of John Beynon's *Passing Show* serial *Stowaway To Mars*, here abridged as *The Space Machine*, with the sex of the stowaway, Joan, changed to John, thus eliminating the sexual tension elements present in the original novel, and rendering it suitable for a juvenile audience. Alerted to its advent by Gillings, Fearn was quickly on the case, and he soon crashed the magazine with a very clever series of articles, tailor-made for the magazine: 'The Chronicles of a Space Voyager'. This was a series of speculative/factual articles on each planet of the solar system, strictly based on modern astronomical knowledge (but leavened with a science fictional framing device) of the planets, described from the viewpoint of the crew of an exploratory spaceship. The device would be much imitated in later years.

Having got his foot in the editorial door, Fearn sent the editor the synopses of a number of science fiction short stories, some of them based on earlier unsold stories. Fearn was commissioned to produce three short stories as quickly as possible.

For the first story, 'Death at the Observatory', he created a modern-day scientific detective, Marlo, called in to investigate an 'impossible' murder at an observatory. Appearing first in *Modern Wonder* No.76 (1938) it was reprinted in the U.S. in *Captain Future* in September 1940, and reprinted as a classic ten years later in the first issue of the same publisher's reprint magazine, *Fantastic Story Magazine*. It would be later translated into Italian and appeared in that country's edition of *Perry Rhodan* magazine in 1982.

Fearn's second *Modern Wonder* story, 'The Misty Wilderness', was rewritten from one of Fearn's Weinbaum-flavour 'Thornton Ayre' stories that had been rejected by *Astounding* at the beginning of the year. In the original, Fearn's villain, Eboni, had been a woman (based on Weinbaum's 'The Red Peri'). Fearn changed the character to a man (in accordance with the requirements of a boys' magazine). The story, an interplanetary detective yarn, duly sold and appeared in *Modern Wonder* No.77 (1938). It was not an ostensibly juvenile story, as was proven by its being reprinted by *Startling Stories* in September 1939.

Its quality was further attested by its being translated and published in a French newspaper, *Ric et Rac,* on 6 December, 1939. With the Second

World War having broken out, this was a truly astonishing coup for an English author, as well as being the first translated science fiction short story to appear in the paper!

The third story that Fearn sold to *Modern Wonder*, 'The Weather Machine', (No.78, 1938) was an adventure story based on the unscrupulous use of a weather-control device. This too was translated into French and published in *Ric et Rac* in 20 December, 1939! Both these Fearn stories would later be freshly translated by Jean-Luc Buard, and published in the French academic journal *Le Rocambole* (No.18) in 2002, celebrated as the first English SF magazine stories to have been translated in France.

Also translated for the French newspaper in 1941 was another *Modern Wonder* SF serial, *The World Behind the Moon* by the much overlooked William J. Passingham, who had earlier had the distinction of placing two other SF serials in *Passing Show*, *When London Fell* (after suffering an invasion by prehistoric monsters) and *World Without Time* in 1937 and 1938. Gillings later described him as "a forceful personality at the third annual convention of the British SF Association [1939] in London," and he would later link up with John Carnell in a failed attempt to launch *New Worlds*.

The other most notable SF serial in this paper was *The Lost Kingdom*, an Atlantean adventure by radio engineer Ralph Stanger, who had earlier appeared in a 1932 *Wonder Stories*.

The magazine was highly successful. However it would eventually fall victim to the war, because as Walter Gillings noted in one of his *Vision of Tomorrow* articles, "the widespread evacuation of its school-age readership, problems of distribution, and other setbacks which gradually throttled the life out of many publications. In an attempt to capture a more adult following, it switched its title to *Modern World* while changing its format to war economy size. Still it could not escape extinction, though it had a good run for its money, and can still fetch a fair price as a collector's item.'

With the demise of *Scoops*, Britain had returned to her reliance on American imports, but the march of British fandom was not to be denied. The American pulps were a focal point that brought many of the fans together, especially *Wonder Stories* (a combination of Gernsback's two earlier magazines) which went as far as to label its August 1935 letter department a 'British Edition'. The Science Fiction League was instituted in the U.S. through that magazine in 1934, and in May of 1935 the first overseas chapter was launched in Leeds, England.

This undercurrent of response generated a flickering spark at the publishing house of George Newnes, an associate company of Pearson's (who had issued *Scoops*). Newnes editor T. Stanhope Sprigg conceived the idea of four specialized pulp magazines, one of them SF. Gaining their addresses from the editor of *Scoops*, he sought to contact their SF writers. The roster of authors was not large.

John Russell Fearn was one of a handful of former *Scoops* contributors to receive the following letter from Sprigg on the 17th of September, 1935:

> Dear Sir,
>
> I understand from Mr. Haydn Dimmock of the *Scout* that you contribute extensively to Science Fiction magazines in the United States. We are interested in an English market for this type of fiction and we write to inquire whether you have available any original stories which you would care to offer us. Alternatively, we should be interested to see some of your recent work already published in America and of which the British Serial Rights are still available.
>
> Yours truly,
>
> Stanhope Sprigg
> EDITOR.

Walter Gillings, a friend and correspondent of Fearn's, then a young journalist living in Ilford, also received a letter. This was on the strength of his being the leading SF fan in the country—he had bombarded editors (including Dimmock) with advice on how to run a SF magazine. Gillings was by then in personal touch with practically every SF writer in the country, and the 'call to arms' soon reverberated all over Britain. Fearn and his recently widowed mother actually moved to Brighton from Blackpool, just to be nearer the scene of the action, and bombarded Sprigg with mss that had fallen back on his hands with the sudden demise of *Scoops*. Eric Frank Russell pitched in with his own inimitable mss, which had yet to create their tremendous impact on the SF world. But the overall response was disappointing to Newnes. The plain fact was that there were only a relative handful of genuine British SF writers. The paucity of good mss caused the magazine to be delayed.

The first three magazines were launched over 1935-36, but the fourth, already identified as *Fantasy*, still failed to appear. As increasing doubts as to the validity of the magazine crept into the mind of its editor, it was eventually shelved, to the chagrin of Fearn, who promptly upped sticks and moved back to Blackpool.

But the spark fanned into flames with the fans, especially Walter Gillings. He had been acting as the unpaid agent and consultant to authors, trying to provide Newnes with material, and was too avid a fan to let eighteen months of work die. In January 1937, he launched the first printed fan magazine in Britain, *Scientifiction*, a thoroughly professional-looking journal of SF news and comment. Through its interviews, it familiarized admirers with such authors as Benson Herbert, John Beynon Harris, Festus Pragnell, Fearn, Russell, and even the great Olaf Stapledon.

Then, through the grapevine, rumour reached Gillings that World's Work, a subsidiary firm of Heinemann's—the book publisher, who had their own press in Kingwood, Surrey, where they turned out pulp magazines—was to publish a science fiction magazine. Actually, the rumour was unfounded and had probably arisen because World's Work was issuing magazines with the titles *Tales of Terror* and *Tales of the Uncanny*. They continued their weird magazines, but no SF magazine was planned until Gillings approached them. The result of his efforts was the commissioning of a trial SF issue of 80,000 words. Some of the material could be of American origin so long as it had not appeared in remainders sold in England. It was because of World's Work reprinting American stories for their magazines that Gillings was somewhat handicapped by having to operate with a reprint rate of payment—10/6d per thousand words top rate.

But Gillings was equal to the task, and the authors rallied around with enthusiasm. The low rate was happily accepted with the thought that a beginning was to be made for British SF. The first issue of *Tales of Wonder* is now a rare collectors item. The cover story, 'Superhuman', was by John Russell Fearn, but had been bylined 'Geoffrey Armstrong' by Gillings without Fearn's knowledge, because of his use of another story under Fearn's own name in the same issue. 'Armstrong' had been chosen because it was Fearn's mother's maiden surname. On being told of this by

Gillings, the genial Fearn accepted the *fait accompli* quite happily. This marked Fearn's first venture into the realm of pen names—something that was to eventually lead to his downfall in the eyes of fans—as will be shown later in this volume. Other stories included Eric Frank Russell's 'The Prr-r-eet', voted the most popular story in that issue, and others by John Beynon Harris, Festus Pragnell (who had a second under the name 'Francis Parnell'), and a second offering from Fearn under his own name, 'Seeds From Space'. Both Fearn's stories had originally been written for *Scoops*, and were quickly revised at Gillings' request. Halifax writer W. P. Cockcroft's 'Revolt on Venus' was another story that had originally been written for Newnes, and Maurice G. Hugi rounded off the issue with 'Invaders From the Atom', which had been extensively revised by the editor.

The issue was successful enough to prompt World's Work to continue *Tales of Wonder* on a regular quarterly schedule.

While suitable new material continued to be at a premium, despite encouragement of such new authors as Charles F. Hall and D. J. Foster, *Tales of Wonder* ran many reprints by established American writers such as David H. Keller, Stanton Coblentz, and Clark Ashton Smith. Later Gillings acquired such remarkable early stories as Murray Leinster's famous 'The Mad Planet' and its sequel 'The Red Dust', and Jack Williamson's debut story, 'The Metal Man', together with the classic 'The Moon Era'. These reprints undoubtedly helped immensely in the development of the magazine, introducing the old-time adventuresome elements that would make the magazine more accessible to new readers not so well versed in the general subject matter of SF. Undoubtedly, however, it annoyed authors trying to sell new stories. After selling a third old *Scoops* mss 'Through Earth's Core' to the second issue, Fearn in particular had several new stories rejected, as did others including L. J. Johnson. Gillings was obsessed with what he perceived as the need to keep his stories "simple" and "plausible to the general public", eschewing anything that was too wildly imaginative. Both Fearn and Johnson vented their ire with articles in contemporary British fanzines, Fearn using gentle satire and mild reproof in his article 'Kintergarden SF' in *The Futurian*, whilst Johnson, writing in *Satellite*, was openly scathing in his condemnation of the 'go-slow' policy. Gillings attempted a rapprochement with Fearn by reprinting his first short story 'The Man Who Stopped the Dust' (1934) which had originally appeared in the premier American magazine *Astounding*. But since Fearn could readily sell his new stories to the American magazines at *four times* the payment rate of *Tales of Wonder*, he eventually gave up after several attempts, and did not appear again after 'Dust' was reprinted in the 8th issue. Instead, he resumed his regular sales to the American magazines.

One author who was able to comply with Gillings' editorial policy (although mostly with reprints) was John Beynon Harris, and the second issue presented something of a scoop, 'Sleepers of Mars,' the sequel to his earlier novel, *Stowaway to Mars*. Some would-be contributors were put off by the low rates of pay, but there were no thoughts of this kind from the writers yet to make their names in the United States, and the magazine presented some masterful stories by such fledgling authors as William F. Temple, remembered especially for his 'Experiment in Genius' and 'Smile of the Sphinx', which would later be reprinted in America. Nor by Eric Frank Russell, whose humorous tales included 'I, Spy!' Even the illustrious Arthur C. Clarke failed to sell Gillings his early fiction—it was too wildly imaginative for the cautious editor!—but made his first professional sale to *Tales of Wonder* with a non-fiction article on space travel and the solar system.

As well as creating new British talent, the magazine further served to stimulate the imaginations and ambitions of younger British fans who contributed enthusiastically to the readers' pages, where Gillings astutely ran many readers' contests for SF essays. Among the prizewinners was young Kenneth Bulmer, later to become one of the pillars of British fantasy.

The success of the magazine served to jog the reluctant Newnes into reviving the plans for their fourth magazine and, in July 1938, editor Sprigg finally brought out *Fantasy,* and the higher rates of pay (twice that of World's Work) attracted new stories by Fearn, Russell, and Beynon Harris.

The first issue compared well with *Tales of Wonder*, where the budget only permitted the use of small illustrations by noted fan artist Harry Turner. *Fantasy*, on the other hand, was comparatively lavish in production, with covers by ex-*Scoops* artist Serge Drigin, a very competent professional artist, whose evident recent study of the artwork in American magazines showed to good effect. It also boasted several interior artists, all of whom worked in Newnes' other magazines. Featured in the first issue was a new novelette by Fearn, specially written for Sprigg, 'The Red Magician', together with other equally good pieces by John Beynon Harris and Eric Frank Russell.

Perhaps the production costs were too high, or there was still a shortage of suitable new material despite the respectable rates of payment, for Sprigg also had to fall back on reprints from early British SF appearing in *Pearson's Magazine* and *Argosy*, such as G. R. Malloch's 'The Winged Terror' a mediocre story of giant caterpillars, which was however impressively illustrated by Drigin on the cover. Fearn appeared to good advantage in the second issue with another strong novelette, 'Climatica', and Eric Frank Russell and John Beynon Harris distinguished themselves by appearing in all three issues—the June 1939 third issue (featuring 'Derelict of Space' by John Beynon) being the last. Sprigg had been mobilized out of the reserves into the Royal Air Force, and with its guiding editor gone, the magazine's continuance looked uncertain. Not previously recorded in any SF histories is the fact that Newnes general editor F. J. Camm at first only *suspended* the magazine, and intended to restart the magazine at a later date. Fearn's letters to William F. Temple in my possession show that he continued to send mss to Camm for some time, even having his story 'Blind Vision' accepted in January 1940. However it would never be published, because Camm finally decided to fold the magazine, making *Fantasy* the first British casualty of the war.

Tales of Wonder, however, lasted until the spring of 1942. Paper rationing had gradually cut down the number of pages to 76 including covers, and Gillings' own call up meant that editing the magazine was almost impossible. The sixteenth issue (by now entitled on the cover as *Tales of Wonder and Super-Science*) was to be the last. Gillings' editorial spoke of the difficulty he was having obtaining new stories by British authors because many of his writers had been caught up in the war. He still managed to feature a new novelette by Benson Herbert, 'The Earth Shall Die!' and a first short story by perhaps Britain's only female SF writer at that time, 'Secret of the Crater' by Marion F. Eadie (who was married to the magazine's talented fan cover artist and illustrator Harry Turner). The rest of the issue was made up of American reprints by Clark Ashton Smith and Miles J. Breuer.

Overprinted at the side of the front cover was a sad announcement:

"Since this issue went to press, we have been obliged—owing to paper restrictions and war conditions generally—to discontinue this magazine while the war lasts. No further issues will appear until peace comes when we hope to restore publication as before."

It was a tragedy for British science fiction, because had the magazine continued, further new British talent would have emerged much sooner than it eventually did. An announcement on page 53 trailed 'Before the Flood' a story by a new author, John F. Burke, which of course never appeared. Burke's notable career in SF writing would have to wait many years—until 1953, in fact.

However, the die had been cast by the these early publications—proof that Britain could support itself in the field, and proof of the determination of these early fans to produce a professional magazine of British science fiction.

Not widely known is the fact that Britain had been very close to gaining another SF magazine in 1940, to be named *New Worlds*. We are fortunate that in 1970, as editor of the SF magazine *Vision of Tomorrow* (the story of which features in later chapters) I commissioned editor John Carnell to write a detailed memoir of his early career. This extract was published as an article entitled 'The Magazine that Nearly Was', in *Vision* in June 1970, and this is its first appearance in book form:

As Walter Gillings' campaign to promote science fiction in Great Britain progressed through the late '30's, so, too did his enthusiasm communicate itself to the small but growing group of aficionados who were becoming linked by correspondence and local groups. I had first met Walter early in 1936, when I was assistant manager in private printing company; a meeting which brought Eric Frank Russell and Leslie Johnson as visitors from Liverpool at a time when they were both active in the newly formed British Interplanetary Society, founded by Philip Cleator. I met them at Liverpool Street station, our only means of identification a copy of *Astounding Stories* prominently displayed under an arm—and the three of us then journeyed to Ilford to the home of the Prophet, where we were more than impressed by both his collection and his seriousness.

Walter's enthusiasm was contagious, his connections with so many other SF personalities phenomenal, so like good disciples, we went out to

spread the gospel and the net began to gather many more enthusiasts—
Arthur C. Clarke, William F. Temple, Ken Chapman, John Beynon Harris,
Eric C. Williams and Sydney J. Bounds to mention a few whose names are
currently familiar. There was also increasing contact between the loosely
knit London group and the active members of the several SF League
Chapters at Nuneaton, Leeds, Liverpool and Glasgow, which had been
promoted by the American *Wonder* Stories. The London link was more
strongly forged when, on October 28th that year, the London branch of
the BIS was formed and held its first meeting in the offices of Professor
A. M. Low, in Lower Regent Street. Nearly all its members were also SF
fans.

After nearly two years of steadily increasing activity, which saw the first
British SF convention in Leeds in 1937 and the first London convention a
year later, 1938 turned out to be a key year in the development of my own
personal involvement with events to come. In March that year, the BIS
was transferred from Liverpool to London, Professor A. M. Low became
President and I became Publicity Director and editor of its *Bulletin*. In the
summer, Leslie Johnson and I partnered a mail order magazine business
called 'Science Fiction Service' with premises in Liverpool (our little yellow
stickers can still be found inside the covers of many collectors' items of
that time) and the Science Fiction Association which had been formed the
year before, was transferred from Leeds to London with Ken Chapman as
Secretary and myself as Treasurer.

It was at this time that the celebrated 'Flat' in Grays Inn Road came into
its own as the centre of London SF activity. Arthur C. Clarke and William
F. Temple, already in residence, were joined by Maurice K. Hanson, from
Nuneaton, bringing with him his lively fan magazine *Novae Terrae*, which
later became the official magazine of the SFA, with myself as editor (primarily
due to time and circumstances). One of the first things I did was to change
the name to *New Worlds* and three issues containing news, articles and
fiction were published before the Association went into cold storage at the
outbreak of the 1939-45 war.

To celebrate all this outward urging, the first London SF convention was
held on a Sunday at The Druids' Hall, not very far from the 'Flat'. At that
gathering, apart from celebrities like John Beynon Harris and Professor Low,
we met for the first time W. J. Passingham, a freelance writer who contributed
fiction and articles regularly to Odhams' *The Passing Show* and *John Bull*.
Blackpool author John Russell Fearn delivered a typically optimistic speech

anticipating a science fiction boom on television and in the cinema, in the not-too-distant future.

Following the success of the many SF serials published in *The Passing Show*, Passingham had written two serials specially for the paper and became so fascinated by the medium that he had joined the SFA, thereafter becoming my guide, mentor and friend into the world of professional journalism. From this friendly relationship came the first tentative prospects of editing a new British SF magazine.

In October 1939 Bill Passingham approached me with the news that he had interested a publisher in the possibilities of such a magazine and arranged for us to have preliminary talks with one of the directors. The company was The World Says Ltd. with offices in Burleigh Street, Strand, where they published a digest magazine, *The World Says*, a pale image of the then current American *The Readers' Digest* before that magazine was produced here. The publisher was a Canadian named Alfred Greig.

Having discussed the situation—including my misgivings over the inappropriateness of the timing—and shown examples of the US magazines, in particular *Astounding SF*, the matter germinated until January 5th 1940, when I was summoned to a second conference, at which Walter Gillings was also in attendance and we were both invited to give our views. Finance, we were assured, was adequate; paper would be supplied from Canada despite the war; the editor would almost certainly be exempted from war service; and, finally, as part of the company's policy, were we prepared to put money into Company shares?

Both Passingham and I agreed to put up £50 each. Whether this had any bearing on my being offered the editorship, I never knew, but plans were formulated, a salary fixed and my entry into the editorial sanctum arranged for March 1st. The magazine was to be called *New Worlds*, published monthly and distributed by the Atlas Publishing & Distributing Company, who had distributed *Astounding SF* for so many years. Prior to that date I was to prepare the initial issues at home by using as many services of the company's office as I needed. No.1 should be ready to go to press in March, with two further issues in preparation.

By early February the initial issue was beginning to round out. Harry Turner of Manchester, already producing art work for *Tales Of Wonder*, had submitted some magnificent cover lettering; artist Chester, who had illustrated many of *The Passing Show* serials, had produced a number of cover roughs and three other London artists, introduced by the publisher, had been commissioned for illustrations as soon as the stories had been selected. At one time it had even been hoped that Fortunino Matania might be tempted to paint a cover illustration but either he was not readily available or, more likely, his fees were too high for our budget.

Unfortunately, my records do not show the story line-up for that first issue, all the material being returned to the authors, but I do remember that one novelette was Robert A. Heinlein's 'Lost Legion', which later appeared under his pseudonym of 'Lyle Monroe' in *Super Science Stories* in USA. Making full use of my membership in the American Fantasy Amateur Press Association—which included such enthusiasts as Donald A. Wollheim, Forrest J Ackerman and others—I had gained the support of writers like Jack Williamson, L. Sprague de Camp, Robert A. Heinlein, John Victor Peterson, as well as most of the British writers who were becoming established or who were planning upon becoming SF writers. I also intended looking for new writers, in much the same way that T. Stanhope Sprigg had done for Newnes' *Fantasy* but unlike his declared middle-of-the-road policy and Walter's 'straight-forward but simple themes', I stated to the authors that I wanted to develop a magazine of the calibre of John W. Campbell's *Astounding SF*, a magazine I had read regularly since 1932 and seen through its various stages of development to its then present stage of leading magazine. I wanted a high literary standard, plus mature thought-provoking stories, feeling that the British reading public would be ready for an advanced SF magazine in view of the preparations that had been made in the previous ten years. On the other hand, I had no intention of deliberately copying *Astounding SF*, feeling that the new magazine would develop its own personality as the right stories came along. The stage looked set for a good initial send-off.

On February 13th the Directors gave a luncheon at the 'Savage Club' to celebrate the completion of the initial work and round out the final plans for launching.

Guests included authors Bruce Woodhouse and Bill Passingham, Sir Frederick O'Connor, president of the company, Professor A. M. Low and myself. Here I outlined the policy I proposed setting up. Plans were also discussed for a possible collaboration with the SFA, the suggestions including two separate kinds of membership, one including a year's subscription to *New Worlds* and SFA membership, the other as Associate Membership at 5/- entitling members to all the privileges planned around the magazine— co-operation with cinema Clubs and special tickets for members when SF films were being shown; a yearly free gift to all members of the 'best' SF book of the year; the formation of a SF circulating library; a monthly printed fan magazine covering news about the genre in general. All very grandiose considering that we now had a war in Europe!

Two weeks later and just over a week before I was due to take up my official editorial residence, the bubble burst. Ostensibly, it was an internal dispute within the managerial organisation of The World Says Ltd; the Directorate split, funds mysteriously disappeared and wages were not paid and by the end of March the company had gone into voluntary liquidation but before then, in mid-March, there appeared (ironically enough) in *John Bull*, the weekly which had a penchant for sifting out the shifty, an article headed HE IS GRAND—BUT SHADY! wherein Man-about-Town Alfred Greig was reputedly stated to be seeking fame and fortune in the literary world, preferably fortune at the expense of other people, the article inferred. It castigated the system of employees buying shares in companies. 'I have always held', the writer of the article stated, 'that it is a most objectionable way of raising finance for private companies by taking it from people in return for employment or directorships. Printers are pressing for payment. Even typists find it hard to get their wages and some weeks have to go without. Greig still prates buoyantly of new publications—no doubt I shall embarrass him by urging my readers not to invest any money in the company while he remains at the helm.'

By then it was too late. The company had closed down, Mr. Greig had folded his prospectus along with his tent and departed for his native Canada and the pieces of the proposed magazine were filed away in my desk to await another day. I was richer by a vast amount of experience and poorer by £50 (most of which had been borrowed) but, as we shall see in a later article, the experience and the expense were worthwhile.'

Soon after, Carnell joined the Royal Artillery, but transferred in 1941 to become an observer for Combined Operations, and spent the next four years with Naval Bombardment on commando raids and major invasions, managing to somehow survive the war.

Photo: First meeting of B.I.S. London Branch, 27 October, 1936. L to R front row: E.J. Carnell, A.C. Clarke, Walter Gillings, Prof. A.M. Low, P. Bois, Jack Happian Edwards, Elizabeth Huggett. Back row: Klemanntaski, Strong, R.A. Smith, T. White, Day, Bein, two unidentified. (Courtesy Peter Weston.)

[Courtesy]   [B.I.S.

P. E. CLEATOR

Philip E. Cleator (ca. 1937)

Practical Mechanics.
March 1939 (uncredited)

Chums (Monthly), May 1931
(uncredited).

Scoops # 10, 1934 (S.R. Drigin).

Tales of Wonder # 1,
June 1937 (W.J. Roberts).

Modern Wonder # 23,
23 October 1937 (uncredited).

CHAPTER 3:
THE NEW BREED

April 30, 1940 was the date when paper rationing came into force in Britain and the fiction publishing industry was thrown into chaos. Previously they had issued several thousand hardcover books a year, but suddenly with paper restricted—and especially the boards used for hardcovers—they were struggling. Now, with the War Economy Standards severely limiting the number of new hardcover books, a new breed of publishers emerged. They scented a golden opportunity: anything new on the market was assured of a ready sale. New companies, as John Russell Fearn observed in a letter to his friend and fellow writer Norman Lazenby, were 'springing up like mushrooms'. These 'mushroom' publishers were usually small operations: one person would act as 'editor,' the other would handle the business of putting the product on the market. The cheapest printing methods were used, and no effort to turn out a quality product was made. Sometimes the paper used was so bad that there was a distinct 'see-through' from the print on the other side; sometimes the paper used changed from white to green or pink as supplies of each 16-page 'signature' (8 pages folded in half) ran out. The resultant thin booklets were usually not worth the effort of reading. At the height of the shortages, any kind of paper was used, and some products looked as if they had been printed on toilet paper (appropriately enough, in some cases), but that didn't concern the publishers unduly: their multi-coloured booklets would still sell! The chief culprit of these 'rainbow' booklets was Gerald G. Swan.

Gerald G. Swan Ltd. seemed to have inexhaustible supplies of paper—of wildly varying grades of quality. Foreseeing the likely shortages, Swan had craftily built up stocks of titles before issuing them onto the market. When the impending war finally came in September 1939, Swan's warehouses were well stocked. As other firms struggled or went to the wall as paper shortages bit, Swan made a killing with a huge diversity of publications, from adult fiction and magazines, to children's annuals (which he called 'Albums', all carrying his distinctive 'GGSwan' drawn logo) and comic books.

Science fiction was not featured heavily in pre-war publishers' lists, but during the war years the occasional SF title began to make its appearance, and the leading (if that was the right word) publisher was Swan.

He had apparently cut a good deal with American pulp publisher Louis Silberkleit, owner of the Blue-Ribbon chain of magazines, to obtain British Reprint Rights to a great deal of their pulp fiction. During the war Swan did have the astuteness to obtain British rights to some 1940-41 editions of *Weird Tales* from The American News Company, but their three 1942 editions failed to make any impact because of very poor shoddy quality paper, and single colour blue covers, giving it a poverty-row appearance. They were not helped by the use of microscopic typeface. Thus the earliest Swan straight science fiction consisted of odd reprints lifted from the American pulp magazine *Science Fiction* and its companion titles. Swan continued to reprint much of his SF from the Blue Ribbon Magazines, who also issued *Science Fiction Quarterly* and *Future Fiction*. Swan's *Yankee Shorts* series was launched in 1941, with *Yankee Romance*, *Yankee Mystery*, then *Yankee Science Fiction* as the third issue. This issue contained four stories from the Summer 1940 issue of *Science Fiction Quarterly*. However, issue 6 of the series was *Yankee Weird Shorts*, with four British original stories. These magazines were pretty mediocre, but sold well enough for Swan to continue in the same vein. Issues 11 and 21 were science fiction, 14 and 19 were weird stories. In 1940, Swan had issued *Weird Story Magazine*, mostly written by William Elliott under pseudonyms, in a pulp format, and he went on to produce several slim booklets (averaging 36 pages, including covers) sporadically. *Weird Shorts: First Selection* appeared in 1945-1946; two issues of *Occult Shorts* came in 1945-46; and *Weird Story Magazine* reappeared as two 1946 booklets with two-colour covers by John Woods and David Williams. Woods had earlier done the cover for *Weird Pocket Library No.1* (1943), featuring Kay Hammond's *The Dark City*.

Swan continued to issue the occasional reprint edition, and issued the Summer 1940 *Science Fiction Quarterly* as a paperback anthology entitled *The Moon Conquerors*. The Winter 1941-42 issue received similar treatment as *Into the Fourth Dimension*. The two lead title novels, by R. H. Romans and Ray Cummings were thus backed up by five and three short stories respectively. The covers—in common with most of Swan's paperback offerings—were printed on very thin stock in blue monochrome. But perhaps his most curious wartime SF offering—now a legendary collector's item!—was a "tuppenny shocker" of just 16 pages: an original SF novelette *They Came From Mars* by Halifax writer W. P. Cockcroft. Its lurid cover drawing by Swan's overworked staff artist Jock McCail showed two aviators being attacked by a giant, six-legged rat, whilst the blurb proclaimed it as 'A Tale of thrills and terror on the red planet'.

Colour covers were usually reserved for his more expensive children's books, and the dustwrappers of numerous American pulp magazine western novels he put into book form. His hardcovers, good value at 5/-, covered a wide spectrum of genres including romances and detective fiction, and the occasional fantasy and SF title. They varied greatly in quality; a few were early works by writers who later became prominent, and are today valuable collector's items, such as *Background For Murder* (1942) by Shelley Smith (1942), and *The Immortal Error* (1946) by Elleston Trevor, a fantasy concerning the transposition of souls. Some were wild and woolly gangster thrillers by his "staff writer" William J. Elliott, but Elliott's prolific output also included *Tomorrow's Spectacles* (1946), actually identified as 'A Romance', but which was a borderline fantasy in that it featured a pair of magical spectacles through which the wearer could visualise what the person viewed would be doing at any desired time into the future. The novel exploited the criminal and comedic possibilities, rather than the scientific. More substantial and interesting was a novel of the supernatural, *Seeker to the Dead* (1942) by the noted weird story specialist, A. M. Burrage. The only 'out and out' hardcover SF novels were Ray Cummings' reprinted time travel epic, *The Shadow Girl* (1946) and the juvenile (schoolboys journey on a spaceship to Venus) *The School In Space* by Reginald Browne (E. S. Brooks). Neither book was identified on the cover or in the blurb as science fiction, though the vivid cover pictures and wording of the blurbs made their SF themes clear enough. Collectors should note that *The School In Space* was reissued several times in different coloured boards, and only the true first edition (in black boards) carried four colour plates by cover artist Jock McCail; *all later editions dropped the plates.*

Other publishers also included a smattering of SF titles among their regular publications. Mitre Press and Everybody's Books were among the more prolific, including Eugene Ascher's occult detective series about Lucian Carolus (*There Were No Asper Ladies*, *Uncanny Tales* (collection), and *The Grim Caretaker*, all in 1943). Justin Atholl had a number of short SF novellas, starting with *The Man Who Tilted the Earth* (1943), cover blurbed as "A one sitting thriller" rather than the SF it undoubtedly was, and Preston Yorke (Harold Kelly) first appeared with *The Gamma Ray Murders*, also in 1943. 'Yorke' later had other SF and weird novels and short stories published, the last in 1953 (*Space-Time Task Force*). Possibly horror and the supernatural figured more prominently than SF during the war years, and whilst they really lie outside the scope of this book, mention can be made of one of the more interesting ephemeral slim paperbacks produced by Mitre Press. *Horror Parade* (1945), was a collection of five stories by the noted professional ghost-hunter R. Thurston Hopkins. Priced at 1/-, its 64 pages measured only five by six inches (rather than the usual seven) and its red and blue cover by H. W. Perl further reflected the effect of wartime shortages and economies.

In 1942 Benson Herbert was invited to edit a fiction line for a technical book publisher, Lloyd Cole. Herbert had been born in Wallsend, on Tyneside (only a hundred yards away from this chronicler!) and he had gone to his local University and gained a Master's Degree in Science. Thereafter he had moved to London. Several of his SF stories had appeared in *Wonder Stories* and *Tales of Wonder*, and in 1936 he had the rare distinction of having a hardcover SF novel issued in England—*Crisis!1992* (which had earlier appeared in *Wonder Stories* as 'The Perfect World'.)

As well as penning a number of mystery novels himself, Herbert supplied a few short SF novellas (*Strange Romance*; *Hand of Glory*; and *Thieves of the Air*, written in collaboration with Festus Pragnell; and *The Red-Haired Girl*). Cole's line also included a couple of juvenile SF stories written by 'Edmund Burton' (Edward Childes).

In 1944 Herbert left Lloyd Cole to set up his own company. Walter Gillings had just been released from the army, suffering from psychoneurosis, and Herbert contacted him with the idea of setting up a joint venture. With Gillings' editorial experience and Herbert's knowledge of publishing, they set up Utopian Publications and launched a new SF line in September of 1944, with an original SF booklet, *Girl in Trouble*, by London fan E.

Frank Parker. With Gillings making good use of his previous contacts with American authors during his *Tales of Wonder* editorship, the series continued using mainly American reprints by such noted authors as Robert Bloch, Stanton Coblentz, Edmond Hamilton, Otis A. Kline, Raymond A. Palmer, Manly Wade Wellman and Jack Williamson. Gillings' favourite author and friend John Beynon Harris also appeared with *Love in Time* ('Wanderers of Time' retitled, but cloaked under the pseudonym of 'Johnson Harris', to protect his good name: Utopian was not the sort of publisher he wished to be associated with!)

Utopian illustrated another aspect of the new breed of publishing with their products. They did not only issue SF booklets—they included westerns and crime on their fiction list—but also on the programme were numerous 'art' studies such as *Futurist Femininity,* which featured nude photographs of Rosemary Andree, 'Britain's most beautiful model.' This was issued with a sealed band about the middle and was priced at 5/-, which was a ridiculously high price at the time when the normal price for one of these fiction booklets was 9d (and even those sported nudes on the covers). The reliance on sex to sell the books was not really necessary, but it did mean that some products would reach an audience they would not normally have done (one wonders how many people picked up some of the SF booklets because of the nude on the cover and the racy titles like *Romance in Black, Love in Time,* and *The Sea-Kissed,* only to be disappointed that there was nothing sexy in the contents!). In many cases, the fiction was of secondary importance to the buyer (although by the end of the war it was necessary to dress the cover model in 'adequate light clothing' if the books were to get distribution).

Author Sydney J. Bounds also became involved with Benson Herbert. The inside story of their relationship was told when I interviewed Syd at a London Book Fair in 1991, the interview being recorded on video.

After remembering him as "a very sharp character", Syd continued:

> I met him when he was a guest at the Teddington SF club. After the war
> he started Utopian Publications, which at first reprinted some old American
> SF and weird stories, and then switched to original material. I began to
> sell him a few stories. At Utopian Publications he started his photographic
> business, producing nude 'art studies' of young ladies, and selling them—the
> photographs, that is! In order to advertise his photographs for sale, he started

a magazine. The actual contents of the magazine didn't particularly matter! The attitude many publishers had in those days was that they never read what they published. Or at least, I would be very surprised if they did—I certainly never read anything of mine that appeared in his magazines!

Benson's brainchild was what was then known as a 'spicy' magazine—nowadays it might be classed as very soft porn. In those days of post-war shortages, publishers were not able to get paper supplies for a new regular magazine, so the way they got around it was to change the title of the magazine with each issue. So one month it might be called *Peppy Stories*, the next month *Snappy Stories*, and so on.

Utopian Publications needed a reliable writer to provide their monthly quota of spicy stories. The gentleman who got the job was Norman (Wesley) Firth, who was known as 'The Prince of British Pulp Pedlars.' Now, it is a lie—I do know this—that Firth was chained to the wall in the basement of Benson's house. He had a room in the basement that contained a bed and his wife. He wrote virtually the entire contents of the Utopian magazines, one after the other—until he suddenly went down with TB. This was a very serious disease in those days: there was no known cure. Within a matter of weeks, Firth had died. Benson had to act quickly to find a replacement.

Since I'd done one or two stories for him, he hired me to supply 30,000 words a month. I realized that the income from this writing was more than equivalent to my £6 a week in the factory—so I immediately quit working there!

But things were too good to last. Utopia Press were subject to two difficulties. Because of the risqué nature of his operation, Benson was regularly raided by the Police, and subjected to fines of up to £200 a time (a lot of money in the late forties.) His second problem was that rival sleazy publishers used to hire professional crooks to burgle his premises and steal his photographs, so they could sell them themselves! The Police—who were not enamoured of his operation—just weren't interested in apprehending the thieves. Eventually, Benson decided he'd had enough.

He moved to Wales and got hold of a printing press, and launched a somewhat different line: publishing poetry by amateur dear old ladies! He was immediately successful, and made a lot of money!

The end of the war led to a publishing boom unequalled to this day, as some of the pre-war publishers returned to set up or restart their companies, and less scrupulous men set out to exploit the market.

With the end of the war, the SF fraternity began to regroup and start, once again, to pressure publishers into issuing a British SF magazine.

Walter Gillings had left Herbert and Utopian Publications in 1946, after he had edited two issues of a reprint fantasy magazine, *Strange Tales* (February and March of 1946). The first issue was especially notable for carrying the first-ever reprinting in the U.K. of a story by Ray Bradbury ('The Tombstone'.)

Herbert himself had also made two reprint selections, *Thrilling Stories* and *Strange Love Stories,* after which Utopian ended their SF and fantasy list and returned to westerns and then saucy magazines, with such titles as *Cowgirl Capers* and *Peppy Stories,* along with sexy 'foto' sets.

Ever since 1943, soon after the folding of *Tales of Wonder,* Gillings had been putting material together in preparation for either relaunching his pre-war magazine or editing a new one. In 1944, he approached Temple Bar Publishing Company and persuaded them to launch a new magazine, *Fantasy* (not a continuation of Newnes' pre-war magazine). It was 1946 before the plans finally came together, and by the time the first issue was put out at the end of 1946, Britain was to see not one, but five SF magazines launched.

The first magazine off the launching pad was *New Worlds.* Soon after demobilization, in January 1946, Carnell met Frank Edward Arnold, another longtime SF fan and occasional author, who had just persuaded a publisher to issue a science fiction line. Arnold introduced Carnell to the company's director, Stephen Frances, and on the strength of his unused 1940 portfolio, was invited to edit a science fiction magazine.

Presented here for the first time are the late Frank Edward Arnold's own recollections (written in 1970) of this pivotal moment in British SF history, extracted from the memoir he wrote for my intended book *The Impatient Dreamers:*

> I vividly remember the reunion, early in 1946, of members of the pre-war Science Fiction Association, all of whom had mercifully survived the war unharmed. The meeting, held at the Shamrock Tavern in Fetter lane, close to our old haunt at Gray's Inn Road, was a cheerful and heartening occasion and I recall that we were less concerned with war-time memories than with

what we were going to do now that the fuss was all over. One surprising development was a general aversion to reviving the old SFA, probably because it had given its committee-men too much hard and thankless work. Another and more urgent point was the need for a new magazine to replace Walter Gillings' *Tales of Wonder*, a wartime casualty. This is where I came in.

A little while before the reunion I had joined a transient Writers' Circle somewhere in Soho, whence I had encountered Stephen D. Frances, then a freelance publisher. Steve was an instant convert to SF and invited me to edit a series of booklets for him, beginning with a reprint of some of my own early stories. Soon after, having read some more copies of *Astounding* and *Startling Stories*, he was on fire with enthusiasm for the new magazine he intended to publish—and for which he had only the paper and printers, no authors, no stories, nothing. By a happy coincidence Ted Carnell had just been demobbed, and I knew he had in his possession the dummy of the magazine projected as long ago as 1940. The three of us got together over a noggin, and thus *New Worlds* was born.

And who better than its editor, John 'Ted' Carnell himself, to tell the full inside story of *New Worlds*? His memoir that follows was first published in *Vision of Tomorrow* for June 1970, as *The Birth of New Worlds*.

It was the last week in January 1946, typically cold and bleak. I had been demobilised from the Army the previous week, still apparently fit and sane after five and a half years' service. A grateful Government had given me a complete civilian outfit, three months pay and allowances and a bonus of £80 (which I had promptly spent on a 9-inch television set). I had just visited my pre-war firm in Holborn, only to find that the printing department had been firebombed out of existence in 1941 and was walking down Fleet Street contemplating my next move, when I met bibliophile and author Frank Edward Arnold. From such a small event the lives of many people, including my own, were to be shaped.

Frank, who was then working in the offices of the daily *News Chronicle*, had been one of our non-combatant anchormen during the war years and had kept in touch with most of the serving science fiction people, even contriving to organise a couple of minicons when sufficient people were in and around London on leave. We had plenty to talk over in one of the Street's celebrated coffee houses. His main news was that he was preparing to edit a series of 'little books' for a publisher 'just round the corner', to be called

'The Spacetime Series', containing short novels. If I still had my plans for the aborted 1940 *New Worlds* on file, he thought we should pay the enthusiastic publisher a visit and sound out the possibility of a regular SF magazine.

There were many realistic arguments against such a visit but Frank convinced me that there was no harm in trying, so we walked along Chancery Lane into Lincoln's Inn and up to the top floor of No. 10 Old Square, where the nameplate read *Pendulum Publications Ltd*. There I was introduced to one Stephen D. Frances, a mercurial young man full of enthusiasm for science fiction (and later to become universally famed as thriller writer 'Hank Janson'). Steve Frances was convinced that SF would rapidly become a universally popular form of fiction—were we not already in the throes of a technological explosion brought on through the exigencies of war? He could see no end to the advancement of science or to the possibilities of science fiction going hand in hand with it. He was also a very astute young publisher.

Every objection I raised was counterbalanced—paper, printing, production, artwork, distribution—leave it to Pendulum. All I had to do was find good material. I finally left the office having been given *carte blanche* to edit and produce the first two issues of *New Worlds*, if possible on a quarterly basis. A flat fee was to be paid to myself out of which I would pay the authors.

At that time Pendulum Publications was already publishing a number of 'series', all edited by freelance editors; there were 'Popular' westerns, thrillers, detective, romance, sport, film, adventure, politics and even a science series. Apart from Frank Arnold's 'Spacetime' series, Steve Frances also gave me the go-ahead to think about a fantasy series as well as a weird fiction series. I left his office with mixed feelings—partly of elation but largely disbelief in the existence of fairy godfathers.

My first job was to re-establish contact with the many pre-war friends, most of whom had been amateur SF authors or at best semi-professional. The Services were beginning to release those around my age group and I found that many had kept up their literary efforts despite wartime journeyings and had unpublished material on file. Bill Temple, who had spent a lot of his spare time in Italy writing a novel which periodically was either blown up or sunk in transit home (it was eventually published in 1949 by John Long as *Four-Sided Triangle*) sent me an unusual fantasy titled 'The Three Pylons'. Some of the regulars were still around—W. P. Cockcroft, Maurice G. Hugi and the indefatigable John Russell Fearn.

Fearn responded to my urgent request for material by sending over one quarter of a million words and in all those first few months produced over half a million, all of which had to be read and from which a selection had to be chosen for that first vital issue. As that began to take shape, my old SFA colleague, Ken Chapman, came out of the Navy and we arranged a meeting in Mooney's Irish House in Fetter Lane (owing to the beer shortage, we were only allowed one half pint on that occasion). Discussing the plans for the new magazine, Ken suggested that we tried to arrange a monthly meeting of all our pre-war colleagues, as this would give me an opportunity of talking to them about editorial requirements. This was quickly arranged in March and I remember meeting Maurice Hugi for the first time. Also present were Harold Chibbett, Bill Temple, Fred Brown, Eric Williams, Alan Devereaux, Frank Arnold, Ken Chapman and several others.

The next month we moved across the road to the 'White Horse' tavern, where accommodation was larger and the supply of beer more liberal. We were soon joined by John Beynon Harris (who was soon to start his 'John Wyndham' career), Arthur C. Clarke, Walter Gillings, Sydney J. Bounds, Harry Kay and most of the former attendees at the Grays Inn 'Flat'.

Those 'White Horse' meetings soon became weekly and were the forerunners of all the subsequent 'London Circle' meetings which continued over 'The Globe' in Hatton Garden, where aficionados still meet regularly on the first Thursday in every month. By no means an insignificant achievement over twenty-four years.

The first professional issue of *New Worlds* took shape and rounded out with two novelettes: 'The Mill of the Gods', by Maurice G. Hugi and 'The Three Pylons', by William F. Temple, plus four short stories, all of which were written by John Russell Fearn—i.e. 'Solar Assignment' by 'Mark Denholm'; 'Knowledge Without Learning' by 'K. Thomas'; 'White Mouse' by 'Thornton Ayre', and 'Sweet Mystery Of Life' under his own name. Cover art and interiors were by Bob Wilkin, one of the many artists employed by Pendulum. It was published in July, price 2 shillings, 64 pages quarto and subtitled 'A Fiction Magazine of the Future'.

Its sales were disastrous. Out of a print run of 15,000 copies, only 3,000 were sold. The postmortem at Pendulum's office (and subsequently at the 'White Horse') was rigorous but the general consensus was almost complete apathy in the wholesale distributing trade. One point, however, I was insistent upon—the second issue, already committed to the printer, needed an eye-catching cover painting. I had never approved the first one; in fact, I never saw it until it was completed, although I liked the original idea.

This stemmed from Frank Arnold—an atomic explosion in the background, nude New Man foreground, futuristic buildings left and ruins of old-style buildings right. However the execution was flat and two dimensional, dull and uninspiring.

I designed the cover of No. 2 from a montage of several American covers. I had (and still have) an original Howard Brown oil painting of the July 1937 *Astounding* which illustrated the Eric Frank Russell and Leslie Johnson story 'Seeker Of Tomorrow'. To this was added a spaceship design from a 1938 cover from *Amazing Stories* and from this sketch artist Victor Caesari evolved a spaceship cover to illustrate 'Space Ship 13' by Patrick S. Selby. While not technically perfect it still had good balance and colour and was a striking improvement over No. 1. Plus a wider variety of authors—a new John Beynon story, 'The Living Lies', plus 'Thornton Ayre' and 'Polton Cross' (both Fearn pseudonyms), W. P. Cockcroft, new authors Patrick Selby and John Brody, and a short, 'The Micro Man' by Alden Lorraine (one of many pseudonyms used by our old American friend, Forrest J Ackerman). Articles by Leslie Johnson and Forrest Ackerman, plus a drum-beating editorial.

That second issue was published in October and was almost instantaneously a sell-out due almost entirely to an all out drive by the Pendulum group. In fact, it was oversold by more than 3,000 copies, which led directly to the publisher deciding to strip out the 'No. 2' on the cover blocks, insert 'No. 1', print 10,000 new covers and replace the cover on the 10,000 unsolds still lying in the warehouse. Even that venture was a selling success and if anyone has a copy in their collection, I can say that they don't have the original No. 1.

So, as the year ended, Britain's SF future looked fairly bright. In December, the long-delayed first issue of *Fantasy: The Magazine of Science Fiction,* edited by Walter Gillings and published by Temple Bar Publishing Co. had appeared, pocket-sized, 96 pages and retailing at only one shilling, (which was something of a blow to the Pendulum controlled *New Worlds*). Walter's editorial policy, now backed by a publisher of considerable repute, was as ambitious as my own and it looked as though the healthy rivalry we expected to grow between us would be good for the authors and entice many new writers to try their skill in this somewhat demanding medium. Frank Arnold's 'Spacetime' series was off the ground with *Wings Across Time*, a collection of four of his own stories and I had produced *Jinn and Jitters*, a collection of five fantasy stories in the Pendulum 'Fantasy' series. It was followed by John Russell Fearn's novel *Other Eyes Watching*, reprinted from the American *Startling Stories* under the pseudonym of 'Polton Cross'.

Listed as a short novel for No. 2 was Lyle Monroe's *Lost Legacy* (Robert A. Heinlein). The weekly meetings at the 'White Horse' had swollen to over thirty regulars and now included Sam Youd (soon to write under the name of 'John Christopher'), John Burke, E. C. Tubb, Kenneth Bulmer, merchant navy officer A. Bertram (Jack) Chandler whenever he was in port, John Newman and many others.

1947 started well enough. Encouraged by the rapidly expanding SF market, Walter Gillings commenced publication of his vitally important bi-monthly news magazine *Fantasy Review*. I had been given the okay to go ahead with *New Worlds* No. 3 due for March publication, although the bad winter that subjected the country to power cuts was only the beginning of a series of setbacks that delayed final publication until the end of October! But the Spring was full of promise. Bill Passingham's eldest son, Kenneth, with a natural flair for artistry, had produced a cover painting I liked—now a prominent Fleet Street journalist, Ken has probably long forgotten his incursion into the world of science fiction under the pseudonym 'Slack'). His painting was a scene from a long novelette titled 'Dragon's Teeth' by John K. Aiken, who had been the former president of the Teddington Cosmos Club. It was the forerunner of two further novelettes, 'Phoenix Nest' and 'Cassandra', the whole making a complete novel of a revolutionary nature for those days. (Ironically, it never saw book publication until 1969, when Robert Hale published it under the title of *Phoenix Nest*).

New writers were beginning to submit good stories; Arthur Clarke submitted a short story, 'Inheritance', which was scheduled for No. 3 under the pseudonym of 'Charles Willis'; Francis G. Rayer, long a technical radio expert, sent his first story 'From Beyond The Dawn', John Brody had his second acceptance with 'The Inexorable Laws'. Yet another newcomer, Nick Boddy Williams, was placed in that third issue with 'The Terrible Morning'. Finally the editorial contents were rounded off with what was to be Maurice G. Hugi's last written work, 'Fantasia Dementia', for he died early in that year at his home in North London.

He was only 43. What we did not know until afterwards was that in 1946 when we had all met for that first post-war gathering, Maurice already knew that he only had a year to live. So British SF lost its first great character.

The Spring lengthened into Summer and the third issue of Walter Gillings' *Fantasy* was published—but not the third issue of *New Worlds*. Delays were caused by printing problems, blockmakers, difficulties in obtaining paper, power cuts and finally Pendulum Publications began to run into financial difficulties. However, during the go-slow period I had still gone ahead preparing No. 4 and had four novelettes scheduled—'World In Shadow' by John Brody, 'Edge Of Night' by John K. Aiken, and from USA, 'Was Not Spoken' by E. Everett Evans and 'Bighead' by William de Koven. The latter was a pseudonym for a then well-known American author but neither my memory nor records throw any light on his true identity. Short stories were accepted from Patrick S. Selby and Norman Lazenby (who was already appearing in *Fantasy*) and I was planning to use that great pre-war Manchester fan artist Harry Turner.

By October, when the long-delayed third issue finally went on sale at a reduced selling price of 1/6d, the publisher had moved to less pretentious premises in Chancery Lane with a reduced staff and an ever-increasing list of periodicals. In November I was given a cheque for the editorial expenses, paid the authors out on my own cheque, then received the Pendulum cheque back marked 'Refer to Drawer'. A stormy session with the publisher's accountant drew an apology and the assurance that if I would present the cheque again, it would be fully met. Which I did, only to have it bounce again. This time there was only Steve Frances left in the remnants of Pendulum's offices, clearing up on behalf of the Official Receiver. The accountant-secretary had disappeared leaving an empty coffer and all that Steve could offer me was a suitcase full of the first three issues of *New Worlds*, which I carried away and stored in my attic until their value increased sufficiently for me to start selling them on the collectors' market. Even then it took over ten years to recoup the £80 editorial fee I dropped in 1947—but by then many new events had taken place and a new *New Worlds* had risen from the ashes of the old. As if in sympathy and at just about the same time, Walter Gillings announced the suspension of his professional magazine, *Fantasy*, after publication of its third issue. So the year closed dismally, with only the cheering commiserations of the ever-increasing band of fellow travellers at the 'White Horse' to carry the glowing embers.

Arnold had seen the fruits of his work appear in April 1946, when the first of the Pendulum 'Spacetime' series of books under his editorship appeared, with a reprint collection of his own American pulp short stories entitled *Wings Across Time*, followed a month later by a novel, *Other Eyes Watching*, by 'Polton Cross' (John Russell Fearn). The first title in the 'Fantasy' series, edited by Carnell, was published in June 1946, an original anthology entitled

Jinn and Jitters; and, in July, the first issue of *New Worlds*.

As previously noted by Carnell, that issue was far from successful; only three thousand copies of the 15,000 print run were sold. Much of the blame was put on the cover by Bob Wilkin. Wilkin was a successful and competent commercial illustrator, but had succumbed to working to a policy of mass-production of quickly drawn comic strips and illustrations for children's annuals, particularly for Gerald G. Swan. His cartoon-like cover was not particularly effective and would have been lost among the welter of magazines then appearing. But, as noted, Carnell had adroitly managed to retrieve the situation.

So, back in 1946, it had looked like Britain had a steady SF market, and the appearance of more titles of varying quality showed that SF was again a genre to be reckoned with.

Hamilton & Co. (Stafford) Ltd. had been established for some three years, issuing diverse 'original' paperbacks and pamphlets, but generally following and copying the products of their competitors. They were quick to spot the initiative of Pendulum's *New Worlds,* and quickly commissioned their mainstay writer Norman Firth to write science fiction for them. A self-styled 'Prince of British Pulp Pedlars' Firth was a versatile hack willing to turn his hand to whatever fiction was in demand—gangster, western, saucy stories and juveniles. Their first SF product was a 48-paged pulp-size effort entitled *Futuristic Stories* in October 1946, followed a month later by *Strange Adventures.* Both magazines were originally priced at two shillings, but trade resistance to the high price quickly forced Hamilton to distribute later copies with a one shilling sticker over the old price. Each contained three stories by author Norman Firth, under his own name and two pseudonyms, Earl Ellison and Rice Ackman. They were generally of an appalling standard, mechanically written space operas, although a couple of the stories showed flashes of wry humour. Both featured lurid and garish space operatic covers (robots and monster respectively) painted by veteran cover specialist H. W. Perl, whose idea of science fiction was apparently rooted in 1930s *Flash Gordon* serials. Each magazine featured a single uncredited full-page illustration unusually executed in scraperboard; these were actually quite good, but the overall impression of both magazines was pretty dreadful, and did nothing to advance the cause of British science fiction.

Hamilton's followed the magazines with two paperback books that were of a slightly better standard—*Terror Strikes* by Firth, and *Strange Hunger* by Michael Hervey (previously known only as a prolific crime writer). Firth's 78-page novella was a routine reworking of Wells' *The Invisible Man*, and sported another lurid (but quite striking) Perl cover. The book, somewhat overpriced at one shilling and sixpence, was printed on very thin cheap paper, which didn't help. Hervey's book on the other hand, was a full 128-page novel printed on much better stock, and consequently carrying the high price of two shillings and sixpence. It was a rather curiously restrained Utopian story, not at all lurid or sensational. Hervey was a talented writer and his earnest and well-written novel had a serious anti-war message. It deserved a better publisher; Hamilton's clearly did not know how to illustrate it, so used a Perl painting obviously originally intended for one of their romance novels, showing a langorous leggy lovely (Perl was much better with "Good Girl Art" than he was with SF!) Unsurprisingly the books would have made little impact, and were probably not perceived as science fiction anyway.

Both *Futuristic* and *Strange* made only one more appearance, in December and the following January, this time reduced to only 32 pages priced at one shilling, with only a single Firth novelette. The uncredited covers were even more lurid, this time being laminated, and were executed by rising young artist Oliver Brabbins, who also probably did the garish comic strip style half-page interior illustrations. SF was decidedly not his forte, and he would go on to much better things in later years. One can safely assume that sales of the magazines were deservedly poor, as Hamilton did not produce any more SF for four years.

These four dreadful Hamilton publications probably did more than any other SF offerings at the time to blacken the reputation of the genre. They were spotlighted and burlesqued by the noted novelist and critic Margot Bennet, who lambasted them in her article entitled 'Space-ships also Leak' featured in the famous monthly *Lilliput*, in which she chivvied "incredible science writers." Unfortunately, she appeared to put them in the same category as *New Worlds* and *Astounding Science Fiction*, at whom she also poked fun, with " . . . green mammoth egg-headed statues and an intrepid pilot on the cover . . . Moral of this scientific pulp seems to be to keep the future with its fatal exaggeration of the present away from your door . . . As for the ice-men, metal-men, fish-men, space-jelly and incredible writers, a bottle of Martian *Sitch* would probably keep them all quiet for a small part of the future, at least."

Of much higher literary tone was *Outlands*, edited by Liverpool fan Leslie Johnson (another person instrumental in the formation of B.I.S.). Although operating on a shoestring budget, Johnson managed to bring together old and new authors for his debut issue by soliciting rejected material considered too unorthodox by other publications. Whilst the sedate blue cover with inset river scene would have looked more at home on a church journal than a science fiction publication, the banner headline 'A Magazine for Adventurous Minds' and the announcement of 'Pre-Natal', by John Russell Fearn could have left no doubts in the minds of fans as to its contents. But even veterans like George Wallis and youngsters like Syd Bounds (his first professional appearance) could not save the magazine. A complete failure to secure newsstand distribution killed *Outlands* before the planned second issue could appear in December 1946.

But December *did* bring *Fantasy* from Walter Gillings and Temple Bar. Digest (5½ by 8 inches) sized, with good illustrations and its 96 pages printed on good stock. The magazine was again led off by John Russell Fearn with his novelette 'Last Conflict', and included contributions from Arthur C. Clarke ('Technical Error'), Philip Cleator, newcomer Norman Lazenby, and Stanley G. Weinbaum's 'The Worlds of If', betraying Gillings' conservatism.

The year 1947 should have seen science fiction magazines settling down to more regular schedules, but it was not to be. With two quality magazines on the market and the war now a bad memory, spirits must have been quite high, but the effects of the war were still being felt by the publishing industry. With more and more publishing houses being launched, the problem of paper supply was getting worse instead of better. Although some restrictions were gradually being lifted, the paper shortage meant that rationing was still in full force. More supplies were coming through, often from Canada or Ireland, but far from enough.

Fantasy appeared again in April 1947 with interesting non-fiction pieces by the editor, and short stories by Clarke ('Castaway' as Charles Willis) and two by Lazenby ('Survival' and 'Haunted House' as J. Austin Jackson) and others by E. R. James and P. E. Cleator, with Eric Frank Russell providing the lead novelette, 'Relic'. There was a gap of four months until August, when the third and final issue appeared. The enterprising

Gillings had obtained 'Time Trap' a new novelette from veteran American writer Stanton A. Coblentz, supported by four short stories by Norman C. Pallant, who also appeared as by Charles Allen Crouch, F. G. Rayer and Clarke, whose story 'The Fires Within' as by E. G. O'Brien would later be sold to *Eagle* (who would think it was a new story). The issue was rounded out with a condensation of Bohun Lynch's 1925 'Menace From the Moon' and a non-fiction feature by the editor under his Thomas Sheridan byline. At that point, although *Fantasy* was selling out its 6,000 copy print run, Temple Bar decided to axe the magazine in favour of using the paper for other more lucrative publications. Gillings once again retired back to fan publishing and concentrated on *Fantasy Review*, which he had started in March 1947. His journalistic experience ensured that the fanzine was anything but amateur in content.

Problems were also besetting Ted Carnell's *New Worlds*. There was a year's gap between the second and third issues and, when the third finally did arrive in October 1947, the editorial put the blame on power cuts and distribution problems (caused by bad weather in the early part of the year) from which the magazine had only just survived. Pendulum was also hit with financial problems and soon went into liquidation, taking *New Worlds* to a premature end with it.

Science fiction publishing was back to square one again, with only the occasional low-quality product put on the market. It is ironic that the most healthy SF production was a British Reprint Edition (BRE) of the American magazine *Astounding*, which had appeared regularly since August 1939 from Atlas Publishing and Distributing Co. The magazine was trimmed down from its American original, missing certain features and replacing some items with British advertisements. It was, nonetheless, a much-needed publication for the fans of 1948. Poorer efforts at BREs were two rag-bag compilation issues of *Amazing* that appeared in 1946-47, and Gerald G. Swan's *Future Fantasy and Science Fiction* which appeared in 1948 as number 11 of the 'Swan American Magazines' series (which included *Science Fiction Quarterly* as number 15 in 1950). Atlas also issued a doctored edition of *Unknown Worlds*, which folded in 1949 after forty-one issues (more than the original, since the BRE used less stories per issue).

With only BREs to exist on, 1948 was a bleak year for SF fans, but proved to be the calm before the storm, and 1949 was to be the start of a deluge that has not been rivaled since. Also, it was the two factions from the recently liquidated Pendulum Publications, director Stephen Frances and editors Arnold and Carnell, that were instrumental in the next step that was to launch the best and the worst science fiction into the British market.

Yankee Science Fiction # 3
(John Woods). Swan, 1941

They Came From Mars by W.P.
Cockcroft (Jock McCail). Swan,
ca. 1944. (Courtesy Morgan Wallace.)

Newnes house advertisement that
appeared in several of their magazines,
announcing *Fantasy*.

Fantasy # 1, July 1938,
(S.R. Drigin artwork).

Strange Tales # 1 (Alva Rogers).
Utopian, 1946

Strange Offspring by Raymond A.
Palmer (photo). Utopian, 1945

New Worlds # 1 (Bob Wilkin).
Pendulum, 1946

Fantasy # 1 (Bruce Gaffron).
Temple-Bar, 1946

CHAPTER 4:
BRAVE NEW
(TREMBLING) WORLDS

Ever since the 1930s, it was always the constant pressure that fans brought to bear on publishers that had led to the issuing of quality SF magazines. Those that arrived without the backing of fans with a solid background in SF were invariably poor comparisons, such as the Hamilton magazines in 1946-47. Without any apparent interest from the publishing world, SF was at its lowest ebb at the close of 1947, and it did not look as though things would get any better.

It was up to the fans again to rectify the situation.

The following essay on the rebirth of *New Worlds* was written for me by Ted Carnell and describes the efforts he and other fans put into the advancement of British SF and the launching of fandom's finest monument, Nova Publications.

The winter period of 1947-48, following the end of Pendulum Publications was a sad one, at least for myself, enlivened only by the regular weekly meetings of authors and fans at the White Horse Tavern in Fetter Lane. Wartime import restrictions were still in force and the only American SF magazines that found their way in were those arranged privately by mutual exchange. The British Reprint Editions did a great deal to reduce the gap but they were mere shadows of the parent magazines.

By the spring, however, optimism was once again on the upsurge, promoted largely by the one-day Whitsun SF Convention held at the White Horse and presided over by Walter Gillings. At the meeting, I was able to inform the delegates that a scheme was being pursued with a view to forming our own publishing company for which they would have the chance of purchasing shares. The idea was started quite innocently at a typical Thursday gathering during the never-ending argument about shortsighted publishers, when a voice asked, "Why not start our own company? We could publish our own magazine." The idea had been heard before, but not by Frank Cooper, a retired R.A.F. officer who had put some of his gratuity into a bookshop in Stoke Newington, with a popular SF section. He had recently joined the regulars at the pub and took up the idea of volunteering to obtain all the necessary information on floating a company.

In fact it was entirely due to his fine efforts that the company prospectus was finally drafted, approved, and sent to a list of some 400 names acquired from various sources. Shares were offered at £1 each, with a minimum of five to be purchased. Nearly fifty enthusiasts subscribed an initial capital of just over £600, which was thought to be sufficient to launch the company. Frank's solicitor handled the formation details, Walter Gillings' wife, Madge, thought up the name Nova Publications Ltd., and by the end of the year the dream was moving into reality.

The first six working directors (spare-time, unpaid), were John B. (Wyndham) Harris, Chairman; G. Ken Chapman, Treasurer; Frank C. Cooper, Secretary; Walter Gillings, Advertising; Eric C. Williams, Subscriptions; and myself, John Carnell, Editorial. A top-class printing house convenient to Stoke Newington was located, paper was coming off the ration, and the blockmakers were glad to welcome a new account. By the spring of 1949, the new company was in business, and *New Worlds* #4 was planned as a trial issue, demy format (8½ x 5½"), 96 pages selling at 1/6d, with quarterly publication ultimately in mind. That issue went on sale in June, with a traditional bullet-shaped spaceship in a breaking orbit near the moon, painted by 'Dennis' (Slack), with interior artwork by White, a young art student lodging at our home at the time. The contents were exactly the same as planned for the defunct Pendulum edition. The issue also featured a lively article by Arthur C. Clarke entitled 'The Shape of Ships to Come', in which he postulated the possibility of dumbbell-shaped spaceships for extra-planetary voyages—used seventeen years later in the epic film *2001: A Space Odyssey.*

To economize, Nova had to do its own distribution, no mean feat for a group of amateurs, but Frank Cooper and his manager, Les Flood, proved to be capable of this monumental task and by July we were confident that we could plan ahead for regular quarterly publication. In fact, issue 5 was published in September of 1949, and issue 6, dated 'Spring 1950', in January of that year. While issue 5 was at press, I had been one of the Guests of Honour at the 7th World SF Convention in Cincinnati, Ohio, going on a partially-assisted passage originated by Forrest J Ackerman (which was ultimately the forerunner of the Trans-Atlantic Fan Fund [TAFF], awarded to a British fan so s/he may travel to an American convention) backed by donations from both sides of the Atlantic, which yielded about half the fare on the Queen Elizabeth. Because it was not possible to take any money to the United States, I was sponsored by 'Doc' Barrett of Ohio, and completely overwhelmed by the generosity of a host of American publishers, authors, and fans toward the first representative from the United Kingdom to make contact in the United States. Most of the post-convention time was spent in Chicago and New York, soaking up the American SF scene, and I returned to England full of ideas and useful contacts.

Soon after the third issue of *New Worlds* had appeared in October 1947, Pendulum Publications had gone into voluntary liquidation. Director Stephen Frances wasted no time in launching his next enterprise, S. D. Frances (Publisher) Ltd., with sole distribution by Gaywood Distributors Ltd. In the autumn of 1948, he began to write and publish a series of tough gangster novels under the byline 'Hank Janson,' a name he had previously used on a short novel, *When Dames Get Tough* (Ward and Hitchon, 1946). The 'Janson' novels met with instant success; the sexy/sadistic portrayal of the tough Chicago newspaperman's adventures, packed with tough action and violence (and plenty of dames), while distinctly unsavoury, were at least better written (though somewhat indebted to Damon Runyon) than most of the paperbacks then offered. Although not the British originator of this style of fiction (Britain already had such authors as 'Darcy Glinto' (Harold Kelly) and the pre-eminent 'James Hadley Chase' [René Raymond] to offer), Frances, as both author and publisher, was able to build up the character as the series progressed. Most publishers of the time kept away from the series format since it would give the author a chance to become extremely popular, and then possibly move on to other better-paying markets. This happened to Modern Fiction Ltd., whose 'Miss Otis' series (first appearing in 1948) was published as by 'Ben Sarto'. Sarto titles had been appearing since 1946, and were mostly the work of F. Dubrez Fawcett, who had created the 'Miss Otis' character. In 1953, Fawcett discovered he could get a better rate of pay from the newly-formed Milestone Publications, and so switched his allegiance to them for a couple of years in 1953-54, taking with him the lucrative 'Miss Otis' series and using the 'Ben Sarto' byline.

The popularity of 'Hank Janson' was a contributing factor in the sudden emergence of hundreds of American gangster novels. The market was suddenly swamped with poorly written trash, all written to a low-standard formula of constant violence laced with sex.

Norman Lazenby showed me a letter dated 9th April 1951 he had received from John Watson, the Managing Director and editor of Muir-Watson Ltd.:

> Lately I have been trying to find out what makes Hank Janson tick.
>
> You may not realize that it is rumoured in the trade that Janson sells almost as many books as all our authors put together. This of course is not quite true, but I believe it is true that he is the biggest seller in the gangster field with our Nata Karta following not so terribly far behind.
>
> Now I think this is partly due to the fact that Janson always focuses his story on the trials and tribulations of a girl. I think he has something here. The kind of people who read our stuff don't give a damn if Johnny, the hero, is tied up and treated rough in the basement of a warehouse, but they just love it when the same thing happens to Grizelda the heroine.
>
> I think we should have a crack at this style of story, which, of course, is no different from what we're doing, except that you keep in mind this 'focus on the girl' angle, while keeping in mind the fact that nobody wants to go to gaol.
>
> Payment will be increased to meet additional work, this increase to start from the story you are writing now, *Just Make a Pass*."

Such was the cynical contempt for the readers in those days! But a short time later Watson got cold feet, and wrote to Lazenby again on 23rd April 1951:

> . . . after consultation with my distributor I decided to discontinue for the time being, publication of our Nat Karta, Hyman Zore, and Hans Vogel lines.
>
> You will appreciate with what reluctance I came to this decision, but in the face of the terrific spate of prosecutions which are taking place all over

the country, and especially after R. & L. Locker were last week fined thirteen hundred pounds in respect of three books which were very little different from our own, I don't see how we can carry on until the authorities decide just what is an obscene book.

Accordingly, Mr. Lazenby, I have to ask you to stop production with the completion of *Just Make a Pass*. We will pay you up to date, and as soon as this position clears itself, I look forward to carrying on in the Karta, Zore and Vogel tradition.'"

In February 1952, Muir-Watson re-entered the fray, with a toned-down *Just Make a Pass* revamped by Watson as *A Guy Named Judas*. He explained his action in another letter to Lazenby:

To do that I had to change the name of the original hero to that of Dana Dallas and to make this acceptable to the reader I have indicated that Dallas was not always the most respectable of characters, this you might do well to bring out in your new manuscript. While this idea was not anything other than expedient, I think that it doesn't do any harm to have a complex character in this Dallas fellow, as I see him now, he is something of an ex-crook, turned into a private detective, but his moral outlook remains that of a man who has operated on both sides of the law.

Most of the gangster novels were passed off under Italian-American bylines that publishers claimed to be real American private eyes, and for a while several mushroom firms flourished, producing endless gangster novels, with the occasional western, foreign legion, and science fiction title.

With 'Hank Janson' so financially successful, Frances felt able to experiment with science fiction again, and by mid-1949 he was preparing a new SF line. In a later letter to me in 1964, written in answer to my query about the origin of the 'Astron Del Martia' byline he revealed:

My intention was to establish a regular science fiction author (at the back of my mind I thought I myself might be this author) and quite deliberately and cold-bloodedly I sat down and worked out a science fiction pen-name, 'Astron del Martia'—which is just about as concocted a pen-name as one could expect to see!

To launch his new byline, Frances needed an established author to write at least the first novel, since he had no experience in writing SF. His first choice was Eric Frank Russell, an author he had read and whose novel *Sinister Barrier* was one he particularly admired. But Russell had no intention of seeing his work abused in this way and, after ignoring two letters, he wrote a scathing reply to the third, making that quite clear.

Frances then turned for help to Frank Arnold, his former editor of the 'Spacetime' series at Pendulum. Arnold in turn contacted John Russell Fearn, who had already supplied material for Frances in his earlier days; six short stories had appeared in the first two issues of *New Worlds*, and the second book in the 'Spacetime' series was by Fearn under his 'Polton Cross' pseudonym. In a letter to me Arnold recalled:

> After we had bought *Other Eyes Watching* for the series, I was in correspondence with Fearn—I never met him, unfortunately—and he sent me a remarkably fine tale called *A Martian Returns*, featuring a noble character named RU. I bagged this one without delay, intending it to be fourth in the series, but by this time Pendulum Publications was in difficulties, and the 'Spacetime' series came to a premature end with only two titles to its name. I returned the typescript of *A Martian Returns* to its author, who was, of course, pretty wroth at the sudden and disappointing end of the effort after a promising start. Also his cheques were somewhat slow in arriving, which did not soften his opinions of Pendulum Publications!

In 1946 Arnold had, in fact, also accepted another Fearn novel, *Four Shall Avenge*, but this was also returned. Both of Fearn's aborted novels would eventually appear years later as by Vargo Statten: *A Martian Returns* as *The Last Martian* (1952) and *Four Shall Avenge* as *2,000 Years On* (1950). Yet another SF novel written around the same time was *Slaves of Ijax*, which Fearn managed to sell without any problems to Hyman Kaner, who published it in paperback early in 1948 as 'a complete mystery romance'. Kaner, however, was well aware that he was really publishing science fiction. He had been writing the odd short SF and weird story himself, scattered throughout his own 64-paged paperback collections since 1946, such as *The Cynic's Desperate Mission* and *Ape-Man's Offering*, and two 'wild and woolly' hardcover SF novels, *People of the Twilight* and *The Sun Queen*. Both novels had appeared in 1946, and were well produced with quite attractive dustwrappers by H. W. Perl—which, however, looked more weird and supernatural, rather than science fictional, and the words 'science fiction' were never used in the flap notes. Later Kaner would also publish westerns by Fearn.

When Arnold contacted Fearn again in 1949, it seemed that he would be unlucky: most of the latter's unpublished science fiction had recently been sent to America. However, never one to miss out on a possible sale, Fearn agreed to quickly write a brand new novel, *Legacy from Sirius*, which he sent directly to Frances.

Retitled *The Trembling World*, it was rushed into print in June 1949 by Frances under the 'Astron del Martia' byline, and became the first ostensibly SF novel to be published as part of the new paperback boom. The novel showed more imagination than the horrendous cover: instructed to 'depict a spaceship', artist Philip Mendoza did just that; his 'spaceship' resembled nothing so much as a naval battleship cruising through space! Mendoza was a talented cover artist then specialising in covers for gangster and western novels, who unfortunately was not familiar with SF. This diabolical cover would not have helped sales, nor would the unknown concocted byline. Had Fearn's quite good novel been published under his own name with a more competent SF cover, Frances' bold claim in the advertisement at the back of the book ('the publishers feel they are pioneering a new type of fiction!') might not have been just a hollow boast.

With poor sales (despite being advertised in *New Worlds*), Frances did not proceed with his SF plans, and instead concentrated entirely on his commercially successful 'Hank Janson' sex-and-sadism gangster thrillers. Fearn's potential as a best-selling SF writer—especially if linked to a good cover artist—would not be recognized until a year later, and then by a totally different publisher . . .

Photo: E.J. Carnell and Frank E. Arnold
presiding at 1952 London Convention.
(Courtesy Peter Weston.)

New Worlds # 3 (Dennis Slack).
Pendulum, 1947

Other Eyes Watching by Polton Cross
(Bob Wilkin). Pendulum, 1946

New Worlds # 4 (Dennis Slack).
Nova, 1949

Photo: Philip Harbottle, Norman
Lazenby, Claire Harbottle,
Matthew Japp, Nini Japp.
St. Annes, 1982

Ape-Man's Offering by Hyman Kaner
(H.W. Perl). Kaner, 1947

Slaves of Ijax by John Russell Fearn
(H.W. Perl). Kaner, 1947

The Trembling World by Astron Del
Martia (Philip Mendoza). Frances, 1949

CHAPTER 5:
THE CRAZY WORLD

Although 1948 was a bleak year for science fiction, it was the turning point of the paperback boom that was to lead to the loss of face that SF suffered in the 1950s.

What follows here is a richly detailed essay that offers a unique insight into the conditions and motivations of the publishing companies. Author Gordon Holmes Landsborough became involved in the paperback industry in 1949, and worked with distinction in the field for many years after. He was one of the few figures who tried to save science fiction from the gutter when it hit an all-time low.

Even so, he had remained a shadowy and unknown figure to the SF community, until I was introduced to him at the Easter 1970 British Science Fiction Convention in London. I was then editing my magazine *Vision of Tomorrow*, and on learning that he had been the first editor of *Authentic Science Fiction* under the alias of 'G. L. Holmes' and Panther Books, I commissioned him to write his memoirs, intending to serialise them. Unfortunately the magazine folded before I could do so.

A later essay in this volume describes his attempts to launch a quality SF magazine in the shape of *Authentic Science Fiction*. But first he looks at what he identified as 'The Crazy World' of publishing:

The ten-year period from 1945 was, from a publishing point of view, so bizarre that what is written here might be dismissed as writer's fantasy or fiction. It is neither.

To understand the period, one must realize that wartime paper rationing lasted for thirteen years—thirteen years of scarcity, with the men there to exploit shortages, as always happens. Paper rationing began on April 30, 1940. During the war years, book publishing limped along, periodicals folded, and newspapers were down to four or six pages. The paper ration was like gold, to be used sparingly, sufficient to keep business alive—if the bombs didn't blow them out of existence.

But when war ended and the 'boys' came home, a new and astonishing breed of publisher mushroomed, an incredible phase in British publishing, whose effect is still strong upon us. These men did a terrible disservice to literature in general, and science fiction suffered woefully because of them.

These opportunists suddenly realized that if only they could lay their hands on paper—any kind of paper—they would be in the money: big money. People who did not live through those times cannot realize the desperate shortages caused by war. We were so starved of printed literature that anything printed sold. I know of one mushroom publisher who issued a sixteen-page brochure (it could hardly be called a book) showing Rita Hayworth, the film actress, in various poses, not very daring by today's standards. They were printed from film stills and sold at a shilling each. A shilling? But that was a lot in those days. *And over 200,000 copies were sold.* Perhaps that gives us an illustration of the artificial conditions prevailing at the time.

A new breed of opportunist publisher, then, came on the scene. They were particularly damaging to the infant science fiction market, which had struggled along to gain even a modest following in the UK.

These publishers, apparently with plenty of capital behind them, began a systematic purchase of any paper that was available. At the time we referred to it as 'black market' paper, but in fact there was nothing illegal about its purchase. If a publisher or printer preferred to sell his ration of paper, it was not against the law. Many found it more profitable to sell and make a profit out of their ration than to bother with publishing. The proceeds of resale could be very rewarding. The 'boys' found paper supplies in other ways. One intriguing one was to purchase reel-ends from newspaper publishers. At the end of a newspaper run there would generally be some paper left on the reels, which did not warrant re-threading for the purposes of a later edition. The 'boys' snapped these up eagerly, then cut them into sheets, for use in their backyard publishing enterprises.

At least a dozen firms specialised in this late 1940s publishing. A few tried their hand at producing periodicals (of abysmal quality), but most concentrated on paperbacks. These were as deplorable as could be possibly imagined: and someday someone should do a research on the paperback product of the time, through the British Museum Library, and produce a thesis that would not only astonish, but outrage those who read it.

Not one of these newcomers to publishing strived for quality. The cheapest possible printing was resorted to—any crude paper was used, and the books were invariably side-stabbed—that is, two nasty wires were inserted through the side of the text, so that it was impossible to flatten out the book. Artwork for the covers was the crudest imaginable, reflecting the deplorable taste of the publishers. They paid the artists only a few guineas, and got a standard worth only that price.

But we buy books for what is written in them, and it was the commissioning of stories that the publishers had most effect and were at their most damaging.

Today, paperback publishers are virtually reprint houses, sometimes paying sometimes huge sums—even into six figures—for the rights of titles bought from hardcover publishers. But in the late 1940s, all these backyard publishers issued 'originals'—that is, they commissioned authors to write specially for them. And here's where the fantasy begins.

Generally they paid about ten shillings per thousand words. Some paid a little more—perhaps 12/6d; often they paid less. I know one publisher who boasted to me that he had bought a manuscript for £5 and published it. He didn't read the manuscript before buying it. The temptation to buy cheaply was sufficient, and that story was inflicted on the public. (It was not science fiction, by the way). Some years back I met the same publisher, but by then he was out of business, working as a clerk in an export house. Perhaps crime doesn't pay, and what he gave that author was a crime in my opinion.

A very few authors were paid rather better rates than this—John Russell Fearn, for instance—but they weren't many. And often, after being commissioned, they had an awful job to get their money out of their exploiters.

Comparatively little science fiction was published in those years by these wretched publishers, and none that I remember did any good for this most imaginative of fiction writing. How could they attract genius at the rates they paid? It will be difficult for people to believe, but the backyard publishers (most of them operating from the most primitive of premises), would for a long period publish almost entirely westerns and sexo-sadistic stories with an American gangster setting á la James Hadley Chase.

They honestly believed that this was the only type of story the public wanted. I had many an argument with them, but they only looked at me with tolerant pity. Like the Wardour Street film producers of that period, they believed implicitly that only they knew the public taste. One of the silliest, glibbest sayings ever mouthed is the one that the public gets the literature (or government) it deserves. It's not true; we get what unscrupulous, uncaring people foist upon a public simply because they have the finance to put it across.

Under these circumstances, new science fiction of good quality could hardly emerge. Reputable publishing houses did not compete for the so-called 'black market' paper and used most of their ration to keep alive their established authors. So it was very difficult for new—let alone good—authors to break into print. The backyard boys never tried to find good writers, and that is the most damning thing that can be said of any publisher.

Hundreds of new titles were produced every year by this fraternity; they were never reprinted. The quality of storytelling was abominably low. The western writers had only the briefest acquaintance with the history of the West, and produced what the trade called 'bang-bang' tales. The private eye, American gangster novel (astonishingly dignified by the term 'sophisticated' by these publishers), depended on endless shootings, knifings, and other forms of violent murder, and sold on covers that depicted gangsters' molls which hinted at debauched sex along with the violence. Yet sex was only lightly touched on in those days; there was nothing like the permissiveness of today. They were just very unpleasant books, and God only knows how they found customers, even in a time of acute book shortage.

If one of those publishers did try his hand at science fiction publishing, he commissioned one of his western or American gangster writers to turn in a story. The result was insultingly bad, and explains why SF never got off the ground in Britain in the late 1940s.

The imagination of this type of writer never rose higher than an interplanetary voyage, with ray guns deployed in place of homely Chicago tommy-guns, with eight-legged, green-faced monsters to be destroyed on whichever planet they landed. Always, curiously, there was a girl on these planets—the female of the species (or they were a long-lost race fighting for survival against monster invaders) never running to more than the normal complement of limbs and was blessed with those organs which gangster writers felt inseparable from attractive fiction. These women were always portrayed on the covers by artists who gave them the most improbably-sized mammaries, generally tastefully covered in what looked like miniature dustbin lids. Most inconvenient, was my thought, when it came to moments of passionate bedwifery.

It was curious that though these crude publishers were so out of touch with the real literary needs of the masses, they yet had an instinct that in SF there was a large potential market. Time after time, each in turn put out so-called science fiction. They would sell out their first books, probably to an unsuspecting public hoping to find imaginative literature in spite of the gaudy covers. But 'once bitten' is a good adage and, when the publishers, delighted at finding a good new market, issued more such trash, it failed to sell. The SF reader wanted more than badly told tales which were really westerns or gangster stories with a supposed interplanetary setting.

Boom or bust was the pattern of science fiction publishing in those days. What an opportunity was lost! If only *one* of them had tried, had paid writers reasonable rates consistent with the big profits that were made out of rubbish, a thriving market might have been established. But what good writer would write for such meagre payments? And if an original, thoughtful SF story had been turned in, it would have been rejected by the stubby-fingered, mentally-calloused publishers who insisted, against all the evidence, that they knew the right formula to cater for the market.

What harm they did! For at least fifteen years, SF was virtually at a standstill. Instead of making the most of the genuine opportunities, these men did not advance SF in the slightest. Rather, they identified it with juvenile rubbish, a reputation it took a long time to live down.

Fifteen years is a long time. A new generation grew up with little opportunity to read good SF. Of course, there were *some* good SF books published by reputable houses, but of necessity it was limited in quantity because of paper rationing and generally appeared only in more expensive hardcover volumes (generally *five times* more expensive than paperbacks), beyond the pockets of young people who are always the future clientele for SF.

Perhaps even more harm was done to SF because there were few or no outlets for new writing, and potential authors who might have enlarged the field were lost to the SF world—what was the good of writing if there was no one to publish it?

They were wasted, those fifteen years from 1940 to 1955, and it was not until paper rationing ended in May 1953, and good paperback publishing houses began to cater for the enthusiast, that the exciting and truly sophisticated SF writing we enjoy today had a chance to be published and create an enthusiastic following. True, there were frequent phases during which phony SF appeared on the market. I am thinking of those writers who tried to impress by writing so obscurely that no one could understand them, and who turned many away in consequence.

Any of today's readers who feel that we have not come a long way with SF writing should read the products of the late 1940s and early 1950s. They would surely change their opinion after such a wearisome exercise.

I came into this curious world of publishing in 1949 for the simple reason that I was flat broke. As a writer and journalist (among other things, I had launched *Reveille* for its first owner in 1940), I was just one of thousands who came through the war to find there were few jobs available in publishing, whether it was newspapers, periodicals, or books. One day I saw an advertisement in *Advertiser's Weekly*: 'Wanted, Production Manager'. I decided I was a production manager, and went after the job.

The advertiser was Hamilton & Co. (Stafford) Ltd., who operated from two adjacent shops on Goldhawk Road, Shepherds Bush, London. It was then I learned that a production manager was required for paperback book publishing, of which I had no experience. The inadequacies of salary—£8/10/- a week—matching my inadequacies in the field, I got the job. But I was married, had three children, and couldn't live on that salary.

So I stipulated that Hamilton's must contract to buy one book a month from me, in addition to my salary. This would bring me a further £18 or so a month, and I needed that 'lolly'.

Before accepting the job at that low rate of pay, I took home some of the firm's products. I read them and I was appalled. Until that moment I honestly had never known of the existence of this type of publishing. I'd been brought up on Penguins, and those *were* books. These weren't worthy of the description.

I was shocked by the deplorably low standard of storytelling. I cannot describe how bad they were. At no other time in history, I am confident, could such wretched examples of craftsmanship have had money invested in them. They were so bad that my first reaction was to turn down the job, with its poor rate of pay. Then came the realization that here was a golden opportunity. With such deplorable storytelling, I could see ways of improving the situation and getting more for myself into the bargain.

I had never written a book before, but as a writer I knew I could beat any of the rubbish I had read before coming to my decision—and that wasn't rating my skills inordinately. So I went boldly to the publisher, made my proposition—and got the job. It was arranged that I should turn in a book a month, *even though my employer had as yet seen nothing of my writing.* Bewildering days indeed!

However, I was assigned to writing westerns—"Anyone can write westerns," said the publisher, amiably. Fortunately, I had read American history for some years, and I think I was able to introduce a note of originality into a list that was indefensibly bad. Later, I even made the grade with hard-cover publishers with my westerns, and some of them were reprinted, and the rights sold for translation so they couldn't have been too bad!

My job as production manager proved to be something of a euphemism. For £8/10/- a week I was everything: editor, sub-editor, blurb writer and, for some time, even proofreader, *and I had to commission and handle twelve to fourteen original manuscripts a month!* Manuscripts rolled in unsolicited, too, and these I had to read because from the start I was looking for talent—except for two writers, there were none on Hamilton's list in those days. One of those two was John Russell Fearn, who had been commissioned to write a series that was a dead ringer on Edgar Rice Burroughs' Martian series. There were four of them—*Emperor of Mars, Warrior of Mars, Red Men of Mars,* and *Goddess of Mars,* all published in 1950. John leaned on Burroughs heavily; his hero was Clayton Drew—Burroughs, you will remember, had a John Clayton as Tarzan. And Burroughs had red men on Mars a good quarter of a century before Fearn did. But more of this prolific author later.

The other good writer wrote American crime-gangster stories. He had been for some years in America, was an extremely nice and gentle man for all his tales of horrific violence, and his writing had quality. He could have made a name for himself in literature, but I think writing one book a month burned him out. One of the casualties of this senseless exploitation.

Each day I would turn into the office. I would read, punctuating, correcting spelling, 'subbing' manuscript after manuscript as I went along. The manuscripts were a little more presentable when I had finished with them, but they were still terrible. It was murderous work, and I do not know how I coped with handling over a dozen manuscripts each month. Then at night forcing myself to write 3,000 words of a western. I think the quality of the product I was handling was so much against my instincts, and the pace at which I had to work was so intense, that I developed a headache that remained with me for years.

Acceptable manuscripts were really half-length books—about 35,000 words. A flood of tacky westerns, American gangster tales, and some SF space opera reached my desk. There was always this interest in SF as a subject, however badly the stories were written. I could sense a market there, but I knew it would never be developed on this wretched standard of writing.

Now, my publisher, for all my critical feelings for him, had many likeable qualities. We battled, but we got on well together. He listened to my blasphemous comments on the quality of his products and there were signs that he could see ahead and might agree to a change in policy.

Six weeks after I had started with Hamilton's, he said I was doing an excellent job and he was going to raise my pay to £16 a week. This was quite big money in those days. He was quite thoughtful and recognized that I could not work at that pace and also write a book a month and keep sane. He asked me not to write any more books for him; we compromised and I continued writing, but at a more leisurely pace.

So he handed over editorial policy to me, and began to talk of publishing more serious science fiction. Here was the chance I had scented; I was being given a publishing list to develop, and I started to work with genuine enthusiasm.

I advertised for writers in various journals—for westerns, American gangster stories . . . and for science fiction. I was able to increase the rate of pay to 15 shillings a thousand words for westerns, but up to £1 a thousand for the other two categories. We were on the way to better things. I began to see a publishing list of quality in a few years' time, confident that better pay would bring better authors and a bigger readership.

I put up the idea of linking our SF books as a recognisable series, for I was sure that a market was there, and that in time quality would bring its due reward.

All for £1 a thousand words? I was very innocent!

Those were the crazy days of publishing, times when good SF writing was almost at a standstill. Yet in 1949 even I did not realise just how crazy this peripheral paperback publishing industry was. What I was to learn in the next years, through my association with Hamilton's and with other less worthy publishers, assumes in retrospect to be a nightmarish period which will never be repeated.

But that deserves careful detailing. At least from it all came something that tried—*Authentic Science Fiction*—and I met Bert Campbell.

Landsborough's efforts were to see fruition in 1951 with the arrival of *Authentic Science Fiction*, but before then, the Crazy World of publishing had already spotted the market for SF, and with no effort to produce quality material, they flooded the market with juvenile rubbish—so even before *Authentic* arrived, there were forces at work that made it look as if it would never succeed.

Futuristic Stories # 1 (H.W. Perl).
Hamilton, 1946

Futuristic Stories # 2 (Oliver Brabbins).
Hamilton, 1946

Strange Adventures # 1 (H.W. Perl).
Hamilton, 1946

Strange Adventures # 2 (Oliver
Brabbins). Hamilton, 1947

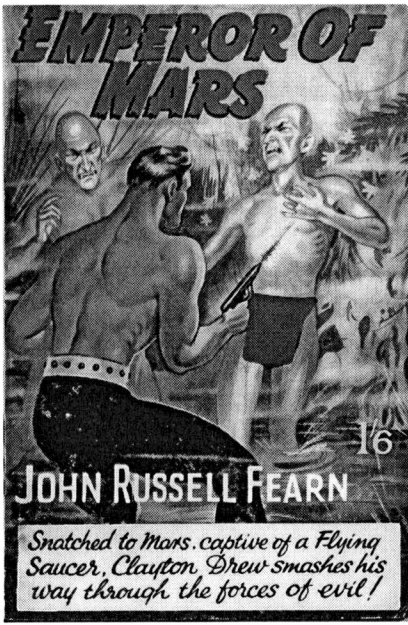

Emperor of Mars by John Russell Fearn
(Terry Maloney). Hamilton, 1950

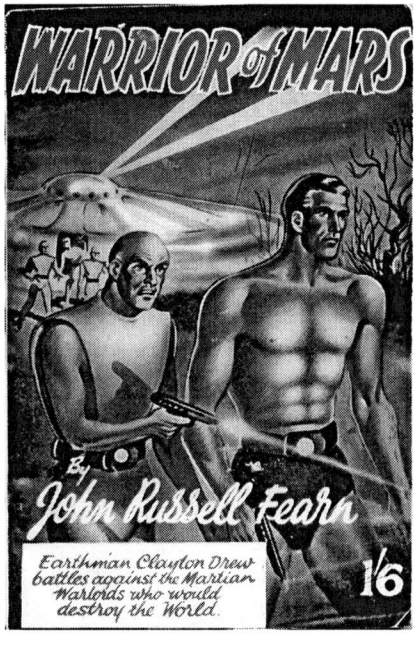

Warrior of Mars by John Russell Fearn
(Terry Maloney). Hamilton, 1950

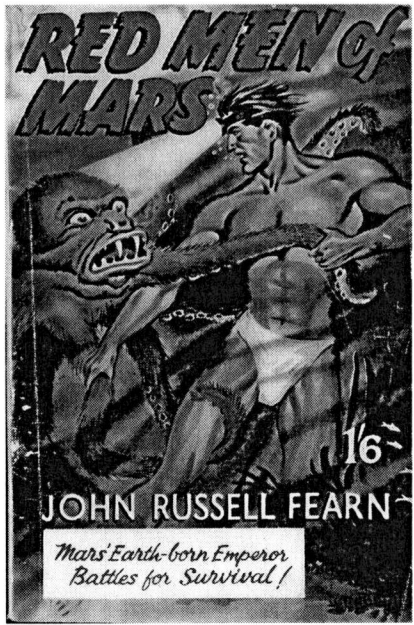

Red Men of Mars by John Russell Fearn
(Terry Maloney). Hamilton, 1950

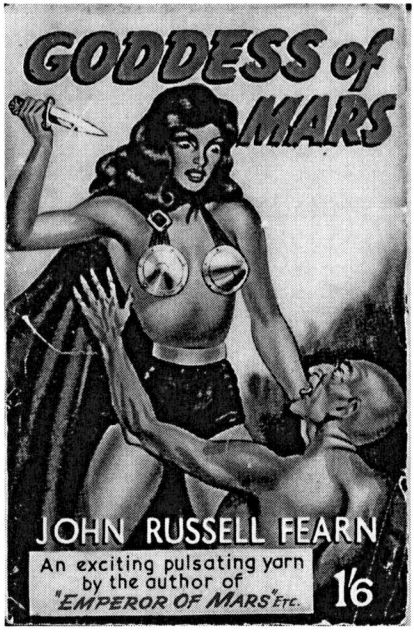

Goddess of Mars by John Russell Fearn
(Terry Maloney). Hamilton, 1950

CHAPTER 6:
INVASION FROM SPACE

In the early summer of 1950, science fiction paperbacks suddenly burst upon the British publishing scene. The field leader was the small London firm of Scion Ltd, who published the novels of John Russell Fearn. Writing as 'Vargo Statten', with dynamic covers by Ron Turner, Fearn became a bestseller. Scion quickly put him under contract to write SF exclusively for them as 'Statten'. His story is looked at in more detail in the next chapter.

Of Scion's several competitors, one of the quickest off the mark was John Spencer Ltd. operating out of Shepherds Bush Road, London. Its Directors were Michael Nahum and Sol Assael (whose brother, Harry, was director of Hamilton & Co.). They had commenced operations early in 1948, issuing a string of pulp-sized booklets, starting with titles such as *Crime Confessions* and *Phantom Detective Cases*, written completely by Norman Firth and John F. Watt under various pseudonyms. By 1949, they had turned to American gangster novels and, in 1950, science fiction. The company was John Spencer & Co., who between them, managed to produce not one, but four SF magazines (presented as short story collections, with no editor named), all of such abysmal quality that they almost single-handedly made science fiction the laughing stock of the literary world.

First to arrive was *Futuristic Science Stories* in April 1950. Inside were stories by J. Austin Jackson and Norman A. Lazenby, names that fans might have remembered from Walter Gillings' *Fantasy* magazine back in 1946-47. Both were, in fact, Lazenby—who also made a third appearance in this issue as 'Martin Gulliver'. The other authors were the relative unknown Frederick Foden and the pseudonymous 'Ray Mason'. The next arrival, *Worlds of Fantasy*, also had stories by 'Jackson' and Lazenby (and again a third as 'Hamilton Donne'), and a couple of further unknown pseudonyms, Frank C. Kneller and D .R. Mencet. A closer look at three of the stories (by unknowns Frank Kneller, D. R. Mencet, and Ray Mason) would have shown that they were certainly the work of one author—one who had no idea how to write a good SF story. The Lazenby stories were poor, but these were terrible! My research indicates that they were the work of Scottish author John F. Watt, who had never written SF before.

In the Autumn they added a third title, *Tales of Tomorrow*. The start of the following year saw the publication of a fourth, *Wonders of the Spaceways*. Each of them had an identical format, and although the titles were different, they were indistinguishable. Essentially, they were the same magazine, but issued under four different titles to get around the U.K. post-war paper shortages and quota regulations. Their early covers were embarrassingly bad, uniformly dull and drab, and were the work of Gerald Facey, an artist who was clearly unfamiliar with science fiction.

Among the early pseudonymous contributors was Sydney J. Bounds, who had been selling regularly since 'Strange Portrait' appeared in *Outlands* in 1946.

Before folding his Utopian Press and leaving to make a new start in Wales, Benson Herbert had introduced Bounds to another publisher of the same type of material as Bounds had been writing for him. Bounds recalled to me what happened next.

> I did a couple of spicy magazines for them, and so I was able to keep going as a freelance writer. Then I was introduced to the firm of John Spencer, ran by Harry Assael. They were launching a line of paperback novels in imitation of the successful 'Hank Janson' line of another publisher, and invited me to write hardboiled gangster novels for them—which I did. They—or their readers—seemed to like my work, and so I did several tough gangster novels for them, under such pseudonyms and house names as 'Brett Diamond' and 'Rick Madison'. I also churned out some short SF stories for their pocketbook sf magazines, *Futuristic Science Stories*, *Tales of Tomorrow*, and *Worlds of Fantasy*. Since they only paid me fifteen shillings a thousand, I wrote the SF stories straight onto the typewriter, and they went out (under pseudonyms) with minimal revision.
>
> At the time, I was not on the phone and Spencer's would send me a telegram; then I'd rush to a call box to learn their latest requirements. After

a while I began to wonder why I was never invited to the editorial office. One evening, while I was travelling to visit friends in that area, I watched for No. 24 as the bus went along Shepherds Bush Road, and lo! It turned out be a second-hand clothes shop!

Payment by Spencer's was usually only 10/- a thousand for all rights. The only authors likely to have been attracted by those rates were those able or willing to work quickly, like Bounds or Lazenby, or perhaps a young beginner, like Peter J. Ridley, a fan trying to make his first sale, who appeared in the first issue of *Wonders of the Spaceways*.

In 1992 I interviewed Norman Lazenby for a magazine article, and I asked him how it came about that, after writing quite reasonable stories for Gilling' *Fantasy* in 1946, followed by his interesting collection *Terror Trap* (published by Shenstone Press in 1949) he had authored such poor stories for the Spencer magazines. He was amused, and his answer highlighted the attitudes of publishers in those days, and also echoed the experience of Syd Bounds:

> Spencers *wanted* that kind of SF action story, so I gave it to them. It's called 'writing for the market' and any full-time writer in 1950, as I then was, had to plough that particular furrow. Spencers used to write me short letters, asking for three or four ten thousand word stories, but they wanted them *in two or three weeks time*! There was nothing else for it but to sit down at the typewriter and knock them out at the rate of about 6,000 words a day. No first drafts or revision. It wasn't necessary to do that in order to sell to Spencer's. Of course, I would work out in my mind some general idea of what the plot was going to be before I started—but once I was pounding the keys that was it. First draft—and Spencer's bought it. A story a day was my motto at the time!

Possibly the Spencer magazines, because they offered no editorial guidance, harmed the progress of British SF writers. However, they apparently found a readership (mainly teenagers) sufficient to sustain them, since they would continue for the next few years. The reasons for this are looked at later.

A number of SF fans, who had chanced to read the magazines, were encouraged to think that they could write better themselves. So they tried a few stories, and inevitably they were accepted. Amongst this small group of readers-turned-authors was John Stephen Glasby.

The magazines had been running for some eighteen months before Glasby chanced on a few copies at the beginning of 1952. Glasby had a scientific background. He was employed as a Research Chemist for I.C.I, and his hobby was astronomy. At a later period in his life he would become the Director of the Variable Star Section of the British Astronomical Association. He saw at once that many of the authors in the Spencer magazines had little or no astronomical knowledge, and were making fundamental blunders in nomenclature and other scientific details.

Working in collaboration with a friend, Arthur Roberts, Glasby had already made a string of sf novel sales to a rival firm, Curtis Warren Ltd, and decided that he could do a lot better than Spencer's short story writers. Roberts was not interested in continuing their collaboration with short stories, so now working alone, Glasby sent in a couple of sample short stories, 'Ghost Moon' and 'Moondust'. Spencer's promptly accepted them with a request for more of the same.

Thus began an astonishing association with the publisher that was to last for nearly twenty years. During this time, Glasby worked without a contract, simply responding to letters from Spencer's outlining their immediate requirements. As he would supply the material, Spencer's would accept it, and either request more of the same or specify something different.

Over the time of his association with them, Glasby would switch back and forth from science fiction to supernatural stories, foreign legion, war stories, westerns and even hospital romances, writing hundreds of short stories and novels. He told me:

> How Spencer's operated was to send me a pencil tracing of the cover for each book and asked me to write a novel (or short story in the case of a collection). At one time in the late fifties I had fourteen of these drawings on hand and was writing one 40,000-word novel every ten days as well as a full time job as a research chemist with ICI! I only wrote the hospital romance and war novels at the insistence of John Spencer. My real interest was in the SF and supernatural 'horror' stories which I enjoyed writing, and which I've tried to concentrate on in recent years between writing non-fiction chemistry and astronomy books.

Later on Glasby would make a very successful return to fiction writing, with a string of new western and detective novels—after, as his agent, I had managed to resell all his old ones—as well as new SF and supernatural stories, including both short stories and novels. Some of his work was anthologised, and he was enjoying great success when he was taken ill and died in hospital in June 2011, aged 82.

Since February 1947, Walter Gillings had been editing a highly professional-looking fanzine on a bi-monthly basis, entitled *Fantasy Review*. Gillings was a top-class journalist, and his magazine was packed with news and reviews of fantasy developments on both sides of the Atlantic—mostly on the American side, since SF publishing there was much more advanced—and literate. The articles included profiles of major American authors such as August Derleth and Jack Williamson, and knowledgeable book reviews by experts in the field. Nothing as good as his magazine had been seen before—nor has it since. With issue 15 (Summer 1949), it went quarterly, and the next autumn, the magazine was renamed *Science Fantasy Review*. Only two further quarterly issues appeared, at which point the next part of the Nova Publications plan came into operation—the production of a second magazine, to be edited by Gillings. So *Science Fantasy Review* was incorporated into the new and professional *Science-Fantasy*.

The first issue arrived in July 1950, dated Summer, and its ninety-six pages included fiction by veteran J. M. Walsh and by the now-regularly appearing (especially in America) Arthur C. Clarke. These stories had been intended for Gillings' previous magazine, *Fantasy,* and he had arranged to buy many of the fine stories that the publishers still had on file. He also included several features from the fanzine *Science-Fantasy Review*, and the whole magazine gave the promise of being a superior production. The second issue arrived in October, boasting one of John Russell Fearn's best stories, 'Black-Out', (which had been announced to appear in the aborted *Fantasy* # 4 in 1947 under Fearn's original title of 'Black Saturday') and excellent stories by Arthur C. Clarke, John Christopher and others.

With sales of both magazines continuing to rise, the year ended on a very bright note for both the Nova enterprises.

One aspect of the SF publishing scene not covered in detail in this volume so far is the comics field. One of the war's far-reaching effects was that all American periodicals were banned from import, thus the success of the British Reprint Edition of American SF magazines during the early 1950s. As previously mentioned, Atlas Distributing Co. was publishing *Astounding* regularly and, until 1949, they also published *Unknown Worlds*. When they finally ran out of stories after forty-one issues, Atlas started producing a BRE of *Thrilling Wonder Stories*. Other American magazines with BREs included *Startling Stories*, *Weird Tales* (both started in 1949), *Amazing*, *Fantastic Adventures*, *Planet Stories*, and one issue of *Super Science Stories* appeared as *Cosmic Science Stories*, all of which arrived in 1950.

The influence of comics at that time was recalled by Gordon Landsborough:

> The British reprint of *Astounding* was printed from metal cast moulds (matrices) flown in from the United States. The technique derived out of necessity from a curious and colourful fragment of United Kingdom publishing history.
>
> After World War II, periodicals were not permitted to be imported from America because of the dollar balance-of-payments problem. That is, except for newspapers. And one very astute Midlands company spotted a loophole in the act.
>
> They shipped over vast numbers—tens of millions—of newspapers from Canada and the United States. The papers were those with coloured comic supplements. When they reached England, the Midlands company solemnly threw away all the newspapers and sold the comic supplements. All perfectly legal, and in that time of shortage, the comics enjoyed enormous sales. In time, of course, the loophole was sealed, and comics were not permitted for import in this manner, and this set the Midlands company a problem.
>
> A big following had been made for American comic book heroes. The Midlands firm wasn't going to lose this support, so they began to fly in matrices moulded from American comic book metal, from which they made their own plates and printed from them in Britain. Because of this, we became accustomed to the American comic book and those cartooned SF heroes, *Superman*, *Captain Marvel*, and others.

Most of the paperback publishers dallied in comics at one time or another; Hamilton & Co., Grant Hughes, Martin & Reid, and Modern

Fiction all tried their hands. Two of the more prolific were Paget Publications and Scion Ltd., who first began in 1948 publishing comics. Scion issued crime, western and science fiction comics, the latter giving an opportunity for Odhams staff artist Ron Turner to freelance with some vivid and attractive self-penned SF comic strips for Scion, beginning with a three-page strip entitled *The Atomic Mole*. The mole was an Earth-boring machine, taking explorers deep into an underground world replete with prehistoric monsters, a la Edgar Rice Burroughs.

Clearly, Turner was an SF buff. In an interview my friend John Lawrence and I conducted with him more than 30 years later, Turner told us:

> I think my initial interest was aroused by reading H. G. Wells, Jules Verne and some of the quasi-scientific romances of Edgar Rice Burroughs, boosted by a diet of the various pulps of the time, such as *Amazing Stories* and *Astounding Science Fiction*. Films such as *Things to Come* and *Metropolis* also made a lasting impression on me, along with the *Flash Gordon* serials. A long way from *Star Wars* of course but they impressed us then in much the same way.

Turner explained how he entered the illustration world through a busy Art Studio:

> I joined Odhams Press in 1938 and began work in their art studios as an office boy. Subsequently I was given menial tasks such as lettering crosswords and drawing chicken runs for a magazine called *Poultry Farmer*. Later, I began supplying various small illustrations for *Modern Wonder* and similar publications. Then, when war came I began working on various projects of a war related nature, purely on 'spec', and in 1940 succeeded in having two of these accepted. But my call-up into the army soon put an end to any further activity, at least of an artistic nature.

After being demobbed Ron Turner found himself 'drafted' into the comic strip field:

> Initially, I had no particular interest in strip work and only became involved when I 'ghosted' for an indisposed studio artist on work he was unable to complete. During this period, 1948-49, most of the artists at

Odhams were engaged in a certain amount of freelance work, some of it handled by Greg Hall, later to become my agent. It was from him, on the basis of this early effort, that I obtained my first SF strip commission from Scion, 'The Atomic Mole'. Further work was forthcoming as a result of this and has continued almost without a break since.

Ron Turner cited some legendary artists as early influences on his work.

I was always a great admirer of *Flash Gordon* creator, Alex Raymond. No one of course could but admire the breathtaking work of astronomical artist Chesley Bonestell, and the photographic realism of his 'I am a camera' technique; probably the most emulated artist of them all in this particular field.

After more than three-dozen comic titles, Scion diversified into the more lucrative book publishing, initially with romances, then adding crime and westerns to their list before turning to John Russell Fearn to launch their SF list. They triggered the SF boom in 1950, described in detail later.

The high watermark of Turner's early comics work was achieved with his *Tit-Bits Science Fiction Comics,* a series of six 64-paged digest-sized sf comic books that appeared in the UK in 1953-54, published by Pearson's. A seventh issue was prepared, but not issued in the UK, although like the others, it was sold on by the publisher and translated and published in the French comic book series *Aventures De Demain* in the late 1950's.

Turner had earlier been engaged as the cover artist for the same publisher's ongoing series of 64-page *Tit-Bits Science Fiction Library,* which eventually ran to 19 issues, all with Turner covers. Turner convinced them to allow him to create a comic book series as a companion to the books, to be provided by him. He painted five of the six covers, and did the majority of the black and white artwork on the stories inside, mostly working from his own scripts. Because he was both writing and drawing the strips, he put everything into them, working at the peak of his inspiration.

All of Turner's dozen stories for the series have a polish and panache that typifies the best of 1950's science fiction. They reflect Turner's own detailed knowledge and careful reading of the genre, with many of the plot elements clearly derived from novels by Fearn and E. C. Tubb, published by Scion and Milestone, for which Turner did the covers. The artwork, however, was uniquely Turner's own, with dynamic vari-shaped panels, and dramatic use of black shadows and silhouettes with minimal use of line. These techniques were pioneered by Turner, years before similar work by such artists as Frank Bellamy and David Lloyd was published to popular acclaim. If there is any discernible influence it was Chesley Bonestell, the leading astronomical artist of the 1950s, whom Turner has freely acknowledged as one of his sources of inspiration.

Whilst the stories (like most comic strips) have a patina of juvenility (probably at the insistence of the publisher) the themes were often highly scientific and quite complex, abounding with force screens, hyperspace concepts, and atomic physics. They are sometimes epic in scope—*Dome of Survival* ranges across the whole of the solar system, and spans millions of years. *The Terror of Titan* details the struggles of a group of freedom fighters to overthrow a 22nd century dictatorship. The rebels set up a base on Titan, where they encounter gigantic, robotic insects—the Scorabs. These creatures were recognisably derived from Tubb's novel *I Fight For Mars* (Milestone, 1953) where Tubb's Martian colonists had to contend with similar creatures—the "Lobants."

Another Turner strip, *The Planetoid Plague*, was similarly inspired by another of Tubb's Milestone books, *Planetoid Disposals, Ltd* (1953), but in both cases Turner added unique twists. His *Inner World* had echoes of Fearn's sub-atomic novel, *Scourge of the Atom* (Scion, 1953) wherein a microcosmic race seek to destroy scientists in our own universe, whose experiments are unwittingly damaging the atomic universe.

In *The Deimos Deadline* Turner came up with a completely original concept: the idea of detonating Deimos in a controlled atomic explosion. The plan is to create a mini-sun that would release the trapped atmosphere of the Martian deserts, terra-forming the planet to make it suitable for colonisation. Equally impressive is Turner's space engineering 'hardware'—spaceships and space suits etc, which reflected Turner's own scientific and engineering knowledge. *The Scourge of the Carbon Belt* features a gigantic mothership that can release self-contained 'pods' able to separate and operate independently of the parent craft.

Pearson's folded the comics when they ended the novel series, but Turner then was invited to take over the character of 'Space Ace', for

VULTURES OF THE VOID: THE LEGACY

Lone Star Magazine. 'Space Ace' was a mediocre SF strip that was ran as a back-up to a featured cowboy strip, Steve Larabee, a character created to help merchandise the publisher's own line of cowboy toys, hence the overall 'western' nature of the comic. But once Space Ace was both written and drawn by Ron Turner, it quickly became the most popular of the two, and the character would eventually be given his own comic. Turner commented:

> Scriptwriting is not my particular forte, though I did find that, as with many other activities, there is a basic principle involved which, if followed, does produce results. If a line of thought is followed through on a given situation, such as the discovery of a mysterious coffin-capsule floating in space, then a story can soon be built around this basic premise. Then it's only a matter of devising suitable characters and dialogue and breaking the story down into frames.
>
> As to inspiration, it can come from a variety of sources. I'd read and absorbed such a tremendous amount of. SF material over the years, that there always appeared to be a fund of suitable themes available. On the basis that everything evolves from a previous event, I suppose it could be argued that no story—or art for that matter—is truly original.

The *Space Ace* feature ran for almost seven years, but one of Ron Turner's most famous characters is *Rick Random, Space Detective*, published by the comics specialist, Amalgamated Press. Its talented roster of scriptwriters included a young Harry Harrison, during his sojourn in the UK, who was later to be famed as the creator of "The Stainless Steel Rat" series of novels. *Rick Random* was produced for the *Super Detective Library*, series, which were digest pocket-sized comics. Turner recalled:

> I mostly remember the *Rick Random* series for the quality of the scripts; a factor of fundamental importance and more likely to produce inspiration than working from inferior material. So I would think the consumption of midnight oil increased in direct ratio to the amount of detail that I put into a particular sequence. Although, of course, the characters in these stories were of prime importance, I must confess that derived far more satisfaction from my creation of the machines and settings than anything else.

Unlike much of the American product, British SF comics at the time—and Turner's particularly—did not tend to feature *super*hero characters. Rather, British heroes were ordinary human beings, who were simply *very* resourceful. There were *some* British superheroes, but they catered for the more juvenile end of the market.

Almost certainly the greatest and most influential of the British SF comic strip heroes was *Dan Dare*, the flagship strip of the weekly comic *Eagle*, and who merits a closer inspection.

Awareness in the growing interest in science fiction by young readers prompted Hulton Press, publishers of the highly successful *Picture Post*, to seriously consider the launching of a new juvenile science fiction magazine. Hulton's plans, however, gelled in a different direction with the arrival of the Reverend Marcus Morris and a brilliant young artist, Frank Hampson. The two men had met a couple of years earlier when Hampson was freelancing artwork to Morris' religious monthly, *The Anvil*, and together had prepared a dummy of a religious and educational comic called *Dragon*, which Mrs. Hampson had re-christened *Eagle*. The lead character was to be one Reverend Dan Dare: Chaplain of the Future, but the religious angle was dropped. *Eagle* became Britain's first top quality and most influential comic.

The high quality of the publication must have helped to turn many a young reader on to science fiction. Your chronicler was certainly one of them. The full colour front page featured *Dan Dare: Pilot of the Future*—and the meticulous clean-cut realism of Hampson, which continued over onto the second page, revolutionized comic strip art. With heavy advance publicity, including plugs aimed at adults in Hulton's adult magazines such as *Picture Post*, the first issue (April 14, 1950) sold an astonishing 900,000 copies.

Hampson evidently had a thorough background in SF, but since he was drawing much of the contents (later he set up a studio, and other artists worked under his guidance), he called in some other writers to help write the plot continuities. One of the earliest was Arthur C. Clarke, who helped plot the first Dan Dare story, which concerned an expedition to Venus and stretched over 18 months (little wonder this story is considered such a classic, and it was destined to be often reprinted long after *Eagle* had ceased publication, along with Dan Dare's succeeding adventures).

The actual extent of Clarke's involvement (which has been confirmed and documented) is, however, hotly debated, and ranges from 'extensive' to 'minor'. Hopefully, it may one day be resolved when his effects and papers are finally documented and released. Subsequent known continuity writers have been identified, and the best of them was Alan Stranks, the versatile writer who was better known for his radio serial 'P.C. 49'; the character also appeared in films and as an *Eagle* strip.

The advent of *Eagle* was noted by John Carnell in his Summer 1950 issue *New Worlds* editorial. After recalling their influence on himself and his contemporaries of many of the early juvenile titles I discussed in Chapter 1 of this book, Carnell commented that since 1939 there had been "no first-class juvenile weekly devoted to futuristic fiction." But he went on:

> It was, therefore, with great personal pleasure, I saw the first issue of the new Hulton Press juvenile *Eagle* heralded in recently with plenty of advance publicity. Subsequently, it gave me a very warm feeling to know this national juvenile weekly is selling out everywhere. Edited by a clergyman, who devised and designed it prior to submitting it to Hulton Press, it carries a strip-cartoon adventure on Venus, and regular science fiction stories with a strong juvenile appeal. Not without a little pride, author Clarke informs me that he has sold a story to the *Eagle*.

Just over a year after its launch as the flagship strip for *Eagle*, *Dan Dare* was adapted as a serial for radio, for Radio Luxembourg. Whilst extremely faithful to Hampson's characters, the radio *Dan Dare* had much in common with the recently discontinued *Dick Barton, Special Agent* serials on the BBC. The scripts were written by people unconnected with the *Eagle*, and very possibly the majority were by Edward J. Mason, (the famous co-creator of *Dick Barton* and *The Archers*). The show was sponsored by the night time medicinal drink 'Horlicks'. Actor Noel Johnson (a former 'Dick Barton') portrayed the gallant Colonel to great effect throughout its long run, and my memory suggests that Dan's sidekick Digby was voiced by John Sharpe who had played Dick Barton's former batman, 'Snowy' White.

It was brilliantly done—a hybrid of Hampson's creations and Mason's *Dick Barton* cliffhanger technique. As a schoolboy, I was a regular listener—and nearly became a 'Horlicks' junkie as a consequence! I was sufficiently inspired to draw and colour my own comic strip versions of the radio serials, and my adaptations eventually ran to more than half a dozen stories over several hundred meticulously inked and coloured large pages. Somehow—I never knew how; possibly my parents had written to them—my curious hobby led to my being interviewed by a reporter and given a write-up (with photo) in the national children's newspaper, the *Junior Mirror*, in 1955!

The piece was noticed by someone at the BBC, and I received a letter inviting me to take part as a contestant in the famous Wilfred Pickles weekly radio quiz show, *Have a Go, Joe*.

The show moved around the country each week, and by an amazing coincidence was shortly to be broadcast from Wallsend Town Hall, a short walk from my home. I was familiar with the show, and knew that Pickles always leeringly asked his unmarried contestants: *"Are you courtin'?"* The prospect terrified me, as at only 13 I had no regular girlfriend—and like most heterosexual schoolboys in those unenlightened times, I didn't wish to be thought gay! I ignored the invitation, and have regretted it ever since.

My unpublished comic strips are in fact the *only* surviving record reflecting the actual contents of the *Dan Dare* radio serials, since Luxembourg's master-disc recording has been lost or destroyed. When the serials eventually finished, I switched my creative talents to even more ambitious comic strip adaptations of Fearn stories, managing to complete a full length adaptation (in ink and colour crayon) of Vargo Statten's *Across the Ages*, followed by *painted* adaptations of two of his best Polton Cross magazine stories, 'Prisoner of Time' and 'Twilight Planet'.

A misspent youth? Not really—decades later, I would put this early experience to good use, when I was invited to write the scripts for *Garth*, the *Daily Mirror's* famous strip cartoon hero . . . but that came much later.

At the height of *Eagle's* success in 1951, Hulton again flirted with the idea of a science fiction magazine. They met with SF writers and editors in London, to discuss their plans. Scientist and author H. J. Campbell was actually appointed as editor and prepared 'four dummy issues' of the new magazine. Editor and agent Walter Gillings was also consulted regarding possible reprint material from his unused *Tales of Wonder* inventory. He passed to Hulton tearsheets of a 1933 *Astounding* story by Jack Williamson, 'Salvage in Space'. Hulton paid Williamson $60 for second serial rights.

Later American bibliographers of Williamson, on learning of the sale from the author's records, have mistakingly stated that the story was published in *Eagle*. It never was. However, Hulton got cold feet and their SF magazine never appeared. Very probably they had decided to put their resources into launching companion comics to *Eagle* instead—*Girl*, and *Robin* subsequently appearing.

Eagle reached an even wider audience than most of the science fiction published, and 'primed' many young readers to the basic tenets of SF—to these readers most of the old iconic plots were new and exciting. Originality of theme was not particularly important, so long as the story moved swiftly and had colour and imagination.

And it was for that reason that 'Vargo Statten' was so successful . . .

Futuristic Science Stories # 15 (Ron Embleton). John Spencer, 1954

Worlds of Fantasy # 7 (Ron Turner). John Spencer, 1952

Tales of Tomorrow # 9 (Gordon C. Davies). John Spencer, 1953

Wonders of the Spaceways # 7 (Norman Light). John Spencer, 1953

Science Fantasy # 1 (Frederic Powell).
Nova, 1950

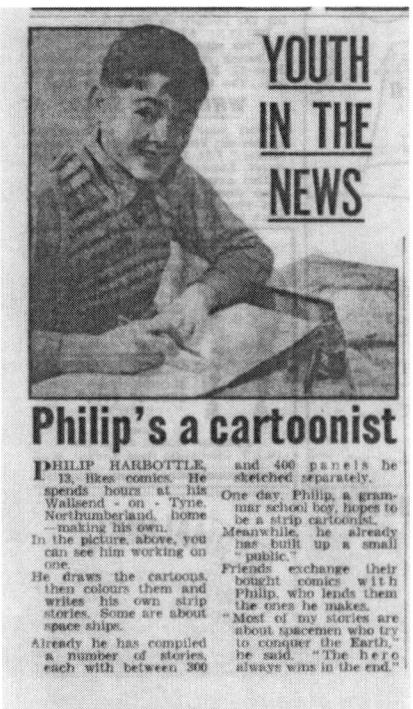

Photo: Philip Harbottle. *Junior Mirror,*
June 22, 1955

Front page: *Eagle* # 15, 21 July 1950 (Frank
Hampson). Hulton, 1950

CHAPTER 7:
THE DELUGE BEGINS

In 1949, thanks to poor distribution and its dreadful cover, the arrival of *The Trembling World* had not set the publishing world alight to the possibilities of paperback SF, and was seen as another one-shot. Although the back pages of the book boasted that this was the first of twelve novels to be written by 'Astron del Martia', the promised arrival of the next title, *Dawn of Darkness*, did not happen for a couple of years, because publisher Stephen Frances had decided to go and live in Spain. He continued to write 'Janson' novels from his new home, and the S. D. Frances (Publishers) imprint was taken over by Gaywood, but without his personal interest in SF to prompt them, there were no more 'Astron del Martia' novels at that time. It would be left to others to launch the boom.

The appearance of 'Vargo Statten' so soon after the arrival of *Eagle* and the John Spencer magazines was the spark that finally mobilized other publishers, but it was only by chance that the three coincided.

Although John Russell Fearn was not the instigator of the publishing boom, he was certainly one of the central characters. For years, Fearn was the *only* British author to make his living by writing science fiction. He had discovered the American pulps in 1931, and had his first story, a novel, *The Intelligence Gigantic*, serialized in *Amazing* in two parts from June 1933. He shot to prominence when he switched to writing for the more influential *Astounding Stories* in 1934. Throughout the 1930s and early 1940s he had, by necessity, supplied most of his imaginative stories to America, but had stories in all of the occasional British SF magazines as well.

Fearn's eventual withdrawal from the United States magazines began in 1943, when his American agent allegedly 'appropriated' some £300 belonging to Fearn. Most of the money had been earned from the Ziff-Davis magazines, *Amazing* and *Fantastic Adventures*, and represented a small fortune for a writer in the difficult war years. Fearn's personal appeal to the publisher and their editor, Ray Palmer, yielded no joy. He confided in a letter to Walter Gillings: 'they had paid the money: what happened afterwards was not their worry'. So Fearn concentrated on other work, including a new detective novel series, *Black Maria* (for British hard-cover publication), which he had been planning since 1940. Abandoning his appeals to Ray Palmer and Ziff-Davis, Fearn turned instead to Leo Margulies and his magazines *Startling* and *Thrilling Wonder Stories*. Thereafter he wrote for them exclusively, and quickly sold them both novels and short stories. By way of gratitude, Fearn dedicated his first detective novel *Black Maria, M.A.* (1944) 'to Leo Margulies.'

In 1949, Oscar J. Friend, a former editor of those magazines and an associate of Margulies, took over the Otis A. Kline Agency. Fearn had renewed contact with him when Friend had invited Fearn to choose his best short story for an American anthology he was co-editing with Leo Margulies, *My Best Science Fiction Story* (Merlin, 1949). Fearn had chosen 'Wanderer of Time', and following this Friend had invited Fearn to write a new SF novel, which he would agent Stateside. Fearn had taken him up on his invitation, and written a new book, *Fool's Paradise*. He took particular care to make this his best work, hoping to gain a foothold in the American book market. A few months later, Frederik Pohl set up the Dirk Wylie Agency, and his British representative, Walter Gillings, contacted Fearn asking if he had any suitable SF novels on hand for Pohl to agent.

Not having had any news from Friend, Fearn accepted the invitation and responded by sending Gillings two novel mss. One of them was *Queen of Venus* (lengthened and revised from a short novel in a 1940 *Marvel Stories*), which Fearn had recently had returned from Diamond Books, an Irish publisher, who had failed before it could be issued. The other was *A Martian Returns* (previously mentioned as a hangover from the Pendulum days). Added to these were copies of his previously issued hardcover books already published in Britain, *The Intelligence Gigantic* and *Liners of Time*.

A successful editor and SF writer himself, Pohl was an astute agent. American and Canadian paperback rights to both published books were soon optioned, but the two companies involved (Checker Books and

Fireside Publications) later ran into financial difficulties and the books were aborted. The two novels in manuscript form, meanwhile, were sent to Ray Palmer, who accepted both. As Pohl had known, Palmer was then busy setting up his new SF magazine, *Other Worlds*, in which he intended to feature short novels.

Other Worlds, using material Palmer had gathered earlier, was launched in November 1949, and still Fearn had received no money. He was then contacted by B. Z. Immanuel, Managing Director of Scion Ltd., who invited him to write a regular series of westerns for the company. Fearn was already selling them (as 'Vivienne Carne' and numerous other personal pseudonyms) a series of Romance novelettes, which they published as small 3d (16 pages) and 6d (48 pages) paperback booklets. These charming little stories were adorned by evocative covers of star-crossed lovers by artist Ron Turner. (The existence of Fearn's and Turner's romance booklets remained unknown for decades until uncovered by my researches into both men's output.) These cheaply produced small booklets had been so successful for Scion that they were now emboldened to branch out into paperback novels. Naturally, their first productions were mainly western and crime novels. Fearn had already written western novels for several hardcover publishers, and so was able to effortlessly switch genres.

With regular money arriving from Scion and no sign of anything from America, Fearn impulsively retyped copies of his two 'pending' American manuscripts. Retitled as *Annihilation* (*Fool's Paradise* shortened and revised) and *Operation Venus*, he submitted them to Scion purely on speculation.

Scion's editor at the time was Maurice Read, who was already familiar with science fiction. He scented the same potential market that Gordon Landsborough had spotted, and immediately accepted both novels with the request for more. In June 1950, Scion published their first Fearn SF title: *Operation Venus*, with an attractive spaceship cover by Ron Turner.

An announcement on the back cover stated that this was the first in a regular series, and announced the second title as *Annihilation*, by John Russell Fearn. But when it appeared in July, that novel carried the byline 'Vargo Statten', thus making it one of the shortest lived secret pen names in publishing!

The credit (or discredit) for the pseudonym goes to Maurice Read. After the first book, *Operation Venus*, had been scheduled alongside one of

Fearn's westerns, he decided that for marketing purposes different author names were indicated. When artist Ron Turner called into his office with his cover roughs for *Annihilation*, he asked him for suggestions. Read's initial idea had been to label future Fearn westerns as by 'Wells Fargo', but Turner suggested that science fiction offered the opportunity for a distinctive and dynamic name. Thinking of static electricity, he suggested 'Statten'. Read then briefly considered 'Fargo Statten', but deciding that this was not 'hard' enough, he quickly changed it to 'Vargo Statten'. Turner made the necessary alteration to the cover byline—but Read forgot to alter the already typeset back cover of *Operation Venus.*

As things turned out, Read's action was to damage Fearn's reputation as a writer of science fiction. Fearn himself, like all writers at the time, had no say as to under what name his books went out.

Coinciding with the advent of *Eagle*, the 'Statten' novels were picked up by a larger audience than was usual for SF, helped along by Turner's attractive covers. Sales were higher than the average paperback issued by Scion, and Fearn could supply them regularly. Eight 'Statten' books quickly appeared in 1950, and in October of that year, B. Z. Immanuel travelled in person all the way to Blackpool to offer Fearn an exclusive contract to write SF for Scion for the next five years.

His astonishing action had been prompted because Hamilton & Co., Scion's biggest rivals, had just published four SF novels by Fearn, that formed an ongoing series: *Emperor of Mars, Warrior of Mars, Red Men of Mars*, and *Goddess of Mars*. The 'open' ending of the last novel clearly indicted that Fearn and Hamilton were intending to continue the series.

Fearn accepted Immanuel's terms—to write only SF, and exclusively for Scion—but negotiated a clause that enabled him to offer first American and Canadian serial rights on any of his new novels to his best and most lucrative overseas market, the Toronto *Star Weekly.*

He then ordered Gillings to withdraw his original manuscripts from the American market as Scion, in the accepted practice of the day, had bought all rights to *Operation Venus* and *Annihilation*. He also asked—not unreasonably—for Palmer to either pay the agreed sum for *A Martian Returns*, which he had now sat on for almost a year, or to return it. Fearn could obviously easily sell it to Scion, but he did not have a copy of the mss. (The mss was slow in being returned, which was why it did not appear as a Statten novel [as *The Last Martian*] until 1952).

At the time, the contract must have looked like a gift from heaven to Fearn and his widowed mother, whom he supported, but it eventually resulted in his total downfall in the eyes of older British fans. Even contact with his old friend and ally, Gillings, was broken off. Gillings felt he had been made to lose face with Pohl, and ended his almost 20-year friendship and correspondence with Fearn.

The advertisement on the back of *Operation Venus* meant that it soon became known that Fearn was Statten, and the fact that *The Trembling World* by 'Astron del Martia' was written by Fearn had been revealed by Gillings in *Science Fantasy Review* (Autumn 1949), where he stated that the real author was 'John Russell Fearn, or I'm a Spaniard!' (Gillings' ancestry was fairly safe, since Fearn himself had informed him at the time of sale.) The arrival of four more novels under Fearn's own name (the commissioned Martian series from Hamilton's, previously mentioned) must have made it look as if Fearn had a monopoly on the SF paperback market. Consequently, many fans put two and two together to make five, being convinced that he was responsible for all the *other* exotic, rubbishy bylines when they started to appear—sadly ironic, since the exclusivity terms of his 'Statten' contract meant that he *could not* have been the author behind them.

His apparently prolific output was pre-judged unread as 'hack' work, although the early 'Statten' books were quite respectable. The speed of their publication is fairly easily explained: *Annihilation*, for instance, was *Fool's Paradise* abridged and retitled, while *The Micro Men*, which quickly followed, had originally been written for America in 1946, but rejected by *Startling*. The fourth title, *2000 Years On* was *Four Shall Avenge*, also written earlier, this time for Frank Arnold and Pendulum. Two other 1950 novels, *Nebula X* and *The Sun Makers*, were partially based on earlier magazine stories that had been published in America. He was still supplying Scion with western novels, a further nine in 1950, but this was achieved with the help of a fellow Blackpool writer, Matthew Japp, who supplied a cast of characters and a 2,500 word plot outline from which Fearn wrote the story—so Fearn was *not* 'churning out' inferior SF material as everyone thought. But many older fans still persisted in making him the scapegoat of the boom that was just about to start.

One of the worst offenders was Curtis Warren Ltd., formed in 1948 as an offshoot of the successful Hamilton & Co. The financial backer was

Joseph Pacey, who was also a director with Hamilton's; co-directors of the new company were D. A. Pacey and ex-Hamilton editor Edwin Self. Self had many years publishing experience, and he spotted an opportunity to develop a line of science fiction novels, copying Scion's lead. He would only stay with Curtis Warren a few months before leaving to start his own company, but he was there long enough to start the SF ball rolling.

Instead of looking for talented writers, he used the standard ploy of these publishers, which was to commission those authors they were already exploiting.

At first, he used only two authors: David Griffiths, who was working at Curtis as a manuscript reader, but who fortuitously just happened to be a science fiction fan and was a regular visitor to the White Horse meetings, and Dennis Talbot Hughes. Hughes had written many westerns, crime, and even romance stories for Curtis, Hamilton's and their third offshoot, Grant Hughes. So, like Norman Firth before him, he was asked to switch to writing science fiction. Despite trying for many years, I was never able to trace Hughes, who remains a mysterious figure to this day.

The Curtis novels were initially unremarkable. Trying to rival the 'Statten' novels, they were, like many imitations, inferior to the originals. The books arrived one after the other in October 1950. Hughes supplied *The Earth Invasion Battalion* and *Murder by Telecopter* under the abbreviated byline 'Denis Hughes', as well as a scientific detective novel, *The Green Mandarin Mystery*, as 'Grant Malcom'.

Griffiths wrote *Laboratory X* as 'David Shaw', and the two of them provided three more novels in the November list, at which time the first 'Marco Garron' books (blatant imitations of Edgar Rice Burroughs' *Tarzan*) appeared; this was a separate and intriguing phenomenon, to be looked at in more detail later).

By early 1951, two more names were introduced: 'Gill Hunt' and 'King Lang'—although these were still the work of Hughes and Griffiths respectively. Some of the stories had quite imaginative ideas, but the speed at which they were written precluded any real quality, and the work of Hughes in particular abounded with the most appalling scientific 'howlers'. He reached his absolute nadir with *Elektron Union* (June 1951) a ludicrous transplanted western. The books weren't helped by atrociously lurid covers that were mainly the work of Ray Theobald. Theobald's idea of science fiction was a peculiar hybridization of *Flash Gordon* and cod

Roman History, with blue-skinned aliens wearing metal helmets and short skirts! Astonishingly, he usually signed his work, and as a result he picked up an enormous number of cover commissions with a great many of the mushroom publishers, once word got around that he was both quick and cheap!

It wasn't until October 1951 that different authors began to make appearances on the Curtis list. Hughes had been switched to writing for another series, which slowed his SF output, and Griffiths realized he was incapable of taking up the slack himself. He therefore conceived a scam involving other aspiring SF authors he had met at the White Horse. His outrageous behaviour has been detailed by Ted Tubb in his preface, so at this point we need only note that he was responsible for the introduction to the Curtis line of early novels by E. C. Tubb. The first was *Saturn Patrol*, which appeared under the 'King Lang' byline, and was followed by *Planetfall* as Gill Hunt (November 1951) and *Argentis* as Brian Shaw (February 1952). This demonstrates the central dilemma posed by the 1950s publishing industry: the mushroom publishers were practically the only outlet for SF, and aspiring authors had little choice but to write for them if they wanted to see their work in print. Quality markets simply did not exist, so it was the paperbacks or nothing, and superior novels—such as Tubb's—were indistinguishable from the bad ones when issued in the same packaging under the plethora of house pseudonyms.

Operation Venus by John Russell Fearn (Ron Turner). Scion, 1950

Annihilation by Vargo Statten (Ron Turner). Scion, 1950

Nebula X by Vargo Statten (Ron Turner). Scion, 1950

The Avenging Martian by Vargo Statten (Ron Turner). Scion, 1950

The Green Mandarin Mystery
by Grant Malcom (Ray Theobald).
Curtis Warren, 1950

Laboratory X by David Shaw (Terry
Maloney). Curtis Warren, 1950

Photo: L to R: E.C. Tubb, David Griffiths,
W.F. Temple, S.J. Bounds. *New Worlds* # 17,
September 1952. (Courtesy Peter Weston.)

CHAPTER 8:
AUTHENTIC SCIENCE FICTION

─◆─

By the time Tubb first appeared, other publishers were jumping on the SF bandwagon, which continued to gather speed in the wake of the tremendous success of the regularly issued Vargo Statten novels with their dynamic Ron Turner covers. One of the more prolific was Hamilton's, under the guidance of Gordon Landsborough who, in his second essay for this book, describes the launching of *Authentic Science Fiction*:

By 1949, when I took over editorial policy for Hamilton's, the end was already in sight for the trashy publishers of westerns and American crime fiction. With incredible folly, the shortsighted publishers were rapidly destroying even that profitable market by virtue of gross overproduction.

Up to 1949, these publishers did not even employ sales representatives. Such were the shortages that they sold most of their product by telephone. It was astonishing to listen to them over the telephone. They would ring up a succession of wholesalers (many of them mushroom firms like themselves) and would quote the titles currently available. It was not a question of trying sales talk to get big orders, either. A wholesaler would state his requirements and the publisher would tell him how many he could have, generally cutting the order because of restricted supplies. Astonishing publishing, but it only lasted about four years.

There were so many identically bad books in this restricted field of (generally) westerns, American crime fiction, and sometimes SF, that there was a glut of titles and the market could not absorb them all. Print runs fell and surpluses were hawked around as remainders. Wholesalers who had queued for supplies now became distant and choosy.

In Autumn 1949, Hamilton's print runs were down to 20,000 for 'sophisticateds' (American gangster stuff) and 15,000 for westerns. The lesson was there for all to read, but these publishers were not the breed to adapt quickly.

I saw that only a better standard of writing would survive. I would have liked to have bought reprint rights to hardcover books, but publishing policy was against this for two reasons. First, there was an objection to paying much more for reprint rights, and secondly, publishing policy was to issue short books of about 35,000 to 40,000 words to sell at the magic price of 1/6d. Good books were far too long.

Within a few weeks of being given control of the Hamilton's list, I had made changes. I discarded the old hacks except for one good writer, and instead recruited newspaper journalists as writers, attracting them with the rather better pay. The quality of writing was better, though I will not pretend that the storytelling would have commanded attention in *The Times Literary Supplement*. Still, we were improving.

I am not sure how I recruited SF writers. I think they came in response to advertisements in the *World's Press News*. A mixed bag, and I have forgotten most of their names but, again, they were an improvement on the gangster writers who had been detailed to 'do something in science fiction'.

At that time, my own experience of reading SF was strictly limited—little broader than Wells and Verne, though I remember having a great fancy for Lovecraft. But when I read the so-called SF works that occasionally appeared on Hamilton's list, I got the shudders. They were so bad they held the seeds of self-destruction.

In any event, I was looking ahead. Paper rationing had existed for a decade, and obviously would not continue indefinitely now that war was ended. When paper was in free supply, competition would put to the wall anyone trying to purvey such inept trash.

My opinions were sometimes explosively expressed. The publisher at Hamilton's took it in good humour and just said, "All right, get better stories." Only then was I allowed to offer £1 per thousand words for good SF, though I had to try to get as much as possible at lower rates!

The way I looked at it, SF readers were above average in intelligence, certainly in power of imagination. Space opera was the last thing the real SF reader wanted. What these benighted publishers were catering to with their space operas was not the true SF fan, but a more vacuous type of readership— jet-propelled western fans. I saw the market of the future in a higher intellectual readership, and from the beginning I planned to go for it, though starting from scratch meant that much duff material did go through at first. Still, it was obvious that, in time, the better writers would be attracted and we could build our future on them.

It seemed to me that with such a mass of rubbish competing for counter space, we had to do something distinctive and different to create a loyal readership. So, having now a settled programme of two SF titles per month, I put a strip across the cover and called them 'Science Fiction Fortnightly'. These first novels were very much of a mixed bag, but I argued that the caption would not hurt sales and in time might begin to assist them.

But almost immediately, my publisher came up with an idea. He said he would like to produce a monthly SF magazine. Curiously, in the balmy days of 1946, Hamilton's had published two SF magazines, Strange Adventures and Futuristic Stories. They had short lives and were dead ducks long before I joined Hamilton's. I have only a vague memory of seeing file copies, but they did not impress me at the time, seeming to make the supreme mistake of identifying SF with juvenility, and that on a depressingly low level of craftsmanship.

I was not overjoyed by the idea of producing a magazine. I had been a periodical publisher and knew that the editorial work of finding suitable writers and producing a magazine of shorts was ten times as great as producing a short novel. I had enough work on my plate for one man—as my headache testified—and did not want to embrace a monthly SF magazine. Besides, where was I to find high-standard authors to fill each issue with only a pound a thousand words to offer? When I insisted to the publisher that the rate should be increased, he winced and changed the subject.

Finally, I came up with a compromise. This was to wed my idea to his. We would produce a 'magazine' in conventional paperback format, but it would consist of one 35,000-word novel with a short editorial feature and an odd article as a filler. The publisher accepted the idea and Science Fiction Fortnightly died, and Authentic Science Fiction was born. The title was the publisher's idea; I was never keen on it, but was never one to argue over trifles. At least the title would carry a note of identification and would attract regular readers for our better-than-average SF stories. And Authentic became Hamilton's biggest steady seller. Within two years, it was selling 20,000 copies at 2/- each, compared to about 13,000 copies of other products selling at 1/6d each. I have an idea that it attained sales of 30,000 at one time after I left Hamilton's.

It was only some time afterwards that I learned why Hamilton's had been anxious to start an SF magazine. A London publisher, Atlas, was having great success with *Astounding,* a science fiction magazine of American origin, which seemed to me well ahead of anything we had in the United Kingdom. Rumour had it that *Astounding* was selling 40,000 copies a month and Hamilton's wanted to get in on the act.

We launched *Authentic* in 1951. Hamilton's agreed to employ artists with some pretensions to SF knowledge, and they were a decided improvement on some previously gaudy and uninspired horrors. Covers are always difficult; whatever cover one produces, there is always someone who will tell you it is terrible. But until *Authentic,* no one had ever said our covers were any good. So as compliments began to flow in, I realized that we were progressing.

Previously, Hamilton's had paid a mere nine guineas for a cover drawing, and it had to be hand-lettered for title, author, and front-cover blurb! Now, payment went up to fifteen guineas, and lettering was done independently.

For all that I am severe on Hamilton's, in many ways they were a cut above the usual backyard publisher of the time. They did pay more (under pressure), they did have an editor (whereas most other similar publishers seemed to exist without one), and they read printers proofs and corrected them.

Most other mushroom publishers of the time accepted material, some odd bod read the stories, then they were sent to the printers for setting. Little or no correcting was done to the manuscript, and when the proofs were returned, many of the publishing houses did not bother to correct them. Contempt for the reader was massive, though it came out of sheer, myopic ignorance for the human audience and its requirements. Shortage of reading matter accounted for sales—and readers were steadily dropping for this kind of production.

In fact, people at the time were remarkably indulgent. After the hardships of war, they seemed prepared to put up with anything. I remember one of our printers misbinding sections of two books. Half of the text was an American gangster story, the other half was science fiction. Each shared the other's cover. I do not know how many thousands went out for sale, yet we never had one reader complain! Perhaps no one noticed the difference!

But that was not *Authentic.* We were still pushing through some titles in addition to the better-standard *Authentic* magazine, on which so much effort was lavished. But sales of these SF titles were much inferior to those of the magazine.

Authentic was astonishing. Within a few months, our mail began to bear stamps from Australia, New Zealand, the United States, and other countries. We were trying, it was appreciated, and there was an immediate warm response. I could feel we were building. Besides, a new breed of author was being attracted to the stable. I remember Bert Campbell suddenly appearing with his black beard and an excellent manuscript. John Brunner floated through my office. A quite useful writer, Bryan Haven, Australian or New Zealander, turned in a few stories. S. Fowler Wright, Bryan Berry, H. Kenneth Bulmer, S. J. Bounds, and many more after I left. L. Ron Hubbard wrote for us. So did E. C. Tubb and William F. Temple. My regret is that I cannot remember many other excellent writers who contributed to *Authentic*.

Names I do remember, however, are Roy Sheldon and Jon J. Deegan. I invented both these names pre-*Authentic*. This was following a practice much pursued by this type of publisher at this time. Deliberately, these names were not restricted to one author, instead, they were used for any old author, the publishers not wanting to employ the author's real name in case the author became highly popular and successful.

The above sentence is really thought-provoking and has to be re-read a few times in order to absorb its implications. But it is true. Apart from a few writers like John Russell Fearn, this type of publisher always insisted on employing a pen name for their authors. Deliberately, they used several writers to that pen name so that it could not belong to any one writer. It was a way of controlling an author who could never achieve fame under a nom de plume, then go to a rival publisher, taking the good name with him. Not that there was much danger of anyone acquiring a big following under those publishing conditions, though it did happen to two or three American gangster writers, more sado-sadistic, presumably, than others. From the beginning of my 'new deal' SF policy, I aimed to use the author's real name, and I cannot say there were any ill consequences as a result.

The trouble was that in spite of improved rates of pay, it was still not enough to maintain the enthusiasm of good writers. Writers are reluctant to spend long hours working on a manuscript, which, in the end, brings only pocket money. But despite my constant urging of the publisher to increase his rates, it seemed that I had pushed him as far as he would go. He stuck at £1 per thousand words, and you do not build literary empires on a quid a thou'.

One author might have been paid more. That was John Russell Fearn. As I have said, Hamilton's had commissioned him to write four Martian books, and I think John was paid 30/- a thousand words. Hamilton's publisher was keen on Fearn and might have commissioned more, but I did not share his enthusiasm.

It seemed to me that Fearn represented the space opera market, writing rather better than most in the field, true, but I wanted infinitely more sophisticated writing to aid the expansion of *Authentic*.

Not that I was without some admiration for Fearn, and I will not attack him as some did for writing down to the market at the time. The critics neither knew the problems facing an author like Fearn, nor did they appreciate the remarkable effort required to turn out the scores of books that he did.

In the late 1940s, there just was not a market for good SF that could keep an author alive. Crude publishers insisted on crap and would not have recognized good SF if it had bitten them. Fearn had to make a decision: he could hawk around a few good pieces and break his heart having them contemptuously returned to him, as happened to so many others at the time, or he could write with his tongue in his cheek and at least live comfortably by his writing. Comfortably? Fearn must have been writing a book a fortnight, a staggering performance. At a later period in my existence, I wrote 23 books, ranging from 35,000 to 50,000 words, in one year. Just try that stint and you will never again criticize a man like Fearn, who did that kind of thing year after year. He was truly formidable, and considering his vast output of work, he attained a remarkably high standard. The big tragedy about Fearn was that English publishers paid him so little that he could never afford to take his time and write the good SF he undoubtedly could have done.

In 1950, Fearn was sought out by Scion (always, curiously, pronounced 'Skee-on' in the trade) and offered a contract giving his exclusive services for five years in the field of SF. Fearn signed it, and 'Vargo Statten' was born. I still think it was a bad deal. I had no respect for this company, which seemed to equate readers (of its gangster series, at least) with considerable mental impairment plus a touch of sadistic requirement. They had a checkered career, finally folding in the mid-fifties. Through his association with them, Fearn became yet another writer mangled by the stubby-fingered men with the checkbooks. As it was, he lived in the bracing air of Blackpool, always kept to delivery dates like the professional he was and . . . survived.

The success of *Authentic* brought with it some undesirable consequences. The hungry boys who ran these fringe publishing companies saw *Authentic* selling well and decided to hop onto the SF wagon. With their usual literary myopia, they made the usual wrong diagnosis, 'Hamilton's was doing well with *Authentic*, therefore any SF would do well,' again.

In 1951, so many (bad) SF books were published, that the market was overloaded. Sales per title were often less than 5,000, leaving a lot to remainder, and virtually this was the end of this type of publisher. By the time they had recovered, paper rationing was over, and more progressive paperback publishers like Penguin, Pan, and Fontana were in the field. Between 1950 and 1955, at least thirteen publishing companies passed away.

But *Authentic* continued to build up strength, and I am quite sure this was because of the generic titling of the series that created confidence among the growing band of discerning SF readers.

Yet all was not well. I had been given editorial policy by Hamilton's; the list would be of my choosing, I was promised. And one of the first things I had done was to turn off the tap of the 'sophisticated' books—those unpleasant sexo-sadistic, American gangster novels.

There were still some in the pipeline, and these I let through reluctantly, but I did not want to handle any more of them. I was put off by the crude craftsmanship of the writers, by their repetitive and unoriginal themes of violence, and I was uneasy about them because I could not believe that they assisted toward better human relationships.

I am theoretically opposed to all forms of censorship, but during the time I handled these sexo-sadistic books, I began to doubt the validity of my own arguments in favour of unfettered writing.

In almost all of these stories, the girl was a nymphomaniac who could be most brutally ill-used. Imagination on the part of the authors often extended to violence during the sex act, or the sex act related to violence and under sordid conditions. Ripping open a nympho's stomach at the climax of the sex act appeared in more than one story I read; beating her almost unconscious and yet she still crawled for sex participation was another theme. I felt such stories, while unpleasant, might have no influence upon balanced readers, but with scores of these stories going out yearly, it seemed to me to amount to a wave of propaganda that could have some effect. I cannot see how it helps humanity if the female half is constantly portrayed as worthless and deserving of brutality.

Perhaps that is why I so welcomed our SF stories. They tried for originality, and they did not carry this propaganda of sexual violence. Another publisher, Gaywood Press, was not so scrupulous. At a time when local

Watch Committees were beginning to pay attention to gangster material, they suddenly introduced a strange brand of science fiction laced with sex and violence. In a series that purported to be about 'the mysteries of the universe', they issued two titles, *Freaks Against Supermen* and *Captive on the Flying Saucers*. The former used sex at every conceiveable opportunity, but at least more-or-less normal sex. The latter title, however, was an outrage on morals, literature, and science. Death by castration in which the victim bled to death and the hero being raped by six nymphomaniacs at once were just two of the more presentable episodes. Mercifully, the series quickly faded out—probably due to the hand of Providence. So I was shaken one day when the publisher came to me and said that he wanted to maintain his list of American gangster novels after all. There was still a profitable market for them. Now Hamilton's was always careful about their 'sophisticateds', blue-pencilling vigorously, yet they were still sexo-sadistic in content; wearisome where they were not nauseating (and I have a strong stomach). The writing was so abysmal, I disliked having to edit them.

I gave thought to the situation, then resigned. The publisher was upset and paid me a handsome tribute— "You've given this company a great boost"—but the gangster rubbish had to go through. He asked me to stay on for three months more and arrange a successor. In spite of the break-up, we were friends, but only for three more months.

I took on two editors for Hamilton's, one to handle westerns and 'sophisticateds' and the other, a very good editor for my enthusiasm, *Authentic*.

The editor I chose for *Authentic* was H. J. Campbell. Bert was exactly the man for the job—or rather, he was too good for it. Bert had written a few SF novels for me before the launching of *Authentic*, and I had been most impressed with this man. He was a scientist first, and a fiction writer (though a good one) secondly.

At the writing of this essay, I have just re-read his Panther SF novel, *Brain Ultimate*, and my respect for him grows even higher. Bert Campbell could have been a master in the field of SF writing, but bluntly, the rewards in those days were enough to put any man off . . . for life.

Bert did an excellent job for *Authentic*. He had literary taste, but he also had a scientific background, which invariably meant an acceptance of sound SF stories only. Bert was rarely satisfied and nothing was really up to the standard of his requirement—which is the hallmark of a good editor.

It must be remembered that Bert had an editorial budget so insignificant that what he achieved was all the more remarkable. Including his own fee, each issue had to be produced for something less than £100, and that included the cover art! He did well, and if the publisher had encouraged him by increasing the editorial budget, they would have had a first-class SF magazine. But they didn't.

I had an admiration for Bert Campbell, though it was not completely reciprocated. Bert, bless him, was a simple soul. He identified me with his restricted budget, and with the squalour of the literary product going out alongside *Authentic*. Bert never seemed to realize that the standards we had were vastly higher than they had been a year or so before, that concessions only came following hard fights, and that it was up to him to fight as I had done to improve upon the gains I had made.

He edited reluctantly, shuddering at the crude publishing world around him, incapable of blaspheming loudly at the worst of intellectual atrocities as I did. But then I'm a crude, crude man. Bert should have had the good fortune to be invited to edit for a major company. Notwithstanding, he made a considerable improvement upon *Authentic* during his term as editor.

In the three months prior to his taking over as editor he wrote several excellent books for me. I remember asking him to write two prehistoric fantasies, and he turned in absorbing works. But what impressed me was the smoothness of his writing at short notice, and the very considerable scientific knowledge he displayed.

A year or two after I had left Hamilton's I ran into Bert, and it was clear he'd had enough of the crude publishing world. He was going to study for (I think) a Ph.D. and then begin a career in some scientific establishment. In this he was successful, and we lost him from SF writing, more's the pity. But I am certain he became a senior scientist somewhere, and a happy man in consequence.

The next editor of *Authentic* was another first-class SF writer, E. C. (Ted) Tubb. But by this time, I think the magazine was already sliding out of existence.

Policy in publishing is so important—make the wrong decision and you have only yourself to blame. When I returned to Hamilton's in the mid-fifties, I could see the end was ahead for *Authentic*.

Now, why did this aspiring magazine die? It was wrong that it should have happened. It grew quickly, strongly, with a general improvement in SF content. It could have gone on growing in circulation and setting top-class standards. But it didn't. It attained a minor peak, then slowly died when it was no longer as profitable as other publications put out by the same company which was by now styling itself as Panther Books.

It was starved to death. The publisher, in my opinion, made a wrong decision. Instead of increasing the budget steadily as sales grew, it was cut. Bert Campbell told me this—it was one reason why he left. He could not produce a first-class magazine on the budget allocated. No one could, and Ted Tubb operated admirably under an unsurmountable handicap.

That *Authentic Science Fiction* lasted as long as it did is a credit to its editors, who had the imagination to see that science fiction could, and should, have been of a higher quality than the publishers were allowing.

Launched in January 1951, the early *Authentic Science Fiction Series* (as it was originally entitled) was a bit of a mixture. The first story was the appallingly titled *Mushroom Men from Mars*, by Lee Stanton, which was followed two weeks later by the first in what was to become *Authentic's* most popular series—*Reconnoitre Krellig II*, by Jon J. Deegan introduced the crew of *Old Growler* and their adventures exploring new worlds for the Interplanetary Exploration Bureau. The 'Inter X' series was certainly a cut above most of the SF appearing in paperback. They were written by Robert G. Sharp, an experienced thriller writer, under H. J. Campbell's editorial guidance. In subsequent issues, *Authentic* began to attract a regular stable of excellent authors, with Bert Campbell (under his own name and as 'Roy Sheldon'), F. G. Rayer, E. C. Tubb, and Bryan Berry appearing alongside regulars Deegan and Roy Sheldon's 'Shiny Spear' series.

A name change to *Science Fiction Fortnightly* lasted only five issues, and with the ninth (May 1951) issue, the schedule was changed, as was the name, to *Science Fiction Monthly*. After four months, the final change to *Authentic Science Fiction* was made. With that issue (#13, September 1951), Bert Campbell took over most of the duties of editor, although the format remained almost exactly the same for another year. In October 1952, a serialized novel was started, *Frontier Legion*, by Sydney J. Bounds, and in January 1953, short stories were introduced, turning *Authentic* into a true 'magazine'.

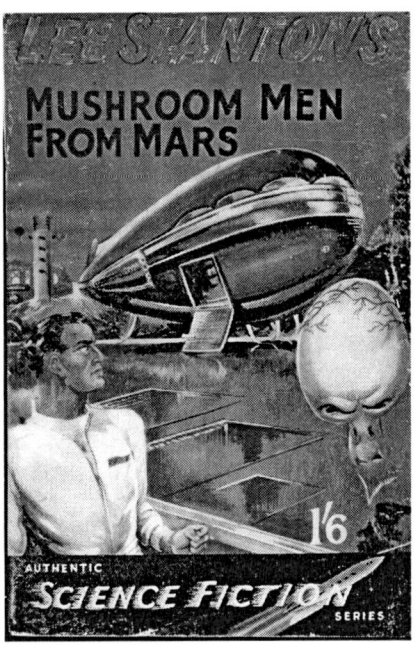

Mushroom Men From Mars by Lee Stanton (D.L.W.). *Authentic SF # 1*, January 1951

Reconnoitre Krellig II (D.L.W.). *Authentic SF # 2*, January, 1951

Aftermath by Bryan Berry (Gordon C. Davies). *Authentic SF # 24*, August 1952

The Plastic Peril by Roy Sheldon (John Pollack). *Authentic SF # 35*, September, 1952

Alien Impact by E.C. Tubb (Gordon C. Davies). Authentic # 21, May 1952

Earth, Our New Eden by F.G. Rayer (George Ratcliffe). Authentic # 20, April 1952

Mammoth Man by Roy Sheldon (George Ratcliffe). Hamilton, 1951

Brain Ultimate by H.J. Campbell (John Richards). Hamilton, 1953

CHAPTER 9:
PRISONER IN THE CELLAR

The sudden increase in the amount of science fiction being issued in Britain was the result of two things: the apparent success of the occasional title that was issued (such as 'Vargo Statten'); and the gradual decline in sales of the other mainstays, gangster novels and 'saucy' magazines. By today's standards, most of these publications would scarcely rate a second glance by those seeking titillation, but in the late 1940s, the sex content of these magazines was the cause of a great outcry by various Watch Committees around the country, coupled as it was with a great deal of misogynistic violence against women—although these committees frequently targeted material unread, simply based on their cover titles and pictures.

The successful prosecution and imprisonment of various publishers, editors, writers, and even printers, had editors reaching for the blue pencil. Violence, it would seem, was another matter and author Norman Lazenby showed me a letter dated September 25th 1950, he received from Edwin Self (an ex-director of Curtis Warren, who had set himself up as a publisher and agent for other companies):

Dear Mr. Lazenby,
Thank you very much for your letter of the 21st regarding the new story.
As it happens October 2nd will suit me very nicely. I will look forward to receiving the MS, on this date and the others at roughly monthly intervals.
I read *Bad Woman* and thought it quite good. Perhaps there was a little too much emphasis on the sex-angle for me—and I thought the one you did for me at Curtis Warren was more what I want—but generally with this type of book there has to be a sex-emphasis and I usually find it works out better

if the central character of the book is a gangster-type with plenty of brutal beatings-up, etc., and, of course, the sex-angle is brought in by his affairs with female characters who have rather minor roles. However, I don't want to interfere with an author who has already done so many of these books and I much prefer to leave the plot, etc. to you.

In the Autumn of 1950, Self had set up his own publishing company, and Lazenby, as one of his former authors at Curtis Warren, received a circular letter dated September 6th, 1950:

> Dear Sir,
>
> I have immediate requirements, both for my own publishing company and for companies with whom I am connected, for 40,000 word MSS. which may come under the following general headings:
>
> Sex Gangster Stories
>
> Science Fiction Stories
>
> Westerns
>
> If you have any manuscripts of this nature available for placing, I should appreciate an opportunity of considering them, and I could promise you a quick decision as to their suitability for my purposes.

Self duly included SF in his lists, at first written by Curtis Warren regulars Dennis Hughes (as 'George Sheldon Brown) and John Jennison (as 'Edgar Rees Kennedy') and who later used the 'George Sheldon Brown' name, but spelt as Browne, with an 'e'! The two Hughes novels, *Destination Mars* and *The Planetoid Peril*, in particular, were atrociously ill-written space opera.

Notice the deliberate concoction of the names to resonate with those appearing from rival publishers, i.e. 'Roy Sheldon' and Edgar Rice Burroughs! Scion followed the same dubious practice with their gangster line, with 'Frank Hanson', being their unsubtle version of Hank Janson.

Self, like many other publishers, turned to other areas in the quest to titillate the audience, as an increasing number of French-flavoured novels, with bylines like 'René Laroche', 'Ramon Lacroix', and 'Georges Louis Delmaine' appeared. Most of these were even claimed to be actual translations from French, but only a few of them were. Self began a series by 'Jean Paul Valois' in 1953, supposedly 'translated' by 'Marc Lavelle', but which was actually the pseudonym of British author, Lisle Willis. (Willis also supplied a couple of wretched SF novels for Self as 'Erle Van Loden', *Curse of Planet Kuz* (1953), which was fully as bad as it sounds, and *Voyage Into Space* (1954). These titles betrayed the fact that his only previous track record in SF was with four short stories with Spencers.

This 'Continental' angle was merely cynical camouflage for a deliberate attempt on the part of these publishers to push sex fiction, for which they thought there was a market. Authors were deliberately commissioned to write unsavoury material.

Fittingly, Self would eventually find himself serving a gaol sentence, and he was not the only mushroom publisher to be gaoled. Other publishers were not quite so reckless, but still wanted to exploit the gullible audience for 'Continental' fiction, which they presumably sensed readers would equate with 'feelthy French postcards'.

Hamilton & Co. commissioned Norman Lazenby to write one of these 'sophisticated' novels for them. When he turned in the mss to their specification, Director Harry Assael's reply, dated 26 February 1949 ran thusly:

> Dear Sir,
>
> Our reader has now had an opportunity of going through your manuscript *Toast of the Latin Quarter* and you will see from the slips attached to the manuscript enclosed there are a very considerable number of scenes "too blue" for us to publish. Had there been fewer of these we should have endeavoured to tone them down ourselves, but feel that since a good deal of rewriting is going to be necessary you are best fitted to undertake it.
>
> We appreciate that the whole theme of your story is a 'sophisticated' one and apart from rewriting the offending passages would suggest you endeavour to 'clean' the theme up so that the risqué element is reduced. For example, if the heroine could pursue the 'perfect' man instead of the 'nice bad man' the implication would not have to be necessarily on sex. There can be romance, of course, with ardent love scenes, but we feel that there is no need for so much 'spice'.
>
> We would add that we enjoyed the story itself and even without the "blue" note there is the basis of an enjoyable yarn.
>
> Would you please do your best to return the manuscript by Monday next, March 7.

Lazenby complied, and the 'toned down' novel was subsequently published in July 1949. At the time, few formal contracts were ever drawn up, and each novel was either commissioned on an individual basis with an absurdly short time allowed for completion, or were picked up from unsolicited manuscripts. Some of the publishers were keeping their eyes on the Watch Committees, and included an indemnity clause making the author entirely responsible if anything of a scandalous or obscene nature brought on litigation.

It is incredible today that these publishers expected authors to write a novel in a fortnight (or less)—and to go on doing so! Typical of these so-called 'contracts' was the agreement with Scion Ltd. that Norman Lazenby was given in July, 1952.

Term of Contract: 18 months, between Norman Lazenby and SCION LTD,,

2 (two) books per month. One American thriller and one Science-Fantasy. Each book to be of 40,000 or 45,000 words. The American thriller to be paid for at the rate of 30/- per thousand words, All Rights. Science-Fantasy to be 27/- per thousand words, All Rights. Rights to cover all translations.

The Author agrees to give SCION LTD., all his output, i.e. two books per month and not to work for or supply fiction to any other Publisher for the period of the above contract.

First book to be supplied on the 1st July, 1952. Pen-name will belong to SCION LTD., payment to be made six weeks after delivery of manuscript.

Standard of work must be good, failing which contract can be terminated. Contract can be altered by the Publisher to two American thriller type books at the agreed fee of 30/- per thousand words, instead of one Thriller and one Science-Fantasy.

For and on behalf of NORMAN LAZENBY

16th June, 1952.

When Lazenby showed me this contract in my 1992 interview, I asked him for his recollections of it, and whether he had employed an agent:

No, I handled all my own stuff. I used to regularly write to all of the publishers, asking them their current requirements.

Often they were overstocked, or couldn't get enough paper—rationing was still on in those days, remember. I only wrote whatever was currently in demand at any particular time—westerns, gangster, romance.

Most publishers were reluctant to commission anything—that is, giving any commitment that they would actually buy what you sent them. Tastes changed so rapidly that sometimes when I supplied what a publisher had asked for, they would reject it and ask for something completely different! I was eventually able to sell rejected mss to one or other of the various publishers.

I had two so-called 'contracts' with Scion, and there was quite a story attached to them. In June 1952, I went to London to see B. Z. Immanuel at Scion's offices. He'd given me a contract for two books a month. Whilst I was waiting to see him, I went into their editorial office and met their editor at that time, Julian Franklyn. The room was small, and was lined with rows and rows of their paperback books. It was an Aladdin's cave of books— you'd have loved it, Phil! I was quite impressed until Franklyn suddenly started swearing! "That bastard Immanuel!" he said—those were his actual words—"he conned me into this set-up! Just look at this place—look at it! He got me here under bloody false pretences . . . bloody this, and bloody that!" The tirade went on. I showed him my contract from Immanuel, and he laughed, ironically. "Watch yourself," he said. "That contract isn't worth the paper it's printed on!" But I had signed the damn thing, and so I wrote two of them, until I got a letter from John Russell Fearn warning me that Immanuel and Scion were in trouble financially.

Whilst paper rationing was still in force, the paperback market did at least offer opportunities for writers—but only if they worked under the conditions dictated by the publisher. Certainly the rates were low, given that they were invariably "flat fees" and none of the publishers paid any royalties, so that even if the books became bestsellers, the author would get no further remuneration. The same if the books were translated abroad (as several, in fact, were).

Most of the later commentators on this period have claimed that the payments to authors were so poor that the authors had to mass-produce in order to survive. And that mass-production led to an execrable standard of work. However, in many cases, this was simply untrue. It was not the authors' poverty that drove them to mass-produce—it was the sheer rapacious greed of the publishers. It was the *publishers* who set the two-books-a-month schedules, and many of them simply didn't care whether the resultant work was any good or not.

With the average working man's wage being a good deal less than £30 a month, any author able to write two books a month, bringing in around £80 to £90, was obviously quite well off, since he was earning *three times the average wage*! The only problem was the terrific mental and physical strain thrown onto the author in keeping up such a punishing schedule— assuming, that is, that he tried to produce his best work.

Authors therefore coped with the problem in different ways.

Some 'hack' authors simply churned out absolute rubbish, the John Spencer and Gannet Press publications were prime examples.

Some 'good' authors—mostly pre-war SF fans with a background knowledge of the medium—simply wrote straight onto the typewriter and turned in their first drafts without any revision. The resultant stories were thus very much below the standard those authors *could* have achieved, had they been able to take their time. But since the fee was the same for good or bad work, it simply wasn't worth the candle, even if the author had been given the time to polish his work. Even so, even the poorest work of these 'good' writers was streets ahead of their 'hack' competitors.

In the field of SF, John Russell Fearn was the most successful and prolific author. Given his tremendous output, critics have condemned him unread. But a surprising amount of his work was perfectly good. This was proven by its extensive translation and reprinting around the world, and the fact that *scores* of his best novels have been reprinted only recently, more than 50 years on, whilst most of the work of his pseudonymous contemporaries has been deservedly condemned to oblivion.

The simple fact was that Fearn had a 'head start' on all his competitors. He alone had a vast amount of both published and unpublished SF magazine material to draw upon. He was able to skim the cream of this large body of magazine work, which served as the inspiration for a whole string of novels published under his Vargo Statten pseudonym. As already detailed in an earlier chapter, several novels were unpublished mss he had written earlier. Other 'Statten' novels incorporated, in modified and often improved form, existing magazine material:

Nebula X (1950) was based on 'The Multillionth Chance' (1946), *The Sun Makers* (1950) was based on 'Metamorphosis' (1937), *The Avenging Martian* (1951) was based on 'Red Heritage' (1938), *Cataclysm* (1951) was based on 'The Devouring Tide' (1944), *The Red Insects* (1951) was based on 'Lords of 9018' (1938). *Renegade Star* (1951) was an expansion of 'Blue Infinity' (1935), *Inner Cosmos* (1952) was an expansion of 'Worlds Within' (1937), *Space Warp* (1952) incorporated the unpublished novelette 'Endless Day' (written for the US in 1946), *Eclipse Express* (1952) cannibalized two short stories 'Eclipse Bears Witness' (1940) and 'Valley of Pretenders' (1939), *The G-Bomb* and *Time Bridge* (1952) incorporated earlier magazine novellas 'Last Secret Weapon' (1941) and 'Prisoner of Time' (1942).

And this is just a *partial* list; there were numerous similar examples. And some of the Statten novels were actually *reprints* of novels Fearn had earlier published in the prestigious Toronto *Star Weekly*, on which he had lavished a good deal of time for this more exacting and higher paying market, and which therefore represented his best work, e.g. *Man From Tomorrow* (1952) was *Stranger in our Midst* (1950), *Across the Ages* (1952) was *Glimpse* (1952) and *Zero Hour* (1953) was *Deadline* (1952).

The Watch Committees managed to flush out many of the bad publications, As well as issuing destruction orders for the books, they were responsible for a number of arrests, fines, and jail sentences, not only for publishers but also for authors and, in at least one case, a printer. But they did not manage to stop the really guilty men. Their concern was with the books, and the morals of the printed page; sadly, they missed the really horrific aspects of the publishing business—the treatment of authors by their publishers.

During my editorship of *Vision of Tomorrow* in 1969-70, I met several authors who had written for those publishers in the 1950s, and they told me some sad stories of the exploitation some vulnerable writers had to contend with. One concerned a sick author for whom his writing was his only source of money to buy medication to keep himself alive. His publisher tried to force the author to work harder by withholding payments, and eventually the author died. Even in 1970, much the same practices were still being carried out by at least one publisher who had stayed in business, forcing an author on expensive medication to keep churning out material for him, to continue his treatment.

Gordon Landsborough's memoir gives a further chilling insight into how some of these mushroom publishers operated:

My parting with Hamilton's in 1951 was friendly. Hamilton's felt they needed to keep their 'sophisticateds' going—the bottom was beginning to drop out of the cheap paperback market—and I did not want to touch the stuff. I handed everything over to two editors and retired to freelance writing. Hamilton's was pretty good; the publisher generously offered to buy westerns from me at £1 a thousand, which was well above market average.

But in the next three years I did many things apart from writing. The publishing world is small, and in my short time at Hamilton's I had acquired a reputation as having ability. Thus, three times I was approached by various people troubled with their publishing interests and wanting my advice on them. So I was plunged into a publishing world that made Hamilton's, by comparison, look as sober and earnest as *The Times*.

Obviously, I cannot give names, even after all these years, for fear of possible libel, yet I can assure you of the truth of what I write now.

I met a publisher who kept a writer in a cellar. It was a dark and chilly place, one of a warren of cellars along an echoing stone passage. The writer sat on a stiff kitchen chair at a small kitchen table, centred under a naked electric lamp suspended from the ceiling. A low-wattage lamp, I remember; the room never seemed more than half-lit. Against a wall was a hospital-type metal bed, and on it was a disorder of army blankets, brown and uninviting, and overcoats and clothes to keep out the night's seeping cold.

The writer was a thin and wasted creature, wan and blinking behind his glasses. I never knew his name. He sat at that table from morning till night, tapping timidly away at an old typewriter. I never saw him eat, though he must have. He was said to work all day and far into the night, and kept working at weekends too.

He was supposed to write two books a week!

They were short books, of course, but . . . 70,000 words a week, ten thousand words a day! I don't know how far he failed (if he did fail) in his target, but the task was beyond human endurance and this boy was in no condition even to attempt it.

The publisher, a man for whom I can say no good at all, paid him £7/10/- a week for his work. But first he deducted £2/10/- because the boy slept on the premises, and then was reluctant to part with what he owed to the unfortunate 'staff' writer.

I saw the boy one day, a washed-out ghost of a creature in daylight, feebly leaning against the publisher's office door, both hands beating gently against it. He was like a moth fluttering there, crying, yet still afraid to draw attention to himself. "I want some money," he was saying. "I am hungry."

The publisher, rot his pulpy soul, safely locked in his office (he locked himself in any time he though there was going to be trouble) shouted brutally for him to go away and work and then he would not starve.

And the writer went timidly back to his cell, and we fed him on some cake that a typist wouldn't eat because of her figure.

Now, the curious thing was that the boy sat all those hours, mostly writing the toughest of American gangster stories! (He probably wrote some SF too, space opera). He mowed people down with Thompson submachine guns, he carried a sawn-off shotgun in his grip and slugged men across the windpipe with his automatic, he was beaten up time after time and staggered back to kick and stamp and gouge and hammer the brains out of his opponents and then crawled off all bloody and took the gang leader's willing moll. That was the world the boy lived in, there in that yellow-lit cellar; a world of subhumans, of shocking violence perpetrated on others! And he the weakest of creatures,

He could not stand up to that fat rogue of a publisher. He had no courage, poor lad—it was only on typing paper. He was sick and he should have been looked after in a hospital. Instead, he was exploited by a man with no conscience.

Within a week I had put my report to the financial backers of this company, and the rogue publisher was out and the company finished with him.

What happened to the boy, I never knew. I hope he stopped writing—one of the hardest jobs in the world. I hope he found someone to look after him. It is because of incidents like these that I have an abiding hatred of publishers who will not pay the rate for the job, who expect writers to work for next to nothing, while they live it up on fat expense accounts.

I have seen too many people destroyed by these exploiters—this boy was one of them. I have seen men sickened and humiliated by these greedy men, beating them down in price, their efforts disparaged so that a bargain can be made.

No, I have no time for them. They are good for no one, not even themselves, judging by the record of publishers who had opportunities after World War II, but faded when competition came. They certainly set back SF for a decade when they could have made a fortune for themselves if they had tried. But greed killed them

From the time I went freelance in 1951, these publishers were dying and knew it. That was why worried people, with finance invested, asked me to look into these companies. Though paper rationing had not yet ended, paper was easier to come by, which meant that more cheap-jack publishers were coming into an already crowded market.

Additionally, though, these publishers were receiving the close attentions of various Watch Committees throughout the country. The Glasgow Watch Committee started in 1949. They successfully prosecuted some publishers for what they considered obscene literature. Then, Brighton magistrates had their attention directed to this 'sophisticated' literature, and books were destroyed and fines imposed. Sheffield came into the picture, and then suddenly all of Lancashire appeared to have gone Puritanical.

By 1953, publishers were reeling before this wave of outraged opinion; they were really rattled and almost in panic. They began to read their manuscripts more carefully, and here is where I always though the situation was hypocritical. The Watch Committees and their ladies got worked up over a scene involving sex, but seemed untroubled by the sadistic violence, where men slaughtered men in atrocious circumstances. Violence is the true pornography.

Cover drawings also became more restrained. What we used to call 'breast-sellers' now went into bras and were almost respectfully covered. I remember the king of them all, 'Hank Janson', a tough American private-eye series, more daring than most in its covers, suddenly realizing they could not get away with it any longer. But they had four covers printed, each a voluptuous and overflowing female, decorating the cover en décolleté. The publisher knew they would never get away with such covers now, with the hounds baying for blood, but neither did he want to scrap the valuable board used for paperback covers.

To our delight (we can always appreciate a smart cookie in publishing) the publisher overprinted the near-nudes, imposing them with a dark silhouette of a man in a cloak and flat hat, reminiscent of a Spaniard. In fact, we called them the 'Sandeman's Port' covers, and they looked very much like that excellent brew's trademark. If you held the covers up to the light you could see the near-nude underpicture. There were no prosecutions in Glasgow, and the 'Hank Jansons' sold well.

Basically, this fringe publishing went out because it did not understand the reading needs of people, but undoubtedly its demise was accelerated by the constant attacks of the Watch Committees. My attitude towards the situation was somewhat ambivalent. I am wary of accepting that the Watch

Committees should be arbiters of public taste, yet I had such a contempt for these publishers that I cheered on the prosecutors.

A minor disadvantage of the situation was that these publishers had a final fling at SF. They stopped or cut back their 'sophisticateds' and they had to do something with their paper. So, hopefully, they committed themselves to more SF stories (along with boxing, foreign legion, football, and an increasing number of romances; the time for experiment was there). The lesson repeated throughout all these years did not change, however. You will never win an intellectual audience with crap.

Curiously, though the signs were all against this type of publishing, there were always mugs being conned into putting money into paperback ventures. One worried and very large printing firm called me in because they had doubts about a printing programme they were financing by virtue of the credit they had been talked into granting a glib publisher. I looked over the programme.

There were twenty-four new titles scheduled for publication each month, the print run was 40,000 each. There were eight 'sophisticateds', eight Westerns, and eight SF novels. I told the printer bluntly and immediately that the thing stank. I knew the state of the market and I knew that it could not take eight SF novels each month. As for 40,000 of each title . . . no one had sold so many in this field since the end of the war, so far as I knew. Twelve thousand if you were lucky—but not with eight new titles competing with each other.

The printer brought me the SF manuscripts. I didn't really have to read them. Some I recognized as deadbeats I had rejected at Hamilton's, others were dog-eared and clearly had gone the rounds. The few I dipped into gave me the palsies, they were so bad.

The whole setup was a con-trick. The publisher was a completely ruthless man who had played this game before and would continue to play it. The thing was to get someone to back the printing of the books, sell as many as you can, then argue with the printer or whoever had financed the deal regarding payment.

In this case, the printer lost £8,000 (a lot of money in the early 1950s). I gave my report that the thing was on the crook, yet the publisher still managed to talk the printer into it. The books were delivered. The print bill was never met. The publisher was a man of straw and it is useless to try and get money out of a man who has made sure he doesn't have any. Besides, when the crunch came, the publisher, still bold as brass, made a proposition to the depressed and unhappy printer. Okay, so he'd made a mistake about the number of titles the market could bear. Well, just give him six months and let him remainder the surplus and there would be enough money to pay off the print bill. God help me if it isn't true, but the printer fell for it. He told me a year later, by which time he could grin at his own folly. He'd left the disposal of the stocks to the publisher, who had disposed of them all right, but not a penny came to the printer.

Science fantasy? It doesn't hold a candle to the truth of paperback publishing in Britain in the 1950s!

I once saw a publisher chased around his desk by an irate author with a fireman's axe. The publisher had chiselled on him, commissioned a work and then refused to pay for it. He had been unusually disparaging about the author and his writing ability, and suddenly the author went berserk. He snatched a fireman's axe off the wall and my regret is he didn't do in the publisher. I never knew anyone could flash out into the street as fast as that out-of-condition publisher without conscience did.

There was another publisher who published some of the worst SF, who was so warped and dishonest that his own wife didn't trust him and kept the keys to the warehouse. He never had enough money because his wife did the company books and held the purse strings tightly. So he was in the habit of burgling his own warehouse.

It was a rather tricky business, this. He used to leave a window unlatched, so that he could open it from outside. There was a bit of an area to cross, for the window was below ground level. With more ingenuity than most of his writers showed, the bent publisher would leave a decorator's plank leaning against the wall of this area. After dark, he would come along, reach down for the plank, prop it across the area, crawl across, open the window, go inside, parcel himself some books, which he sold to a pal around the corner.

One night he was crawling across the plank when a dispassionate voice invited an answer to the question, "And what d'you think you're up to?" It was a cynical London bobby. Explaining things from the middle of a plank presents difficulties in the way of plausibility, and his statement that "this was his business and if he chose to enter via the window, then what of it?" only resulted in his being marched down to the police station. His wife gave him hell when she got the story!

Destination Mars by George Sheldon Brown (Ron Turner). Edwin Self, 1951

Conquerors of Venus by Edgar Rees Kennedy (Ron Turner). Edwin Self, 1953

The Yellow Planet by George Sheldon Browne (Ron Turner). Edwin Self, 1954

Voyage into Space by Erle Van Loden (Ron Turner). Edwin Self, 1954

The Red Insects by Vargo Statten (Philip Mendoza). Scion, 1951

The G-Bomb by Vargo Statten (Ron Turner), Scion, 1952

A Thing of the Past by Volsted Gridban (Philip Mendoza). Scion, 1953

The Lonely Astronomer by Volsted Gridban (Ron Turner), Scion, 1954

CHAPTER 10:
BLAST-OFF
FOR SPACE OPERA

By the end of 1951, it seemed that everyone and his dog was publishing paperbacks, and there were an ever increasing number turning out science fiction.

Curtis Warren Ltd. was the most prolific, still relying on Dennis Hughes and David Griffiths to write them all, although in mid-1951, Hughes began to fall back on his production due to his involvement with writing another series. The byline 'Marco Garon' (originally 'Garron') had first appeared in November 1950 with two novels, *The Missing Safari* and *The Lost City*. The books, with a large banner headline 'Azan the Apeman' were unashamed rip-offs of 'Tarzan the Apeman', and obviously commissioned after the hugely successful Mark Goulden/W. H. Allen (later Pinnacle Books) reprints of Edgar Rice Burroughs' *Tarzan* novels began to appear in 1949, bringing them to Britain in mass-market paperback for the first time. They had begun with *Tarzan and the Lost Empire* and were an immediate hit. Goulden gradually introduced Burroughs' other SF series characters, their sixth title being *A Princess of Mars*, with the ninth introducing *Carson of Venus* (1950). Unprecedented for the time was that the publisher reprinted and reissued many of the titles, and the series was so successful it continued unbroken until 1955, with a late flourish in 1958.

Curtis Warren quickly published another two pairs of 'Azan' novels, *Tribal War* and *White Fangs* (January, 1951), and *King Hunters* and *Jungle Fever* (March, 1951).

The 'Azan the Apeman' banner was such a blatant copy that E.R.B.

Inc. (trustees of the Edgar Rice Burroughs estate) threatened Curtis with prosecution unless the books were taken off the market, and Curtis was forced to destroy stocks (although they somehow only managed to destroy under two-thirds of the print runs—making the 'Azan' novels a rarity in collecting terms).

Hamilton's had been considering commissioning their own Tarzan clone, but the prompt legal action caused them to drop the idea.

The 'Azan' novels themselves do have a peculiar appeal for those unfamiliar with the original, and the character's fluency in the English language does have a far more logical basis than picking it up from books. The author was almost certainly David Griffiths, and if E.R.B. Inc. had not threatened prosecution, the series would have been developed much further than the six that did appear.

Not wanting to lose the byline, Curtis Warren quickly brought Dennis Hughes into the writing seat and a new series of jungle adventures began. The 'Rex Brandon' novels were fast moving and cliché-ridden, but strangely enjoyable, with Hughes' best high-speed writing style. The new series was possibly based upon Alex Raymond's *Jungle Jim*—or, more likely, the 'Jungle Jim' *films* starring an aging Johnny Weismuller. These films were only loosely based on Alex Raymond's comic strip character, and were essentially a vehicle for Weismuller to reprise his earlier role of Tarzan (for which he was now too fat—but as Jungle Jim he got to keep his shirt on!) but this time it did not appear to upset either the artist or film producers, as the 'Azan' series had done E.R.B. Inc.

In order to capitalize on their earlier series, Curtis Warren issued the new series under the byline of 'Marco Garon' (only one 'r' in 'Garon'). The first pair of 'Brandon' books was issued in May 1951, *Jungle Allies* and *Death Warriors*, and were successful enough for the publisher and author to continue churning them out—a further six titles in 1951, and another four in 1952. Most of these novels have decidedly fantastic elements, and are infused with the same weird imagination Hughes displayed in his many 'science fantasy' novels. All of them are set in the African jungle, except for the last one, *Mountain Gold*, which, exceptionally, is a 'straight' adventure set in the Yukon.

With Hughes tied up on this series, it meant that the Curtis SF line was severely depleted. There were two options open: detail another Curtis regular author to write SF, or rely upon unsolicited manuscripts.

Judging by the mixed quality of the subsequent product, it appears that Curtis did both. A number of new bylines began to appear alongside 'Gill Hunt' and 'King Lang'—'Neil Charles', 'Rand Le Page' (laughingly billed as 'the French Master of Science Fiction'), and 'Berl Cameron' ('America's Ace Writer') were examples. The same group of authors were behind them all; two of the more prolific being Brian Holloway and John Jennison. And amongst the late-1951 crop were E. C. Tubb's first three novels (*Saturn Patrol*, by 'King Lang'; *Planetfall*, by 'Gill Hunt'; and *Argentis*, by 'Brian Shaw', commissioned by David Griffiths, who was a regular visitor at the White Horse, where he met Tubb). Another new author was John Brunner, who entered the writing field with *Galactic Storm* (as 'Gill Hunt'). At seventeen, Brunner had launched himself on a career in which he would later be internationally recognized as one of Britain's leading writers. But this first effort, written while he was still at school, became something of an embarrassment to him, although the £27/10- he (eventually) received paid for his first typewriter. This was after he managed to follow it immediately with sales to American magazines, including the prestigious *Astounding*. Although he acknowledged the book's existence, he refused to confirm the title until Robert Reginald proved his authorship in 1979 through the records of the Library of Congress (the book had been imported into the United States, requiring disclosure of its true author). Actually his authorship had already been an open secret in British fandom after he had been introduced as its author at the 1951 British SF Convention. In later years, *Galactic Storm* has become one of the most sought-after collectors' items of the period.

By mid-1952, Dennis Hughes was once again writing most of the Curtis SF novels (once the 'Rex Brandon' series ended after twelve books) and was to become one of the most prolific writers of science fiction of the day. The quantity of titles obviously meant that the quality of writing suffered a great deal, and Hughes' background in SF was probably zero, but when he moved away from space opera to allegorical science-fantasy, some of these books were surprisingly readable; not great literature, by any means, but certainly a cut above most of the crap. (Sturgeon's Law applied long before he put it into words!).

Both the publisher and author seemed to know what they were doing, because these allegorical fantasies were actually published with the cover logo of '*Science Fantasy*,' whereas the straight SF novels were simply labelled 'Science Fiction'. Even more curiously, each of these Science Fantasy novels actually began *as* straight science fiction, and continued as such until the *exact half way mark* in the book, and then 'went peculiar'! No other publisher sought to imitate this technique (assuming they were ever aware of it), which makes these Hughes novels rather unique.

Land of Esa and *Twenty-four Hours* (both as 'Neil Charles') in particular have a quite electrifying frisson despite the high-speed prose style and, after wading through the rest of the dross, any book that shows even the slightest pretensions to imagination shines out like a gem. The books were also distinguished by being written around some quite amazing bad-taste, Bug-Eyed Monster covers, painted with brilliant panache by a young artist named Gordon C. Davies (who later graduated to gracing the covers of Heinlein paperbacks in the 1970s).

Curtis Warren was a prime exponent of having authors write stories around pre-prepared covers, although the novels were often halfway towards completion before the cover arrived, and the author had to quickly write in an explanation, resulting in some marvellously contrived situations suddenly cropping up in otherwise logically-written stories.

Of a slightly better class than the Curtis Warren average was Hamilton's *Authentic* series. Some non-*Authentic* novels were still being published under the Hamilton imprint, such as *Duel in Nightmare Worlds*, by B. Flackes and *Space Beam*, by John Robb, but these were not up to the standard that Gordon Landsborough and Bert Campbell were striving for—a fact proven by sales figures of some 10,000 copies less than the magazine was selling.

But still by far the most popular line was the 'Vargo Statten' series from Scion Ltd. John Russell Fearn continued to deliver the goods in the eyes of his (many) new fans, and Fearn's background in SF, dating back to 1931, as a fan and writer, meant that he was able to recapture the 'sense of wonder' in his novels that had thrilled young American and British fans back in the 1930s. In fact, as stated elsewhere, many of the 'Statten' novels derived their basic plots either from stories Fearn published or wrote in the 1930s and '40s, and Fearn's strict adherence to six hours of writing a day helps to explain how he managed to keep up his terrific output.

The sudden appearance of Tarzan-type adventures from Curtis Warren prompted other publishers to try their hand, and Scion Ltd. was no different when it came to jumping onto bandwagons. They realized that their rival's big mistake had been to call their character 'Azan the Apeman', a crudely obvious rip-off of Burroughs' hero. If they had applied a little more common sense and used a dissimilar name, they would probably have gotten away with it.

They invited Fearn to write such a series, and two 'Anjani' novels (*The Gold of Akada* and its sequel, *Anjani the Mighty*) appeared under the byline 'Earl Titan' in May and July 1951. Fearn made a surprisingly good job of imitating Burroughs, borrowing particularly from *The Jewels of Opar*, but mixed with his *own* original action sequences. With their attractive Ron Turner covers, both these books eventually became expensive collectors' items, and were notable enough to be reprinted in the US (2004) and in the UK (2010).

However, Scion did not continue the series, partly because Fearn told Scion he was not happy doing them, but mainly because the 'Statten' novels were selling in far greater quantities, and Scion did not want to reduce the number appearing in favour of a series with lower sales. But having discovered that there *was* a profitable market for jungle adventure stories, another Scion regular was drafted in by the publisher, Victor Norwood.

He had been writing prolifically since 1950, and was a writer who went along with prevailing practices simply to make some quick money, not even knowing or caring under what names or titles his work was published. Known work included numerous westerns as 'Jim Bowie'. Because Norwood's real life travels in the Amazon had received newspaper publicity, Scion allowed him to retain his own name for his jungle novels, which began with *The Untamed* (1951). His real-life experiences gave the series some authenticity, and 'Jacare', Norwood's 'Jungle Lord' was sufficiently different from Tarzan not to trouble the Burroughs estate—as a feral child brought up in the jungle he was dumb! A dynamic Ron Turner cover helped ensure the book's success, and the series eventually ran to six books between 1951 and 1953—though Burroughs pastiche collectors should note that the last title, *Drums Along the Amazon*, did not feature Jacare.

A fascinating non-fiction account of Norwood's real-life adventures in the Amazon can be found in his book *A Hand Full of Diamonds* (Boardman, 1960), a sequel to his earlier book *Man Alone,* detailing his earliest adventures in Guiana and Brazil.

Completing the quintet of Tarzan rip-offs were novels by John King and John Raymond. 'King' was the pseudonym of Ernest McKeag, and his two novels for Harborough Press in November 1951 owe more to his days as an editor at Amalgamated Press and boys' adventure story writer in the 1920s and 1930s, than to his later output of the '50s (gangster novels and stories of Parisienne lowlife for Modern Fiction Ltd.). The 'Shuna' (or more properly, Esh'una) stories were another step away from the normal—more a mixture of Rider Haggard and Arthur Conan Doyle's *The Lost World*. Shuna and her lost tribe are safely hidden away on the top of a plateau in South America. Collectors who steer clear of the 'lost world' novels and only collect space opera from this period are hereby alerted: the second novel of the series, *Shuna and the Lost Tribe*, is out-and-out space opera, wherein a rogue asteroid slices the top off the Mato Grosso and carries Shuna, the tribe, and the city (all intact!) off into outer space! Both titles had vivid covers by the noted artist Reg Heade, which has made them collectors' items today.

The 'John Raymond' novel appeared from John Spencer & Co. in November, 1951, and may have been a reject from Hamiltons. During 1951, Spencer's awful magazines had only appeared irregularly and, with no issues in the eight months after March, it looked as if they had run out of steam and the SF world was granted a reprieve. But they returned in November with more mindless drivel and, it would seem, the idea for a new series. The Raymond novel, *Zamba of the Jungle*, carried the banner 'New Jungle Stories'. If this was an example, then it was lucky no more appeared, since there was nothing 'new' about the clichéd plot (although it is quite an amusing story, especially where millionaire-adventurer Jacob P. Smirkle decides to find out if there is any truth in the story that elephants are afraid of mice! One wonders if the undoubtedly ill-paid author wasn't cooking a snook at the publisher and readers).

The non-arrival of more 'New Jungle Stories' was amply made up for (or down for, in Spencer's case) when they launched their SF novel line in late 1952. Their first story was the work of Gerald Evans, who had previously sold a few stories to *Thrilling Wonder Stories* in America, and Gerald G. Swan in the United Kingdom. His title, *The Black Sphere*, as by 'Victor La Salle', is discussed in the next chapter.

'La Salle' quickly followed this story with *Suns in Duo* (this one written by Thomas Wade) and others, and he was soon joined by 'Karl Zeigfried' (sic). These novels were as good as the magazines (that is, terrible!).

John Spencer was just one of the many companies to leap onto the SF bandwagon—as soon as one introduced SF into their line, other publishers followed.

One example was Archer Press, who issued 'An Exciting Science Fiction Novel' *Planet War* (1952), by the strangely named 'Fysh' (probably a pseudonym of Spencer hack Leonard G. Fish). The book's ghastly cover by Gerald Facey gave a good indication of its content. It is difficult to find words to adequately describe this novel, so instead I will simply quote the publisher's blurb verbatim:

> "Planet War" introduces CAPTAIN JOHN FORREST the number one Space Ship pilot, working under the direct orders of SPACE-MARSHAL CONNORY, discovers a new planet on his regular run to the planet JUPITER.
>
> Captain Forest lands on this planet only to discover the most AMAZING CREATURES living on any planet so far discovered by Space-Marshal Connory's fleet of space ships.
>
> The creatures on this planet were so far advanced in the Science World, as we call it, that even Captain Forrest, who has flown the most Scientific Space Ships, and landed on planets millions of miles from the Earth, was struck by these so called creatures' way of life.
>
> After you have read the "Planet War" there is **no doubt** that you will want to follow CAPTAIN JOHN FORREST on his hazardous trips, in this series, in which he and Space-Marshal Connory struggle for supremacy on these far-away planets.

Unsurprisingly, however, no one *did* want to follow the further adventures of the gallant Captain, a man "who had almost before he could walk learnt how to handle a space-ship." For which we can all be truly thankful.

Surprisingly, the book's publishers, the Archer Press, did at least somewhat atone for their crime by later publishing a handsomely produced reprint edition of Lester Del Rey's good quality U.S. magazine *Space Science Fiction* between December 1952 and August 1953. Here fans could read stories like Philip K. Dick's 'The Variable Man' and T. L. Sherred's 'Cue for Quiet' to help assuage the stench of rotten Fish. Unfortunately the magazine folded in the U.S. after its eighth issue.

Gaywood Press Ltd., previously distributors of 'Hank Janson' and 'Astron del Martia' for Stephen Frances, tried their hand at SF in late 1950, and secured the writing talents of Ralph L. Finn. The back covers of his books quoted praise from *Reveille*, *The People*, *Cavalcade*, *The Sunday Times*, etc. "Ralph L. Finn can write—and tell a good story," said *Reveille*.

The approbation was justified. Finn was actually a very accomplished author, having won awards in 1943 and 1946 for Best Short Story; and he had written some intriguing and literate 'timeslip' fantasy hardcovers for Hutchinson, notably *The Lunatic, the Lover and the Poet* (1947). But his two paperback novels that were published in January 1951, *Freaks Against Supermen* and *Captive on the Flying Saucers*, were very different. Finn had been tempted to write them because the publisher had offered him £75 each (almost twice the going rate). Finn later went on record as saying he had dashed them off in a couple of weeks as potboilers.

Included in his brief was a request that both books should be liberally laced with sex. It seems that Gaywood—who were one of the worst offenders with sex-gangster titles—had conceived the idea that they might attract the same audience with their SF, and so slip it past the Watch Committees, whose gimlet eyes were trained on gangster novels.

Freaks Against Supermen was by far the better of the two stories. The human race is all but exterminated by a mysterious Sickness, apart from one man—a reclusive scientist, who eventually finds a woman and her daughter. Through them he creates a new race of mutant supermen, who in turn create a servitor race, known as Freaks, who eventually revolt against their masters. Given the circumstances (repopulation of the Earth), the sexual and biological elements in the book were possibility justified, but the same could not be said of *Captive on the Flying Saucers*.

Its hero finds himself aboard a spaceship, the captive of the 'Visians' a dwarf race from Venus. He is then forced to undergo multiple rapes from tiny female Visians ('the ritual of delight') to test his virility and suitability to mate with the Visian Queen. This book was by turns titillating and sadistic, with ludicrous brushed-in space travel and SF elements.

So blatant were they that word of the books' sexual content soon got out in the Trade, and to the attention of a couple of Watch Committees, who ordered their destruction locally. With the fear of prosecution, the alarmed publishers quickly changed their tack. Their 'respectable' 'Astron del Martia' byline was quickly revived out of cold storage. Fearn could not be approached because he was now under exclusive contract to Scion, so they had to commission their gangster hacks to write routine sexless space operas. *Space Pirates* (1951) was followed by *Dawn of Darkness* (even worse than the first book), and early in 1952 came *Interstellar Espionage*, which was simply awful. A further 'Del Martia' title, *Shades Over the Sun*, was announced but mercifully never appeared.

People who should have known better attributed these further inferior Astron Del Martia titles to Fearn for many years afterwards, which did little to enhance his reputation. Anyone with half a brain, who had read any Fearn, could have realized that Fearn was not the author had they read just a few pages of any of these later Del Martia books. But he was condemned *without the books being read*.

In his landmark reference book *The Encyclopedia of Science Fiction and Fantasy (Volume Three)*, published by Advent in 1982, and for many years the 'bible' of science fiction, even people like Donald H. Tuck would write under Fearn's entry, "Works shown below as by Astron Del Martia are listed here only for convenience, as only *The Trembling World* is known to be Fearn; the others may or may not be." Because of this pathetic cop-out, the false attribution persisted in print for years, probably helped by the fact that *Interstellar Espionage* was reportedly a sequel to *Spawn of Space* by 'Franz Harkon', which was one of two failed efforts made by Scion in 1951 to cash in on their own success with Vargo Statten'. The latter novel, along with *Sister Earth*, by 'Arnold Brede', were mediocre efforts, but the known Fearn/Scion link made him an obvious choice—of people who chose not to read the books—when it came down to who was to blame for them.

In 1952, Fearn had been invited to speak at a convention held in Manchester, and during his speech, he *pointedly disassociated himself* from having anything to do with *all* these inferior titles, but his audience seemed to be later afflicted with collective amnesia, even though the relevant part of his speech *had* been printed in a contemporary fanzine!

The culmination of this collective amnesia and sheer stupidity came in 1985 when a new edition of *One Against Time* by Astron Del Martia was actually reprinted in Italian, with an attribution to Fearn, and a nonsensical long introduction by Riccardo Valla (an Italian 'expert' on SF) compounding the calumny.

Fearn, as 'Vargo Statten', continued to appear with increasing regularity: eight titles in 1950, ten in 1951, and fourteen in 1952. During 1952, there was a hiatus: Scion Ltd. copped a heavier than usual fine for their gangster obscenity, and the directors argued about who should pay the fine, eventually splitting into three splinter groups.

First off the mark was a new company, Milestone Publications, with backing from various ex-Scion personnel. They were reportedly promised credit by a paper merchant who was the boyfriend of Dail Ambler, who had written for Scion's gangster series under her own name and as 'Danny Spade'. Editor Maurice Read was one of those who had 'jumped ship'. By offering slightly higher rates and taking only First British Serial Rights, he set about systematically poaching Scion's most successful authors, intending to continue using their series characters and bylines. One of those recruited was E. C. Tubb, who had been writing for Scion under the byline 'Volsted Gridban'. In the following essay, which I first commissioned for *Vision of Tomorrow* in 1970, 'Ted' Tubb describes how he came into the SF magazine and paperback world and, with a writer's insight, describes how the various changes affected the authors.

In June 1950, I received a letter from E. J. Carnell, then the editor of *New Worlds*, in which he stated that he was pleased to accept my story, 'No Short Cuts', for his magazine and, by so doing, provided me with the greatest euphoric thrill an aspiring professional writer can ever know—that of his first acceptance.

It was a year before the story was published, and by the time it saw print I had already written several others and was launched on a professional career. The early '50s were a good time for aspiring authors to make their mark because, with four magazines hungry for material and with a rash of pocket books appearing on the stands, there was a high demand for stories by those with background knowledge of the medium.

While the magazine editors acted as selective filters, many of the pocket book publishers lacked the knowledge of how to tell a good science fiction story from a bad one and, in truth, many of them simply didn't care. They had a production schedule to maintain, and their critical faculties were low. Also, the habit was to use a plethora of 'house names', pseudonyms which belonged to the publishing company and behind which the author lost both identity and responsibility—a situation which encouraged carelessness in writing and laid the emphasis on speed of production rather than quality.

Speed was important for another reason: the rates were extremely low. The first pocket book I wrote, *Saturn Patrol*, published by Curtis Warren under the pseudonym 'King Lang', which was 36,000 words long, earned the sum of £27. Two others which carried the names 'Gill Hunt' and 'Brian Shaw', the same—and for that sum, the publishers demanded all rights, which meant that no matter what happened to the book later, the author received no further payment.

The irony of this is best illustrated by the late Bryan Berry, who sold a book to a publishing firm under these conditions and received about £35. The firm then sold it to America for ten times as much. On protesting, the author was given the sop of a commission for another book for the same firm—under the same conditions.

To protest against this practice was, at the time, useless. They set the rules and if you didn't like them, you didn't have to submit. If you didn't submit, there was always someone else who would.

My three stories for Curtis Warren had been both in the nature of an exercise and an education. I had not written anything that long before and neither had I used the formula they wanted. This was to have twelve chapters each of three thousand words, each chapter, if possible, ending on a high point. It was a mechanical technique and led to stories that were more a series of episodes rather than a closely plotted story. But I enjoyed writing them and found the concentration on action easier to handle than the interplay of deep characterization, a style both difficult to do within the confines of the length and unwanted by the publishers. Fast-moving adventure stories against colourful backgrounds—a formula that is still the best for easily-assimilated entertainment.

I could write this style of fiction and so had no trouble selling my next pocket book to Hamilton's *Authentic* series, *Alien Impact*, also the usual 36,000 words in length, earned £31/10/-.

Another firm publishing at the time was Scion, and the editor there had more venturesome ideas. He also realized that unless the quality of the product improved, the firm had little hope of surviving among the crowding sea of competition. He was also willing to pay more. *Alien Universe*, 38,000 words long, earned £42. *Reverse Universe*, 40,000 words, the same. The increase was small but important.

Scion, at the same time, had Fearn writing for them on a contractual basis under the name 'Vargo Statten'. It was thought that hard, gritty-sounding names were essential for the successful sale of the product and my first two stories for them carried the name 'Volsted Gridban'. This, it was felt, had the right associations and also the firms wanted to retain the anonymity of their authors. Having no choice in the matter, I could do nothing but agree, even though by this time I was writing not just to bang out a quick story for quick money, but to do the best I could for the medium in which I was writing.

The editor of Scion moved to take up a position with a new firm, Milestone, and two things happened at the same time. I was asked to write for the new company and this time paid by the thousand words instead of a flat rate. But more important, I received a contract for each book. The terms were not much better than before, but the contract did contain 'escape clauses' and was an improvement over the old system.

The editor also wished me to retain the, to me disliked, name of 'Volsted Gridban' because he thought that it had a reader-following and wanted to take advantage of this fact. Scion had other ideas. As the name was their 'house name', they insisted that Milestone drop its use. This they did, but not until I had written a couple more stories carrying it. One of these, *Planetoid Disposals Ltd.*, I always remember with a wry amusement because it was the only one I wrote to 'orders'.

The editor, I forget his name [probably Maurice Read—PH], had an idea. He was enthusiastic but unversed in science and the conversation, or rather his monologue, went something like this:

> It's in the future and we have these men, real hard, tough types who can stand anything. They are the miners, sort of. And then we have the others, police, if you like, and their ships can travel faster than the others. So we get . . .

Something like the Spanish Main with pirates and freebooters and a Royal Navy who have steam, as compared to sail. And the young son who grows up to avenge his father, and so on.

The essence was that I had to invent a faster-than-light drive which produced a mounting strain so that only the really tough could withstand higher velocities, a second faster than light travel system and a means of killing the hero while permitting him to live.

I did it. I can't say that I'm proud of the story, but I was, and still am, amused by it. Simply, no doubt, because of its associations. And for the 38,000 words, I received £45.

As Milestone had to drop the 'Volsted Gridban' name, I took the chance to insist they use one that would remain my property. As I had been appearing in *New Worlds* under the pseudonym 'Charles Grey', that was the one approved and all further Milestone books written by me appeared under that name.

At Scion, Fearn continued to write both under his own label, 'Vargo Statten', and also that of 'Volsted Gridban', but the editor, Alistair Paterson, still wanted to use me. Again an improvement had been made. Books were accompanied by a contract and my own name was used. The lengths had increased and payment was now £56—and only English rights were taken.

By this time, I was consciously trying to write the best material I could within the limits of the medium. The demand was always for fast, quick, entertaining action—in fact, the mixture as before, but now it could be smoother, with greater attention paid to detail and characterization. And, because of the vociferous readers who had a firm grounding in elementary science and the background of science fiction, care had to be taken with stated scientific fact and development. That I succeeded is proved by the resale of many of the books from both companies to America and the Continent.

Then, in mid-1954, came the end of an era. For reasons totally unconnected with science fiction, the pocket book market collapsed and, with others, both Scion and Milestone went into liquidation. Almost overnight, it seemed, the market for that type of story vanished. In a way, I regret its passing for, to me, there will always be a readership for colourful adventure stories set against exotic backgrounds. The type of story I wrote, not simply because the publishers wanted them, but because I enjoyed writing them, and still enjoy reading those of similar nature.

As Tubb mentioned, although Scion had splintered, the three offshoots continued to flourish. For such authors as Tubb, that meant he now had two markets (the third could not be taken seriously, for reasons explained later) to sell to.

Tubb has explained the effects this had on him—for John Russell Fearn, the effect was also immediate. Once again, he found himself owed some £300 by Scion, and immediately terminated his contract, calling in the Society of Authors to collect his debt. His success was well known among other publishers, and once it became known that he was free of his binding contract to Scion, he was innundated with commissions. He was asked to write novels for Curtis Warren, Hamilton & Co., Milestone (as

'Vargo Statten'), Pearsons, and even John Spencer wanted him (but with only 10/- a thousand to offer, they could not afford him!).

Two novels, *Dark Boundaries* and *Z Formations*, were sold to Curtis Warren, appearing early in 1953, while *Fugitive of Time* was sold to Milestone, now helmed by Scion's former editor Maurice Read. He also poached cover artist Ron Turner, who prepared a cover for it. For Hamilton's, Fearn wrote the first of what was to be a new series (to appear under his own name) about a futuristic 'fixer' named Simon Oscar Slade (SOS), but by the time the first novel of this new series had been written (*Moons For Sale*), Scion Ltd. had found new financial backers. The firm was relaunched from a different address (moving from 37A Kensington High Street to 6 Avonmore Road, in London—formerly their warehouse). Scion's former director B. Z. Immanuel retained the old premises for his own publishing ventures.

Scion was now under the directorship of Lou Benjamin, who realized that he was in danger of losing all his old stable of authors to other companies. Fearn was quickly paid the £300 he was owed, and was offered *pay in advance* for his work (which was unheard of in those times). His contract (only two of the five years stipulated had passed) was rewritten to allow Fearn a little more freedom with his writing. Basically, he could now write anything for any publisher, *provided it was not science fiction*: that was to be reserved for Scion exclusively (apart from the Toronto *Star Weekly*, as before). With the offer of pay in advance, Fearn withdrew his Milestone and Hamilton novels (at Scion's insistence) and passed them on to Scion.

In retrospect, Fearn might have been better off freelancing, but given the publishing climate at the time, and with his widowed Mother to support, he could scarcely be blamed for 'selling out' again. Any author in his place would have done the same.

Scion then set about stopping Milestone from using the 'Vargo Statten' and 'Volsted Gridban' bylines—and succeeded, but only after two 'Gridban' novels by Ted Tubb had slipped through—his previously mentioned *Planetoid Disposals Ltd.*, and *Fugitive of Time*. This was *not* the Fearn story (which later appeared as *Zero Hour* from Scion as by 'Statten'), but as Milestone had already secured a cover by Ron Turner, they asked Tubb to write a novel, and used Turner's cover on it. Typical of the publishers of the day, they retained Fearn's title, *Fugitive of Time* (the artist had already hand-lettered it on his painting). That neither the cover, or the title, reflected Tubb's story in any way was immaterial to them! (And to complete the complex tale, Ron Turner also did the cover artwork for *Zero Hour* as well—same scene, but different cover!).

Scion craftily gave Fearn the 'Volsted Gridban' byline as well, their idea being that as he would be writing under his two names for Scion he would be unable to capitalize on his new contract clause to write non-science fiction for other companies. *Moons For Sale* became his first 'Gridban' novel in May of 1953.

Scion was but one of the companies suffering under the eagle eye of the Watch Committees, and the industry was slowly but surely beginning to crumble. A final peak was to be reached in 1953, followed by a rapid decline, sending the paperback mushroom industry crashing. Only the more reputable firms would survive.

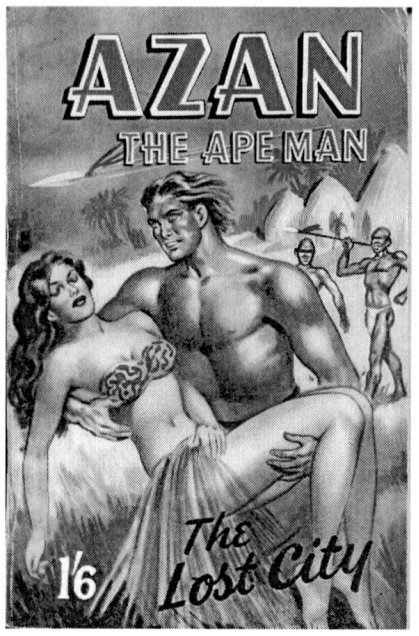

The Lost City by Marco Garron (Terry Maloney). Curtis Warren, 1950

The Missing Safari by Marco Garron (Terry Maloney). Curtis Warren, 1950

The Gold of Akada by Earl Titan (Ron Turner). Scion, 1951

The Untamed by Victor Norwood (Ron Turner). Scion, 1951.
(Courtesy Morgan Wallace.)

I Fight For Mars by Charles Grey (Ron
Turner). Milestone, 1953

Shuna and the Lost Tribe by John
King (Reg Heade). Harborough, 1951.
(Courtesy Morgan Wallace)

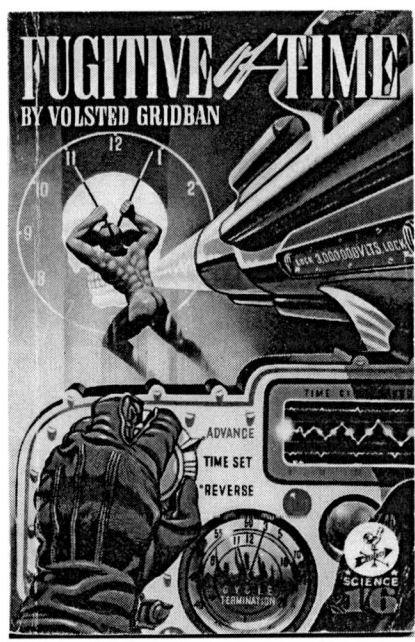

Fugitive of Time by Volsted Gridban
(Ron Turner), Milestone, 1953

Zero Hour by Vargo Statten (Ron
Turner). Scion, 1953

CHAPTER 11:
CHILD OF THE FIFTIES

By the beginning of 1952, Britain had six legitimate SF magazines.

Authentic was still a short novel series—it did not begin to print short stories until January 1953—but the improvements that Bert Campbell was bringing to the magazine were beginning to pay off. *Authentic* became part of the movement towards better science fiction.

Hamilton & Co. and their director, Harry Assael, showed a little more foresight than most of their competitors, who were still producing the same old rubbish.

Hamilton's had managed to resell a couple of their crime novels to America, where they were reprinted by Lion Books. Lion were an enterprising outfit (they had discovered and nurtured the dynamic crime writer Jim Thompson) and their books bore a distinctive Lion's head logo. Hamilton's appropriated the idea, changing the lion image to that of a panther for their new imprint, Panther Books, in April 1952.

These books were of a slightly better production than the plethora of other publications. The success of the line was greater by January 1953, when the page count went up from 128 to 144, and again in March to 160, and the number of titles up from four a month to five (and then six a month in 1954), including regular SF stories. The better presentation attracted the better writers.

Kenneth Bulmer supplied a steady stream of action-packed novels, the best of which was probably *The Stars are Ours* (1953), writing as H. K. Bulmer. John Burke also contributed some excellent early novels, writing as Jonathan Burke. Bert Campbell also wrote for the Panther line, as well as editing *Authentic*. Ted Tubb's homage to Jack Williamson's *Legion of*

Space was published as *The Metal Eater* (1954, under the 'Roy Sheldon' house name). Bryan Berry, a very promising young writer, also wrote some excellent novels (including a trilogy as by 'Rolf Garner') before disappearing completely in 1955, which led many to believe he'd met an early death.

Even S. Fowler Wright allowed Panther to separately reprint his two famous short novels, *The World Below* (1953) and *The Amphibians*—retitled as *The Dwellers* (1954)—from their compilation together as *The World Below* (1929). Another coup for Panther was an original collection of stories by a famous American SF writer, *L. Sprague de Camp's New Anthology*, edited by H. J. Campbell (1953). Evidently Campbell had earlier met de Camp (or his agent) at a Convention when he was in America, and received their permission to select this anthology (which has never been reprinted, making the Panther edition a prime collectable). Campbell also bought some excellent American stories from agent Forry Ackerman, assembled in *Tomorrow's Universe*, whose eight stories included fine work by Charles Harness, Chad Oliver, Ross Rocklynne, A. E. Van Vogt and de Camp.

However, *New Worlds* and *Science Fantasy*, now published by Nova Publications, were still the leading British magazines, and once again, John Carnell takes up the story of their two-pronged attempt to raise standards:

By Spring 1951, *New Worlds* was beginning to become editorially interesting. Authors John Christopher, Ted Tubb, Jim M'Intosh, Peter Phillips, Francis G. Rayer, Peter Hawkins, Sydney J. Bounds, and others were beginning to be published regularly, strengthened by such favourites as John Beynon, Arthur C. Clarke and A. Bertram Chandler. Illustrations were improving—Bob Clothier, who worked in the art department of the company which paid my bread and butter, had a flair for outre drawings and, because we worked under the same roof, it was easy for us to liase. Alan Hunter, a technical illustrator who lived on the South Coast, had submitted black-and-white work which I considered suitable and began to receive regular commissions, and the great Gerard Quinn had submitted his first fantasy work and had been talked into trying science fiction art instead.

While the editorial side was progressing well, however, problems began to beset the company, just when bi-monthly publication was being planned for *New Worlds*. Paper costs began to rise, printing and block-making too. The company was forced to increase the selling price by 6d. Simultaneously, difficulties arose with *Science-Fantasy*; Walter Gillings finding it more and more difficult to devote as much time editorially to the magazine as he wished. In the event, *Science-Fantasy* #3 was delayed almost a year and the Winter 1951-52 edition came out under my editorship with a farewell from Walter which now, many years later, reads obscurely, and does little to emphasize the fundamental differences of opinion that were then contributory causes for his relinquishing the editorship.

It was then my plan to change the magazine and lean the content more towards fantasy fiction, making a division from the 'straight' SF of *New Worlds*. I also introduced a series of 'Guest Editorials' by prominent writers, giving them full rein to express opinions on any point concerning fantasy fiction and these proved consistently popular. Also, artist Gerard Quinn found his element in SF art, and began to develop a style that was to lead him to full-time professionalism. Briefly, too, we made the acquaintance of Reina Bull, wife of a London publisher, and artist in her own right, who had a style reminiscent of the great Margaret Brundage, and her cover paintings for *Weird Tales* in the middle-30s. Reina produced some paintings for both magazines at a time when the Festival of Britain was in full swing and the first International SF Convention was held at the Royal Hotel in Bloomsbury.

In November 1951, *New Worlds* went bi-monthly; another step in the original planning. Both magazines saw a steadily increasing circulation in 1952. By the middle of the year, *New Worlds* was selling 18,000 copies per issue and *Science-Fantasy* 14,000, and the directors began to think in terms of yet another step already planned—to publish complete novels in paperback format and sell them through the existing magazine distribution system. The first three 'Nova Science Fiction Novels' were to be John Beynon's *Stowaway to Mars*, Malcolm Jameson's *Bullard of the Space Patrol* (compiled and edited by Andre Norton from the stories which had appeared in *Astounding*), and Raymond F. Jones' *Renaissance*. The plan seemed to be tying in with the apparent 'boom' in the SF then being 'enjoyed' by many publishing houses (and forgive the quotations which are engendered by hindsight). Hardcover publishers such as Museum Press Ltd., T.V. Boardman & Co., Grayson & Grayson, Sidgwick & Jackson Ltd., Dennis Dobson Ltd., Weidenfeld & Nicholson Ltd., William Heinemann Ltd., and many others were listing SF regularly, while on the paperback front, Hamilton & Co. (Stafford) Ltd., publishers of *Authentic Science Fiction*, had started an SF series; Cherry Tree Books, owned by Kemsley Press, were commencing mass market distribution of all kinds of fiction, including SF; and John Russell Fearn, under his 'Vargo Statten' name, was proliferating with Scion Ltd., and E. C. Tubb was beginning to make his mark.

The signs and portents all looked good for an increase in Nova's activities, but the wish to publish all our publications at 1/6d instead of 2/- sent the directors looking for new printers with special rates which included paper. After considerable investigation, it was decided to place the contract with The Carlton Press, whose offices were in Racket Court, Fleet Street, and handy for editorial supervision by myself (I was then managing a commercial printing and stationary company in Holborn). The changeover period was to be from April 1953—the March issue of *New Worlds* and the Spring issue of *Science-Fantasy* being the last under the old regime. But the new printer did not keep to the prearranged schedule. In fact, when proofs of *New Worlds* #21 did arrive, the issue had to finally be dated June. The production was so shoddy that the directors complained bitterly. Delivery was also affected for the first Nova novel, *Stowaway to Mars*, which was also a poor production. So, from the crest of a wave in March, the company was down in a trough by summer.

While H. J. Campbell and Ted Carnell were struggling to keep good British SF alive, what of the other end of the market; those publications that were issued for no more than a quick profit?

In 1954, I was a 13-year old teenager who had only recently discovered science fiction books and magazines. I could not afford to buy new books—and in any case most publishers had ceased to issue new SF material—but lots of the older pocket books were still available cheaply at my local second-hand bookshops.

In those days I was a very real enthusiast, but had yet to discover organized sf fandom. Nonetheless, amongst my close friends and my Wallsend Grammar School classmates, there were at least fifteen other SF devotees. All of us read sf voraciously, and organized expeditions to all the second hand bookshops within a six-mile radius. (i.e., that we could reach on foot.) Between us, we must have bought, read and swapped nearly all of the material that was issued in this "boom and bust" period of British SF.

Later commentators, faced with trying to explain away the fact that Fearn's books alone sold five million copies, have sneeringly suggested that this vast readership was made up of uncritical teenagers, with no background knowledge of the medium. In other words, that we read rubbish uncritically, and enjoyed anything and everything. *That is absolute nonsense.* We *were* critical, and we *were* selective in our preferences. Just because our youthful enthusiasm caused us to read—or start to read—all the SF we could find, it did not mean that we enjoyed it all.

We *hated* some of it. The early John Spencer magazines, the early Curtis Warren product, practically anything published by Gannet Press and the worst of the mushroom publishers. After we'd been caught out, we learned to avoid it—although we were all guilty of trying to unload crap onto an unsuspecting friend: "I'll swap you these six Gill Hunts/Spencer mags for your one Vargo Statten/E. C. Tubb!"

Where other material was available from authors and publishers I knew I would most likely enjoy, I soon learned to avoid the Spencer magazines. But occasionally, with nothing else available, I would buy the odd copy. I can still remember the pleasant shock I got when I read a battered copy of *Futuristic Science Stories* # 8 (October, 1952). Amongst the dung-heap of hack material, one story stood out like a beacon: "Moondust" by 'A. J. Merak,' a byline I had never previously encountered. To my surprise, I thoroughly enjoyed the story, and thereafter I would *always* buy a Spencer magazine wherein I saw the name A. J. Merak featured!

Like most readers and collectors, I never knew that the admirable 'Merak' was a pen name of John Glasby until 1979, when I published the first major study of the Spencer publications, compiled by SF scholar and researcher, Mike Ashley. Writing in *Fantasy Reader's Guide* # 1 (which I published under my Cosmos Literary Agency imprint) Ashley declared: "Research can be infuriating, but it can also be immensely rewarding. I shall never forget the day when I finally received a helpful response from the man behind the pseudonyms A. J. Merak, Ray Cosmic (sic!) and others."

John Glasby discovered Spencer's in March 1952, soon after he had started writing SF—that month saw his first sale to Curtis Warren (*Satellite B.C.*, under the Curtis house name of 'Rand Le Page') and he found them disappointing. As he told Ashley:

"The authors appeared to have no astronomical background. They were using the wrong terms, e.g.: talking about the galaxy when they meant the solar system. I decided I would write a couple and sent them in. They were accepted with a request for more."

After his debut with 'Moondust' and 'Ghost Moon' Glasby became a prolific contributor to the magazines. Whilst not in the first rank, his early work was much better than the usual Spencer's fare, drawing on his knowledge of scientific background and love for astronomy. He had been a regular reader of *Astounding*, and much of his work was heavily influenced by A. E. van Vogt. Coupled with a natural flair for storytelling, these qualities—when the author chose to exert himself—led to sales to other, better markets, including *Authentic* and *Nebula*.

In 1952, Spencer's had decided to experiment with a line of science fiction novels, in an attempt to compete with their rival publishers, spearheaded by Scion's immensely popular Vargo Statten books. For some extraordinary reason, UK publishers had decided that weird, harsh-sounding 'Germanic' names were *de rigeur* for science fiction authorship, and so Spencer's selected 'Victor La Salle' and 'Karl Zeigfried' for their own particular house names. The latter was probably an unconscious misspelling of "Zeigfreid."

They began to solicit novels from their regular contributors, and their first title was *The Black Sphere* by Victor La Salle (actually Welsh author Gerald Evans). Evans had been an occasional contributor to the wartime American SF magazines, and had originally written his novel for an overseas market, where it had failed to sell at the time. Needing some quick money, he dug it out of a drawer and decided he might as well try it with Spencer's. It sold immediately, at their bottom-line rate of 10/- a thousand words. The author was therefore expecting a cheque for £20 for his 40,000-worder, but was disconcerted to receive only £19. Later, when he purchased a copy of his novel on the bookstalls (Spencer's never provided author copies!) he discovered why: Spencer's had arbitrarily deleted an entire 2,000-word section from the middle of the novel, without any attempt at rewriting. His novel had been ruined, and the dismayed Evans never wrote another. The explanation of this outrage was simply a matter of cynical economics.

Scion Ltd had set a benchmark in publishing 40,000-word novels (for which they paid authors £40) in 128 page books (including covers), at a price of 1/6. They were printed in multiples of 16 page "signatures." Scion were able to make a healthy profit because Fearn's 'Statten' novels were guaranteed best sellers. Spencer's, less confident of their own inferior imitation product, decided to save on production costs and author payment by reducing their format to only 112 pages!

Notwithstanding, the line was successful enough for Spencer's to add a second author, 'Karl Zeigfried,' and after issuing four 112-page titles, they reluctantly switched to using the standard 128 page format (probably at the insistence of their distributors, and also because some larger publishers, such as Panther Books, were starting to issue books with *144 pages* for the same price.)

John Glasby recalls how he was first approached to write SF novels for Spencer's:

> I'd already written a number of short stories for Spencer's after they agreed I could write the contents of an entire magazine by using five or six pseudonyms. Then they asked me if I would write 40,000-word novels for them. As I'd already written novels for Curtis Warren I agreed to give it a go. I remember that I wrote them directly onto the typewriter with no revision, each one being completed in ten days!

Glasby wrote only four novels for Spencer's first SF series: *Dawn of the Half-Gods* as by Victor La Salle (October 1953), *The Uranium Seekers* as by Karl Zeigfried (December 1953), *Twilight Zone* as by Victor La Salle (February 1954), and *Dark Centauri* (April 1954) as by Karl Ziegfried.

Dark Centauri proved to be the end of Spencer's first SF novel series (despite the 'No.9' legend on the spine and cover, it was in fact the *13th* novel in the series (or even the 14th, if one counts Spencer's one-shot 1951 'Tarzan' imitation, *Zamba of the Jungle*). Spencer's were never a publisher to worry overmuch about accuracy or minor details!

The John Spencer magazines were still being issued regularly, and were still using the same stable of authors, along with some original (that were often very *un*original) stories by new aspirants. The Spencer magazines did provide a market to authors who had stories that were not up to other magazines' standards, or for authors who were so prolific that they were swamping the limited British market. So some good stories did get through into the magazines, usually when Ted Tubb sent in some stories. John Glasby and Lionel Fanthorpe were introduced to the Spencer pages in 1952; in years to come, these two were to write 90% of the total Spencer output, from SF to romances! Fanthorpe had seen the magazines and sent in a poem, a parody of John Masefield's *Sea Fever*.

Spencer's did not want the poem for their magazines, but invited

Fanthorpe to write SF stories for them instead. His first appearance was with 'Worlds Without End', in *Futuristic Science Stories* #6, under his own pseudonym 'Lionel Roberts'. Fanthorpe was only seventeen at the time, working as a lowly-paid apprentice dental technician, and he spotted an opportunity to make some easy money. He continued to write stories occasionally, and contributed a novel, *Menace from Mercury*, as Victor La Salle, but he is much better known today for his infamous later work, from the late 1950s up to 1966 (a period outside the main focus of this book), when he wrote the vast majority of titles in the SF and supernatural series that Spencer's published under their Badger Books imprint. Fanthorpe became a 'cult' figure for his atrocious books when he revealed his extraordinary working methods: having his family members transcribe his books from a tape recorder, written from verbalised stream of consciousness dictation! This was a case of the biter bit—an author exploiting his publishers!

On a much higher level than the Spencer magazines was the Scottish magazine, *Nebula Science Fiction*.

Nebula was a new magazine in the field, edited and published by Peter Hamilton, an eighteen-year-old Scottish fan who had only recently left school. The following memoir which I'd commissioned for *Vision* in 1970, takes a closer look at what was to become one of Britain's most popular magazines, and is by author Kenneth Bulmer, one of its leading contributors:

> When, in the autumn of 1952, a new science fiction magazine appeared on the bookstalls of Britain, few, if any, readers could have foreseen that it would become what many fans regard as the best-loved British SF magazine.
>
> The name of the newcomer was *Nebula Science Fiction* and it announced this in round block capitals printed in red across a white strip at the head of the cover. At the foot, another white strip contained, in red, the names: James, van Vogt, Ridley. The cover picture remained completely free of lettering of any kind, apart from the artist's signature. This format was retained throughout the entire forty-one issues of *Nebula's* life. Sometimes the bottom strip gave the contents, sometimes blurbs like: '**All Star Issue**,' or 'Voted Britain's Top Science Fiction Magazine,' and, with greater frequency until it became standard, 'For Reading That's Different.'
>
> Rumours and news about *Nebula's* impending debut had been rife for many months before it actually appeared, so that this first issue could contain a letter

section with congratulatory letters from leading fan personalities of the day. This was to be a strong feature of *Nebula*, this continuous involvement with fandom and its generous catering to fannish affairs.

'Robots Never Weep', by E. R. James, led off, a long story, filling no less than 103 of the 120 pages. The legend '120 pages' appeared in the top right-hand corner of the cover, immediately above the price '2/-' and the proud 'Vol.1., No.1.' The size was 5 3/8" by 8 3/8", the same as *New Worlds*, which contained only ninety-six pages. However, the *Nebula* typesize was larger, thus reducing the discrepancy of quantity.

At the time, when *Nebula* burst on the scene in September 1952, *New Worlds* published its 17th issue and was already established in the format it had used to such good purpose (later *New Worlds* would reduce size slightly and go to 126 pages), and was publishing material that would make the names of many British writers. *Authentic* was still in its small size, publishing the mediocre stuff that would not improve until Bert Campbell, assuming full editorship, took a better grip on the magazine's policy.

So it was that *Nebula* entered on its 41-issue life at a time when SF itself had little inkling of what lay in store for it, and when all the guidelines lay in the pulp traditions of magazine SF. The new magazine was very welcome.

No giant publishing corporation or combination of enthusiastic fans lay behind this venture, nor was it a cynical opportunistic publication by purely commercial publishers, printed by what the trade terms 'Kipper Box Printers'. Instead, it was the brainchild of Peter Hamilton, a young Scottish fan who loved SF to such an extent that he plunged all of his slender resources into his own professional magazine. Appearing at a time when the bookstalls were flooded with garish trash masquerading as science fiction, *Nebula* at once became a quality production and formed the third limb of responsible British SF development—*Nebula, New Worlds*, and *Authentic*. A child of the fifties, it was born in 1952 and died in 1959. It created a special kind of charisma that, in the view of many writers and readers, no other magazine ever had.

Continuously, Peter Hamilton worked at increasing the quality of his magazine in every department, engaging very often in intimate dialogue with his readers, urging them to cooperate in the development of *Nebula*.

His first editorial carried the title 'Here We Are', but the second and each subsequent one bore the title 'Look Here . . . ' It appeared on page two—as *Nebula* was numbered without counting the cover—and was invariably lively and honest, with genuine feeling of communication between editor and reader.

For the first twelve issues, noted fan Walter A. Willis wrote a fan column titled 'The Electric Fan'. From number 14, the title was changed to 'Fanorama'. Issue 13 did not carry a Willis column and the rabbit foot gropers may find something significant in that fact.

Many currently prominent SF writers had early stories—often their very first—published in *Nebula* over the years. Brian Aldiss, for example, had his first story accepted by Peter Hamilton. Robert Silverberg was another, as was Bob Shaw. Fans struggling for authorship were always helped by Peter, as Brian Aldiss says: "He was a sympathetic editor to a beginner. He was also a patient editor." Among those who had material published but did not continue were Tony Thorne, David Irish, Len Shaw, Ken Potter, Nigel Jackson, and Paul Enever.

But of the better-known writers of the time, nearly all at one time or another were pleased to have their material published in *Nebula*. Perhaps one of the most interesting was Bert Campbell, the bearded editor of *Authentic*, who had stories in issues 3 and 7.

No really notable series grew out of *Nebula*, and perhaps this was the unhappy result of the continued uncertainty of publication. Each issue was greeted with relief that the magazine was carrying on (very much as *Tales of Wonder* during the war years, and *New Worlds* later) and often there were long lacunae between issues. Beginning as a quarterly, the schedule ostensibly went bi-monthly with issue 5, but issue 9 appeared late in August 1954, instead of June. Similarly, only three issues appeared in 1955. Then, in May 1957, the great announcement was made: *Nebula* was going monthly!

In fact, from July 1957 through October, monthly issues did appear. Then came a gap until January 1958. From that issue, number 26, right up to February 1959, Nebula maintained a regular monthly schedule. That took the saga up to number 39. Issue 40 appeared in May and issue 41 in June. After that, there were no more . . .

One reason surmised for the final failure of *Nebula*, quite apart from Peter's precarious health and the lack of adequate financial resources, was his attempt to reach an American audience directly through United States distribution, which backfired, leaving him at a serious financial disadvantage.

The covers of *Nebula* were painted by many different artists, including those well known in the field like Quinn and Rattigan, Clothier and Hunter, and the cover artist Peter was proud to claim he 'discovered'—the late, greatly lamented Ken McIntyre.

Starting with issue 10, a back cover was run in black and white, mostly drawn by the late Arthur 'Atom' Thompson. This gave a tremendously individual flavour to the magazine and added a dignity no amount of back cover advertisements could hope to equal. Many of the finest interiors were drawn by the superb and underrated Harry Turner with his distinctive style.

The most prolific and popular author in *Nebula* was E. C. Tubb, who managed the not inconsiderable feat of appearing consecutively from number 2 to number 11, and who consistently won the Best Author Award. He published thirty-one stories, twenty-seven under his own name, two under the house name of 'Stuart Allen', and two under other bylines ('Lloyd' and 'Seabright'). Kenneth Bulmer published fifteen stories (six as 'Philip Stratford'); William F. Temple, 14; Brian Aldiss, 13; Philip High, 12; and Eric Frank Russell, 10.

The only serial *Nebula* ran, 'Wisdom of the Gods', by Kenneth Bulmer, ran for four instalments between issues 32-35.

Other familiar names appeared at this early date in their writing careers: Harlan Ellison, John Rackham, John Kippax, Dan Morgan, James White, Arthur Sellings, and the evergreen Sydney Bounds, who put in five appearances.

It would be impossible in this short space to deal with any fairness or clarity the many memorable stories appearing over the years. Perhaps something of what *Nebula* meant can best be summed up by Ted Tubb's feeling words:

"Many authors came to regard *Nebula* as not just another market, but as something with which they could have a peculiar affinity . . . Authors wrote for *Nebula* with financial reward taking secondary place; the desire of submitting a good story being of primary importance . . . The editor was always willing to experiment and print stories which other magazines may have found unacceptable. The end result was a form of gestalt in which the writers and the contributors felt as if *Nebula* was 'their' magazine, and all that became a happy, well-integrated family."

In every issue, including the first, under circumstances I have already outlined, appeared a readers' column, and this carried many a high controversy and many a spirited discussion on any and every topic as Peter nursed along his readership. Ken Slater's book column carried news of the publishing world of the day in review format, and Forrest J Ackerman's 'Scientifilm Previews', all the latest gossip, hot from Hollywood—most of it about films that never saw a studio or scriptgirl in their hothouse lives.

John Newman wrote many fine scientific articles and, as half of 'Kenneth Johns', provided comprehensive coverage of current scientific topics in their popular inside cover feature, which presented photographic items unique at the time.

Other articles by Donald Malcolm and A. E. Roy, together with cover artist Barr, helped inject some of the typical Scottish flavour Peter imparted to the magazine.

Arthur Thompson contributed occasional cartoons and a fine pictorial reportage of the 1955 Cytricon, with personalities like Ted Tubb, Sydney Bounds, Ken McIntyre, Ted Carnell, Ken Bulmer, and Bert Campbell, being caricatured.

The page count varied at the beginning, but settled down from issue 13 to 112 pages. In its life, *Nebula* published 231 stories and a four-part serial, and these were written by an impressive sixty-nine authors.

During the proceedings of the 1953 SF Con held at the Bonnington Hotel in London, and despite the unexpected attendance of L. Ron Hubbard and the London Circle Ballet, Peter Hamilton made a decided impact with his quiet good humour and obvious dedication to SF. As a teetotaller, Peter was duly bemused when the con committee succumbed en bloc to write another scarlet page in SF history.

Although *Nebula* often looked amateurish in format, this did create a sense of friendship, and as Peter paid his contributors a tidy sum more than the other prozines, *Nebula*, despite its name, was never nebulous.

Those forty-one issues take up about a foot of shelf space. In those twelve inches are stored many fine stories, much joy and entertainment; they hold the fruits of a great love of and dedication to SF. They are, in a very real sense, an enduring monument to one fan's effort.

Peter Hamilton dropped out of the SF scene and efforts to trace him have proved unsuccessful, although it is believed that he later went into the record business and ran a number of record shops and a small recording company. He should know that while *Nebula*—the magazine—did die, *Nebula*—the essence of what *Nebula* meant—can never really die, can never be forgotten.

Nebula had been launched by Hamilton with the help of his parents, who ran a printing firm. These were troubled times for printers, many of whom experienced occasions when their presses stood idle. Crownpoint decided to become publishers themselves, to take up the slack. Peter

Hamilton intended to publish a series of science fiction *novels*—he had already purchased two before he took advice from distributors to turn it into a magazine (following *Authentic's* lead). The novels became instead the lead stories in his first two issues. Hamilton (just out of school, rather than the nursing home he wryly mentioned in his first editorial) kept the magazine running as best he could. He succeeded in obtaining extensive foreign distribution to the United States, South Africa, and Australia, but a crippling increase in export taxes and other restrictions led to Hamilton folding the magazine, heavily in debt. The earlier hiatus in 1955 had been caused by an upsurge in business for the family printing works and the 'fill-in' publication was forced to take a back seat. Hamilton took complete control, finding a new printer, and resuming his bi-monthly schedule until going monthly in 1957.

Although it never really achieved the international recognition it deserved, *Nebula* was undoubtedly the best-loved of all British magazines among the British fans and authors. In 2000, I managed to trace Peter Hamilton, who had indeed enjoyed a successful career in the music and recording business after leaving publishing, and was now enjoying his retirement in quiet anonymity on a Scottish island. He was delighted to learn that he had been remembered, and pleased to learn of the later success of his authors.

Nebula was just part of the 'revolt' against awful science fiction. The pulp paperback firms were on the way out, and, with paper rationing coming to an end, decent publishers were able to take over the market. The rapid collapse of the 'mushroom' companies would prove one thing: readers had only bought and read their products because there was nothing else available.

The Stars Are Ours by H.K. Bulmer
(John Richards), Hamilton, 1953

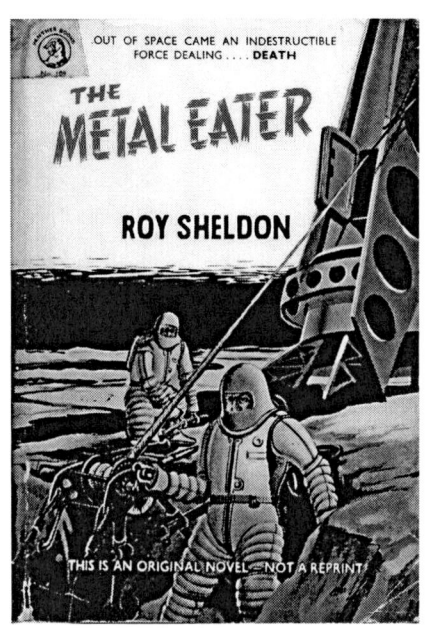

The Metal Eater by Roy Sheldon (John
Richards). Hamilton, 1954

The Metal Eater by Roy Sheldon (John
Richards). Hamilton, 1954

New Worlds # 8 (Bob Clothier).
Nova, 1950

Nebula # 1 (Alan Hunter).
Peter Hamilton, 1952

Nebula # 11 (James Rattigan).
Peter Hamilton, 1954

Nebula # 12 (Bob Clothier). Peter
Hamilton, 1955

Nebula # 40 (Eddie Jones).
Peter Hamilton, 1959

CHAPTER 12:
AMERICAN INVASION

Ever since the late 1940s, some UK publishers were already looking to the American SF field, justifiably doubtful of ever finding British talent among the hack writers.

Seeking to emulate the continuing success of Atlas Publications with *Astounding Science Fiction*, two Midlands firms in particular, Thorpe and Porter (Leicester) and Pembertons of Manchester began acquiring the UK serial rights to some of the other (many) American SF magazines. They were mostly issued as truncated 64 page versions of their US originals, with most (not all) of the advertisements replaced by UK advertisers or the publishers' house ads.

In 1950, with the British SF 'boom' firmly underway, they quickly spread over the UK newsstands like a rash, much to the annoyance of some hack writers, whose inferior work now had worryingly superior competition.

Thorpe and Porter's more successful titles included *Amazing Stories* (32 issues 1950-55), *Fantastic Adventures* (24 issues 1950-54), *Future Fiction* (14 issues 1951-54) and *Weird Tales* (28 issues 1949-54),

Pemberton's had most success with *Planet Stories* (11 issues 1950-54), *Startling Stories* (18 issues 1949-54), and *Super Science Stories* (14 issues 1950-53),

First off the mark to reprint American *novels* as opposed to magazines, were World Distributors Limited of Manchester, part of the successful Pemberton group of companies. At least eight of their ten titles were reprints, with six of those of American originals noted.

Their paperback books were issued two titles at a time, labelled 'A World Fantasy Classic', appearing between Fall 1950 and Spring 1951. With 160 pages at 1/6, they were superior in format to most of their 128 and 112 page competitors.

The first four novels were all world first book editions, reprinted from American SF magazines.

The Whispering Gorilla by David V. Reed was reprinted from the February 1943 edition of *Fantastic Adventures*. It had originally appeared as *The Return Of The Whispering Gorilla* by David V. Reed. The cover art had been skilfully copied from the original Robert Gibson Jones magazine cover.

This fascinating novel was actually a sequel to 'The Whispering Gorilla' a novelette by Don Wilcox, which had appeared earlier, in the April 1940 *Fantastic Adventures*. Whilst this was acknowledged in the 1943 magazine, no reference was made in the book. The book's title has caused it to be erroneously recorded in reference books as an expanded rewrite of the original novelette—which had been written by a different author, Don Wilcox (who knew nothing about the UK edition at the time).

The original fast-paced novelette by Wilcox told how the dying body of Carpenter, a newspaper reporter, is found by a Doctor Devoli, a scientist experimenting in increasing ape intelligence. Carpenter's brain is transplanted into a gorilla body by Devoli.

In the sequel, set in wartime Africa—to where Devoli has returned to resume his experiments with gorillas and care for Carpenter—David Vern (who wrote as David V. Reed) picked up the story three years later.

Both stories were minor classics of the pulp genre, and some fifty years later I would be pleased to edit and introduce a new book edition, containing *both* stories together, with a Ron Turner cover!

Tharkol, Lord of the Unknown by Edmond Hamilton was retitled from the lead novel in *Startling Stories* for May 1939, where it had appeared as *The Prisoner of Mars*. The cover art was copied (with some changes) from a black and white Hans Wesso illustration in the original magazine.

Tharkol was typical Hamilton space opera, loosely based on *The Prisoner of Zenda*. A Martian scheme to steal Earth's oceans by 'matter-casters' is averted by Philip Crain, a Martian hybrid, son of the former ruler of Mars, and an Earth woman. Interplanetary war is avoided when a compromise involving the transfer of polar ice caps (to be melted on Mars) is agreed.

The Beast From Beyond by Manly Wade Wellman had its original source in the Summer 1944 *Startling Stories* (as *Strangers On The Heights*.) The cover was adapted from a black and white A. J. Donnell illustration in the original magazine.

This novel was a rather uneasy mixture of Charles Fort, H.P. Lovecraft and somewhat mystical SF. Investigators into devil worship in South America discover disembodied alien intelligences dwelling on the tops of mountains. But it was well-written, like most of Wellman's work.

The Monsters of Juntonhein by Edmond Hamilton was also from *Startling Stories* (January 1941 issue, as *A Yank at Valhalla*). The cover art had been adapted from a black and white Hans Wesso illustration in the original magazine.

Apart from the wrong spelling of 'Jutonheim' in the title, there wasn't much wrong with this book. Hamilton was at the top of his form, with a terrific retelling of Norse mythology, buttressed by full-blooded science fictional explanations. The action built up nicely to the inevitable climax— Ragnarok! Only the juvenile dialogue and treatment (tailored for the magazine) detracted from this being top-flight SF.

It can be seen that these novels had been quite carefully selected (almost certainly by an American agency) and care taken by the publisher's with their illustration (breaking with the mushroom boys' attitude of sticking any old picture on the cover).

But the next pair of titles showed a ghastly departure!

The Metal Monster by Belli Luigi was not American, coming instead from a diabolical Australian 'Scientific Thriller' paperback series published by Transport Publications, who were the Aussie equivalent to John Spencer. (Australia was concurrently suffering its own mushroom era.) Its original title had been *Crime Flies* by Belli Luigi (1950), and the idiotic cover was adapted from its original.

This book marked a terrific drop in quality. It was one of a series of 'scientific thrillers' featuring Detective-Sergeant Bill Douglas and his young scientist sidekick, Peter Denny. Here they investigate a master criminal who is employing a flying robot to steal jewels (sic) and commit murder. Its juvenile tone jarred oddly with scenes of unpleasant sadism (the robot is prone to beat men's skulls to a bloody pulp with its metal fists, and *go on* doing it after they are dead).

The Master-Mind Menace by Belli Luigi had the same diabolical provenance. This time Bill Douglas is investigating a criminal scientist who has discovered how to transfer minds from one body to another. Various petty criminals are put into the bodies of hitherto responsible members of society. The villain finally ends up in a dead body. The author of these almost unreadable books was very possibly G. Clive Bleek, a prolific writer for the Australian cheap paperback markets.

Why had the UK publishers chosen to reprint this rubbish? Almost certainly because they had been cheap, and had been offered to them as part of a "package deal" of Australian stories culled from early issues of the Australian pulp SF magazine *Thrills Incorporated* (to which Bleek was a regular contributor). *Thrills Incorporated* was a low-quality Aussie counterpart of *Wonders of the Spaceways*. Just about its only virtue was that it offered a market for native Australians, and later helped start the career of Norma K. Hemmings. The material was reprinted by Pembertons in two luridly juvenile issues of a British pulp-sized magazine *Amazing Science Stories*. Despite the inclusion of a couple of stray stories from the American *Super Science Stories* (Pembertons were then issuing a British Reprint edition), they were a throwback to the Hamilton magazines, and sank without trace.

The next two 'World Fantasy Classics' mercifully returned to the superior American source.

Shadow Over Mars by Leigh Brackett (Mrs. Edmond Hamilton) was a rousing novel in the *Star Wars* tradition from the Fall 1944 issue of *Startling Stories*. Its Earthman hero battles against Big Business interests exploiting Mars, fulfilling an ancient prophecy in liberating the oppressed Martians. Brackett, of course, later wrote the first treatment for the film *The Empire Strikes Back*. The fact that the novel was never reprinted in America until 1961 (as *The Nemesis From Terra*) makes this a valuable collectors' item.

Devil's Planet by Manly Wade Wellman also came from *Startling Stories* (January 1942 issue). It was a futuristic detective-mystery set on water-starved Mars, with a rich assortment of characters, including Wellman's 'petal-pussed' Martians (featured in several of his early pulp stories).

The last two novels, published early in 1951, were atrocious space operas by a completely unknown author. 'Karl Mannheim'.

When The Earth Died was a wearisome story of refugees from a disintegrated Earth (after an atomic war) where after various ridiculous adventures on the moon and in space, the last two survivors eventually settle on Venus to begin a new life, Adam and Eve style. One curious feature of the novel was that the characters—much given to rambling rhetoric—actually criticize each other for their own waffling!

Vampires of Venus was a sequel to the above novel, taking place 20 years later Their parents now dead, two children set out to explore the other hemisphere of Venus, hoping to find humanoid life, only to discover a race of Martian bat creatures—who, of course, had previously visited Earth in flying saucers. This turgid tale was even more dire than its predecessor, and the introduction of 'Lukrils' (giant vampire birds featured on the cover) did little to improve the narrative.

The identity of 'Mannheim' remains a mystery, mainly because no one has troubled to find out. At the time, many (including myself) assumed they were also reprints from Australia, but this was not the case. The Germanic pseudonym and the cover tie-in suggests they may have been commissioned UK 'originals' (the publisher was running a concurrent gangster series).

Their sheer mediocrity seems to have put the mockers on what had began as a promising American series, and the line was discontinued.

The Withy Grove Press had been publishing their line of 'Cherry Tree' paperbacks since before the war. These had been almost entirely detective and mystery novels, although they had included a couple of SF reprints by S. Fowler Wright: *Deluge* and *Dawn*. In the late 1940s the imprint was taken over by the Kemsley Press, the famous newspaper chain. The earlier plain two-colour covers were replaced by attractive full colour artwork, and their range was widened to include other popular genres—including science fiction.

Kemsley Newspapers had international connections, and had done their homework before launching their 'Fantasy Books' series in 1951. With attractive covers by Terry Maloney, Ron Embleton and Ron Turner, they quickly issued twelve books of a generally excellent standard, with only a couple of duds. On the inside cover, under a full colour astronomical painting by Maloney, they boldly proclaimed their intentions:

Are you reading
FANTASY BOOKS
Famous American books published in the United States
at not less than 10/6 and 15/- are beautifully produced
In Fantasy Books at only 1/6
Out of this World
The vogue for the kind of the new kind of adventure story known as
Science Fiction has been sweeping America for some years and now has
hundreds of thousands of devotees in Britain. Under the general title
of FANTASY BOOKS the publishers of Cherry Tree Novels have now
produced twelve titles of these unusual and gripping books—stories
which are indeed, "Out of this world."

All of their titles were American reprints except for one 'original'.
Vanguard to Neptune by J. M. Walsh, but even this book had originally
appeared in *Wonder Stories Quarterly* back in 1932. *Sinister Barrier,*
by Eric Frank Russell had first appeared in book form in England in
1943, but the Cherry Tree edition was reprinted from the expanded
1948 American edition, along with the author's introduction. The line
included a true American historical 'classic', *Ralph 124C41+,* by Hugo
Gernsback. Amongst the other American books, the most notable
included titles by John W. Campbell, L. Ron Hubbard, Murray Leinster,
Frank Belknap Long and a Don Wollheim anthology of classic pulp
stories

Sadly, at the time these books were lost among the 'King Langs' and
'Gill Hunts', all fighting for newsstand space. To the disappointment of
knowledgeable fans, Kemsley did not continue the *Fantasy Books* line into
1952.

Today, two of their titles are valuable collectors' items: *The Thing and
Other Stories* by Campbell was a collection originally published in the US
as *Who Goes There?*, but which had been shrewdly retitled by Kemsley. Its
lead story, "Who Goes There?" was retitled as 'The Thing' to tie-in with the
recently released Howard Hawks film based on it, and Maloney's superb
cover was clearly based on the film, and even used its full title, *The Thing
From Another World.* This has identified it to collectors as the only Hawks
film tie-in edition. The second collectable title was Hubbard's *Typewriter in
the Sky and Fear,* now valuable because of the later notoriety of its author.

But even though these paperbacks were not the success Kemsley had hoped for, they were a harbinger of the American invasion to come.

More significant were the ever-increasing number of hardback series that appeared throughout the early 1950s from reputable publishers. The phenomena was immediately noticed and commented on by John Carnell in his November 1952 *New Worlds* editorial:

> Certainly not even the most enthusiastic visionary of a year ago could have visualized the rapid build-up of interest in bound volumes published in this country, in such a short space of time. Science fiction, as we know it, grew up in the United States, through a teething stage in magazine form, which lasted nearly twenty years, reaching adolescence in 1938, and not maturing until 1946. Even then, only visionary Americans who were connected with the writing of science-fiction had a glimmering of the possibilities inherent in the field of books. A few of them—ably supported by leading authors in the field, for whom there had been no other outlet than magazines for their specialised art—launched their own publishing houses to bring the best novels and serials into permanent form.
>
> This gave various authors' agents the incentive to explore wider fields, and science fiction began to appear in such national American papers as *Colliers* and *Saturday Evening Post*. Helped by atomic bomb experiments at Eniwetok and rocket experiments at White Sands, the appeal of science-fiction steamrollered into American radio and films, and leading American publishing houses began to explore the possibilities of the 'new' literature as a substitute for the expiring field of 'thrillers'. By the spring of this year 'science-fiction' as a name and a recognised literature had become established across the Atlantic.
>
> Inevitably the 'new' field was explored by British publishers, helped along by authors and agents in this country who had been closely allied with the American movement. That there was resistance to the coming fashion, even reluctance to admit its existence, was only natural. Consider—the American field had had a softening-up process for nearly thirty years, while British reading audiences hardly knew what a science fiction magazine meant. But, experiments and enquiries throughout the country plus the fact that *New Worlds* itself had survived the barren-years, elicited the fact there was a vast reading potential for science fiction in Great Britain. Our two advertisers of a year ago have now been supplemented by many others who list regular bound volumes, and the next six months will see many more entering the field. The

material ranges from new stories by known British authors, anthologies, and the pick of American novels appearing in British editions, down to 'annuals' and 'space trails' for juveniles.

Even the newspaper book-reviewers have been jockeyed into recognising the field—if not acknowledging it. From here on the barrier is down—science fiction has come into its own.

At first, it looked as if Carnell's optimistic forecast that SF would become established in hardcover publishing was a correct one,

As previously noted, hardcover SF novels had always appeared sporadically in Britain—but they were rarely, if ever, actually *labelled* as science fiction on their covers or inside blurbs.

In fact, the first time the words 'Science Fiction' were employed on the jacket of a hardcover book had been when World's Work had published John Russell Fearn's first novel, *The Intelligence Gigantic*, in 1943—boldly labelled as "A Master Thriller Science Fiction novel!" The same publisher—who had of course earlier published *Tales of Wonder*—had in fact put out Eric Frank Russell's *Sinister Barrier* several weeks earlier—but without any cover blurb (though "science fiction" *was* mentioned in the inside blurb). The same SF cover label appeared on the publisher's hardcover editions of Fearn's next two SF novels, *The Golden Amazon* (1944) and *Liners of Time* (1947), but had disappeared for his *The Golden Amazon Returns* (1948) but with the inside blurb referring to it as a "science fantasy". World Work's final foray in their 1940s SF programme was with *The Call of Peter Gaskell* by George C. Wallis (1948), again without any cover label, and with the inside blurb referring to this lost-race story as a "Romance." However the title page declared it to be A MASTER THRILLER SCIENCE FICTION NOVEL (this time without the exclamation mark).

A diligent search of the bookshelves of the most avid collectors of SF will reveal a surprisingly large amount of hardcover SF and fantasy published by 'respectable publishers' in the UK both during the war and in the decade following. Apart from the wonderful early novels of H. G. Wells that were kept more or less constantly in print, such eminent authors as Olaf Stapledon and S. Fowler Wright were prominent, along with others such as Anthony Armstrong, Pat Frank, John Gloag, Bruce Graeme, Neil M. Gunn, Gerald Kersh, David Lindsay, H. P. Lovecraft (sic), George R. Stewart and so on. And there are a lot of hidden gems by lesser-known authors, such as *The Curry Experiment* by A. A. Rayner (Locker, 1947) a quite remarkable early anticipation of human cloning that is not even listed in *any* of the SF references and encyclopaedias). But the important point is that they were not usually *identified* as such. Instead, the blurbs referred variously to these books as fantasy, imaginative fiction, a parable, or as in the case of *The Curry Experiment*, 'imaginative story-telling'. (Collectors are hereby alerted to try and seek out this rewarding book!).

But as the 1950s progressed, the science fiction label on the jackets of British hardcovers became the norm, rather than the exception. It is these 'generic SF series' that I propose to look at next.

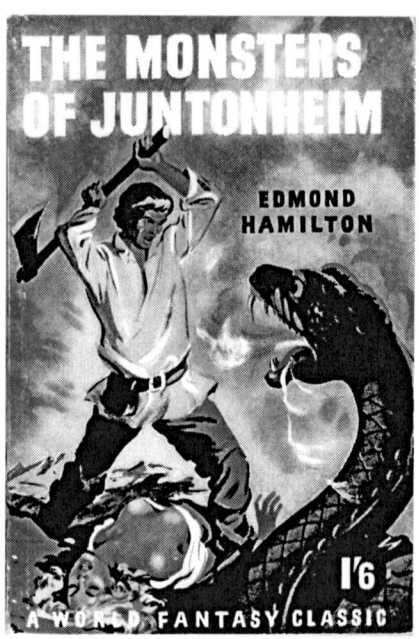

The Whispering Gorilla by David Van Reed (R.A. Osborne). World Distributors, 1950. (Courtesy MAW)

The Monsters of Juntonheim by Edmond Hamilton (R.A. Osborne). World Distributors, 1950. (Courtesy MAW)

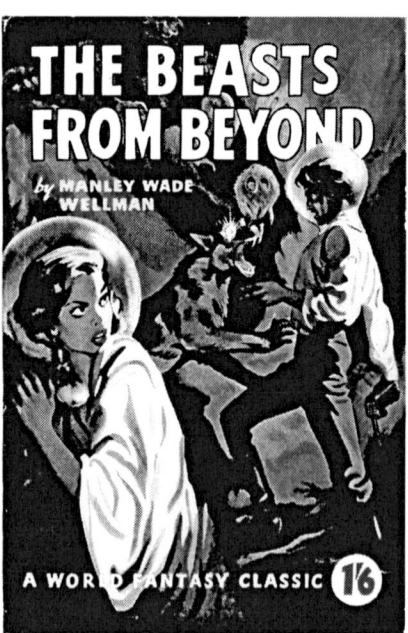

The Beasts From Beyond by Manly Wade Wellman (R.A. Osbourne). World Distributors, 1950. (Courtesy MAW)

Typewriter in the Sky by L. Ron Hubbard (Ron Embleton). Kemsley, 1952

The Thing From Another World by John W. Campbell (Terry Maloney). Kemsley, 1952

Vanguard to Neptune by J.M. Walsh (Ron Turner). Kemsley, 1952

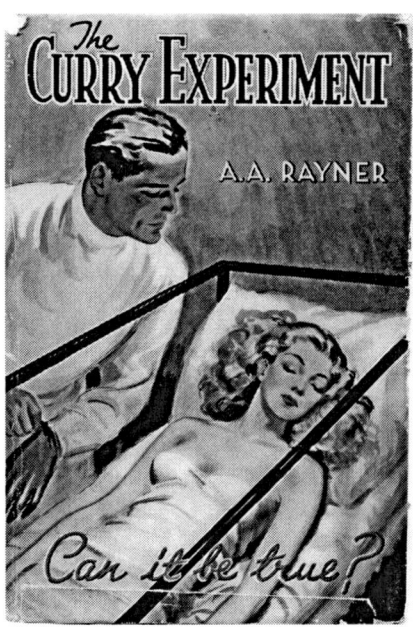

The Intelligence Gigantic by John Russell Fearn (W.J. Roberts). World's Work, 1943

The Curry Experiment by A.A. Rayner (unidentified). Locker, 1947

CHAPTER 13:
BRITISH HARDCOVER SF

One of the earliest harbingers of the coming boom in hardcover SF was *Tomorrow Sometimes Comes* by F. G. Rayer, published in June 1951 by Home & Van Thal. Although not identified as SF, the deliberately evasive blurb read: 'It is not fantasy—it is based on an extension of scientific knowledge already in existence, and recent research.' Or, in other words, science fiction, as the generic cover by *New Worlds* artist Bob Clothier clearly proclaimed! In fact, the book was a novelizing of a series of short stories that had recently appeared in *New Worlds*. But the publisher did not follow up this promising start.

It was the venerable firm of Grayson & Grayson who were first off the mark with a bold and sustained *clearly labelled* line of science fiction hardcovers. Initially, these were all American reprints, and appeared to have been carefully chosen. This was a determined assault on the SF market: no less than three American titles were released simultaneously in July 1951: *The Voyage of the Space Beagle* by A. E. van Vogt, and two anthologies, *Men Against the Stars* edited by Martin Greenberg, and *The Best Science Fiction* edited by E. Bleiler and T. E. Dikty.

All three had darkly attractive pictorial dust jackets by 'C.W.B.' The jackets announced that they were part of the publisher's new 'Adventures in Science Fiction' series, and carried their punchy manifesto:

> From America, land of Science and the Machine, comes a new kind of book. Foreshadowed in the works of Jules Verne and H. G. Wells, Science Fiction answers the age-old query: "What next?" Science Fiction is written by men with the scientific "know how"; men who, however far their imagination

may range, convince by their attention to detail and to the fundamental truths of Science's magic world. Science Fiction is exciting, convincing.

Gone were all the tortuous apologetic euphemisms: here was the real thing, and not afraid to speak its name! It was a breath of fresh air, and deserved to succeed. It did, too, being sustained across the next six years, and inspiring countless imitations by other publishers, as noted below.

From their fourth title, E. B. Mudge-Marriott did most of the dust jacket cover art in bright, attractive pictorial designs, with iconic SF imagery. The actual technical details and SF 'hardware' were a little vague and naïve at times, indicating that the artist was not too familiar with SF or astronomy, but he made a decent stab at it. His work would attract the attention of several other publishers, who would also secure his services when they followed Grayson's lead. Other experienced artists used included Harold Johns and E. J. Pagram.

The success of this opening salvo was not immediately apparent, as the rest of 1951 passed without any follow-up titles. However, the following year *The Best Science Fiction* was reprinted in March, and was followed by *Possible Worlds of Science Fiction* edited by Groff Conklin (June), *I, Robot* by Isaac Asimov (July), *Best Science Fiction Stories: Second Series* edited by Bleiler and Dikty (July). The year finished strongly with perhaps the finest of all the early American SF anthologies. *Adventures in Time and Space* edited by McComas and Healy. Unfortunately with only 11 (out of an original 33) stories, the UK edition was severely truncated, but the selection was still an excellent one. Unaccountably, the publisher missed an opportunity by not buying any of the remaining 22 stories to make up another selection.

The 1953 programme consisted entirely of American anthologies, beginning with *The Galaxy Reader of Science Fiction* edited by H. L. Gold. The ubiquitous editorial team of Bleiler and Dikty had two titles, *The Year's Best Science Fiction Novels* (April) and *The Best Science Fiction Stories: Third Series* (September). Judith Merril offered a more eclectic choice of stories in *Beyond Human Ken* (July).

It was somewhat ironic that when a British hardcover publisher had finally had the gumption to launch a successful line of SF books, they should ignore British authors and look to America for their titles. What an opportunity was missed! 1954 looked like continuing Grayson's obsession with American anthologies, beginning with Groff Conklin's *Strange Travels in Science Fiction* (January). Then, in February came the unexpected: an original British single author collection: John Christopher's *The Twenty-second Century*. Unfortunately this was not followed up: all four remaining titles were again American anthologies—Martin Greenberg's *The Robot and The Man* (May), Groff Conklin's *Strange Adventures in Science Fiction* (June), and two from John W. Campbell, Jr., *The First Astounding Science Fiction Anthology* (March) and *The Second Astounding Science Fiction Anthology* (November).

It was back to America for all four 1955 titles, with two more anthologies from Bleiler and Dikty, *The Year's Best Science Fiction Stories*: Fourth Series (January), and *The Year's Best Science Fiction Novels: Second Series* (December). Groff Conklin edited *Science Fiction Adventures in Dimension* (March). *Costigan's Needle* by Jerry Sohl (November) was only the second novel to be used.

As will be noted further on in this chapter, a strange blight settled over British SF in 1956. The end was in sight for Grayson's series, only two titles appearing in 1956, both of them American anthologies: *The Best Science Fiction Stories: Fifth Series* edited by Bleiler and Dikty, and August Derleth's *The Other Side of the Moon* (April). One further title, Murray Leinster's rather pedestrian novel *Operation: Outer Space* was held over, and eventually sneaked out in January 1957.

Grayson's long run of initial success had both positive and negative consequences for British hardcover SF publishing. The positive aspect was that it set other publishers scrambling to follow suit; the negative was that there was an overwhelming concentration on American authors, and on anthologies.

Grayson's lead was quickly followed in September 1951 by T. V. Boardman. The firm's founder had American roots and they were noted for publishing a very strong line of American detective fiction in both hardcover and paperback editions, with strikingly painted covers by the talented Denis McLoughlin that made them instant collectables. They opened their SF programme with American reprints, but refreshingly they were all widely varied novels, and not anthologies. *The Princess of the Atom* by Ray Cummings (September) *The Big Eye* by Max Ehrlich (October), and *What Mad Universe* by Fredric Brown (November).

They were followed in January 1952 by a rather pedestrian original

British novel, *Wrong Side of the Moon* by Francis and Stephen Ashton, dealing with an early attempt at space travel. Francis Ashton had earlier authored two much more imaginative prehistoric science fantasies, *The Breaking of the Seals* (!946) and *Alas, That Great City* (1948), published by Dakers.

Their next title was much better—John Carnell's anthology *No Place Like Earth*, a strong selection of 10 stories, of both American and British origin, and headlined by two stories by John Wyndham (one as John Beynon) and Arthur C. Clarke, who also provided an introduction that ably promoted science fiction as a legitimate literary form. Four of the stories had first appeared in *New Worlds*, and another four had been reprinted there.

Strangely, Boardman did not issue any further SF titles in 1953, continuing to concentrate on their hugely successful detective novels. But they returned to the fray in 1954, with an impressive run of six American titles. Fredric Brown's *Project Jupiter* (August), Frederick Pohl's outstanding original anthology *Star Science Fiction* (August). *Children of the Atom* by Wilmar H. Shiras (September), Isaac Asimov's *The Caves of Steel* (September), *Double In Space* made up of two stories by Fletcher Pratt (October) and E. E. Smith's *Triplanetary* (November).

Boardman's experiments were successful enough for them to reissue some of their earlier titles in paperback in 1955, including *No Place Like Earth*, *The Big Eye* and *What Mad Universe* and a paperback original edition of *The Best From New Worlds* edited by Carnell, with a cover by Gerard Quinn, and which also afforded E. C. Tubb his first anthology appearance with 'Rockets Aren't Human'.

Boardman also continued publishing SF hardcovers throughout 1955, an eclectic mix of strong American titles that included *This Island Earth* by Raymond F. Jones (February), *The Currents of Space* by Isaac Asimov (April), *Alien Dust* (May) by E. C. Tubb (assembling a series of connected short stories that had originally appeared in *New Worlds*, plus one from *Nebula*), *The Coming of Conan* by Robert E. Howard, (November), and *First Lensman* by E. E. Smith (November).

But despite their being augmented by some outstanding dust jacket cover art by the likes of Harold Johns, Ron Turner, and E. J. Pagram, the line eventually petered out as 1955 ended, along with those of most of their competitors, as a tremendous SF 'slump' panicked the trade. One late

Boardman SF title, Shepherd Mead's *The Big Ball of Wax* (October) was in fact packaged as a mainstream novel with an arty two-colour cartoon cover! Their last title, *The Sword of Rhiannon* by Leigh Brackett, despite its "First printed in Great Britain in 1955" was in fact not released until September 1956.

Another early entrant into the SF field was Rupert Hart-Davis who published Ray Bradbury's collection *The Silver Locusts* in September 1951, a re-titling of his *The Martian Chronicles* published earlier by Doubleday in the U.S. But this was not 'packaged' as a genre SF novel, for in truth there was no need. Bradbury was an exceptional writer who transcended genres, and who commanded the respect and plaudits of even the most acerbic critics. Bradbury had earlier had a collection of weird stories, *Dark Carnival*, published by Hamish Hamilton in 1948 to considerable acclaim.

Hart-Davis followed with Bradbury's other great early SF titles, *The Illustrated Man* in June 1952, *The Golden Apples of the Sun* in September 1953, and *Fahrenheit 451* in March, 1954, and they would continue to publish his later titles throughout the 1960s. The books carried the obligatory 'arty' dust jackets of the mainstream, and were a big success, Hart-Davis reprinting the titles at regular intervals.

"The rockets and spaceships of these fiercely vivid stories are the props of the fable, human nature and human suffering the realities," wrote the critic of the *Scotsman*, and the dust jackets of Bradbury's books began to carry well-deserved heavyweight endorsements by the likes of Christopher Isherwood and Marghanita Laski. The books were quickly picked up for reprinting by the Science Fiction Book Club, with Corgi issuing paperback editions.

In May 1952, Curtis Warren suddenly began issuing all their genre novels—including their SF line—simultaneously in both paperback and hardcover editions. Their first title was *Humanoid Puppets* by Ray Barry (Dennis Hughes). Designated as 'Lion Library' editions the books were 128 pages, priced at 6/-. But at first this was hardly value for money, as Curtis were still publishing rubbish, as exemplified by their next hardcover title, *Black Infinity* (June 1952) by 'Berl Cameron' (David O'Brien, on this occasion). But, as noted in an earlier chapter, the standard soon began to creep upwards as the year progressed, when Dennis Hughes' 'peculiar' science-fantasies began to appear with increasing frequency, such as *The*

Queen People (July, 1952), and the following month saw John Glasby's first hardcover title, *Time and Space*. By 1953 the page count had risen to 160 pages, and the more interesting of Curtis' hardcover titles—such as John Russell Fearn's two titles *Dark Boundaries* as Paul Lorraine (January 1953) and *Z Formations* as Bryan Shaw (March 1953), and *Ferry Rocket* (January, 1954) by 'George Kinley' (Edmund Cooper)—were very good value. Also collectable are the best of Hughes' pseudonymous science fantasies such as *Twenty-Four Hours* (July, 1952), *House of Many Changes* (August, 1952), *Blue Cordon* (September 1952) and *The Land of Esa* (October 1952). The Lion Library eventually ran to over 50 hardcover titles, ending in March 1954, and whilst the standard varied widely from rubbish to quite good, the many vivid bad taste BEM covers executed with great panache by artist Gordon C. Davies, has led to these books becoming collectors' items today. However, at their time of publication, with their small print runs going straight to the lending libraries, their influence on the larger publishers was negligible. With one exception—their immediate rivals, Panther Books.

Panther had earlier experimented in November 1952 with trying to compete in the mainstream SF hardcover market, issuing two 192-paged titles, priced at 8/6: *Beyond the Visible* by H. J. Campbell and *Born in Captivity* by Bryan Berry (the better of the two books). With blatant 'pulp' covers by George Ratcliffe, they failed to interest the main bookshops, and Hamilton's hastily reissued them in paperback in January 1953, priced at 2/- to reflect the greater page count than their 128-paged 1/6 editions. But Hamilton were not to be beaten by this initial setback. In January 1953, Panther increased the number of pages in *all* their genre titles to 144 (by craftily increasing the size of type, rather than wordage, so they would not have to pay authors more!) and emulated Curtis by issuing them simultaneously in paperback and hardcover, and priced at just 6/-.

The 'Panther Library' hardcover SF series eventually ran to an impressive three- dozen titles between 1953-54. It only came to an end because Hamilton's completely changed their whole publishing ethos: they decided to follow the practice of their larger mainstream competitors and *reprint* in paperback books previously issued in hardcover by other publishers, including much non-fiction. Since public libraries had a long-standing policy of not stocking hardcover books that had recently been issued by another publisher, Panther reverted to being a paperback publisher only. And as a reprint operation, they stopped buying new genre fiction, including science fiction. Initially, there were a few exceptions to this—for a while they continued to publish some new westerns (mostly by the prolific American author Lauren Paine) because these had been the most profitable line in their earlier operation.

Virtually ignored for many years, the Panther hardcover series is now becoming increasingly collectable. Whilst many titles were what has become designated as 'routine space opera' there were quite a number of excellent and unusual titles. These are touched on elsewhere in my discussion of Panther's paperback operation, so need not be detailed here. The books were further enhanced by some attractive and colourful dust jacket cover art (also used on the paperback editions), mostly the work of the admirable John Richards, who also did many covers for *Authentic*, often under the pseudonym of 'Davis'. Richards went on to become the Art Editor for Corgi Books, and his outstanding covers helped Corgi to become one of the leading publishers in the UK. Also very collectable are the pair of hardcover titles with Ron Turner covers—*The Great Ones* by Jon J. Deegan (April 1953) and *Deep Freeze* by Jonathan Burke (March, 1955)

Two other interesting Panther hardcover titles by Ralph L. Finn have been overlooked by bibliographers. They were published as 'Romance' books, but in actual fact are absorbing fantasies, very well written. The main protagonist of *Death of a Dream* (November, 1954) murders a man who has married his ex-girl friend, and who then goes on the run, a fugitive from justice. He meets another girl, and falls in love. He is then captured, tried for murder, and executed—only to wake up and discover that he has been dreaming (a fact of which he, and the reader, had been unaware). Frightened in case his dream may come true, and he might yet murder the man of whom he is jealous, he leaves town. Then he meets the girl of his dream. The story can be interpreted as mental time travel into an alternate reality. Finn's other similar title was *I Sent You Red Roses* (November, 1954) a haunting reincarnation love story fantasy that has pleasing resonances with Robert Nathan's classic *Portrait of Jennie*. It is perhaps worth recording here that following the filming of Nathan's book in 1949—starring Joseph Cotton and Jennifer Jones—Sampson Low did a film tie-in edition. This handsome hardcover edition, with film stills on the reverse of its dust jacket, was not included in Tuck's *Encyclopedia*, although its earlier 1940 edition from Heinemann was. Based on J. W. Dunne's time theories, it deserves to be a prime collectable.

Like Curtis Warren's Lion Library, these Panther hardcovers had limited print runs that mainly went into the Lending Library system, making them difficult to find today.

Good hunting!

Weidenfeld and Nicolson entered the 'genre SF' lists in spectacular fashion in September 1952 with two American reprints, *The Weapon Shops of Isher* by A. E. van Vogt and *New Tales of Space and Time* edited by Raymond J. Healey featuring such leading authors as Isaac Asimov and Ray Bradbury. Both books were slightly larger than normal size, 8 inches by 5.1 inches, as opposed to the standard 7.5 by 4.9 inches, and priced at 9/6. They had stylish atmospheric cover art by Pagram, and their back cover announced that they were to be the first in a series designated as the publisher's 'Science Fiction Shelf'. This would prove to be one of the more sustained series, stacking up a respectable 16 titles to 1955.

Two more van Vogt titles followed in 1953, both in the same attractive format, *The House That Stood Still* (January) and his most famous book, *Slan* (June). The last title to use the larger format was something of an anomaly—an original British novel by Hazel Adair and Ronald Marriott. Hazel Adair was a successful mainstream novelist who was beginning to write for television. *Stranger From Space*, a very simple story, had been a serial on Children's Television, which was then novelised. Weidenfeld did not identify it as a juvenile. American anthologies were still very much favoured by all the British publishers—or else were being pushed by agents, hoping to then sell novels by some of the writers featured. Groff Conklin's anthology *Invaders From Earth* (in standard size) was also published in July.

A cheaper-looking 'arty' two-colour dust jacket was also adopted along with the change in size, and applied to the first English edition of Isaac Asimov's *Foundation* in October. The following month saw the inevitable American anthology, *Prize Stories of Space and Time* edited by Donald A. Wollheim.

1954 maintained the high standard of material, with Clifford Simak's award-winning *City* in January, along with van Vogt's *The Weapon Makers*, the sequel to his earlier *The Weapon Shops of Isher*, with another attractive Pagram pictorial cover, albeit in two colours. February brought a surprise (but short-lived) full colour pictorial dust jacket for P. Schuyler Miller's collection *The Titan and Other Stories*. It's companion title, in the cheaper two colour jacket was another, and even better, American collection—Henry Kuttner's *Ahead of Time*.

The year concluded with two anthologies edited by August Derleth, *Beachheads in Space* (May) and *Worlds of Tomorrow* (October) and Henry Kuttner's fine series of the telepathic 'baldies' *Mutant* (assembled as a novel).

The series unexpectedly and disappointingly ended in February 1955 on another high note—Raymond J. Healey's (sic) *9 Tales of Space and Time*. It had been a good effort by an enterprising publisher.

Passing mention should be paid of how the sudden boom in SF attracted the attention of established authors from outside the genre, who were tempted to 'get in on the act'. The most notable of these was Dennis Wheatley, who had been a bestseller thriller writer for Hutchinson since the 1930s. Although best known for his supernatural horror novels such as *The Devil Rides Out* (1935), many of his titles actually blurred into science fiction, such as *They Found Atlantis* (1937) and *Sixty Days to Live* (1939). But all of his SF and weird novels had been confined to Earth, and it was not until 1952 that he ventured into outer space with *Star of Ill-Omen* (August). The naïve blurb writer proclaimed the book as "another of those fine feats of imagination, rivalling the stories of Jules Verne and H. G. Wells" i.e. code-speak for "this is SF but we can't bring ourselves to say so in case it puts you off!" The book *was* SF, and of the most blatant kind. The author had evidently hastily swotted up on popular astronomy and the many 'revelatory' so-called non-fiction books about Flying Saucers, especially Frank Scully's *Behind the Flying Saucers* (1950). The result was ludicrous. Amongst Wheatley's 'fine feats of imagination' was the idea that Martians would have evolved to be three times bigger than human beings because their planet's gravity was only a third of Earth's! The blurb went on to reveal that the book dealt "with the greatest mystery of our age—and one for which the world's most brilliant scientists have so far failed to offer any concrete explanation—the appearance, origin and purpose of the Flying Saucers." The less said about this book the better!

By 1953 a bandwagon had definitely begun to roll as another venerable publisher, John Lane's the Bodley Head, entered the fray, labelling their selections as. 'The Bodley Head Science Fiction Club', complete with spaceship logo. Their lists were dominated by reprints of recent American books, mostly anthologies.

They opened in February with *Adventures in Tomorrow* edited by Kendall Foster Crossen, and followed it in August with *Crucible of Power* edited by Martin Greenberg. Billed as '3 science fiction novels' they were actually three novelettes by Jack Williamson, Norvell W. Page and Norman L. Knight. This was one of the earliest examples of the 'three long stories' anthologies.

October 1953 brought another pair of the seemingly obligatory American anthologies, both edited by the established pairing of Bleiler and Dikty, *Men of Space and Time* and *Imagination Unlimited*. The following month brought their first novel, Wilson Tucker's minor classic *The Long Loud Silence*. Tucker was better known in the UK for his detective novels, but the quality of his SF novel was recognized when the British Publisher's Guild issued it in a simultaneous paperback edition.

1954 brought only a single 'Science Fiction Club' title, another Kendall Foster Crossen edited anthology, *Future Tense* (April). Evidently the Bodley Head's enthusiasm for SF was waning, because their next two SF titles, Bertrand Russell's original collection *Nightmares of Eminent Persons* (May) and *The Long Way Back*, an original British novel by the noted mystery novelist and literary critic Margot Bennett were published as mainstream titles, with obligatory arty dust jackets. Whilst Russell's collection was admittedly more properly fantasy—as had been his earlier 1953 collection *Satan in the Suburbs*—the fact that Bennett's fine novel was SF was demonstrated when it was subsequently selected for reprinting in Sidgwick and Jackson's Science Fiction Book Club, which made a nonsense of the publisher's caution. Its sale may have nudged Bodley Head into resuming their 'Science Fiction Club' imprint, as they issued another four books between March and May, 1955.

Category Phoenix (March) edited by Bleiler and Dikty contained three stories, reprinted from 1952 issues of *Astounding* and *Galaxy,* all billed as 'novels': 'Firewater' by William Tenn, 'Category Phoenix' by Boyd Ellanby, and 'Surface Tension' by James Blish. But the remaining three 'Club' titles were all novels: Steve Frazee's *The Sky Block* (April) was a US reprint, but *Angelo's Moon* (May) was a British original, an ambitious if not entirely successful first SF novel by Alec Brown. The last title was another US reprint, *Hellflower* by George O. Smith, which scarcely deserved its original printing in *Startling Stories*, much less its reprinting in UK hardcover. Bodley Head thereafter folded their Science Fiction Club, which had not really brought anything innovative.

Like other established publishers, Heinemann had already been publishing SF for some years previously, but always with carefully worded blurbs referring to it as "Wellsian", "parables" etc. as did their contemporaries. Apart from regular H. G. Wells reprints, and a 1951 edition of S. Fowler Wright's collection *The Throne of Saturn* (the blurb of which cunningly contrived to avoid referring to the contents as SF by calling them "stories based on scientific possibilities in the future"), their most notable titles included the "Antigeos" series by Paul Capon. Capon was better known as a detective novelist, but had switched genres with some panache, his first SF novel *The Other Side of the Sun* (1948) having been serialised on radio by the BBC. It had a sequel, *The Other Half of the Planet* (1952). Heinemann had been publishing the occasional juvenile SF novel since the late 1940s, most notably Capon's *The World at Bay* (1953) Another 1952 SF novel was the borderline *The Boy Who Saw Tomorrow* by established mainstream novelist Ian Niall. This was not identified as SF, nor were Gerald Kersh's *The Great Wash* (1953) and *Men Without Bones* (1955). This was understandable, since Kersh was by then well established as a mainstream author who transcended all genres, and simply wrote interesting books.

But suddenly, in November 1954—when the hardcover SF boom was already well on the wane with most publishers—Heinemann started including a bold planet Saturn logo with the legend 'Heinemann Science Fiction' on their jackets, and promoted their books as part of a new SF series. The inside back flap of the attractive full colour jackets by Mudge-Marriott (poached from Grayson & Grayson) set out their admirable manifesto:

> Science fiction has a long and mixed history. It has had one great master in Wells and a number of competent practitioners. Today it exists at many levels—a vehicle of pure escape and relaxation, of creative reverie, of social comment and reflection, of alert scientific speculation, and of excellent entertainment. It is as well written as any prose produced today.
>
> The purpose of this series is to present novels and short stories which will combine some or all of these qualities at a level thoroughly acceptable to any

reader of good fiction. We can be certain of one thing about the future: it will be more various, more surprising, than the past has ever been. To that future science fiction presents a key.

Possibly they had also been prompted to enter the field because of the success of Capon's books, which by then included a juvenile all-out SF novel *The World at Bay* (1953). Whatever the reasons, they opened their SF programme with the concluding part of Capon's Antigeos trilogy, *Down to Earth*. The dust jacket announced three titles as forthcoming, and surprisingly the first two were original British novels: *Utopia 239* by Rex Gordon and *Dark Dominion* by David Duncan appeared in April 1955. Some thought Duncan was new to SF, but he was already an experienced novelist who had published some 'borderline' unidentified SF with other publishers, such as *The Shade of Time* (1948), issued as a detective thriller. 'Gordon' too was already a published author under his real name of S. B. Hough.

Heinemann followed this promising opening with a string of excellently varied American reprints: *Bring the Jubilee* by Ward Moore (June), *The Space Merchants* by Pohl and Kornbluth (September), and *Lest Darkness Fall* by L. Sprague de Camp (October). The publisher showed considerable enterprise by doing the first hardcover book edition of Poul Anderson's minor classic *Brainwave* (November, 1955). This story had initially appeared as an incomplete U.S. magazine serial in Lester Del Rey's short-lived but admirable *Space Science Fiction* as *The Escape*, before Ballantine published it complete as a paperback original in 1954. This made Heinemann's edition an instant collectable. Another top-class US writer Clifford Simak, appeared in January 1956 with *Time and Again*, a masterly time travel story originally serialised in *Galaxy*. Sadly, it was the last title in their labelled SF series, which they abandoned thereafter. The juvenile book *Phobos, The Robot Planet* by Paul Capon had appeared three months earlier, but did not carry the 'adult' Saturn SF logo, and so was not strictly part of the series.

Not that Heinemann abandoned SF per se. Even as the labelled SF series was breathing its last, Heinemann published a 241-paged anthology of 21 short stories at the hefty price of 15/-. This was *A.D. 2500*, billed on the perfectly ghastly two-colour arty cover (surprisingly by Mudge-Marriott, but evidently 'painted' under instructions) as 'The twenty-one prize-winning short stories in the *Observer* Competition 1954.' It was introduced by Angus Wilson, who presumably had also judged the newspaper's competition. This had invited its readers to submit stories that envisaged life one thousand years hence. In his long and earnest introduction, Wilson 'banged on' about the deficiencies of most SF genre authors in writing about 'the human condition' and creating believable characters and good characterization, etc, etc. All valid points, no doubt, but the present collection was trumpeted as solving these deficiencies, and *A.D.2500* was "a collection of science fiction short stories by writers untouched by the stock conventions of the genre," which Wilson adjudged as "refreshing. It should convince many a superior reader that science fiction can be serious literature." Needless to say, the book—and its authors—sank without trace, apart from two writers who *had* been touched by the conventions of SF, namely Brian Aldiss and Arthur Sellings!

Heinemann also later published three SF novels by writers who *had* been part of the earlier series: *Another Tree in Eden* by David Duncan (June 1956), Paul Capon's adult SF novel *Into the Tenth Millennium* and Rex Gordon's minor classic *No Man Friday* (both November 1956). Many thought that Gordon's book later inspired the Byron Haskin film *Robinson Crusoe on Mars* (1964) but he was not credited. Both books were marred by 'arty' dust jackets. The art directors of all these hardcover publishers unaccountably seemed to equate decent full colour artwork with lower quality SF or juvenile titles—an annoying convention that has persisted for decades.

World's Work (also part of the Heinemann group) had re-entered the fray in May 1953 by issuing their numbered 'Master Science Fiction Series' featuring four of John Russell Fearn's 'Golden Amazon' novels, chronologically third to sixth in the series they had started in 1944. Fearn had sold them the novels between 1946 and 1948 (when they had been first published in the Toronto *Star Weekly*) but due to paper shortages, they had sat on them, whilst continuing to publish their already established line of 'Master Thriller Westerns' that included Fearn's own more recent 'Merridrew' series. *The Golden Amazon's Triumph* (No.1. 1953) *The Amazon's Diamond Quest* (No.3. 1953), *The Amazon Strikes Again* (No.4, 1954) and *Twin of the Amazon* (No.6, 1954), were interspaced with three American reprints: *David Starr, Space Ranger* (No.2, 1954), and *Lucky Star and the Pirates of the Asteroids* (No.5, 1954) by 'Paul French' (Isaac

Asimov) and *Seetee Shock* (No. 7, 1954) by 'Will Stewart' (Jack Williamson). The series ended with Williamson's novel, not because of poor sales, but because World's Work had decided to phase out *all* their fiction titles, and concentrate entirely on non-fiction).

Robert Hale had published Lewis Sowden's *Tomorrow's Comet* in May 1951, a SF novel about the threatened destruction of the Earth, but this had been carefully labelled as 'A Tale of Our Own Times'. But in 1954 they threw caution to the winds with spaceship dust jackets and the bold label 'A Modern Science Fiction Selection'. Their selections were first class ones: *West of the Sun* by Edgar Pangborn (August 1954), *Planet of the Dreamers* (January 1955) by John D. MacDonald and *Mission of Gravity* by Hal Clement (June 1955).

Another surprise entrant was Cassell & Company Ltd. Like most established publishers, they had been issuing the odd fantasy title since the 1940s, including 99% by John Gloag (1944), Gerald Heard's *The Great Fog and Other Weird Tales* (1947), *The Doppelgangers* (1948), *The Lost Cavern and Other Tales of the Fantastic* (1949), and *The Black Fox* (1950), which titles had at least been identified as fantastic fiction or weird fiction, but Michael Harrison's allegorical SF novel The *Brain* (1953 was presented as mainstream fiction. However they finally entered the SF label arena with three top-class American anthologies: *Great Stories of Science Fiction* edited by Murray Leinster (1953), *Looking Forward* edited by Milton Lesser (1954) and *Startling Stories* edited by Samuel Mines (1955).

After many years of virtually ignoring SF, it may seem surprising that English hardcover publishers were suddenly coming up with so many excellent American choices. However, the answer lay not with the astuteness of the publishers, but with knowledgeable literary agents. Elsewhere in this book, Gordon Landsborough pays tribute to the substantial role paid by Laurence Pollinger in promoting good SF throughout the post-war decade, helping to stem the tide of so much rubbish. He was quite evidently knowledgeable about the American field, and his firm of Pearn, Pollinger and Higham was probably behind most of the better choices. Further support for this supposition has been recently provided by the researches of latter day anthologist and horror fantasy expert Stephen Jones.

In his superb monograph, *H. P. Lovecraft in Britain*, published by the British Fantasy Society in 2007, Jones revealed much of the behind the scenes transactions that helped to bring American fantasy—and

Lovecraft's in particular—to Britain. Having gained access to the editorial archives of publishers Gollancz, Jones revealed that Pearn, Pollinger and Higham had been linking up with Oscar J. Friend of the Otis Kline agency in America since 1949, and had been trying to place the collection *Best Supernatural Stories of H. P. Lovecraft*. In the event, as Jones revealed, they were unsuccessful and Lovecraft became established in Britain because of direct communications by Victor Gollancz himself (who had discovered Lovecraft's work whilst on a trip to America in 1950) with August Derlerth, Lovecraft's US publisher and rights controller, via his Arkham House imprint. Jones' monograph reveals how Gollancz went on to publish British hardcover editions of all Lovecraft's fantasy, beginning with *The Haunter of the Dark and Other Tales of Horror* in 1951.

We can reasonably infer that it would have been Pollinger, through his link-up with Friend and other American specialist genre agencies such as Scott Meredith, and Frederick Pohl, who was responsible for the American selections of Kemsley's Cherry Tree 'Fantasy Classics' series and World Distributors' 'Fantasy Classics'. Kemsley's titles had included Friend's own SF novel *The Kid From Mars*, first published in *Startling Stories*, of which Friend had been the editor in the early 1940s. And most of the best of the World Distributors series had first been published in *Startling* during Friend's tenure. After making this breakthrough in the paperback field, Pollinger then succeeded in selling quality American material to the hardcover houses.

In this endeavour he was soon joined by John Carnell. In his position as editor of Britain's leading SF magazine, *New Worlds*, Carnell was uniquely placed to know all of the best writers—on both sides of the Atlantic. Increasingly, British publishers began to ask his advice, and Carnell quickly drifted into becoming an agent himself, whilst continuing to edit his magazines.

Museum Press had published Edmond Hamilton's *The Star Kings* in August 1951, billed as 'Science Fiction at its Best'. This was a label that would persist for years on diverse British editions, constantly repeated—presumably in an attempt to differentiate it from other publishers' inferior offerings! It was used so often it eventually became meaningless. Museum Press had already printed an edition of *The Lurker at the Threshold* by Lovecraft and Derleth in 1948, followed by a reprint of the Arkham House collection *The Hounds of Tindalos* by Frank Belknap Long. Both books were ostensibly presented as supernatural and weird horror stories, which they undoubtedly were, rather than as SF. Despite being attractive editions, they did not sell well and Museum did not follow them up at the time.

The Star Kings looked like remaining a one-off, until September the following year, when they published another Hamilton title, *City at World's End*. This time they meant business, identifying that title as the first in their 'Science Fiction Club' series. John Carnell was approached by Museum Press to edit this series, which steadily developed into a substantial line of books—which led much later to some confusion amongst non-fan booksellers with the totally different 'Science Fiction Book Club' which commenced shortly thereafter. The Museum editions were not in any way a book club, but straightforward ordinary trade editions. The label was simply an attempt to attract reader loyalty to their line, their house ads offering to supply details of their new and forthcoming SF publications. Museum (or Carnell) eventually phased the label out in favour of 'Books of the Future'.).

Under Carnell's guidance their SF line quickly flowered to produce a string of first-class titles, mostly by American authors, or UK writers whose books had already appeared first in the US. The only exceptions were a few titles by Carnell himself (anthologies) and John Burke (who worked at Museum as an editor, and wrote as Jonathan Burke). Dust jacket art was upgraded to full colour, and apart from the occasional dud, was of a good standard by experienced SF artists such as John Pollack, Gerard Quinn, John Richards and E. B. Mudge-Marriott.

Carnell's first titles in 1953 were *The Blind Spot* (March) a creaky but atmospheric old pulp yarn that had been pushed by American agent Forry Ackerman, who wrote a typically overblown introduction for it, and the much better *The Puppet Masters* by Robert A. Heinlein (April). The books were successful enough to be followed by *Dreadful Sanctuary* by Eric Frank Russell (October) and *The Humanoids* by Jack Williamson (December).

1954 brought a further five titles between February and October: Carnell's own all-British anthology *Gateway to Tomorrow*, Russell's *Sentinels From Space,* Williamson's *Dragon's Island, The Starmen* by Leigh Brackett (Mrs. Edmond Hamilton), and an original British novel, *Pattern of Shadows* by Jonathan Burke.

1955 continued the parade of strong titles: *World Out of Mind* by J.

T. McIntosh, *Gateway to the Stars*, another all-British authors Carnell anthology, *Assignment in Eternity* by Robert A. Heinlein, *Alien Landscapes*, a first collection by Jonathan Burke, and *Born Leader*, another McIntosh novel, in September. But the end was in sight. Despite opening in February 1956 with *One In Three Hundred*, one of McIntosh's best novels, the year petered out in September with an obscure French translation, *The Trembling Tower* by Claude Yelnick. The dust jacket was downgraded to two colours on non-glossy-stock, and the book (a quite interesting inter-dimensional thriller) was not identified as SF. The uncredited translator was John Burke.

Sidgwick & Jackson gradually emerged as one of the leading quality SF hardcover publishers. After having great success in 1950 with the groundbreaking non-fiction book *The Conquest of Space* by Willy Ley, beautifully illustrated by Chesley Bonestell in November 1951 they turned to science fiction with *The Sands of Mars* by Arthur C. Clarke, reprinting a plate of Mars by Bonestell as cover illustration. Clarke had already won international acclaim with his trailblazing non-fiction books *Interplanetary Flight* (1950) and *The Exploration of Space* (1951),

Whilst the publisher proclaimed Clarke's book as "A full-length Science Fiction Novel" they did not follow it up until September 1952, when they published his juvenile novel *Islands In the Sky*, beautifully illustrated in scraperboard by *New Worlds* artist Gerard Quinn. But the success of other publishers such as Grayson & Grayson served as a spur, and following consultations with John Carnell, Sidgwick & Jackson became a major player early in 1953.

Their SF programme was led off in March by Arthur C. Clarke's novel *Prelude to Space*, with an attractive dust jacket by Gerard Quinn. The back cover featured trailers for two forthcoming SF novels, *The Man Who Sold the Moon* by Robert A. Heinlein and *The Demolished Man* by Alfred Bester, and invited readers to write for details of their newly formed Science Fiction Book Club. The titles were originally selected by a team of four (Arthur C. Clarke, J. G. Porter, E. Shanks, and, inevitably, Ted Carnell). The Club's books were initially priced at 6/-, but quickly dropped to only 4/6, half the price of the average trade editions. The books were very well made, printed from the original publisher's plates, and the only thing not to like was the unattractive billboard cover. But the books were projected to sell because of the quality of the selections, which as well as publishing some of the best titles issued just a couple of years earlier, included the odd 'classic' title.

The first title was George Stewart's noted classic, *Earth Abides*, which had won the International Fantasy Award in 1951 as Best Novel, and within the next two years books by Ray Bradbury (*The Martian Chronicles*) Olaf Stapledon (*Last and First Men* and *Odd John*), Isaac Asimov (*I, Robot*), Alfred Bester (*The Demolished Man*), and others by F. G. Rayer, Andrew Marvel, A. E, van Vogt, and Kurt Vonnegut were reprinted, together with Carnell's own anthology *No Place Like Earth*.

The back of the dust jacket of *The Man Who Sold the Moon* (June, 1953) carried the headline 'Science Fiction' and retrospectively claimed Clarke's three earlier titles as part of their ongoing series, announcing Bester's *The Demolished Man* as being in preparation.

When this appeared in November, it was accompanied by another American reprint, Judith Merril's *Shadow on the Hearth*, a moving first novel telling of the effects of a nuclear holocaust from the viewpoint of an ordinary woman. The back covers of both their dust jackets informed the reader that:

More and more people are reading
Science fiction
. . . first-class entertaining reading which gives you something to think about. Sidgwick and Jackson specialize in this branch of writing and have already published three novels of the age of space travel by the leading English writer,
ARTHUR C. CLARKE
Chairman British Interplanetary Society

After listing their titles to date. The advert concluded with a further plug for the Science Fiction Book Club, which offered "the best science fiction books at specially low process."

April 1954 saw the first English edition of Clarke's masterpiece *Childhood's End*. Its accompanying title was *Hole in Heaven* by F. Dubrez Fawcett. Astute fans would immediately have been alerted that the book represented a new departure because the attractive full colour artwork that had hitherto characterized the series was replaced by an 'arty' design in just two colours. Sure enough, the inside flap announced: *This book is the first of a series of Science Fiction novels by British writers edited by Angus Wilson.*

Wilson was a famous academic with a genuine predilection and liking for science fiction, who had commendably been doing considerable behind the scenes proselytizing for science fiction in literary circles. The following year he would persuade the august national newspaper *The Observer* to run a competition for the best new science fiction stories, from which entries he introduced a selection of 21 prize-winning stories that was published by Heinemann the following year.

In his 'Editor's Note' introducing his first selection, Wilson argued that for all its many virtues, the chief fault of much SF that prevented its gaining serious literary recognition, was that most of its writers neglected the human condition and afflicted readers with poor characterization and dialogue—which few would argue with. Fawcett's novel, telling of a man whose body is 'possessed' by an extra-dimensional alien, 'Nemo', was presented as happily meeting this more exacting 'good human interest' criteria. Wilson was presumably unaware at the time that Fawcett was one of the most prolific hack writers of gangster sleaze, churning out novels under a slew of pseudonyms such as 'Ben Sarto' and 'Hank Spencer' for the mushroom publishers. He or his publishers may have found out soon afterwards though, which may account for the fact that no more SF novels by British writers with his recommendation ever appeared!

Instead, Sidgwick and Jackson's next SF release in May was Robert Heinlein's famous American collection, *The Green Hills of Earth*, happily reinstating a beautiful full colour dust jacket (by Gerard Quinn). It was followed in September by Heinlein's noted juvenile novel, *Starman Jones*. October saw a sparkling first collection of short stories by Arthur C. Clarke, *Expedition to Earth,* which Clarke generously dedicated to his friend and first editorial mentor, Walter Gillings.

After this splurge of titles, there was a long hiatus, and 1955 saw only a single American title in October: Judith Merril's splendid hefty collection of 19 stories, *Beyond the Barriers of Space and Time* with an introduction by another American luminary, author Theodore Sturgeon. Whilst mainly drawn from the top regular science fiction magazine specialists such as Asimov, Bradbury, Dick, the much-underrated British writer Peter Phillips, Sheckley and Wyndham, Ms Merril also included fine stories from *Esquire*, the *New Yorker* and *Saturday Evening Post* by 'outside' literary figures, and even a story by Agatha Christie! A betraying sign that the publisher was about to withdraw (albeit temporarily) from the SF fray was the book's dire two-colour billboard text cover. A final American novel, the dynamic *Tiger! Tiger!* (aka *The Stars My Destination*) by Alfred Bester, with a disappointing two colour cover (that was at least illustrative) did not appear until June 1956, by which time the SF slump had set in good and hard.

The man who had spearheaded Sidgwick and Jackson's admirable SF initiative was Herbert Jones. A fascinating sidelight showing his commitment can be found in Alistair Paterson's editorial in the second (February 1954) issue of the *Vargo Statten Science Fiction Magazine*:

> Another gratifying indication that Science Fiction is commanding a new and wider respect is that such an august body as the *Publishers Advertising Circle* should devote one of their lunchtime meetings to discussing 'The Facts about Science Fiction'. Three viewpoints were presented respectively by Mr. Arthur C. Clarke as author, Mr. Herbert Jones of Sidgwick and Jackson as publisher, and Mr. Eric Williams of *Books and Careers* as bookseller. Mr. Arthur C. Clarke needs no introduction, holding as he does a high place in the respect of readers for his *The Exploration of Space*, and also his chairmanship of the British Interplanetary Society. In his talk he annihilated quite a few fallacies, not the least of these being that Science Fiction was an American Invention. He emphasized the point that it was only because of the rise of so many Science Fiction magazines in America that people were under this quite false impression.
>
> At the same meeting Mr. Herbert Jones, whose firm Sidgwick and Jackson is doing such excellent work to further the cause of Science Fiction, spoke of his firm's aspirations in the field. He also pointed out that the Autumn Export Number of *The Bookseller* had, for the first time, made Science Fiction a separate reference section of fiction publishing. Mr. Williams, of *Books and Careers*, found that if Science Fiction titles were exhibited in a shop window with special showcards, then a stream of people would come in to buy books in this tradition. He believed that such accompanying announcements were essential as his experience showed that Science Fiction buyers would only show their enthusiasm when encouragement to do so by the bookshop. All of which is vastly gratifying to the Editor of a magazine whose principal aim is to encourage the reading of Science Fiction—and British Science Fiction in particular.

Hodder & Stoughton issued some very good titles without ever really being part of the 'SF boom'. They published only one author ('Charles Eric Maine'), and only identified their books as stories "of the very near future".

'Maine' was the pseudonym of David McIlvain, a radio and TV engineer, who had been an active fan since before the war, publishing his own fanzine *The Satellite*, in association with his friends Sam Youd ('John Christopher') and John Burke.

His first SF novel *Spaceways* appeared from Hodder in August 1953, and was a novelization of the author's January 1952 radio play. The inside back flap of the dust jacket carried a still from the Hammer Films version then in production (with a screenplay by Paul Tabori). The low budget film, starring Eva Bartok and Howard Duff, was not a big success, but it did help Maine's career, and shaped his strategy of exploiting several different markets.

By the time Hodder published his second novel, *Timeliner* in January 1955, Maine was very well known to SF fans who had encountered his short stories and novelettes in *Authentic, Nebula, Planet Stories* and *Spaceway*. The novel had been developed from his November 1953 *Authentic* (and *Planet Stories*) novelette, 'Highway i' and its radio adaptation as 'The Einstein Highway'. *Timeliner* was an excellent fresh take on time travel, and won acclaim from reviewers, including Leslie Flood in *New Worlds*, who hailed it as 'one of the best novels of its type written in England that I have ever had the pleasure to read'.

'Festival of Earth', a novelette in the December 1954 *Spaceway* provided the basis for his third novel, *Crisis 2000* (dated 1956, but published in November 1955). McIlvain realized that by incorporating strong crime thriller and suspense elements around his SF premises, he could reach a wider audience, as exemplified by his next novel, *Escapement* (July 1956) being picked up for filming as *The Dream Machine*, in 1958. McIlvain had earlier written the screenplay for *Timeslip*, filmed in 1955, adapted from his own radio play, which he then novelised as *The Isotope Man* in 1957.

Hodder eschewed colourful illustrative dust jackets for these novels, using arty two colour graphic designs. Surprisingly, their strategy was very successful, and because of this, new SF books by 'Maine' continued to be published by them regularly, well into the 1960s, unaffected by the SF 'slump' which cut down the blatantly SF lines of their competitors.

Rich & Cowan were another major entrant into the hardcover SF market. They had had considerable success before the war with Russell Thorndyke's famous 'Dr. Syn' historical books, and were now part of the giant Hutchinson group. They had issued Thorndyke's supernatural *Master of the Macabre* in 1948, and had also published many novels by S. Fowler Wright—but mostly detective thrillers under his Sydney Fowler pseudonym., although these had included his future war spy-novel set in 1990, *Adventure in the Blue Room* (1948), presented in a plain billboard cover as a crime and mystery novel. But in March 1955 they launched their own SF labelled series, with a spaceship logo on the spine, beginning with *Seeds of Life* by the well-known émigré American SF writer John Taine (E. T. Bell). This was followed in June by another American import of somewhat lesser standard, the American space opera *The Man with Absolute Motion* by 'Silas Water' (Noel Loomis) with a very colourful but atypically vague cover by Ron Turner.

Thereafter, Rich & Cowan appeared to use an admirable policy of issuing a British novel alongside each American import. Their next two titles in August were headed by another superior American import, Philip K. Dick's collection *A Handful of Darkness*. Well below it was an 'original' British title *Scream From Outer Space*, a first novel by John Robert Haynes, a would-be space epic that harked back to the bad old days of Flash Gordon. The blurb writer (who may well have been the author himself) rather gave the game away:

> In John Robert Haynes we have a space-fiction author who shuns the obscenely horrific without, in any way, sacrificing such essential qualities as a highly imaginative plot, exciting action and sound characterisation . . . *Scream From Outer Space* will carry the reader along at space-flight speed until the final climax has been breathlessly reached.

Their two October 1955 releases were a new edition of Alfred Gordon Bennett's 1939 giant ant classic *The Demigods* (with a striking cover by Eisner, who had done many atmospheric covers for their detective line) and John Taine's last novel, *G.O.G. 666*, with another fine Eisner cover.

November 1955 saw just a single original British novel *The Man With Only One Head* by Densil Neve Barr, an imaginative take on the last fertile man theme. Thereafter Rich & Cowan paused to take stock.

The long delay until their final two titles in June 1956, appeared to suggest that they decided to end their SF line, and were simply using the last two novels in their inventory. This was a great pity as the pair were of a good standard: Philip K. Dick's intriguing *World of Chance,* and a British original by S. Makepeace Lott, a first SF novel by an established detective author. His *Escape to Venus* was a very dense and ambitious dystopian novel involving a colony on Venus, which strove a little too hard to be literate. That Rich & Cowan had decided to throw in the SF towel was evident in the stridently defensive tone of the novel's blurb:

> There is no nonsense here of death-rays, ten-headed Martians or strolling on airless planets with gravity a hundred times as strong as on Earth. S. Makepeace Lott scorns the clap-trap of the comic-strip and delves into questions which are real, . . . etc., etc.

However, sales cannot have been all that bad, because Rich & Cowan later reissued many of their titles in cheaper editions, and they would be reprinted in paperback by other firms in later years. It was just that nearly all of the British publishers decided to shut up the SF shop!

Eyre & Spottiswoode produced only six titles in the period under discussion, most of them very good ones indeed, but they were so widely spaced they made little impact. Their initial entry was a van Vogt collection, *Destination: Universe* in May 1953, complete with a simple but eye-catching spaceship cover that left no doubt to its genre origins, and a rather pretentious blurb. But the publisher did not follow it up until August 1954 when the British original novel *Satellite E One* by Jeffery Lloyd Castle appeared, with a rather better space cover showing the then-popular conception of a wheel-shaped space station. Castle was later identified as an aircraft designer, and a member of the B.I.S. The publisher billed it as "scientific fiction" and it was a sincere, if plodding, attempt to fuse human interest and the conquest of space.

Then came a long hiatus, punctuated only by the first UK publication of the American Jack Finney's *The Body Snatchers* in September 1955, but this was presented as a 'fantastic thriller'.

Several more months passed, and then the publisher really pushed the SF boat with a large (476 pages) handsome volume, with an attractive Val Biro otherworldly jacket, *Stories For Tomorrow,* edited by William

Sloane, an anthology reprinting 22 of the original 29 American stories. It was copyrighted 1955, but released in January 1956. The stories by Blish, Bradbury, Christopher, Clarke, Russell and others were generally excellent, with a good introduction. The only problem was that the book was grossly overpriced at 18/-. This led to its being remaindered, and copies can still be found around to this day as a result. The book had been quickly followed in March by a splendid Eric Frank Russell collection, *Deep Space* (reprinted from an earlier US edition). The attractive jacket shamelessly pirated Heineman's recently discontinued "Saturn" SF logo, and was even painted by their former artist E. B. Mudge-Marriott.

But the disastrous sales of the overpriced *Stories for Tomorrow* appeared to kill off this promising line of titles, although the publisher issued a last hurrah in November 1956, with the ambitious *Sometime, Never*, a collection of 'Tales of Imagination' featuring three original novelettes by the distinguished trio of William Golding, John Wyndham, and Mervyn Peake.

An even briefer 'noble failure' late entry in the SF stakes during this period was the firm of Max Reinhardt. They did everything right: attractive Mudge-Marriott dust jackets, their own distinctive SF logo and two superb American titles: *Shadows in the Sun* by Chad Oliver (October 1955) and *Born of Man and Woman* by Richard Matheson. But the line did not continue. A third title was announced, *A Woman's World* edited by Helen Winick, but in more of than 50 years of collecting, I have never seen this anthology—nor does it seem to have been recorded anywhere.

The boom in science fiction, whilst it lasted, was not confined to the literary medium. The B.B.C. had regularly broadcast science fiction serials on the radio and to a lesser extent on television, although television had the greater impact. Television's biggest SF event had been the two serials by Nigel Kneale, *The Quatermass Experiment* (1953) and *Quatermass II* (1955). Although they were both filmed in 1955 and 1956, amazingly neither was put into book form at the time. They would be eventually be published (as scripts) by Penguin Books in 1960, along with the third serial *Quatermass and the Pit* (1958-59).

Radio's biggest success had been the decidedly space operatic adventures of Captain Jet Morgan and his crew on their *Journey Into Space*. This had millions of listeners, and whilst veteran fans treated its success with considerable surprise and condescending wry smiles, it was massively popular. The serial cried out to be novelised, and this was soon done by its author, Charles Chilton. No large publisher went for it, and it was left to the genre library novel specialists Herbert Jenkins to publish the books, beginning with *Journey Into Space* (1954), followed by *The Red Planet* (1956). Despite claiming massive sales for the first book, which the blurb of *The Red Planet* proclaimed had been selling "a thousand copies a week" Jenkins did not try to introduce other SF into their lines of westerns and detective novels, apart from the slightly dodgy *Satellite In Space* (1956) by Professor A. M. Low. Chilton's later third serial *The World In Peril* would eventually appear in 1960.

Reference has been made elsewhere to the burgeoning juvenile market, spearheaded by *Dan Dare* in both comics and on the radio. It was reflected in hardcover books too, most notably by Lutterworth, who issued four titles by an established children's writer, Mary E. Patchett, *Kidnappers in Space* (1953), *Adam Troy, Astroman* (1954), *Lost on Venus* (1954) and *Send for Johnny Danger* (1956). Don Tuck's *The Encyclopaedia of Science Fiction and Fantasy* informs that before writing her books, Patchett had joined the British Interplanetary Society, having realised that many children were fascinated by the concepts of space and space travel. That she had researched the field was clear from her books, which were a deserved success, and reprinted in the very competitive US market, where there had always been a strong juvenile tradition. One of the established American juvenile SF series was *Tom Corbett, Space Cadet,* by Carey Rockwell, a spin-off from a television series. Publicity Products in the UK reprinted the first two titles in 1953: *Standby For Mars* and *Danger In Deep Space.*

Another commercially successful juvenile series, decidedly *not* well researched, and astronomically and scientifically atrocious, was that written by W. E. Johns, of *Biggles* fame. Like Patchett, Johns (or his publisher, Hodder) decided to produce SF for children, which resulted in *Kings of Space* (1954), *Return to Mars* (1955), and *Now to the Stars* (1956). Despite being (rightly) torn to shreds by *Authentic's* outraged book reviewer, Johns' *Biggles* cachet ensured that the books were successful enough to produce another seven titles through to 1963.

Hulton Press, the publishers of the *Eagle* comic, and owners of the *Dan Dare* copyright, made two ghastly bungles over the exploitation of the character's book rights. Properly handled, these could have had tremendous potential. Their first bungle came in 1952, when—almost certainly following a recommendation by Arthur C. Clarke—Hulton commissioned Clarke's friend and talented British SF writer William F. Temple to prepare and edit a *Dan Dare Space Book*.

Temple put in a great deal of effort into making the book a top quality production by commissioning stories and articles by his friends within the SF community, and writing a short 'Dan Dare' novel for it himself. When he fulfilled his commission and delivered the finished article, it was a big, fat affair that featured his own 'Dan Dare' novel and two stories by John Russell Fearn (an old friend and mentor of Temple's from before the war). Temple had contacted Fearn at just the right time, when he was temporarily free of his contract with Scion and able to freelance. According to Temple's account to me many years later, *Eagle* editor Marcus Morris practically had a fit when he saw the delivered book, with its riches of genuine quality written science fiction, and ordered nearly all of it to be scrapped apart from Clarke's own non-fiction article "Is Space Travel possible?" even though it had all been approved and paid for out of the advance that Hulton had paid Temple.

Morris hurriedly re-edited the book, which shrank drastically in size and ambition. Temple's novel and both Fearn's stories were jettisoned, along with much other material from the regular SF community. Temple was furious when the book appeared as a travesty of his own original packaging, and with no credit to himself.

But Temple's own novel; was not entirely lost (though Fearn's stories, unfortunately, were). He'd retained a carbon, which enabled him to astutely *rewrite* it, changing Dan Dare to his own hero, 'Martin Magnus' and it was published by Frederick Muller as part of a well-received trilogy of hardcover SF novels: *Martin Magnus, Planet Rover* (1954), *Martin Magnus on Venus* (1955) and *Martin Magnus on Mars* (1956).

A couple of years later, Hulton published their own series of hardcover novels, to feature several of their leading *Eagle* characters, including 'Dan Dare'. Instead of commissioning Temple to write the novel—or some other experienced contemporary SF writer—they handed the job to one of their continuity writers, Basil Dawson. The resultant book, *Dan Dare on Mars* (1956) was a complete flop—as indeed had been the earlier book, which had been intended to become an annual. After a reasonably promising beginning, Dawson's novel fell away into a routine shoot 'em up in space finish. It sank without trace, becoming an underserved collectors' item today.

But by far the most significant juvenile hardcover series was that produced by Hutchinson in their own labelled Science Fiction series. Slightly larger than standard book size, and handsomely produced, all but one of its twelve titles were reprinted from the American publisher Winston's famous *Adventures in SF* juvenile series. Each book had vivid illustrated endpapers by one of Britain's top illustrators, Ron Embleton. These portrayed in iconic fashion robots, aliens, spaceships etc giving no doubt as to the book's contents. The images had actually been closely based on, and adapted from, similar images drawn by Alex Schomburg on the American editions. The novels were adroitly pitched at teenagers, and were all written by seasoned American SF professionals. The books set a standard that was unmatched by any other juvenile publisher. Several other Winston titles remained unreprinted, but Hutchinsons called a halt in 1956, in common with most other British publishers as the great SF slump gripped the market.

The arc of the Johns' series (1954-1963) was precisely mirrored by the "Kemlo" series by E. C. Elliott (R. A. Martin) for even younger children, published by Nelson, beginning with *Kemlo and the Crazy Planet* (1954). Whilst having an even more ludicrous scientific premise than Johns (children born in space can be acclimatised to breathe in a vacuum!) and again thereby incurring the wrath of *Authentic's* reviewer (Ted Tubb) the author was skilled at evoking the sense of wonder in very young children. Augmented by jackets and illustrations by Bruce Cornwell and other artists who had worked on *Dan Dare*, the series eventually ran to 15 titles.

Another more successful series of hardcover titles aimed at younger children was that written by the famous astronomer Patrick Moore, for no less than three different publishers, beginning with *Master of the Moon* (Museum, 1952), *Destination Luna* (Lutterworth, 1955) and the 'Maurice Gray' series for Burke, beginning with *Mission on Mars* (1955). Moore's juvenile SF titles would continue to be published by Burke into the 1960s.

Several other small publishers also rushed out opportunist SF titles. But they lacked the wit or resources to look for first-rate material, and instead commissioned some of their current writers in other genres. Sound familiar? The results were only marginally better than some of the earlier attempts by the mushroom publishers. They are not really worth a detailed analysis, but a representative sampling would include a series of execrable 'scientific thrillers' published by library publishers Wright & Brown alongside their mystery titles, written by their crime fiction hack writers, principally Nigel

McKenzie, who 'authored' inter alia, *Invasion From Space* (1954). *Terror in the Sky* (1955), *World Without End* (1955) and *Day of Judgement* 1956 and a few more in the following years. I vaguely recall that one of those featured an exciting chase above the surface of the Moon—*in a helicopter!* Even N. Wesley Firth would be spinning in his grave!

A little above Wright & Brown's efforts were two books put out by Hemmel Locke: Philip Wilding's *Spaceflight Venus* (1955) and *Shadow Over The Earth* (1956). This publisher had earlier published an SF novel by the distinguished journalist and novelist Sir Philip Gibbs, *The Key of Life* (1947, reprinted from *The Grand Magazine*, January 1936 issue). Blurbed as 'an imaginative romance' the book seems have escaped the attention of SF encyclopaedias and reference books! The Wilding novels had colourful space-action covers, which gave them a somewhat juvenile appearance, and both were rather plodding narratives very much in the vein of *Journey Into Space*, which had probably inspired them. The first book gave Venus an atmosphere identical to Earth's, save that it was "a little thin, rather like mountain air." Add beautiful dusky human Venusian girls on the style of South Sea Islanders . . . and little more needs to be said, except that Wilding had also written *Scream From Outer Space* (1955) for Rich & Cowan under the pseudonym of John Robert Haynes.

Whilst some publishers had thrown caution to their winds and 'came out' as unashamed purveyors of 'Science fiction', other publishers could not quite bring themselves to overcome their long-ingrained hang up to avoid such declarations. And, considering the opprobrium for the genre being generated by the lower class paperback publishers such as John Spencer, Curtis Warren and Gannet Press et alia, this was scarcely to be wondered at!

But the publishers sensed there was a *market* for science fiction, so they were on the horns of a dilemma. The august firm of Michael Joseph had been enjoying great success with John Wyndham's masterly novels *The Day of the Triffids* (1951), and *The Chrysalids* (1953). They had successfully marketed them as 'mainstream' novels, whilst their blurb writers—faced with the inescapable fact that they *were* science fiction, had successfully disguised them by claiming them as a '*modified*' form of science fiction, something that was somehow different and better than what was 'unhappily known as science fiction', instead of admitting that they were simply *very good* science fiction novels, as distinct from very bad ones! Given the prevailing publishing climate, the ploy was quite understandable, and one that Wyndham himself—having successfully shed his earlier SF-identified John Beynon (Harris) persona and 'reinvented' himself—was anxious to maintain. As a true literary craftsman, he was not happy to be identified with some of his lesser contemporaries—again, understandably.

But in 1953 Michael Joseph bit the bullet and launched their own distinctive SF series in an ingenious manner. Their jackets proclaimed them to be 'Novels of the Future' and what was more, they were 'under the general Editorship of Clemence Dane', a respected literary figure. The jackets eschewed the 'technicolor film poster' look of their rivals but were instead 'tasteful' two colour 'billboard' covers with a few arty graphics. Their books were higher priced than most, at 9/6, possibly indicating that they paid higher advances for their superior material. It was not just a cynical ploy, but a determined and sincere attempt to advance British SF publishing.

Top American authors such as C. M. Kornbluth (*The Mindworm*, 1955) appeared alongside British talent like John Boland, Arthur Sellings (Arthur Lay), and most notably John Christopher (Sam Youd). Christopher's first SF book, *The 22ⁿᵈ Century* had appeared from Grayson and Grayson in 1954, but Michael Joseph secured his follow up novel *Year of the Comet* (1955). The author then shot to international fame and fortune with his next Joseph title, *The Death of Grass* (1956), which many hailed as reading like John Wyndham—only better! John Wyndham himself continued to write his masterly bestsellers, such as *The Kraken Wakes* (1954) and whilst his books were integrated into the 'Novels of Tomorrow' series by being advertised as part of it on many of the other books' jackets (the blurbs of which by now were incautiously referring to some of their authors as science fiction writers) this label was conspicuously *missing* from Wyndham's *own* books.

Joseph's commendable series, began in February 1955, was successful enough to outlast all of its competitors, running through to 1957, when it was quietly dropped. But they continued to successfully publish John Wyndham's new novels on their own merits throughout the 1960s.

The other quality hardcover SF publisher to emerge towards the end of the boom was Faber & Faber. Bruce Montgomery (under his famous detective novel pseudonym of 'Edmund Crispin') published *Best SF* in 1955, the first in a series of annual anthologies. *Best SF 2* followed in 1956, and the series would run for over ten years. Despite a hefty price tag of

15/-, and the fact that nearly all of the (mostly American) stories were drawn from *already anthologised* stories that had appeared in the UK, the books were well received, owing to their undoubted quality. Faber's titles were not really part of the boom, the publishers wisely deciding to simply go their own way—and as a result they were able to attract some of the best emerging new British writers who, whilst always writing within the SF genre, sought to improve upon it. These better writers would only emerge in the late fifties—after the boom and bust was over—and they would continue their careers in the decades that followed. The most important such writer was Brian W. Aldiss, whose collection *Space, Time and Nathaniel*, Faber published in 1957—his first SF book in a long series of outstanding titles. These later developments are therefore outside the scope of this book, but have been well documented elsewhere.

Aldiss was preceded on the Faber list in 1956 by the American writer James Blish, whose books *Earthman Come Home* and *They Shall Have Stars* were warmly reviewed by Brian Aldiss in his influential review column in the *Oxford Mail*. Building on this platform, Blish would never look back, but his earlier Nova paperback *Jack of Eagles*, had sank without trace!

Considering the general high quality of the *majority* of the hardcover titles, it is difficult to pinpoint why the early 1950s hardcover 'boom' came to an early end. It must have been a combination of several complex factors. The opprobrium against SF that had been generated by the mushroom paperbacks had peaked in 1953, but by 1955 the boom had all but died out. The one notable exception was the Science Fiction Book Club, which, with its lower overheads, continued with its regular monthly selections for almost three decades, dying only when its new publishers lost interest.

So what had caused the great hardcover SF extinction by 1956? Had the products of the mushroom publishers, by some perverse 'reverse logic' actually been sustaining the better SF hardcovers, and had their removal somehow caused a slump in sales? It seems unlikely. Quite possibly part of the answer lay in the gradual slump in the use of circulating libraries, which for many years had been the main purchasers of hardcover genre fiction. These were situated throughout the country, not only in big chains like Boots' famous Circulating Library, but in many High Street newsagents and small shops. With the easing of paper rationing and the vast increase in the amount of respectable paperback fiction becoming readily available from bookshops and other outlets, people ceased to use these 'library' outlets. Another possible factor was the preponderance of American anthologies, all of them very much alike and with the same coterie of authors. The opportunity to encourage the better British authors to raise their game from the mushroom publishers was mostly missed.

Yet another, more prosaic explanation, is that publishers may simply have found that their SF lines did not sell as well as their other genre staples: detective stories and westerns! SF publishing involved more trouble and expense than these genres—the need to employ outside editors and consultants to ensure quality, specialist cover artists, and possibly higher rates to reflect the fact that two agents fees had to met for American material. If all these extra cost factors were not reflected in extra sales over and above their other genre products . . . than it simply wasn't worth the candle!

But the mini-boom in SF hardcovers, whilst appearing to end in failure, *actually sowed the seeds from which a vigorous British SF publishing industry was to spring up.* For within a dozen years, a majority of the titles issued were very successfully *reprinted in paperback*, as part of a steady presentation of SF by all major publishers that has continued ever since. The signs and portents for this later success were already apparent in the 1950s, as the larger and more respectable paperback publishers began to assert themselves with the easing of paper supplies. They all of them began to include a smattering of SF titles in their lists.

In 1954, Pan Books had reprinted Charles Eric Maine's *Spaceways*, followed by *Prelude to Space* by Arthur C. Clarke, and Robert A. Heinlein's *The Man Who Sold The Moon* followed in 1955.

Penguin Books had always published a fair number of more literary fantasies, but the big SF breakthrough came in 1954, when they reprinted John Wyndham's *The Day of the Triffids*, and *The Kraken Wakes* the following year.

The most enterprising UK publisher, in both quality and quantity of SF titles was Corgi Books, published by Transworld. Up until the mid 1950s, their books were identical to the American editions of Bantam Books, with whom they were initially tied. Between 1952 and 1956 they had issued a dozen top class SF titles, by the likes of Ray Bradbury, Fredric Brown, Arthur C. Clarke, Edmond Hamilton, Richard Matheson and George R. Stewart. They would go on over the following decade to be one of the most consistent SF publishers, along with Panther Books and others.

The Voyage of the Space Beagle by A.E. Van Vogt (C.W.B.) Grayson & Grayson, 1951 (Courtesy Peter Weston,)

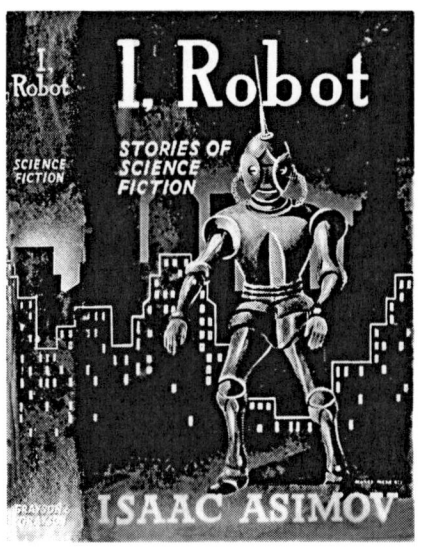

I, Robot by Isaac Asimov (E.B. Mudge-Marriott). Grayson & Grayson, 1952. (Courtesy Peter Weston.)

Alien Dust by E.C. Tubb (Gerard Quinn). Boardman, 1955. (Courtesy Peter Weston.)

The Weapon Shops of Isher by A.E. Van Vogt (E.J. Pagram). Weidenfeld & Nicholson, 1952. (Courtesy Peter Weston.)

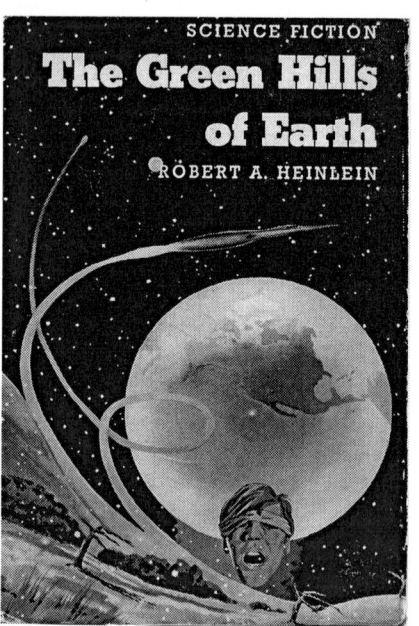

Assignment in Eternity by Robert A. Heinlein (John Richards) Museum, 1955

The Green Hills of Earth by Robert A. Heinlein (Gerard Quinn). Sidgwick & Jackson, 1954

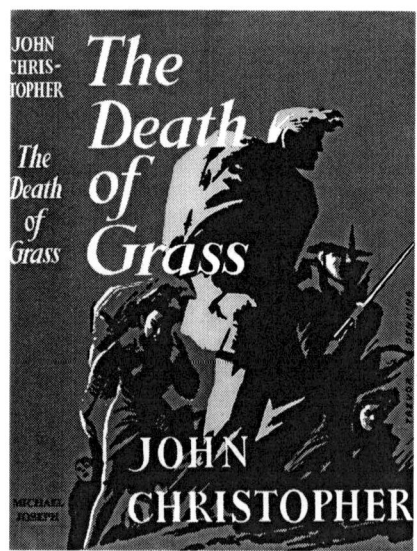

The Death of Grass by John Christopher (Trevor Denning). Joseph, 1956

The Space Merchants by Frederik Pohl and C.M. Kornbluth (E. B. Mudge-Marriott). Heinemann, 1955. (Courtesy Peter Weston.)

World of Chance by Philip K. Dick
(Ley Kenyon). Rich & Cowan, 1956

The Great Ones by Jon J. Deegan (Ron
Turner). Hamilton, 1953

Mammalia by John Lane (Gordon C.
Davies). Curtis Warren, 1953

Deep Space by Eric Frank Russell
(E.B. Mudge-Marriott).
Eyre & Spottiswoode, 1956

CHAPTER 14:
BURN-OUT
FOR SPACE OPERA

This reliance on American reprints did not mean that there was an absence of talent in Britain. Far from it. But many British authors were selling their novels to the Americans first, since the market in the United States was so much larger and better established, and did not wish to see their efforts abused by the British paperback publishers.

But talent was proliferating in the pages of *New Worlds* and the other selective markets, and authors like Eric Frank Russell, William F. Temple, Ted Tubb, John Brunner, Ken Bulmer, and a host of others, were writing some of their best work. Other, newer authors included 'Charles Eric Maine' (the late David McIlwain), who began supplying radio plays to the BBC; John F. Burke, better known now for his horror anthologies and for his television and movie novelizations; Lan Wright, who supplied some excellent serials to *New Worlds*; Irishman James White, later author of the highly successful *Sector General* series; and many others, far too many to list here.

With such talent available, it is a shame that the quality of so much SF appearing in Britain was generally low. Hamilton's 'Panther Books' series, which from 1952 offered both hardcover and paperback presentation, was attracting the best freelance work, with several authors, including Kenneth Bulmer and John Burke, writing for them. Burke's novels, in particular, showed a steady improvement, and his last two novels for Panther, *Twilight of Reason* (1954) and its sequel *Revolt of the Humans* (1955) were excellent. The first novel was an early major exploration of alien symbiosis, whilst the sequel described how mankind is able to overcome its parasitical alien oppressors, with a splendidly ironic ending.

Scion still had Fearn and Tubb, the latter also writing for Milestone under his personal pen name of 'Charles Grey'. These three publishers were leaps and bounds ahead of the others.

One new series might have given them a run for their money: a monthly series published by C. A. Pearson Ltd., under the banner, 'Tit-Bits Science Fiction Library'. The format was that of a small sixty-four page booklet priced at 9d, but the typeface was so small that the books were over 30,000 words in length, so they were hardly any shorter than the standard 128 page paperbacks. There were nineteen 'issues' in all, starting with *The Hell Fruit*, by John Russell Fearn (writing as 'Lawrence F. Rose'), followed by the same author's *Cosmic Exodus* as by 'Conrad G. Holt'. After securing the services of his Scion cover artist Ron Turner, Pearson's intention was that Fearn would write all of the series under the two names. *The Hell Fruit* introduced an unusual detective character 'Earmar Brown' (Earth mother, Martian father!) who Fearn intended to develop into a series, as a science fiction version of 'The Saint'. The 'Holt' byline was to be used for 'one-off' SF novels. But they lost him in May when he resumed writing for Scion under contract. Fortunately this happened before the books could be published, so Pearson's delayed the series until September 1953 whilst they searched for other authors. The most notable writers they found were E. C. Tubb as 'Carl Maddox', Ken Bulmer (as 'Philip Kent'), and the early work of 'John Rackham', the pseudonym used for many years by John Phillifent. The format may have worked against the series, and it eventually folded in March 1955.

Of possible interest to collectors of this series is the companion comic, 'Tit-Bits Science Fiction Comics', which ran in the same pocket book format for six irregular issues in 1953-54. The covers and the lead story in each were the work of the talented Ron Turner (who also did most of the covers for Scion and Milestone, among others, including the 'Tit-Bits' novels).

Another popular SF comic—although pitched at an even more juvenile level—was *Spaceman*, featuring the lead character, 'Captain Future' (no connection with Edmond Hamilton's hero of the same name apart from the borrowed title), Drawn by Norman Light, this comic ran for fifteen issues, and gave rise to a new science fiction magazine. Light was a long-time fan of American SF magazines, and was inspired to 'up' his game by editing his own. His *Worlds of the Universe* was a single, undated issue appearing in November 1953 in conventional paperback format. It was published by Light's own publishing partnership, Gould-Light (also publishers of *Spaceman*). The cover and interior illustrations were signed as 'Marcus' but were obviously the work of Light himself. Whilst they were vigorous and executed with some panache, they were done in a blatant comic strip style, which immediately gave the magazine an unfortunate juvenile appearance.

The editorial was full of hope and enthusiasm for SF and, in particular, the encouragement of British writers. The plan was to publish three stories per issue, possibly introducing serials later, but there were no further issues. Although the editorial boasted that the magazine's lead novelette, 'Waters of Eternity', was supposedly by 'promising young writer Mark Denholm', it was, in fact, by John Russell Fearn, apparently moonlighting from Scion—but Light must have obtained this from Fearn earlier in the year, when he was freelancing. The 'Mark Denholm' byline, and the style of the story indicated that this was unpublished material that had been written for Carnell's *New Worlds* in 1946. The other two (much inferior) pieces were pseudonymous works by Thomas Wade, who had been supplying John Spencer magazines with a plethora of stories under pseudonyms since 1951, and may well have been supplying storylines to Light for his *Spaceman* comic.

Its juvenile packaging and the Wade stories helped consign the magazine to oblivion, except for die-hard collectors of curiosities. However, collectors should note that there were *two* variant issues of the magazine. The editorial in the genuine first edition mistakingly designated Fearn's story as 'Waters of Electricity'. This was spotted early in the print run, and corrected to 'Waters of Eternity'. The true 'first' edition is therefore something of a rarity . . . an interesting fact that has so far never been picked up by dealers or other collectors!

Light, Turner, and the other, better cover artists such as Jim Holdaway and Ron Embleton were still able to showcase their talents as SF strip artists in several comic books which continued to enjoy a vogue in Britain when the pocket book (as paperbacks were then known) field collapsed in the mid-50s. These comic strip artists had been attracted to the paperback cover market by the better rates of pay.

Wade also wrote many of the John Spencer novels and, along with Lionel Fanthorpe and John Glasby, was responsible for the majority of the latter-day magazine stories. But the magazines were finally beginning to fail, and sales were slowly but surely dropping. The end finally came in the summer of 1954, when Spencer's folded all four titles at once. Their passing went unmourned. It seems incredible that fifty individual issues appeared altogether (*Futuristic Science Stories*, 15; *Tales of Tomorrow*, 11; *Wonders of the Spaceways*, 10; *Worlds of Fantasy*, 14), and just goes to prove that anything on the market would sell. The majority were juvenile readers, and those that bought the first issues were now four years older and (hopefully not having been put off SF for life) had outgrown endless Martian/Venusian invasions and moved on to higher quality magazines like *New Worlds*, or to *Authentic* and *Nebula*, which were publishing a more vigorous story with greater emphasis on atmosphere and excitement. One of the most popular authors of this type of tale was Ted Tubb, who was a prolific contributor to all three magazines. Tubb also featured prominently in another new magazine, which was launched in 1954.

During 1953, John Russell Fearn had been supplying a steady stream of novels to Scion, and was as popular as ever. In an article entitled 'The Elevated Fan' in the June 1954 issue of London fanzine, *Eye*, Stuart Mackenzie wrote:

> Today, they tell me, J. R. Fearn, writing as 'Vargo Statten' and 'Volsted Gridban', sells a quarter of a million books per annum . . . there has grown up, and this is true, a sub-species of fan which so likes the work of Fearn that they want to start a fan club in his honour. There is even a fanzine which supports this remarkable desire.

The success of the novels prompted Scion to launch a new SF magazine, initially entitled *Vargo Statten Science Fiction Magazine*, in January 1954. The first three issues were pulp sized, then changed to digest size with number 4, and expanded the title to *Vargo Statten British Science Fiction Magazine* at the same time.

Although the masthead gave 'Vargo Statten' as editor, with Alistair Paterson as 'Associate Editor', the magazine was at first entirely edited by Paterson. The avowed editorial policy was to publish stories only by British authors and to devote a minimum of 10% of its pages to the workings of British fandom. This was quite a surprise to fans, but they responded generously; once again, Stuart Mackenzie summed it up in a letter appearing in the third issue:

> The deliberate statement by the editorial board that it aimed at 'popular' science fiction publication was honest and, I believe, sincere. That the magazine caters amply for the non-iniate science fiction reader is an undoubted fact. If one is to judge by the reported sale of the Scion science fiction novels, an awful lot of people read them; presumably they must like them or they wouldn't be repeat buyers. There is a definite marketplace in this country for the simpler type of science fiction story; at present, no other magazine is aimed at this definite market and therefore I can only wish you every success.

The magazine was unashamedly slanted by Paterson to the more juvenile section of SF fans. Fearn continued to write prolifically for the magazine, but unknown to Paterson or his publishers, he was simply making good use of his cache of old material which had fallen back into his hands when he had quit writing for the American magazines more than ten years earlier. Paterson made one fundamental mistake with the magazine: he requested his authors to 'write down' to the so-called teenage level, and aspiring author Brian Aldiss was one of the authors who refused to contribute after his first attempts were returned for 'revision'. But after six issues, a new publishing regime dispensed with Paterson, and handed over the editorial seat to Fearn. The magazine immediately acquired a more pleasing and less divisive personality of its own.

One particularly poor entry into the SF magazine field at that time was the return of Gerald G. Swan. Swan had published the odd SF and weird magazine since 1940, the SF mostly derived from American publishers, Blue Ribbon Inc., and their latest effort was no different: *Space Fact and Fiction* relied almost totally on stories from *Future Fiction* and *Science Fiction Quarterly*, originally published back in 1941-42, with the occasional original, although most of these had been written in the mid-1940s and held in Swan's vast inventory (they accumulated stocks of stories as well as stocks of paper!).

Swan also had been reprinting the occasional novel from these magazines, which sometimes led to amusing results. *The Man on the Meteor*

(1952) by Ray Cummings was reprinted from *Future Fiction*, October 1941. The story concerned the miniature world of an aquatic civilization, while the cover depicted a man mounted on a giant grasshopper being pursued by kangaroos! The Hannes Bok cover illustration for this novel was also from *Future Fiction*, where it had illustrated 'Pogo Planet', by 'Martin Pearson' (Donald Wollheim) from the same issue, and must have caused some funny looks on anyone buying the book! Collectors of Hannes Bok may be interested to know that some of his illustrations appear in *Space Fact and Fiction*.

The magazine ran for eight issues between March and October 1954. The standard of the stories and the production (arrayed in comic-sized format) was never very good. In fact, two of the original stories, 'Forced Landing on Elvarista' and 'The Black Menace of Zenolius', both by Reginald Brown (who is not to be confused with 'Reginald Browne', a pseudonym of noted children's and *Sexton Blake* author, Edwy Searles Brooks) are particularly poor. Surprisingly, there were a couple of good pre-Scion Fearn stories in the magazine as well; 'First of the Robots' in No.4 was a new story (written early in 1950) and 'Across the Ages' (as by Dom Passante) was a 1941 reprint from *Science Fiction*. Unsold copies of the magazine were later sold as a book; Swan removed the covers and shuffled the issues, then sold them as *Space Fact and Fiction Album*. (This curiosity is now something of a collectors' item).

A discussion of the poorer magazines and stories leads (neatly) to the introduction of Gannet Press, which, in my opinion, published the worst SF novel ever to reach the public.

There are quite a few contenders for this title; others would include *Planet War*, by 'Fysh'; *Return to Mars*, by 'Elton Westward'; *Adventures on the Planets*, by 'Simon Querry'; and *Tremor*, by Frank Lederman. The last was (accidently) truthful in its cover blurb, proclaiming the book to be a 'Nerve Wrecking Experience'; anyone who has managed to read the book will know this to be quite true!

Gannet Press was the new company launched by B. Z. Immanuel, who had been Managing Director of Scion Ltd. for many years. When Scion split in Autumn 1952, Immanuel retained the old premises on Kensington High Street and launched Gannet Press in May 1953.

By the time the company was launched, Immanuel found that his previous stable of authors had already been snapped up by the newly-formed Milestone, or the re-floated Scion. So, Immanuel was forced to solicit material from second-and third-string authors, and others he knew to be highly prolific (Immanuel was a businessman pure and simple, with no literary taste at all, although he probably acted as 'editor' as well). He managed to get gangster stories from Michael Barnes and Victor Norwood, and invited Norman Lazenby to write for him. Lazenby was a highly prolific writer and had produced almost everything from fairy tales to soft porn; he had also written SF, his first appearance in Walter Gillings' *Fantasy*, and he had also sold to *New Worlds*, which proved he was capable of writing good stories. In 1949, he had a number of stories published as an original collection by Shenstone Press, entitled *Terror Trap*. In 1949, Francis G. Rayer had anonymously edited an anthology for Tempest Publications: *Worlds at War*, and Lazenby was invited to write the follow-up volume, but it did not appear. Lazenby then had thirteen stories in the John Spencer magazines under various names, none of which showed his earlier promise. Lazenby nearly wrote a great deal more SF, and was invited to write a regular series of novels for Scion, but was put off by the 'scare' when they split.

Immanuel wanted an SF line for Gannet, especially since his only experience was the highly successful 'Vargo Statten'. He contacted Fearn, who was then freelancing, but he curtly refused. Later Fearn told Lazenby (with whom he was corresponding), "I've withdrawn from Immanuel completely. I dislike giving three months credit for payment." By then Fearn was already back under contract with Scion.

Immanuel then contacted Lazenby, who turned in a number of gangster novels and one science fiction. This became Gannet's first SF title when it appeared in the July 1953 list as *Brains of Helle*, by 'Bengo Mistral', but it was also the last by Lazenby, since a better market arrived and he started to write for them . . . "SF was a sideline for me, and as it was harder work than the other stuff, I naturally did the easy work, being a lazy so-and-so!"

That same July list included the first SF book by 'Vektis Brack', entitled *The X People*, which was terrible. The Gannet line must be considered the worst overall SF line ever; more imagination seems to have gone into inventing bylines that into the stories, with awful stuff like, *Far Beyond the Blue*, by 'Drax Amper' and *Trouble Planet*, by 'Mark Steel' appearing—but there are a couple of surprises: *Castaways from Space*, by 'Brack' and

Global Blackout, by 'Karl Vallance', aren't too bad at all. I have a distinct recollection that Michael Burgess once told me that they were actually written by Michael Harrison, an established novelist who had written the novelization of *The Bride of Frankenstein* in 1936 (as Michael Egremont) and had published two hardcover SF novels under his own name: *Higher Things* (1945) and *The Brain* (1953). How and why he would have linked up with Gannet is hard to understand. Perhaps, like Ralph L. Finn, he had needed some quick money!

Castaways from Space was the third Gannet SF title. The fourth was *Pirates of Cerebus*, by 'Bengo Mistral', and every tortuous sentence is the essence of rubbish. The package begins badly with a terrible illustrative cover by Ray Theobald, who was one of the worst SF cover artists of the 1950s, alongside Gerald Facey, who also did covers for Gannet. The story is even worse—this novel is a must for any literary masochist who thinks he has already read the worst SF novel . . . for, believe me, this one is *the* worst! Anyone trying to find a copy today, however, will have to pay a hefty collectors' premium: the novel achieved a considerable curiosity value and cachet after I first exposed it in my earlier book. But as a cure for depression it will be worth every penny! But for now, here are some typical examples of this mind-numbing narrative. I quote from it verbatim, including misplaced apostrophes, non-existent words, etc. And, by popular request, I am including *additional bonus passages* other than those quoted in my original book!

Morganus Thaellier, the Chief Control Commissioner of Troublesome Planets and Asteroids, nodded briefly.

Being in charge of such affairs, he knew exactly what to do with a planet suddenly gone amok—like Astra Bella appeared to have done.

"Speed up the breakaway radioactive sun heading towards Saturn," Morganus ordered immediately, speaking into the telecasting tube on his desk and conveying his order to the Planetary Disposal Squad Headquarters on Mount Kilimanjaro, a large mountain somewhere East of Terrus. "And divert it's course so that it collides with Astra Bella and vapourizes it harmlessly in space as soon as possible."

Then the officials went off to lunch and a spot of skiing on the Glacier, chatting away cheerfully together with not the faintest idea in the Universe as to how close they had been to destroying Magoth the Wizard, sworn enemy of the Four Planets, and most dangerous being in existence in the whole Galaxy!

None of these worthy but unimaginative civil servants as much dreamed for one instance that by destroying Astra Bella they would be destroying also the fossilizing remains of what had been the only walking tree in existence that was the actual creation of human interference with the slowly moving evolutionary processes of nature!

The basic 'plot' involves the activities of the evil Wizard, Magoth, who has escaped from the penal asteroid of Halma, his intention being to take control of the Four Planets of the Dominion. His plan involves soaking the planet Berengaria (the solar system still has fifteen planets despite the hard-working Planetary Disposal Squad . . .) in rays which will speed up the evolution of reptile life and mutate them into fire-breathing dragons who will lay to waste the planet, although the planet will not realize it because Magoth intends to *cast a spell* to immobilize everyone. The author seems to have picked up the SF aphorism 'a wizard of science' and interpreted it quite literally!

The book's hero, Casper Carlyon, is a very unusual hero indeed: "Carlyon, like all Martians, a brown-skinned giant of six hectares high," who "was out on a trading mission bound for the outland belt to exchange tinned synthafood for ores and wild beast hides."

My dictionary (the author seems not to have possessed one) defines a hectare as a unit of area, equal to 10,000 square metres! And Bengo tells us that Carlyon is "six hectatres high." What *was* he trying to tell us?

Casper is a "pilot of the 'Articus' Route Space Transport between Mars and the outland planetary belt beyond the Atmosphere", and is searching for Regina Zelda (beautiful damsel in distress), heiress apparent to the Dominion, and links her disappearance and the escape of Magoth after finding her spaceship trapped in an invisible barrier that surrounds the "Galactic Circle" that was built "to protect Dominion from cosmic rays and breakaway meteors."

The thought of Regina Zelda, loveliest and most delicately nurtured of all the inhabitants of the Four Worlds, in the power of the loathsome being such as he knew Magoth to be, was more than he could bear to think about.

Carlyon had only seen Zelda two or three times in his life at public functions, at which, as Heiress apparent, she had officiated, but her haunting, exquisite beauty, her high spirits and vitality had made a tremendous impression on him.

Carlyon then makes up his mind to rescue Zelda from Magoth's clutches:

"Head for Cerebus, the first inhabited planet beyond the Atmosphere," Carlyon ordered briefly, his shrewd eyes scanning the telescreen for traces of other craft airborne in the intense blue vastness of outer space. "We'll land there and take a look around for signs of Gargon or Magoth."

Gargon is an "ace pirate chief," who "had escaped with Magoth's connivance," and was "believed to be hiding out on one of the uncolonised outland planets far out in space." And Cerebus?

Cerebus, though definitely believed to possess some types of life, both animal and vegetable, was not on the duly accredited trade routes of the Dominion, because it was too far out to be worth exploitation. Hence it was an ideal hiding place for outlaws and escaped renegades such as Magoth and Gargon, because it lay outside the regular spaceways and was not scheduled for tax collection or trading purposes.

Landing on Cerebus, they discover it to be infested with flesh eating plants, and witness a terrifying scene:

The plant, having by now finished its cannibalistic orgy, had turned and with a curious shuffling movement of its roots—the tips of which it deliberately withdrew from the soil—of walk not unlike some humanoid with ropes binding his ankles or a long robe which rendered free and agile motion difficult, had made its way to the body of the humanoid, a blue-skinned Plutonian whose orange hair in an unkempt mop shone vividly on the lush green vegetation of the clearing. With weird excited whistling sounds the plant bowed over the body. Its four now scarlet flowers closing in on the body greedily, petals caressing, with the almost tender movements of a kiss, the blue skin of the dead pirate.

Those petals must have possessed the rasplike surface of a sabre tooth's tongue. For immediately they drew blood.

In less than a quarter of an hour, the body had been devoured, flesh, hair, bones and even the elaborately decorated battle harness of thoat and mammoth hide embossed with uncut lumps of torquils uvonium and platinunumite nuggets,

"Let's get out of here, and quick at that," Bera gasped, turning to go, "I can't stand another momement of this."

Amen to that . . . Finally encountering Magoth, they whip out their atomblasters and fire directly at him.

The beams flashed forward, then spluttered and zig-zagged upwards harmlessly into the sky, crackling and spluttering as if the beams had struck some invisible but impenetrable wall.

"Fools of Spacelanders," Magoth sneered triumphantly, his evil face split by a grin of enjoyment at their dismay. "Think you and your puny weapons of avail against me, thoats? I am indestructible and behind my invisible barrier of gyres am safe from every weapon yet invented by the inner Galaxians."

Magoth escapes, taking Zelda with him, and leaving Carlyon and his crew to be devoured by the cannibal plants. But the resourceful Carlyon escapes their ravages, cutting them to pieces with the "whirring propellers" on the front of his spaceship. There follows a sequence of ludicrous adventures, in which they are tricked and captured again by Magoth—when attempting to retrieve "the ignition key" for their spaceship from around his neck—but, inevitably, Magoth gets his just deserts. When it looks as if he will escape by levitating himself away from them, the "flying sorcerer" (sic) is foiled when Carlyon gets in a lucky shot, which strikes the wizard in the shoulder, causing him to fall:

Hurtling plummetwise to the ground, Magoth landed right at the feet, or rather roots—to express things more correctly—of Sela, the chieftainess of the jungle denizens.

Unable apparently to believe her eyes, or petals—which served all the flesh-eating plants in place of humanoid senses like taste, touch, sight and smell—Sela dived lovingly over Magoth, caressing him with her crimson, velvety petal tongue exactly as a sabre-tooth might caress its cubs.

But, judging by the agonized howls and shrieks issuing from the black huddled shap on the soft mossy ground below them, these caresses were not to the wizard's liking at all!

Carlyon's party hurries "away from the carnage, passing on their way the sight of Sela huddled greedily over the gory remains of her belated breakfast. Green boughs entwined lovingly around the grisly bleeding debris of what had once been the all-powerful wizard Magoth . . . " They reach their spaceship, then:

"We'll have to look mighty slippy then, Cap," Alpha commented grimly, returning from the conning tower, "because it looks as if the plants have broken their truce, and having eaten the first course of their breakfast from the outlaws, have suddenly decided to have us by way of a second course!"

For sure enough, a single file of some twenty or thirty trees, waddling awkwardly, and obviously bloated by their recent feast of flesh, appeared in view and were making straight for the ship.

"I'll take off immediately," Carlyon said tersely dashing for the control tower. "You all keep below."

But he found he was not alone as he took up position before the control board, inserted the ignition key and revved up the engine warming her up for immediate take-off into space.

Zelda, her soft comely breasts rising and falling rapidly beneath their torn flimsy coverings, stood beside him, her eyes alight with tenderness.

"I shall be with you this time, Rega, in death even as I hope we shall yet be together in life back home on the Four Worlds," the future Ruler of the Domination told him, softly moving closer to him as she spoke.

She had called him Rega, the name always given by the future Ruler of the Four Planets to her chosen consort to be!

. . . she wanted to make him her mate and father of her children to be.

. . . The plants were by now dashing for the ship, intent on seizing it before it could escape from their ravening clutches.

The ship began to rise just as the first plant reached it and flung itself on to the whirling propeller.

Aided by the power of its "whirling propeller," the ship streaks into space "at a speed faster than sound." As the ship gains height, the crew put on oxygen masks (de rigeur in leaky spaceships) and the plants lose their grip and fall back to the planet, "whistling eerily in space."

The hero's vessel then makes a rendezvous in space with the Space Patrol, "just before sundown."

In charge of the Space Patrol is "General Vigo, a tall, snowy-haired albino from Urinal, fourth satellite moon of Saturn," This masterpiece of astronomical mythology prompts the idea of a sequel to *Pirates of Cerebus* in which the Space Patrol streaks to the rescue of two asteroid miners being attacked by space pirates. Just as all seems lost, one prospector hears the sound of whirling propellers, turns to his companion and shouts, "We're saved! Here come the Urinals!"

The author of this classic was one B. Ward, who remains untraced, and is likely to remain so, since who would want to do so? However, lovers of his work may also wish to seek out a few of the John Spencer magazines: 'The Pirates of the Black Moon', in *Futuristic Science Stories* #7 (1952) is in fact, an earlier version of the novel, and also has a wizard. Other known stories are: 'Weird Planet', in *Worlds of Fantasy* #8 (1952); that issue also contained an uncredited story by Ward, 'Space Adventurer'; an earlier story, 'Aftermath', 'credited' to 'Edward' Ward, ran in *Tales of Tomorrow* #2 (1951). All four stories are abysmal!

Reading *Pirates of Cerebus* today, it is no wonder that the paperback field collapsed so rapidly when it did, and science fiction lost face. But there was not much time left for the 'Bengo' type books, and soon they were to be a thing of the past, as the 'mushroom' industry collapsed as quickly as it had started.

Menace from the Past by Carl Maddox
(Ron Turner). Pearson, 1954

The Living World by Carl Maddox
(Ron Turner). Pearson, 1954

Scourge of the Carbon Belt
(by Ron Turner). Pearson, 1953

Worlds of the Universe (Norman Light).
Gould-Light, 1953

Space Fact and Fiction Album
(David Williams). Swan, 1954

*Vargo Statten British Science Fiction
Magazine* # 4 (Ron Turner). Scion, 1954

Global Blackout by Karl Vallance
(Ray Theobald). Gannet, 1954

Pirates of Cerebus by Bengo Mistral
(Ray Theobald). Gannet, 1953

CHAPTER 15:
THE END OF AN ERA

In June 1953, paper rationing was finally a thing of the past and the publishing industry was able to heave a collective sigh of relief. At long last there was a chance for the better breed of publishers like Pan, Penguin, and Hutchinsons (Arrow) to show their worth, rather than fight for newsstand space shoulder-to-shoulder with the mushroom product—and this was to be the latter's last stand.

The mushroom companies were suffering blow after blow from the Watch Committees, and it was a miracle that they had not all collapsed a year earlier. Many had fallen by the wayside, such as Grant Hughes, Tempest Publications, and Muir-Watson Ltd., but the others continued to weather the storms of outrage.

In 1952, some of the larger companies were beginning to show signs of strain. Scion had been fined heavily and split, and among the others who were later hit by 'porn fines' was Gaywood Distributors, who distributed many of the smaller company lines, including 'Hank Janson' and 'Astron del Martia'. The directors of the company were both imprisoned for six months, in 1954.

An Official Home Office document (distributed to police and booksellers) in my possession shows that between 1950 and 1953, approximately 1,500 (sic) of these gangster and related sexploitation books (listed alphabetically by title, with author and publisher given) were the subject of destruction orders made by various Magistrates Courts in Britain. The number of destruction orders imposed on individual titles varied from just one or two, and all points in between up to around 50. A few titles had even more, and three titles managed to clock up *more than seventy* destruction orders. *Swan Song for Paula* by Larry O'Brien (World Distributors) had 74, *Baby Don't Squeal* (S. D. Frances/New Fiction) by the infamous Hank Janson (who featured heavily in the lists) had 76, topped only by *Love From Las Vegas* by Hans Vogel (Muir Watson) which had 77. Most of the more pernicious titles averaged around 30-35 destruction orders.

Undoubtedly some of these 1,500 titles should not have been included, victims of some over-zealous Watch Committees, possibly being targeted mainly for their suggestive title or cover, and the publisher imprint or byline. Undoubtedly, that had to be the case in respect of 2 orders for John Russell Fearn's rare gangster title, *Don't Touch Me* under Modern Fiction's 'Spike Gordon' house name. In my possession is a copy which Fearn had even inscribed 'to my beloved Mother'! And Gordon Lansborough himself would have been puzzled and amazed to find some of his 'Joe P. Heggy' and 'G-Man Greer' crime thrillers for Hamilton also garnering just a couple of orders. But make no mistake: the *majority* of these orders (featuring in much higher numbers) were fully justified. As Gordon Lansborough has noted elsewhere, violence is the true pornography. Many of these pernicious books followed a formula, involving the heroines being forcibly held by gangsters and slowly stripped of their clothing, with lingering descriptions of revealed flesh. The women's assailants then proceeded to grope them, before either raping them and/or (and this is true) branding them on their stomachs with red-hot heated pokers or burning cigarettes. If you don't believe me, try and find a copy of World Distributor's *Don't Cross Me, Honey* under their 'Rod Callahan' house name, or any one of hundreds of other titles.

Gaywood had been commercially successful as both publishers and distributors, handling the outputs of other small companies and printing houses, such as Arc Press, Kaye Publications, Comyns (Publishers) Ltd., and Paladin Press Ltd. The paperback industry was still financially successful with small payments for authors and printers competing for business, and there were always people of no literary pretensions willing to invest their money in the industry. So, 1953 turned into another peak year for mushroom publishing, and there were over 100 SF books alone.

But it couldn't be sustained. With respectable publishers now able to obtain paper supplies, the public had a much wider choice of reading matter, and the print runs of these minor publishers gradually dropped as their market contracted. By the end of 1954 they became almost extinct.

Increasingly throughout the early 1950s, British hardcover publishers were trying out 'branded' science fiction lines. Mostly, they reprinted already-published American material, and this was usually (but not always!) greatly superior to the native British product.

One of the later entrants was the venerable publishing house of Ward Lock Ltd, who had always had a penchant for fiction. In the immediate post-war years, they had specialised in doing hardcover editions of popular 'genre' novels—westerns, romances, and crime fiction. These were very popular with the private Circulating Libraries that flourished in Britain at that time. By the early 1950s, Ward Lock had also instituted a paperback line, 'Target Books', which reprinted a selection of their own hardcover titles. Until 1954, they had avoided science fiction, although a couple of their crime thrillers had borderline SF elements (e.g. *Operation Superman* by Hector Hawton (1951) which they labelled as a 'scientific thriller').

However, by 1954 nearly all of the British hardcover houses were jumping on the SF bandwagon, following the successful lead of firms like Grayson and Grayson, and the Museum Press. As noted, most of these publishers were reprinting American SF, but Ward Lock decided to stick to home-grown writers.

Their first two titles appeared in July 1954: *Colonists of Space* by Charles Carr, and *The Wheel in Space* by Rafe Bernard. Both jackets boldly proclaimed the 'Science Fiction' banner. The author names were unknown. 'Carr' was the pseudonym of crime and western writer Sydney Charles Mason, who had been detailed to try SF. Nothing is known about Bernard, excepting that it was probably the real name of a journalist, since the same byline turned up thirteen years later on one of *The Invaders* TV novelizations.

Both books betrayed the fact that they had been written by SF 'rookies', their SF elements evidently having been researched by studying recent titles, particularly the many non-fiction studies of space travel currently popular. 'Carr' described the voyage of the first interstellar expedition, in the spaceship *Colonist*. The ship's crew contains a large number of unscientific 'ratings' hovering on the edge of mutiny. The author seemingly had only the vaguest notion about interstellar distances and the speed of light. By constantly accelerating, the ship reaches another solar system, and no reference is made to the light barrier, or time paradoxes. The crew merely experience slight physical and mental discomfort. They reach the planet 'Bel' and set up a colony. They then learn of a catastrophic world war after they had left, which has destroyed life on Earth, making a return trip unfeasible—they have no alternative but to become 'Colonists of Space'.

The main inspiration for the novel seems to have come from the movie adaptation of *When Worlds Collide*. However, even if completely lacking in originality and scientific plausibility, the novel was competently written. It also had a rather striking colour dust jacket, which, whilst unsigned, was (to me, at least!) clearly the work of artist Harold Johns.

Johns had previously worked under the direction of famed artist Frank Hampson, on the superb SF comic strip *Dan Dare*, serialised in the *Eagle* comic. After two years, he had left the Hampson studio to freelance. Unlike author Carr, Johns knew SF, and the jacket illustration, showing the ship having landed on a strange rocky planet, was quite attractive.

Bernard's novel *The Wheel in the Sky* showed much more attention to scientific detail, and describes the building of Earth's first manned space station, a thousand miles into space. The story is packed with astronautical expositions, and was clearly inspired by current non-fiction books by Clarke, Willy Ley, and others. However, the author betrayed his lay credentials by referring at one point to a 'flaming meteor' in space, thus anticipating the similar howler in the film *Conquest of Space* (1955) The story, set in the near future, was a kind of cold-war soap opera in space, and was competently written. Again, the most impressive thing about the book was its Johns cover, showing the partially constructed wheel-like space station in orbit.

Their third SF title was by another new name, 'John Elton', who was actually journeyman crime and romance writer John Marsh. *The Green Plantations* appeared after a six-month gap, in January 1955, and was a seriously flawed story. The flaw was a glaring one: 'Olloid' is an Earthlike inhabited planet said to have remained unsuspected and hidden behind Mars since the dawn of time! The Olloidian similarly did not suspect the existence of Earth. An unexplained aberration in its orbit had suddenly exposed the existence of each planet to the other. The sheer stupidity of this idea, and apparent ignorance of basic celestial mechanics, marks out 'Elton' as another of Ward Lock's genre writers detailed to try science fiction.

Weakened by a self-inflicted atomic war, Earth is conquered and colonised by the Olloidians. However, they cannot live for prolonged spells on Earth without an alien chemical compound, produced by a plant on the 'Green Plantations' back on their home planet. This Achilles Heel enables Earth insurgents to throw off the alien yolk. By far the best thing about the book was its cover—another beautifully coloured and balanced painting by Harold Johns, done in the 'Dan Dare' style, with Hampsonian spacesuits and alien spacecraft.

The fourth hardcover title in Ward Lock's 'Science Fiction' series was *Conditioned for Space* by Alan Ash, published in April 1955. 'Ash' had never been heard of before, and was destined never to be heard of again—at least under that name. This was an atrocious space opera. It may have been by the same author as *The Green Plantations,* since the author blithely introduced another new planet ('Ektolon') into the solar system, this time without rhyme or reason. The alien planet is inhabited by beautiful but evil warrior-women (who speak perfect English) intent on invading Earth in flying saucers. The whole thing is pervaded by a ludicrous 'camp' atmosphere, and the book oddly anticipated the later Hollywood 'turkey' film *Queen of Outer Space* (1958). The novel is at least action-packed, and the author attempted to spice up the stodge by having his hero being a man of the present who is deep-frozen to be revived one hundred years into the future, when the novel is set. He is given a mechanical heart, which is supposed to help him become 'conditioned for space'.

This book had a new cover artist: Ron Embleton, an up-and-coming young British artist noted for his strong figure work and beautiful colouring. He was not very good on scientific scenes, so tended to illustrate 'action' sequences on his SF cover work. This showed a beautiful girl watching two men astride grotesque alien fish duelling with spears. It gave a fair approximation of the lurid contents.

Four titles had been issued between July 1954 and April 1955—none of them any great shakes as SF novels, but with attractive cover art. Sales were sufficiently encouraging for Ward Lock to decide to reissue the first two books in their 'Target Books' paperback series, in June, 1955. These releases were followed up in July with another hardcover Charles Carr title, *Salamander War,* a sequel to his first book. It described the trials and tribulations of the human colonists on their adopted planet of Bel. Following in the tradition of *After Worlds Collide* (1934) there is conflict between different surviving human factions, and their conflict is complicated by mysterious aliens —the 'Salamanders'—beings who exist at high temperatures, and who seem to be constructed largely of pure energy. They were vividly depicted on another eye-catching Harold Johns dust jacket. Despite some imaginative touches, the story was not particularly inspiring, and it maintained the mediocrity of what had gone before.

It was at this point, someone at Ward Lock evidently realised they had been publishing crap. The next development was surprising: they appointed author Lance Sieveking to edit their SF line. He was a respected radio producer, who had worked for some thirty years at the BBC. He was himself a successful author, though not known in the SF field. He *had* written a few borderline SF tales pre-war, but with a 'literary' flavour. Sieveking's tastes ran more to Wells than *Flash Gordon*. His editorial brief was clearly to make over the Ward Lock space opera series into something more literary and respectable. The jackets of the books proclaimed a new title for the series—it was no longer labelled as 'Science Fiction' but (rather pretentiously) as 'Modern Novels of Science and Imagination: advisory editor: Lance Sieveking'. To underline the changes, Sieveking promptly chucked out the previous writers—admittedly no great loss.

September 1955 introduced a new writer, Robert Conquest, with a first novel, *A World of Difference*. Conquest was a highly literate figure, a poet and University-educated diplomat. He was, however, an SF 'buff' and became well-known in the following decade for his literate and stimulating run of SF anthologies, co-edited with his friend Kingsley Amis—the 'Spectrum' series. *A World of Difference* had a complicated plot of political and scientific adventure in the future, centred around the discovery of an interstellar drive. It was however, decidedly "non-pulp."

Sieveking's own novel, *A Private Volcano* (October, 1955) came next. The author probably thought his central idea—a mysterious element ejected from a volcano that has the property of transmuting metals to gold, with resultant catastrophic effects on society—was original. In fact, a very similar idea had already been comprehensively done in J. R. Fearn's 'Vargo Statten' novel *The Catalyst* (1951). However, the treatment of the theme could not have been more different: whilst the Fearn novel was a wild and woolly cosmic romp, Sieveking stayed down-to-earth and concentrated on character and the human side in an unusually literate and interesting fashion.

When the Moon Died by Richard Savage (November, 1955) was a quite imaginative 'mainstream' treatment of classic SF themes—explorers from another universe discover a devastated Earth in the far future, wrenched from the solar system. They find a tape recording left by a historian, which tells of a double catastrophe—how mankind had been on the brink of destroying itself until scientists had taken control, cowing the people by destroying the moon as a warning of their power. But the scientific utopia degenerates into a spiritless anthill, and rebels against the system repeat the mistakes of the past, until mankind encompasses his own destruction. There was nothing original in the framework of the story—once again, Fearn had used the identical 'cosmic explorer of the ruins' device several times, and J. Jefferson Farjeon had written a gloomy SF novel with a very similar outlook, *Death of a World* (1948). But Savage's novel was very well written and worked out. Donald Tuck has identified 'Savage' as the pseudonym of journalist and novelist Ivan Roe, who was better known for his excellent detective novels.

Pursuit Through Time (January, 1956) by Jonathan Burke concluded this particular series. John F. Burke had written numerous SF novels for Panther Books. Burke was a noted pre-war fan, and his novel dealt comprehensively with time travelling into the past in order to alter the future. Burke was a careful writer, whose imaginative plots were always worked out in human terms, and never sensationalised. This interesting novel was in many ways a direct precursor to John Varley's 1977 classic story 'Air Raid' (later expanded and filmed as *Millenium*) and the James Cameron film *Terminator* (1984), but Burke has never received any credit for his idea of time travellers snatching people about to die by natural accident, so as to minimise repercussions on the space-time continuum. Burke's central theme of altering the future by removing key figures (such as emerging dictators) was of course heavily indebted (as are most subsequent time tales) to Jack Williamson's 1938 classic *The Legion of Time*.

As a group of novels, Sieveking's selections were markedly superior to what had gone before. Unfortunately, either Sieveking or Ward Lock's art editor decided that the covers had to become more 'adult' or 'arty' to reflect the improved intellectual contents of the books they illustrated. All collectors and lovers of paperbacks will know what this meant—the covers simply became absolutely bloody awful! For some reason, British publishers always equate sketchy, shoddy illustration with 'good' books. It is specious reasoning, and the Ward Lock series probably faded out because of it. Had the later titles been illustrated by Harold Johns, they would today almost certainly be collected and remembered.

Burke's novel was particularly ill-served with an arty, drab cover that was frankly repulsive, rather than attractive. Sieveking's two-colour jacket consisted of pretentious line drawings of two utterly boring intellectual-type faces and a pathetic attempt to portray an erupting volcano (10% volcano, 90% smoke!) The artist was 'credited'—Audley Southcott. The remaining three covers used three colours, but in a deliberately drab way. All by the same artist, wisely only one of them (Conquest's) was signed, and then only by the initials "J.S." The real fault lay with the publisher's art editor. Ward Lock seem to have realised this, because whilst they released *The Green Plantations* and *Conditioned for Space* as 2/- paperbacks in their 'Target' series in June 1956, they waited a full year until 1957 before paperbacking only two of the Sieveking-edited books, *When the Moon Died* and *A Private Volcano*, selecting the titles with the least repulsive covers. The Burke and Conquest novels had to await republication by other publishers several years later as had the last of the first series novels, *Salamander War*. The reason for this latter omission remains a mystery, as it had an attractive cover. It may have been because of poor sales of the first hardcover edition, which, perhaps significantly, had not been re-issued as a 6/- edition.

One of the biggest (numerically speaking) publishers of both paperback and hardcover SF books in the early 1950s was Curtis Warren Ltd. Since 1950, they had issued SF, and by 1954, had over 100 titles on their lists, making them the most prolific SF publishers in the '50s. Since mid-1952, they had also issued all their books in a hardcover library edition, and with some six new titles each month, it certainly seemed that Curtis was the most financially successful of all the pulp companies, along with Hamilton & Co., both of whom had the same financial backer.

By 1954, the Curtis SF line was still mostly the work of Dennis Hughes, who managed to produce over forty SF novels in a four-year period, making him one of the most prolific authors of the 1950s. Unfortunately, much of his SF was rubbish; only in some of his later bizarre novels designated as 'science fantasy' did he display any real imagination.

Curtis Warren continued to publish until November 1954. The previous eleven months had seen a slight decrease in the number of their SF novels, but did include as their last title, *Challenge*, by H. K(enneth) Bulmer. By then the company was already sliding out of existence, despite a late change to a smaller sized format.

Bulmer had actually submitted the novel to Panther Books, and was only paid a small amount of what he was owed for the novel—and only then because he was one of the authors who went to the liquidation meeting held by Joseph Pacey in November. One author who missed being paid was Sydney Bounds, who also attended the meeting to aid Bulmer in his claim for payment. He had sent a 10,000-word novelette to Curtis, who subsequently published it without telling Bounds, and without paying for it. His story, 'Terror Stalks the Séance Room' as by Clifford Wallace appeared in Curtis' attempt at a digest-sized, crime/suspense and borderline weird/SF magazine entitled *Suspense Stories*. Its contents page billed the stories as 'The Best in Mystery and Detective Fiction'. In format the 96-paged magazine resembled the early *Nebula*, and was very well printed and produced, being let down only in the quality of its interior illustrations. Amongst the pseudonymous contributors was the well-known Liverpool fan and aspiring author Dave Gardner, recycling some of his fan fiction pieces, such as 'When Johnny Came Home' as by D. G. Carson. Undated and unnumbered, the magazine had three bi-monthly issues between July and November 1954, folding when the company collapsed.

After Curtis Warren and Hamilton & Co., Scion Ltd. was the third biggest company of the 1950s.

In January 1954 Scion had launched the *Vargo Statten Science Fiction Magazine*. They had been fined in Autumn 1952 and, in Spring 1954, they were fined again for publishing pornographic gangster stories; this time it was apparently only one novel that caused the outcry, but the fine was crippling. A new company was formed, comprising the staff nucleus, operating under the name of the Henry Squire Co. However, their letterhead gave their address as that of the Gaywood consortium controlled by Reginald Carter. The consortium refloated the company as 'Scion Distributors Ltd.' Alistair Paterson was retained as editor and attempted to continue the activities of the firms Squire had inherited.

Carter was another of the wide-boy characters of the period: he was the publisher of 'Hank Janson' and acquired a number of other companies to cash in on the gangster boom. Along with other publishers such as Kaye and Ralph Stokes, he had an exclusive distribution deal with Gaywood and all these various firms had tried SF in their time, the first title being the 'Nerve Wrecking' *Tremor*, by Frank Lederman, from Kaye Publications in 1952. Almost certainly written by a gangster hack, this was a dreadful space opera with unpleasant sex and sleaze undertones. In 1953, both Comyns and Paladin started to produce SF novels, written by Ken Bulmer and Peter Hawkins (both under the pseudonym 'Karl Maras') and by E. C. Tubb as himself, as his name had by then acquired a big following. The Tubb novels were particularly good (especially *Alien Life*, which he would later revise at my request), but very badly printed on coarse paper. The last of these novels, *Beyond the Solar System*, by 'Claud Haley', was published by Arc Press in 1954, but the book, with its vivid Norman Light cover, looks as if it may have originally been sold to John Spencer & Co., only to be resold by them when they killed their SF line in the summer of 1954.

The newly founded Scion Distributors continued to publish the novels of 'Vargo Statten' and 'Volsted Gridban' (both still written by Fearn) as well as the magazine, but changes were soon made. With the paperback market collapsing, Squire found by summer 1954 that they were in trouble. The continual buying of small companies was poisoning the conglomerate, and the situation was further aggravated in 1954 when 'Hank Janson' became the centre of a court case at the Old Bailey, where some of the books were actually used in evidence against the authors and publishers in an effort to stop the publication of sex-and-gangster stories. Whilst his publishers had received jail sentences, Frances escaped punishment because the actual specific titles on which the prosecution was based could not positively be attributed to him, the Janson byline being by then used as a house name.

Purely for the record, it can be noted that Frances himself did write three SF novels under the Hank Janson name: *The Unseen Assassin* (Top Fiction, 1953), *Tomorrow and a Day* (Alexander Moring, 1955), and *One Against Time*, Alexander Moring 1956). The last named was reprinted in 1969 by another publisher as by Astron Del Martia. None of them had any real merit, though only the first one, *The Unseen Assassin* had the trademark Janson sleazy sex sequences of women being raped and brutalized, and the astronomical details of the book are ludicrous, with the solar system abounding with unknown planets. One detail, of interest to sleaze hounds, is that Frances seemed to have invented the orgasm machine—a cabinet of mechanized rubber and plastic that moulds itself to the body (Frances euphemistically refers to it as a 'toner') a curious anticipation of Roger Vadim's 1968 film *Barbarella*. But the only really memorable thing about the book is its cover, ostensibly by artist Reginald Heade.

When Frances decided to introduce science fiction into the Hank Janson line, Heade complained to his agent, Charles Montague (Greg) Hall that he had never tackled the genre, and was unhappy about doing it. The ingenious agent came up with the ideal solution—Heade would paint the girl in the foreground, and the painting would be passed to his other client, Ron Turner, who was the greatest SF stylist in the country. Turner painted in the futuristic city and skyline, and passed it back to Hall. The finished painting was passed to the publisher who was none the wiser. Not surprisingly, however, Heade hadn't signed it.

Following the action of the courts, that arm of the Squire/Carter Empire, New Fiction Press and Top Fiction Press, was forced to close down, but the 'Hank Janson' byline was continued by Alexander Moring Ltd., who printed their books in France and Holland, and shipped them to Britain.

Squire also found that in taking over Scion, they had also inherited a large debt to their printers, Dragon Press of Luton, who printed books for most of the mushroom companies. To offset the debt, Squire handed over to Dragon Press their best assets, the 'Vargo Statten' magazine and novels. Fearn himself, still contracted to Scion throughout all these moves, was part of the deal. Editor Alistair Paterson was let go, and Fearn took over the magazine from the seventh (September 1954) issue, after which the magazine became simply, *The British Science Fiction Magazine*, at Fearn's insistence. He also had the byline 'Volsted Gridban' stopped, but was contractually bound to continue as 'Vargo Statten'.

With Fearn in control, the magazine took a turn. Paterson had antagonized fandom and authors by having them 'write down' to younger readers. Under Fearn, the magazine openly catered to fandom, with an expansion of its 'Inquisitor' column by arch-fan A. Vincent Clarke. 'Harry Cohn' (Manchester fan David Cohen, a friend of Fearn's) ran a 'Personalities in Fandom' column, which included a well-deserved homage to Forrest J Ackerman in the fourteenth issue; the quality of the fiction improved as encouragement was given to new writers such as Ron Deacon, Peter Baillie, and Barrington J. Bayley. The magazine was beginning to acquire a definite personality, but Fearn was fighting a lost cause, labouring under a crippling handicap imposed by Dragon Press, which was inexperienced as a publishing company. They misinterpreted a falloff in the magazine's circulation (the natural 'settling' to a firm level) and slashed Fearn's budget by more than half. At only 12/6d per thousand words (for all rights) Fearn didn't stand a chance against other editors who offered a minimum of 25/- a thousand for first British rights only.

So, while the new authors contributed, few established authors bothered because of the miserly rates. The prolific Ted Tubb still appeared, following two three-part serials (*The Inevitable Conflict* and *Forbidden Fruit*) with nine short stories, although he insisted on using pseudonyms for the latter. Ken Bulmer appeared under the pseudonym 'Chesman Scott', and even Fearn (who had been supplying 'new' stories under the 'Statten' and 'Gridban' bylines, using the last of his old American stockpile) limited the number he supplied; his two serials under the 'Statten' name were reprints from the Toronto *Star Weekly* for which he had already been very well paid, and for short fiction he astutely reworked his old wartime American stories under numerous pseudonyms. A standard Ron Turner cover design was adopted for the sake of economy, and a further name-change was made with issue 13 to *The British Space Fiction Magazine*. And somehow the magazine survived through 1955.

During his Dragon editorship period—because he was asked to write in other genres, including detective, romance and westerns—Fearn only published three 'Vargo Statten' novels, including *Creature from the Black Lagoon*, an adaptation of Universal's classic 1954 monster movie. Fearn was a film buff all his life, and during the war had even worked as a professional cinema projectionist. His novel was closely patterned on the film script, but still captured the visual style and excitement of the film brilliantly. Dragon broke precedent and issued the book in both paperback and hardcover editions. Collectors should note that the paperback, published in September 1954, was the true first edition. The hardcover edition, using the same plates and John Richards 'monster' cover, has hitherto been widely recorded as having been published simultaneously. But it was not in fact issued until February 1955 (when it was recorded in *Whitaker's Cumulative Book List* as a 'new impression'). The novel is usually missed in cinema reference works because of its obscure publication, but the book now commands fantastic four-figure prices from OP book dealers, and has even been auctioned at Sotherby's in New York!

As noted, Dragon requested Fearn to write novels for them other than as 'Statten', and Fearn turned in two excellent scientific detective thrillers featuring his character Dr. Carruthers, whose previous books had appeared from Stanley Paul in their hardcover detective series, as by 'Hugo Blayn'. The first of these was *Vision Sinister*, which Dragon put out under the house pseudonym 'Nat Karta', a notorious gangster byline, which they had inherited from Scion. Fearn understandably complained bitterly, so his second 'Dr. Carruthers' title, *The Silvered Cage*, reinstated his 'Hugo Blayn' byline. Both books were ingenious 'impossible crime/locked room murder' novels, and are now valuable collectors' items and highly rated by detective fiction aficionados. (I arranged for their reprinting by F. A. Thorpe, under Fearn's own name, in 2005). Fearn also wrote numerous pseudonymous romances, which were very successful, two of them later being reissued in hardcovers. He was writing westerns under the name 'Jed McCloud' when his novel contract ran out in October 1955.

Fearn had recently become engaged to Carrie Worth, the widow of a Blackpool businessman. He had ambitions to advance his career outside of the paperback jungle, so he refused to renew his contract. The 19th and last issue of *The British Space Fiction Magazine* appeared in February 1956, when a national printers all-out general strike led to Dragon folding as publishers, and their unused novel manuscripts were sold to Brown-Watson Ltd. There were no more 'Vargo Statten' stories and the byline that had launched hundreds of imitations and a paperback SF boom never appeared again on an original novel.

Fearn retired from the British paperback jungle, and concentrated on sales to the high-paying Canadian magazine, the Toronto *Star Weekly*, where his popular 'Golden Amazon' SF series was still going strong, with the stories being issued in paperback by Canadian publisher Harlequin Books. In November 1956, he married his fiancée Carrie Worth, and sought to launch a new career as a dramatist, writing stageplays, television scripts, and radio plays. He was Actor-Manager of his own theatrical group, 'The Good Companions'. By 1959, he had returned to writing detective and western novels, in addition to his theatrical and science fiction work for the *Star Weekly*. He also made both amateur and professional films, the latter including a short drama made for the N.S.P.C.C featuring himself and his wife as erring parents who go out for the evening, leaving their very young children alone at home.

This amazing burst of energy and creativity was to have a tragic result. In September 1960, Fearn died of a sudden heart attack. His passing went unnoticed by British fandom, and it wasn't for some time that people realized that they had lost one of their most dedicated writers, when I reported the fact in one of Ken Slater's Fantast (Medway) catalogues. He left a grieving widow and an incredible cache of manuscripts, which were only rediscovered in 1982, since when I have been arranging their posthumous publication (as detailed later in this book). Until his later posthumous success, Fearn was perceived at the time as having been one of the authors who were, in the words of Gordon Landsborough, "mangled by the stubby-fingered men with the cheque books."

The national printers' strike was the final blow to the junk paperback publishers. Only the better houses survived. The Squire companies were almost dead by the time the last 'Karl Maras' novel appeared in December 1954. The worst of them all, Gannet Press, was sold to Birkenhead-based printers, Merseyside Press, who continued to print novels under the new 'Teal Press' imprint. An attempt at a weird magazine was made in late 1955 with *Weird World*, but this only lasted for two issues before the strike killed it, and the proposed companion SF magazine, *Fantastic World*, never appeared.

But this was not the end of Gannet: after the printing strike was over they re-emerged and moved into the dubious field of 'men's magazines'. They launched a 60-page digest-sized magazine *Fiesta*, containing near-nude photographs and suggestive texts. The title became notorious, and under successive owners was to run for more than 40 years and spawn many competitors—another unsavoury legacy of the 'Vultures of the Void'! The 'underground' market for nude photography and 'art studies' available in 'plain brown envelopes' had been around for years (page Benson Herbert's Utopian Press) and had in fact always been closely aligned with the publishers of sleazy gangster fiction. Sometimes, as with Herbert, books and magazines were issued simply as a cover or marketing device for their underlying sleazy photographic operations. Barrington Gray, for instance, actually issued in 1953 a paperback 'special edition' of the venerable 'banned' book, *Awful Disclosures of Maria Monk*. Revealingly, *nowhere in the book was any publisher or printer listed*, but inside its demure cover of a young nun at prayer were four glossy pages advertising dozens of 'English and Continental nude art books' available from the address of 'The English

Magazine Co, Ltd'. This dubious enterprise was hilariously satirized at the time by Spike Milligan in his BBC radio series *The Goon Show*, with Peter Sellers posing as a 'keen art student' in his 'Major Bloodnok' persona!

With Gannet and Scion among the last of the pulp companies to fold, the 'mushroom boom' was finished, and the cheaply-produced, garishly-packaged paperback novel finally vanished from the newsstands.

An era had ended, as ignominiously as it had begun.

In 1970 Gordon Landsborough reflected on its passing in a tailpiece to his memoirs, which until now has remained unpublished:

> It's curious, but though I have always been attracted to science fiction and have always nibbled at it in my publishing career, I have never seriously tried to write for this market. And the truth? What I could write wouldn't satisfy me. I'm not capable of the inventiveness, the rich imagination that is demanded of good SF. I'm no Asimov, and if I can't be I won't try.
>
> Yet in my second spell at Panther (1955) I remember starting a story that began, 'A practiced sweep of his hand before him, and his electronic zip smoothly opened him to the marble basin that hadn't changed functionally in the course of centuries. As he leaned there in relief he asked wearily of no one, "All this progress yet still our bodies have all their bothersome habits. Why can't we do something about functions?" And from a cubicle someone unseen moaned, "You can say that again, brother." No, not Asimov. And I think I must have been taking the mickey, and no action will be taken if anyone wishes to continue this saga. Incidentally the title of this story was 'The Electronic Fly'.
>
> I was, in any event, too busy reading SF (and other stories) to find time for the deep thought required to write to self-satisfying standards. A curious effect of all that editorial reading was a feeling that outside our own *Authentic* no one was writing any good SF at all. The truth was that I saw so much of bad SF writing, particularly on the part of other publishers in this fringe field, that it seemed to me at times that only bad SF was published. I just didn't have much time to seek out the better stuff that was buried in the mire. And yet I must have done because by 1955, when I was pushing Hamilton's 'Panther' series into the big league, I was a John Wyndham fan, I'd read Bradbury, Heinlein, Asimov and others. I'd read some American SF paperbacks, too—a big improvement on the John Spencer-Curtis Warren SF standards—but already I detected a formula approach to much of the writing. I had too little time for leisure reading, and was only vaguely aware of trends

and movements in the SF world, particularly the SF magazine world.

There were always comings and goings. I wonder how many commercial (as distinct from fanzine) magazines were published in the early 1950s? I seem to remember quite a number, from *Vargo Statten's SF Magazine* to *Science Fantasy* and *New Worlds*.

'Vargo Statten' was, of course, our old and prolific friend, John Russell Fearn from Blackpool. Scion had given him that name, just as they dug up names for all their authors. I don't know why it was, but the vogue at the time for SF *nom de plumes* was generally highly Germanic. 'Karl Ziegfried' and 'Volsted Gridban' (ah, the joyous imagination behind those names) are examples to support this thesis, and I am sure I could think of others if they were worth remembering.

I didn't think much of the *Vargo Statten* magazine, but then I felt it was in a direction away from the rich future of SF publishing. I believe some of the other publishing companies also turned out so-called SF magazines—I seem to remember John Spencer having several—but as they were written down more for the juvenile market they didn't last.

New Worlds and *Science Fantasy* were much nobler efforts, of course. Here editors were trying, though I will say that at times the writing was so obscure I couldn't pretend to understand some of the stories.

I knew the editor of *New Worlds* well—John Carnell. 'Ted', as we knew him in the war years, has contributed far more to the present healthy state of SF writing and publishing in the U.K. than he has been credited with. John Carnell wouldn't lower his standards at a time when the commercial interests were destroying the market with their rubbish; all those years—and how long they seemed—he kept his patience, struggled on a shoestring and strove for better writing. It must have been heartbreaking, yet I never saw John in any mood other than genial and pleasant.

I first met John Carnell aboard a Dutch ship travelling across the Indian Ocean. It was manned by a Javanese crew, and we were chased up the coast of Madagascar by a Japanese submarine. John had something to do with the Signal Corps, I think, but somehow had got himself attached to the Navy and as such was issued with a daily tot of ship's rum. On occasions he was gracious enough to give me a sipper.

Just like John, even aboard a crowded troopship he was in publishing—he brought out a ship's newspaper. As I had a typewriter with me, the cunning Carnell enlisted me on the editorial staff but ensured that any work that went through my typewriter was his. Through the years as a publisher I have met him, sometimes in his role as literary agent (I bought two William F. Temple 'Martin Magnus' SF books from him in 1968), sometimes because of *New Worlds.*

Another man who has made a more forceful contribution to SF publishing than is generally realised is Gerald Pollinger, the literary agent. As a member of the British Interplanetary Society Gerald had an acute interest in SF, and I can tell you he pushed SF manuscripts with vigour in an effort to see them in print. I will never forget one day Gerald saying to me, "But there's no problem in putting a man on the moon. If they wanted to, they could do it in a dozen years." That was in 1955. I didn't believe him.

1955 came and with it a virtually new era in publishing. Paper was in plentiful supply because rationing had ended in June 1953 (though printing facilities were still hard to come by, and Pan Books bought a tank-landing-craft so they could print in France and sail their books to England).

With Panther Books and, later, Four Square Books I published little SF—Heinlein for Panther, I remember—but the late 1950s were awkward times. There wasn't much demand for SF, and I am convinced it was because of the rubbish prior to 1955. It had completely soured the market and we had to live down the reputation that SF was for moronic juveniles. The Trade told me flatly they didn't want SF, they'd had their fingers burned. Yet today millions of SF hardbacks and paperbacks are sold annually, the Trade's cash registers tinkling happily, so the market was there all the time.

What we were waiting for around 1955, though we did not realise it at the time, was the emergence of a good SF writer. When they appeared, the market was created. But good SF writers take time to emerge and must have encouragement, so it was not until the end of the 1950s that publishers and the distribution trade began to see a change that suggested possibilities. The early sixties threw up some exciting authors, but it is not my mandate to write on that period.

After *Authentic* I never really made any great efforts to publish SF—odd forays, that was all. The occasional SF book when I was managing Four Square paperbacks, though I did revive the *Tarzan* series and quite quickly sold a million copies: hardly the sophisticated SF I wanted to publish in the 1950s. I went into children's paperback publishing, and here I published an excellent Arthur C. Clarke—*Dolphin Island*—but also virtually rewrote eight Tarzans and four Edgar Rice Burroughs Martian series. I was planning to enlarge the children's SF list and bought two W. F. Temple's for it, but then sold the company at the end of 1969.

Possibly the most dramatic indication of SF's possibilities (and one largely forgotten now) came in 1954. The BBC televised an SF serial, *Quatermass*. The inventive fantasy gripped the nation. It was the most successful TV serial that had ever been screened. All it indicated was that young and old were fascinated by science fantasy, which so many said was limited in its appeal.

The crazy years of publishing ended about 1955. One day others may tell of the astonishingly vigorous SF that grew out of that dunghill.

By March 1956, the pulp period was finished, but Britain had four surviving SF magazines: *New Worlds, Science-Fantasy, Authentic,* and *Nebula.* The first two were still edited by John Carnell. There had been a hiatus in 1953, just as Nova was trying to expand their programme. John Carnell takes up the Nova magazines story once again, at the point where things seemed to go from bad to worse:

Our new printer continued to procrastinate—we discovered that he was, in fact, only an agent with no presses of his own, who 'farmed' everything out to other printers who only kept their word to him when he had paid previous invoices. Issue 22 of *New Worlds* went on being delayed, proofs finally turning up in August. Even then production continued to be delayed and each month I would phone to alter the dateline on the issue. By November, when delivery was definitely promised, we had decided to label it Winter 1953-54, but the year ended without any copies of the magazine being available.

While this crippling situation was continuing, events were occurring elsewhere which were to have a profound effect on the magazines, the company, and myself. Quite by chance, I met a colleague, Maurice Goldsmith, who was a freelance science reporter at the time, working on assignments for the Odhams Press national weekly, *Illustrated.* Over a beer and a sandwich, he suggested we work out a picture-story spread about SF, including Nova covers and company information, a conference of authors, and a fan get-to-gether. The author conference was arranged at Arthur Clarke's home in North London, and comprised Arthur; William Temple; John Beynon Harris (John Wyndham); Sam Youd (John Christopher); David McIlwain (Charles Eric Maine); Bertram Chandler, who happened to be in port at the time; Ted Tubb; and myself. We arranged a fan gathering with the Medway SF Club at Gravesend, Kent, where there were some leggy camp followers who would make good photographic copy. The whole built up to an interesting four-page spread, which, at least, did not discredit SF.

As we learned later, the appearance of the article coincided with investigations being made by Maclaren & Sons Ltd., a technical trade publishing house that was looking for new outlets. One of their directors, John Copeman, followed up the *Illustrated* story, and called to see Frank Cooper at his new shop in Holborn for a general discussion of the SF field. Frank, perhaps looking a little deeper into his crystal ball than usual, was not overly keen on the possibilities of a takeover bid being made at that time, despite Nova's growing difficulties, or a rival entering the lists, so was not very helpful. John Copeman, however, persisted by discovering my address and inviting me to lunch with his co-directors for a general discussion.

The outcome of that discussion was that I was offered a full-time editorial post to produce a new monthly SF magazine. The prospect was dazzling, but I felt that my commitments and loyalty to Nova were far too strong, and the goodwill which had been built up over the previous years far too great to want to become a rival to my own friends and colleagues. I explained this in turning down the offer. Maclaren's then pursued the possibility of recapitalizing Nova Publications and of incorporating the magazine within the framework of their new publishing group, whose offices were on the border of Fleet Street and the Strand. To this effect, a shareholders meeting was called towards the end of the year, at which all these proposals were evaluated. These were: that the existing shares lost their voting power but received a fixed interest of 6% per annum; that Maclaren's, under one of their holding companies, took over the entire administration of all Nova's affairs; that a new Board of Directors was formed, comprised of three Maclaren directors, and John Beynon Harris, Leslie Flood, and myself; that I become a fulltime, salaried editorial director to produce *New Worlds* on a monthly basis and *Science-Fantasy* bi-monthly.

There was a great deal of discussion, some opposition, considerable disappointment at the thought of a fan-oriented company ceasing to exist as such, but final agreement to the fact that if any circumstances could make a success of British SF magazines, these appeared to be the most promising. The meeting voted in favour and the wheels were put in motion for myself to join the parent company in February. The first of the monthly issues of *New Worlds Science Fiction*, as it was then to be called, were to be ready for distribution in March.

Meanwhile, what of the existing and abortive issue 22, which was still in the hands of the Carlton Press at 'Racket' Court? An advance (sic) copy was sent to me in the middle of January, showing the enigmatic date '1953' on the contents page and, as such, completely useless for 1954 distribution. I refused delivery on behalf of Nova Publications and when Carlton Press rattled the sabre and began to utter threats, put the whole matter in the lap of Maclaren's, who turned it over to their legal department. At one time in the months that followed, an injunction was brought against the printing works who had actually printed the magazine for Carlton Press, to stop them from selling the issue in bulk to obtain their payment and when, some eighteen months later, the case was settled out of court and in Nova's favour, the entire print run was destroyed under supervision. The only surviving copy to my knowledge, is the 'advance' copy I received. I suppose it could be one of the rarest of collectors' items.

Looking at it now, and just for the record, the contents were: 'This Precious Stone', by 'H. J Murdoch' (a pseudonym of Jim M'Intosh); 'Only an Echo', by Alan Barclay, 'Come Away Home', by Francis G. Rayer, 'The Perfect Secretary', by J. F. Burke; 'All Glory Forgotten', by Kenneth Bulmer; and 'Museum Piece', by John Christopher; an article 'Radiac', by John Newman, editorial by myself; book reviews and the Literary Line-up. The cover painting, spaceship in orbit around Mars, by Gerard Quinn, was subsequently used on *Science-Fantasy* #13, and all the editorial matter and blocks were used in various issues of *New Worlds Science Fiction* during 1954, as any checklist will show.

Once I had taken over editorial residence with the Maclaren group, things moved fast. Immediately to hand were departments in advertising, copy layout, accounts, publicity, distribution, a photographic studio, plus a warehouse and complete distribution facilities. This meant that communication lines were short and under one roof so I could concentrate mainly upon editorial matters. To this end it was decided that we should strengthen the already existing story material by publishing three-part serials in *New Worlds SF*, buying from the fast-developing American book market to start with, and thereby bringing 'name' authors. The first book obtained was Cyril Kornbluth's *Take-Off* (still a favourite of mine), which commenced in new-deal #22. Arthur Clarke's story, 'The Sentinel', from which part of the background idea in the film *2001: A Space Odyssey* was developed, headed stories by Wyndham, Christopher, and M'Intosh, and a science article by Maurice Goldsmith indirectly acknowledged the debt I owed him.

Under the guidance of the parent company, which had been publishing for over seventy years, the trade took kindly to the new set-up, and with circulation assured, I was able to devote more and more time to editorial matters. Further American serials were arranged—Wilson Tucker's *Wild Talent* and *The Time Masters*, and Charles Dye's *Prisoner in the Skull*; much later a serial which became Philip K. Dick's first major hardcover novel, *Time Out of Joint*. Before the latter, however, British authors provided new serials for *New Worlds SF*, the first being Ted Tubb's *Star Ship*, followed by Kenneth Bulmer, John Brunner, Charles Eric Maine, James White, and others who were fast becoming prominent. At the same time, I began to buy new stories unpublished in the United Kingdom from the United States for both magazines—Robert Sheckley, Lester del Rey, C. M. Kornbluth, Judith Merril, Horace L. Gold, and our first Australian contributor, Frank Bryning. The plan was to make *New Worlds SF* as international as possible, and at the same time to show potentially new British writers the quality of stories we required and give readers the very best SF available. *New Worlds SF* at last had entered its golden age, which only began to falter in 1959, when import restrictions were lifted and our Commonwealth market began to disintegrate.

Science-Fantasy, fitting in well as a bi-monthly, was wide open for experimental ideas, leaning primarily towards fantasy but, despite a far higher literary standard than *New Worlds SF* averaged, never had quite the same popularity. It may have been because the policy fell somewhere between the fantasy of *Unknown Worlds* and the macabre of *Weird Tales*. It may have been because the stories were generally light in texture, and a leaning towards horror might have increased circulation. Introducing stories by American authors Fritz Leiber, Jerome Bixby, Wilson Tucker, Mildred Clingerman, Marion Zimmer Bradley, and Britain's own John Brunner, Brian Aldiss, and J. G. Ballard, still did not produce the sales figures we would all have liked.

To offset this, it was decided to relaunch 'Nova Novels', this time as a regular paperback series. The first two titles published were A. E. van Vogt's *The Weapon Shops of Isher* and Wilson Tucker's *The City in the Sea*, followed two months later by Theodore Sturgeon's *The Dreaming Jewels* and James Blish's *Jack of Eagles*. The titles were good ones; the covers by Gerard Quinn were tasteful and well suited for a better-class paperback market. The plan was to publish two titles a month for eight months a year. The first two appeared in November 1954, the second two in January 1955. The only trouble was that we could not get adequate distribution! The magazines went through the newspaper/magazine distributing channels to end up mainly in newsagents, where paperback sales were limited to westerns, thrillers, and romances; paperbacks had to go through book buying channels to end up primarily (then) in bookshops and on the big railway station bookstalls. The big book buyers like W. H. Smith & Sons, Wymans, and others, only just beginning to experience the first impacts of the paperback explosion, were not sympathetic toward science fiction, and refused to buy. So the series was discontinued, virtually stillborn. If we had launched it five years later, it would have been overwhelmingly successful.

Thus it was that as the paperback boom came to a grinding halt in February 1956, *New Worlds SF* was going through a golden age, with a hardcore of British talent, supplemented by a strong selection of American reprints. *Science-Fantasy* was publishing many excellent stories, the makeup of the magazine enabling authors to develop ideas and storylines to a greater standard. Carnell did British SF the greatest of services with his magazines—a fact insufficiently acknowledged by the SF establishment.

Sadly, however, the magazines began to fall in circulation in the early 1960s, and a meeting of directors in December 1963 concluded with the decision to fold the magazines and finish Nova Publications. The magazines were picked up by another company, Roberts and Vinter, and opened yet another chapter in their history (a chapter that changed the face of science fiction totally), but it was only through the original fans who launched Nova that the chance ever arose, and John Carnell closed his memoir with a tribute "to all the founder shareholders of the original company and to the many SF friends who contributed advice, assistance, criticism, and enthusiasm when they lacked hard cash. It was their ideal which accomplished the fact. I can only be eternally grateful to them for the opportunity of acting as their managing editor."

With the close of his 141-issue period between 1946 and 1964 as editor of *New Worlds*, Carnell took up another challenge, an original anthology series, *New Writings in SF*, which he edited between 1964 and 1972, for twenty-one volumes, right up until the time of his death on March 23, 1972. Carnell, more than anyone else, had proved that British SF was comparable in standard to the best anywhere in the world.

While *New Worlds SF* was forging ahead, and planning a third magazine companion, *Science Fiction Adventures*, in 1957, that was the year that *Nebula* finally went monthly. The long and honourable history of the magazine has already been covered by Ken Bulmer in his earlier essay. The quality of the magazine was shown by a peak circulation of

50,000, but the unsteady foundation on which *Nebula* was based began to crumble, and an attempt to gain newsstand circulation in the United States failed, after which the magazine was forced to fold in June 1959 after forty-one excellent and fondly-remembered issues.

Nowadays, there are no magazines left that survived the 1950s. *New Worlds* did survive, appearing sporadically over the years, but in several unrecognizable formats compared to that from the 1950s. Perhaps the last pages in the history of that magazine are yet to be written. Certainly only a few of the paperback publishers survived after 1956. Modern Fiction Ltd. carried on for a few years on the strength of their successful 'Ben Sarto' gangster novels, and Harborough Press continued into the 1960s, reprinting controversial and provocative mainstream hardcover novels under their 'Ace Books' UK imprint, but only three of them survived for any significant length of time.

One of the survivors was Brown-Watson Ltd., who moved their premises to Digit House, and began to issue their novels under the Digit imprint in 1957. Their lists included a number of SF novels, excellent reprints from America, including Asimov, Heinlein, Kuttner, Williamson, etc., coupled with a number of original novels of widely varying quality. A number of former Nova writers like Bulmer and Rayer sold 'fix-up' novels based on their magazine stories, but Digit were still prone to revert to type, and provided a late market for forgettable novels by Thomas Wade and a few others of the former era. They were never quite able to shake off their down-market image, and their financial backers were apparently unable or unwilling to upgrade sufficiently to compete with their larger competitors. In the 1970s, they resorted to reprinting their old westerns reissued under various new series headings and imprints such as 'Sabre Books'. Eventually they became a producer of children's books and TV tie-in annuals, the company changing hands many times since its launch back in 1945.

Astonishingly, John Spencer & Co. survived into the 1990s, diversifying into technical manuals, and occasionally reissuing some of their old fantasy and western and detective novels, often under new titles and bylines, or licensing them for reprint abroad (naturally without the knowledge of, or payment to, their authors). They became notorious for their retrograde 'Badger Books' imprint, which they launched in the late 1950s, and which ran for many years, mainly because they had no competition at the lower ends of the market.

After they had folded their SF magazines in 1954, they had begun a new magazine, *Supernatural Stories* in May 1954, closely followed by *Out of This World* in October. These two magazines were written almost single-handedly by John Glasby at first, but both stopped in 1955. *Supernatural Stories* was relaunched in 1957, along with a new SF series, and for the next nine years, Lionel Fanthorpe kept up an output of stupendous proportions, which produced around 150 books. Even more prolific was John Glasby, who also wrote quite a few SF and supernatural selections, as well as writing thrillers, romances, westerns, and almost all of the World War II line into the 1970s.

Hamilton & Co. provided the final link to the 1950s. Panther Books, following their 1955 revivification by Gordon Landsborough, continued for many years as a reprint publisher, spending large sums to secure the paperback rights to hardcover best sellers in all genres, eventually becoming part of the giant Granada Publishing Group, and then as Grafton Books after being taken over by the giant Harper Collins empire. They were the last link between SF and the mushroom publishers, so although their products effectively ended in February 1956, the fall of *Authentic Science Fiction* completes their story, and the final editor's essay (which I had originally commissioned for *Vision of Tomorrow*) is provided by Ted Tubb, who took over from Bert Campbell. Campbell had resigned after years of struggle and thirty-eight much-improved issues, in order to pursue his career in scientific research.

Ted Tubb describes his period of editorship:

> Early in 1956, Bert Campbell, owing to the pressure of other commitments, resigned as editor and suggested that I take over. I had been writing a great deal of the magazine and, as he put it, "you've been filling it so how about running it?" The opportunity was too good to be missed, and in March 1956 I became editor of *Authentic Science Fiction*.
>
> For the first time, I had an opportunity to see the other side of the picture. Up until then I had been a freelance writer, submitting material which was either accepted or rejected and that, as far as I was concerned, was the end of it. The editing, selecting, choice and all the other details which go into the production of a magazine was something I knew nothing about.
>
> Fortunately, there was one thing I did not have to worry about—the

firm had a very good printer who was used to working to instruction. What was left was the choosing of stories, articles, artwork, the balancing of the magazine and the necessity of making sure that all the material fitted into the space available. The system used did not include a 'dummy'. The result was that I had to be extremely careful as to word counts and page numbering, all of which took time.

The policy of the previous editor had been to use a great deal of 'feature' material in each issue, at times as high a proportion as one feature to each story, a balance which I felt to be undesirable in a fiction magazine. However, adjusting it wasn't as easy as I'd imagined. For one thing, submitted material of a good quality was low and for another, the money available to buy it was limited. The maximum that I could spend on the contents of any one issue, aside from artwork, was £100. Artwork came under a separate department and, while it was available, was a great asset, but the quantity was limited to two full-page illustrations an issue. The use of features, with supplied photographs, had eked out this allowance, cutting them down meant losing that advantage.

I offset this a little by the use of filler blocks, small illustrations which could be used many times to fill out the end of a page and so relieve the solid mass of typescript which would otherwise have become overpowering. I also experimented with various typefaces for the title headings and used repeat illustrations for the various departments such as the editorial, book reviews, etc. As regards the use of alternative typefaces, I had to compromise. The printer could only use what he stocked, so again I was limited as regards to layout.

The biggest bugbear was in the submitted material.

I used a simple system by which every manuscript received was noted in a book, the title, author, date of receipt, date of acceptance or rejection, and it was a wise precaution. Another asset for any editor is patience. A third, which he quickly learns, is how to scan a typescript. I specify typescript, stories sent carefully written by hand do not even get read. It is hard but true, and there are good reasons for this practice. For one thing, it is very hard to read the majority of people's handwriting, for another it is equally impossible to run a word count, and even if the story is the best thing ever written, it still has to be typed in order for the printer to set it.

So first, sitting before a heap of submissions, came the initial check. Handwritten, single-spaced, typed both sides of the paper—all out. I used to send them back with an explanatory note.

Second came the appearance of the manuscript. The dirty first page, the rusted staples, the dog-eared corners. This, if nothing else, told me that it had been around for some time. They were scanned, but the odds were against them and never once did I find a useable story among them

The remainder were given the same treatment—scanned at first, read through if the initial impression was good. And if anyone says that such a practice is unfair, let me say that I quickly found that there was no other way to do it. If a story is interesting, it will hold the interest from the beginning. Many of them did that, to sag in the middle and flop at the end. Some, perhaps, picked up halfway through, but then it was too late. Others showed promise and, all too rarely, one stood out and grabbed the interest.

Because of the limited funds available, and because I wanted to provide the maximum wordage, I was forced to adopt a sliding scale of payment. Maximum was two guineas for First British Serial Rights, payment on publication. The lowest was a little less, a new author did not get as much as an established one, adjustments were made as to length, etc. In order to cut out some of the quite unnecessary and time-wasting work I had to do, I published the correct method of submission in an editorial, but that, too, was wasted effort. Effort that was not wasted but which had to be done was the necessary revisions I had to do in order to adapt many of the stories for publication. I felt that it was better to accept and revise them than to return for rewrites. For one thing, it saved time and, being a writer myself, I knew how it felt to be asked to do more work for the rewards offered. Revisions were always minor and consisted of tightening beginnings, cutting out a line or two of narrative and repetitive dialogue, altering scientific discrepancies where they occurred (for example, changing the word galaxy to solar system when it was obvious that was what the author meant). Always, when doing this, I was careful not to impress my own ideas on those of the author or to add material of my own.

The main necessity to revise was mostly to adjust the length. Because of the system used, this was important and I quickly discovered that many authors had no real idea as to the length of submissions. To overestimate was as common as to underestimate and as bad from my point of view. I had to gauge just how many pages a story would fill, to allow for title headings, to arrange the material in order of final presentation, to provide space for artwork and also to provide various items that could be dropped if my assessment was wrong. In a sense, it was like fitting a jigsaw together and though arduous, it was interesting and a challenge to see if things came out exactly as planned.

In March 1957, the magazine changed size and format in a bid to attract a larger readership. With less pages, it still carried an average of 50,000 words of fiction plus extra artwork, the editorial, a feature article, and book reviews—and still operating on the same budget. The editorial, book reviews, answers to any letters, and various feature items were all part of the editorial duties and at times I also had to include fiction of my own, both in order to fill out the magazine and to remain within the budget. The hoped-for surge of sales did not, unfortunately, materialize and, as an economy measure, interior illustrations were dropped in September of the same year.

Dropping the artwork meant finding more wordage to fill the vacant pages and the word count of that issue was 53,250 plus departments. The next was a thousand more, but that issue was also the last.

Authentic Science Fiction died not because it was losing money, in fact it made a profit, but because the publishers decided that the money tied up in it could be put to better use in the publication of paperbacks, in their 'Panther Books' series.

I was sorry to see it go. Despite all the work and the subtle danger haunting a writer who becomes an editor; the unconscious refusal to use ideas he has read, the sharpening of his critical faculty, the satiation of too much too soon, and the disheartening compromise which has to be made when you publish the best available instead of the stories you want, it was a wonderful experience.'

The passing of *Authentic* severed the last links with the early 1950s publishers, and closed the doors on what had certainly been an extraordinary ten years of publishing, a period of lost opportunity, but definitely an era of entertainment.

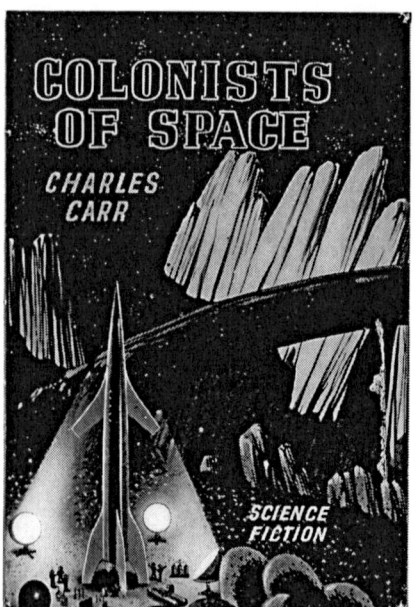

Colonists of Space by Charles Carr (Harold Johns). Ward Lock, 1955

Conditioned for Space by Alan Ash (Ron Embleton). Ward Lock, 1955

The Unseen Assassin by Hank Janson (Reg Heade and Ron Turner). Top Fiction, 1953

Creature from the Black Lagoon by Vargo Statten (John Richards). Dragon, 1954.

Photo: John Russell Fearn
and Carrie Fearn, 1957

Photo: L to R: Sam Youd, David
McIlwain, William F. Temple, Bertram
Chandler, Arthur C. Clarke, E.C. Tubb.
Illustrated (weekly), 12 September 1953

The Dreaming Jewels by Theodore
Sturgeon (Gerard Quinn). Nova, 1955

"Dead Weight" by Douglas West
(Josh Kirby). *Authentic SF # 78*,
Hamilton, 1957

CHAPTER 16:
'A ROSE BY ANY OTHER NAME'

The foregoing chapters have—with deliberate intent—concentrated on the 'Crazy Years' of British science fiction publishing, and on the mushroom publishers and their products in particular.

Many thousands of present day SF fans are probably only dimly aware that such material was ever produced. This volume is intended to hopefully redress that gap in their knowledge, thereby giving them a chance to make up their own minds as to the merits of the stories, without dismissing (as one famous critic did) over 100 of the best of these titles as the work of 'Grub Streeters'. He added, 'none of their writings have established themselves'.

Like most sweeping statements, this generalization does not hold up upon more detailed investigation. However, the same critic was on firmer ground when he added:

> The lesson to be learned from these excellent gentlemen of the pre-Moorcock era is twofold; that while they all had to battle individually (as any writer must) and reach various levels of compromise which affected their quality, they also had to suffer collectively under the opprobrium of writing anything so odd as SF; and that although their battles somewhat aided their successors, readers of today have already forgotten about it. Just as I've forgotten about the twenties and the flourishing SF of the Edwardian era—because I never knew or cared.

This statement succinctly sums up currently prevailing attitudes on this period of British publishing. And while he is right, it seems to me that such opinions have—perhaps unintentionally—helped to perpetuate the idea that *all* of the science fiction published in the early 1950s was bad. That the British publishers of the 1950s were guilty of dragging SF into the mud is undeniable. But were their accomplices, the authors, all equally guilty?

Before examining the assertion (penned in 1970) that none of the writers of the early 1950s 'established themselves', mention must be made of other British SF writers of this period who had a much greater influence on modern SF, and who made an infinitely greater contribution to the present day respectability which SF enjoys. Among this much smaller group of writers were Eric Frank Russell, John Wyndham, and Arthur C. Clarke. All three were actually involved in the crazy years, yet have escaped being 'tainted' by them. They were able to operate powerfully outside the 'ghetto'.

Russell, a brilliant and influential writer, aimed mainly at the American market, and so most of his 1950s writings were outside the scope of this book. His major success in Britain did not come until the later fifties, and his earlier editions, such as *Sinister Barrier* (Cherry Tree, 1951) and *Dreadful Sanctuary* (Museum, 1953), were lost in the mass of mediocrity.

John Wyndham, as the critic also points out, similarly began in America, writing under the pseudonym 'John Beynon Harris'. However, he courageously struck out under a purely English style, writing as John Wyndham in 1949, and his novel *The Day of the Triffids* is justly famous today. *Triffids* and the novels that followed won over the Establishment critics, and opened doors that allowed later authors to come through doors that might have remained closed. Yet, when his early classic, *Stowaway to Mars* was published in paperback by Nova in 1953 as part of the paperback explosion (as by John Beynon), it *sank without a trace*, and remained out of print in England for over twenty years, until Walter Gillings and myself brought about its republication with an attribution to John Wyndham, since which time it has remained constantly in print.

Arthur C. Clarke towers above all of the writers mentioned in this book. His achievements are such as to require little explanation here. Nor could I improve on the masterly assessment made by Brian W. Aldiss in *The Shape of Further Things*:

'Clarke alone in the American magazines talked in an English tone of voice, his space heroes returned to London rather than New York . . . He has fought and won his own battles, too. And bigger battles, at that. If the going is better for the rest of us as writers, much of this is due to Clarke.'

All three could have written for the likes of Scion, Curtis Warren, and the others. They chose not to, and everyone can be mightily grateful for that. But other writers of worth either did not possess their genius, or never had the opportunity to even attempt to follow their example. Just think . . . if Clarke's *Childhood's End* had been published under the pseudonym 'Bengo Mistral,' the whole course of British SF might have been changed!

But, interestingly, the stigma which was attached to British paperback SF in the 1950s—which has effectively inhibited its reprinting in England—was really only confined to Britain and America. In continental Europe, readers were unaware of the odium associated with cheapjack British publishing. Further, although these countries had their own traditions and SF history, there was little cognizance of Western 'popular' SF literature. But, just as the pulp era of American SF ofttimes painfully but finally triumphantly spread the seeds of SF appreciation to Britain, so the product of 'The Crazy Years' (analogous to Britain's 'Pulp Era') spread across the English Channel. Starting in France, it spread like wildfire; no doubt, the more acerbic critics when confronted with this historical fact would liken the phenomenon to that of weeds being transported into an adjoining garden!

One of the prime movers in the popularization of SF in France was Georges Gallet, a fan from pre-war days who had actually succeeded in launching a science fiction magazine when the war broke out. Returning from service, he started Le Rayon Fantastique in 1951, a paperback series published by Hatchette of Paris.

Gallet can fairly be recognized as a Gallic equivalent to Carnell or Gillings. His series introduced a mixture of both American and British authors to the continent: Williamson, C. L. Moore, Sturgeon, Temple, Wyndham, Clarke. The success of Le Rayon Fantastique prompted the Fleuve Noir Press to bring out another SF series, Anticipation (still going strong), a handsome series of thick, chunky paperback editions with colourful card covers, initially printing original French SF. Then they began to feature translations of 'Vargo Statten' novels with increasing frequency. The 'Statten' novels were a huge success. Long after 'Vargo Statten' had ceased to be published in England, with the fadeout of Scion, translations were featured in the French series.

The French editions were in turn translated into Italian, Danish, Portuguese and German. There is reason to believe that 'Statten' was, in fact, thought to be French, so that the stories were judged on their own merit, and did not suffer from any preconceived stigmatization. The contents page of French and Italian SF magazines were, by 1958, boasting stories by all the leading American and British SF writers, including Asimov, Heinlein, Clarke, Wyndham . . . and 'Vargo Statten'!

The success of 'Statten' opened the door for E. C. Tubb, who went on to blaze an even brighter trail across Europe. Every single one of his many Scion, Panther, Curtis, and Milestone novels saw one or more translations, long after their original English publishers had disappeared. Other good writers, such as Kenneth Bulmer and H. J. Campbell, were similarly translated. Inevitably, given a booming European market and a shortage of indigenous writers for a 'new' type of fiction, a few unscrupulous agents unloaded a handful of the poorest British novels published under house names—especially to an insatiable German market, where standards were lower. But there were no translations for 'Bengo Mistral' and others of his ilk.

In 1960 Fearn (who had been selling his novels through The Richard Steele Agency, having reclaimed their copyright from the defunct Scion Ltd.) suddenly died from a heart attack at the age of fifty-two. The 'Statten' byline faded out, although 1950s novels by Tubb and others continued to circulate and flourish.

Childhood's End by Arthur C. Clarke
(Deborah Jones).
Sidgwick & Jackson, 1954

Sinister Barrier by Eric Frank Russell
(Terry Maloney). Kemsley, 1952

Heure Zero, Part 1 (*Zero Hour*) by Vargo
Statten (unidentified). Aredit, 1975

Heure Zero, Part 2 (*Zero Hour*) by Vargo
Statten (unidentified). Aredit, 1976

Planeta Maldito (The Catalyst) by Vargo Statten (unidentified). Tecnoprint Grafica, S.A., 1957

Den usynlige Fjende (Decreation) by Vargo Statten (unidentified). NYT Dansk Forlag, 1958

Saat Der Vernichtung (Pandora's Box) by E.C. Tubb (unidentified). Moewig Verlag, 1960

Objectif Pollux (Star Born) by E.C. Tubb (unidentified). Ditis, 1960

CHAPTER 17:
VISION OF TOMORROW:
DEATH OF A DREAM

During the 1950s, I had become a great fan of the works of both John Russell Fearn and E. C. Tubb, two prolific British authors who had first introduced me to science fiction in 1954. By 1958, I had discovered that Fearn had enjoyed an earlier career in the American pulps, his first novel *The Intelligence Gigantic* having been serialized in *Amazing Stories* in 1933. More than one hundred and twenty of his stories had been published in nearly all of the SF pulp magazines through to 1948, and I was striving to obtain a collection of all his work, my intention being to publish a complete bibliography and tribute book.

Eventually discovering his address in August 1959 from his then-current publisher, the Toronto *Star Weekly*, I wrote to him at his Blackpool home with details of my researches, asking him to confirm a number of hitherto-unattributed pseudonyms I had guessed to be him, and asking him to reveal any new ones I had missed. I was thrilled to receive a swift and cordial reply:

> "Many thanks for your long and pleasant letter of the 28th August, but to take care of all the details asked for may occupy some little time—so please accept this letter as an interim acknowledgement whilst I get myself 'organized'.
>
> I'll reply in full at a later date, and if it takes a little time don't be disturbed. I'll answer in full at the earliest opportunity.
>
> Meantime, many thanks for your interest, and with best wishes.
> Sincerely yours,
> John Russell Fearn."

Fearn kept his promise and sent me a longer letter in December, with much useful information, promising a further letter to "bring your information more up to date." Alas, it was the last letter I would receive from him.

Dismayed by the premature death of Fearn (at 52) in 1960, before I had his promised further reply, and before I could meet him, I had tirelessly researched Fearn's work, unravelling dozens of hitherto unrecorded pseudonyms (mostly outside of the SF field), and had promoted and analysed his stories (and those of Tubb, who was very much alive, and still writing) both in fanzines and in self-published pamphlets. As I accumulated more information, these pamphlets grew in size and elaboration, until in 1968 (with the help of my mother, who gave me £200 to meet the professional printing costs) I published an entire 50,000 word printed book, *The Multi-Man*, which was both a biography and annotated bibliography of Fearn.

This book—and my earlier 1964 pamphlet, *E. C. Tubb—An Evaluation* came to the attention of Australian Ron Graham, who, whilst becoming a successful mining engineer and owner of the Graham Group of companies in New South Wales, had by repute the largest collection of science fiction books and magazines in Australia. And by a quirk of fate, John Russell Fearn was also his favourite author . . .

Following the publication of *The Multi-Man*, there was a flurry of interest amongst a few UK publishers in reprinting Fearn's work, led by Peter Haining, Senior Editor at New English Library. I was asked to supply a copy of Fearn's Vargo Statten novel *Creature From the Black Lagoon*, which Haining had remembered reading, and also to assemble for them a representative collection of his short stories from the pulp magazines. I passed my selection (*Deserted Universe and Other Stories*) to Haining, also providing him with Mrs. Fearn's Blackpool address. I left it to him to approach Mrs. Fearn for the necessary copyright permissions. Although I had been corresponding with her husband up to the time of his sudden death, I had never received any replies to my subsequent letters and enclosures to his widow—somewhat to my chagrin and puzzlement.

What I did not know at the time, was that following her husband's sudden death from a heart attack (coming only 5 years after the death of her first husband) Mrs. Fearn had herself fallen seriously ill, her condition exacerbated by her profound grief at being twice bereaved in a short space of time. She also suffered from severe arthritis in her right hand, which made holding a pen and writing letters an extremely painful business. Little wonder that my letters—and countless others from fans and publishers alike—had gone unanswered.

Haining later told me that not only had his own letters gone unanswered, but that although he had even tried sending a representative to call on Mrs. Fearn, to discuss matters, he had been refused admission to her home. (Mrs. Fearn later denied this story to me.) Haining concluded that nothing further could be done, and eventually he returned my book and pulp magazines (after craftily photocopying their entire contents for possible use in his own series of anthologies).

It was also at that time that I was amazed to receive an enthusiastic airmail letter from Ron Graham, in Sydney, Australia. Ron was a successful New South Wales businessman, and long-time collector of science fiction. He told me that he had been a life-long fan of Fearn's work, and that he had read *The Multi-Man* and shared my sentiments for the best of Fearn's work to be restored to print. He enquired as to the progress on publishing *Deserted Universe*, which I had optimistically announced as forthcoming, at the end of my book.

I replied to his letter, telling him of the impasse with Mrs. Fearn. Back came a long reply, informing me that Graham was independently wealthy, and was prepared to finance—or co-finance—the publication of Fearn's work himself. Would I be prepared to act as his British representative, and to try to persuade Mrs. Fearn to change her mind? You bet I would!

I telephoned Mrs. Fearn, and spoke to her for the first time. After an awkward initial exchange, she recognised me as having been a former correspondent of her husband—"he did speak about you"—and became more forthcoming. I learned that the reason she had rebuffed the New English Library had been two-fold. Firstly, Haining had not made it sufficiently clear that the royalties from the sale of her husband's books would in fact be paid to her. She had been given the impression that others—including myself—would cash in, without her receiving a penny. Haining had incorrectly assumed that as a writer's widow, Mrs. Fearn would be *au fait* with publishing contracts and conventions.

She wasn't.

Secondly, her own solicitor, whom she had consulted, had actually advised her to *refuse all requests for the reprinting of Fearn's work*, on the grounds that she did not possess any contractual evidence of his authorship for stories appearing under pseudonyms! The *only* exception was his "Golden Amazon" series of novels, published in the Toronto *Star Weekly*, all of them published under his own name, with the copyright notice © *John Russell Fearn*! Her solicitor had wrongly advised her that this was the *only* property she was free to consider offers to reprint!

When I pointed out that this was untrue, and that in the course of my researches, I had already proven Fearn's authorship and title to his pseudonymous works, Mrs. Fearn remained adamant that she would only consider giving permission for the Amazon stories to be reprinted—nothing else. She gave as an additional reason the fact that the Amazon had been her husband's favourite creation, and that if anything should be reprinted, it should be the Amazon, as a tribute to his memory. She and Fearn had married in 1956, by which time he had stopped writing for the pulps, and was concentrating on Amazon novels for the Toronto *Star Weekly*. She had in fact never seen much, if anything, of his earlier magazine work.

I reported the conversation to Graham, who indicated that he would open up formal negotiations with Mrs. Fearn, now that I had established contact. He also advised me that he was interested in publishing novels by such authors as E. C. Tubb and Ken Bulmer, and on learning that I knew these writers—and several others, including William F. Temple—he authorised me to approach them on his behalf.

By 1968, under Carnell's successor as editor, Michael Moorcock, *New Worlds* was pursuing an editorial policy of what became known as the 'New Wave', catering for a very special new readership. Britain no longer had a professional traditional science fiction magazine, a situation that both Graham and I deplored. But it came as quite a surprise to me when Graham told me he wished to publish a new science fiction magazine, and that I should be its editor.

At that time, I had no thought that I would ever be working full-time for Graham, Ever since leaving school in 1959, I had pursued a career in Local Government. Now, at 27, I was working as the Assistant Registrar at a large Technical College in my home town of Wallsend. After three years of our working together, I had recently become engaged to Maureen Doyle, a college departmental secretary. I was head over heels in love, and was actively househunting. None the less, I accepted his offer, believing (rather naively) that I could edit it on a part-time 'hobbyist' basis.

Mindful of the economics and the risk of launching a new magazine, I suggested it should be a reprint magazine, to keep costs to a minimum (i.e using reprints at half the prevailing cost of new material). I had in mind as a model the US pulp, *Fantastic Story Magazine*, which had been very successful in the previous decade, featuring a reprinted novel, together with a mixture of both new and reprint short stories. I proposed to reprint carefully chosen stories by well-known American, as well as British and Commonwealth authors, and to only include such new material as the limited budget permitted. However, my suggested magazine would be in paperback format—along the lines of John Carnell's successful *New Writings In SF* series published by Corgi books. I subscribed to the prevailing view that the traditional magazine format was "dead in the water."

Graham welcomed the idea, and advanced me a sum of money in order to buy reprint rights for him to stories of my choice. I approached Tubb and Bulmer, and bought from them reprint rights to some of their best stories that had appeared in *Nebula* some ten years earlier— 'Into the Empty Dark', 'The Captain's Dog', and 'Talk Not at All' by Tubb, and 'Advertise Your Cyanide' by Bulmer. William F. Temple also provided his original unsold version of 'Echo', a different version of which had recently appeared in the American *Famous Science Fiction*. I also bought reprint rights to Frank Edward Arnold's 1941 pulp story, 'The Twilight People' (mainly to encourage him to write new stories for me, which he promised to do—but never did. Or, at least, he never completed anything of which I was aware.) I had met Frank at the 1965 World Convention in London, and we were in regular correspondence.

Ken Bulmer promptly sent me an excellent unsold novel, *Miniman*. Ted Tubb agreed to accept my commission to expand and rewrite one of his earlier (1954) paperback novels, *Alien Life*—one of my own favourites from his early work. For the proposed magazine, for which I also intended to use American authors, I bought reprint rights to Jack Williamson's 1939 *Thrilling Wonder* short story 'Passage to Saturn', and attempted to trace Donald Wandrei in order to reprint his 1927 *Weird Tales* classic 'The Red Brain'.

I reported progress to Graham, and was astonished to receive a letter saying that he was now contemplating publishing a magazine containing *all-new stories only*. The purchased reprints could still be used, but instead of being used in a magazine, they could now go into a reprint paperback anthology, which I would also edit.

Graham invited my comments and proposals for the new magazine, which he proposed to call *Vision of Tomorrow*. We exchanged several letters, batting ideas backward and forward—including suggested title logos—and the policy for the magazine quickly took shape. It was Graham's sincere, if somewhat idealistic, intention to give a real opportunity for not only British writers but also Australian, Commonwealth and European writers. To reinforce this, American writers would be barred from appearing in the magazine: *I was expressly forbidden to solicit any American mss.* The percentage of stories—subject to availability for the issue on hand—was to be 50% British, 40% Australian, and 10% Commonwealth or European. John Bangsund, a prominent Australian fan, and editor-publisher of *The Australian SF Review,* a highly literate fanzine, was to be hired by Graham as my Australian contact. It would be John's job, as Associate Australian Editor, to solicit and obtain Australian mss, which he would then airmail to me; but the actual decision on buying the Australian material would be mine alone, as the actual editor of the magazine.

All of my letters to and from Graham had been numbered at his suggestion, beginning with 'No.1' and the rapidity of our progression and agreement can be gauged in the following letter I received from him:

LETTER No.9   14th November, 1968
Dear Phil,

I have just received your letter No.10. Firstly, may I say that I was delighted with your design *VISION.* I think this is absolutely tops. I decided on this name myself after much thought. Merv Binns was responsible for the "OF TOMORROW" part.

By now Phil you will have read Letter No.8 and what follows is based on the premise that you will accept the Editorship offered there.

I have now decided definitely that the policy of the magazine will be to print new stories only. Perhaps an exception might be made for Temple's story, but not at least for issue No.1, which will be all new stories only. I would like a new Tubb story for this first issue if you can obtain mss and I will have John get stories from A. Bertram Chandler and John Baxter and perhaps Jack Wodhams for the first issue.

I am seeing issue No.1 as extremely important and it will be worth spending a little extra on this in the way of artists and stories.

If you do accept the editorship you will be completely responsible for the mag except for policy decisions—such as printing new stories only. The decision to have the magazine printed in Britain has been made to enable you to have true liaison with the printer and to be able to get and correct galley proof, paste up the pages for the printer, fill up odd spaces, etc., with some appropriate piece of information or an advertisement (perhaps for our own paperbacks).

We will publish Fearn of course, but in paperback form only, not in the magazine.

Features:

Book Reviews: Yes, and we will probably adopt your idea of having John Bangsund look after this.

Letter Column: No; idea wiped.

Featured Author: Yes; good idea.

Features: I think we will adopt your idea of an article about science fiction Phil and moreover I think that I am competent to do this, and would very much like to as my contribution to the mag. I am probably extremely egotistical, but I feel that I could do this equally as well as Sam Moskowitz.

Glad to note you have contacted Ken Slater and that you are good friends still. I visited Ken when I was in Britain last and have been dealing with him for years. I had already spoken to him about our proposals.

As I mentioned in Letter No.8, I am hoping to be in Britain for the SF Conference next year in company with your goodself and would of course endeavour to meet as many fans and authors as possible and spread the word about *Vision* and our paperbacks.

In conclusion Phil, again many thanks for your conception of *Vision* with which I am delighted.

Anxiously awaiting your reply,

Yours sincerely,
Ron Graham (signed).

I agreed to all of Ron's proposals, and set about looking for material. As an active fan since 1964, I had regularly attended the Annual BSFA Easter Conventions, and had made many contacts within the field, both fan and professional. One of my first contacts was John Carnell, then the leading SF specialist agent.

In recent years Carnell rarely has been given proper credit for the vital role he played in launching and establishing SF in Britain during and after the war—something that the foregoing chapters of this book irrefutably demonstrate. A number of his former clients became mega-successful only after leaving his agency, and have tended to denigrate him as a 'small-time operator' who, rather than helping their career, actually held back their progress and recognition by placing them in lowly markets. This is grossly unfair. It is of course a fact of the literary market place that agents who specialise in genre fiction can only take their clients so far, and that there will inevitably come a time when a truly talented author will need to move to a larger, "general" agent to earn larger rewards and attendant recognition. But that is no reason to bite the hand that fed and nurtured them.

It was largely Carnell who helped to create the UK genre markets in the first place, and he was internationally known and respected. He had worked tirelessly for some 25 years, as both editor and agent. When I came to know him well, in 1968, it was apparent to me that this dedication had taken a toll on his health. He was, as ever, charming and urbane, but his once dark hair and neat moustache had whitened, and I sensed that his relinquishing of the editorship of the Nova magazines a few years earlier had not entirely been dictated by falling sales. Now his only editing was of the quarterly paperback collection, *New Writings in SF*, published by Corgi Books, which he had successfully launched. But he was still as active as ever as a literary agent.

He was of immense assistance to me. After a long telephone conversation, he responded to my SOS for mss by sending me a batch of material, which I read through. Presumably the material was stuff he had on hand that had been rejected by himself for his quarterly *New Writings*. However, some of it was excellent, especially stories by Douglas R. Mason, which I bagged without delay, but a lot I felt obliged to reject. As an inexperienced editor, I didn't just reject a mss, with a printed rejection slip (standard practice) but I sent a long critique explaining *why*. I also explained why I had accepted the mss I had, and was enthusiastic about them. I detailed the type of story I was looking for.

I was *not* looking for space opera, or old-fashioned stories. I was *not* looking for a new variant of my childhood idol, John Russell Fearn. I was looking for stories that were literate without being obscure, with strong human interest, modern, and inventive. Whilst it was perfectly true that I had spent a large part of my life researching the pre-war science fiction of Fearn and his contemporaries, which I found fascinating and rewarding (and still do!) it was *as an artefact of the past, and its contribution to the formation and establishment of the genre.* I was keen for it to be reprinted, and honoured *in its context, for what it was.* For a magazine publishing new stories only, I was looking for an entirely different approach. I was desperately keen to discover new writers.

One mss excited me particularly—'Sixth Sense' by Michael G. Coney, an entirely new writer. Coney's story was about the human condition; the 'SF element' involved telepathy, but it had no resemblance whatsoever to the old-style pulp adventure stories. It was exactly the material I wanted for *Vision.* The second of three Coney mss, 'A Judge of Men', was more conventional, with a greater reliance on SF tropes and trappings. It had something of the flavour of a 1930s Stanley Weinbaum story—but it just about passed muster because of literate writing and human interest. I wanted to encourage Coney and be favoured by more mss so I bought this as well, but in so doing I urged Coney to move away from this type of conventional SF, and to write more in the style of 'Sixth Sense'. The third mss was a fantasy, seemingly set in a Cornish fishing village. It seemed incomplete, as if it was part of a larger work, and was not really science fiction. It was, however, very well written. I returned it with reluctance, but indicated how it might be rewritten. (When Coney's 'Sixth Sense' later appeared in *Vision's* first issue, it was immediately selected for anthologization by Don Wollheim for his *World's Best SF* series.)

There were two mss by Brian N. Ball, a writer just then becoming established. One story was 'The Fauntleroy Syndrome', a sardonic, humourous satire about a future society ruled by women where men were kept as pets. It wasn't a great story, but it was useful filler material (I had been warned by Ted Tubb—himself an ex-editor—that finding enough good material would be a nightmare. So from the beginning, I was prepared to buy 'borderline' stories to have in a reserve inventory.) Ball's other story was much longer, and more complicated. It entirely revolved around an elaborate pseudo-scientific gimmick, striving for cosmic significance that was vitiated because the central gimmick was based on pseudo-science. In rejecting it, I told Carnell that it had reminded me of an old Nat Schachner story in the pre-war Tremaine *Astounding*. It was *not* the material I wanted to publish.

There were a few other stories I rejected, but I bought another two. One was an excellent offtrail story by Eric C. Williams, 'No.7', and another story that had the fresh approach I was looking for was 'Moonchip' by John Rankine (Douglas R. Mason).

Carnell's reaction was—to me—almost overwhelming. He wrote and then telephoned to say that he believed that I had what it took to be a successful editor. He had been impressed with my analysis of old-fashioned sf, and the need to move on, whilst retaining the two best elements of the past—a sense of wonder and entertainment. He said he was happy that someone would now be taking over his mantle.

At the time, I felt immensely flattered. In retrospect, the episode seems slightly chilling. It reminds me now of 'Sinbad the Sailor' who was doomed to carry the Old Man of the Sea on his back—unless he could trick someone else into accepting his burden!

I was now the only editor of a monthly sf magazine in the U.K. What had been riding on Carnell's back for years was now riding on mine. I little knew the tribulations that lay in store for me. If I had, I would have resigned immediately!

Carnell put me in touch with Walter Gillings, whom he knew was about to make a comeback with *Cosmos Science Fantasy Review*, a revival of his famous fanzine of the late 1940s. My first telephone call with Gillings lasted well over an hour, and I found a staunch ally and good friend. Wally had been through it all himself several times, and he became my mentor. A professional journalist, Wally surprised and delighted me by turning my telephone call into an excellent write-up ('Dead Author Inspires New SF Venture') that appeared in the first issue of his new magazine, dated April 1969.

Carnell also offered his services for story illustrations, but the only client he had at the time was a beginning young artist, Brian Finch. I accepted his offer. I asked after Gerard Quinn, and although he was not his client, Carnell freely gave me the address and telephone number. Another phone call, and Gerard kindly agreed to do both interiors and covers for me. I also contacted another young artist, Alan Vince, whom I had known because of our mutual admiration of the work of Frank Hampson, creator of "Dan Dare."

Ken Bulmer sent me an unsold novelette he had on hand, 'Swords For a Guide', to tide me over whilst he worked on something new. Ted Tubb informed me that he had nothing on hand, as he had abandoned short stories in favour of novels, but he promised to write new stuff especially for me. "It may take me a little while to get back in the groove."

My first issue had now taken shape, and I farmed out the stories I had selected for black and white interior illustrations to Carnell, Alan Vince, and to Gerard Quinn, whom I hoped to use as chief artist. Entirely for expediency, and to save money, I also executed a few small illustrations myself (as 'James'—my middle name.) I also asked Quinn to design a title logo for the magazine (which I would also use as a letterhead) and to paint the cover of the first issue, illustrating an excellent story that William F. Temple had written especially for me—'When In Doubt—Destroy!'

No sooner had the first issue been closed, when Ted Tubb finally responded to my urgent pleas for mss by sending me three splendid stories at once: 'Full Five', 'Lucifer!' and 'Quarry'. He had just missed out on making the first issue—to our mutual disappointment. I asked Quinn to illustrate all three stories, and to paint me a cover for 'Quarry', which would be the lead story in our second issue.

At the time everything seemed to be going well, apart from the fact that Graham was making heavy weather of his negotiations with Mrs. Fearn's solicitor—to whom she had turned over his letter. So I took another approach. I tracked down some of Fearn's former publishers and made enquiries about specific Fearn novels they had published. Two publishers were prepared to sell reprint rights, and sign an indemnity that they had bought the copyright from Fearn. They were Hyman Kaner (for *Slaves of Ijax*) and Paul Hamlyn (successors to Newnes and C. Arthur Pearson) who claimed to hold the rights to *Cosmic Exodus* and *The Hell Fruit*. Hutchinson's, who had taken over Stanley Paul, claimed that they held the paperback rights to Fearn's hardcover scientific detective novels (although royalties would need to be shared with the author's estate.) It now looked as if we had the basis of a paperback line, both new and reprint, which would also include the new magazine, *Vision of Tomorrow*.

The first bundles of mss began to arrive from John Bangsund, which

I examined eagerly. Graham had decreed that both John and I should send him copies of all letters we exchanged between us, to keep him fully informed. He would then send funds to John to pay for the stories I selected at our standard rate (£4 a thousand for 1st serial rights only—equivalent to one cent a word.) The rate had been suggested to me by Bill Temple, who said that as the only magazine in the UK, there was no need for me to pay more (even though that advice was not in his own best interests as a contributor!). It was typical of the help and advice I was to receive from Britain's SF professionals.

John's initial selections contained some awful rubbish, clearly written by fans or novice authors, but a fair number proved acceptable, either as 'borderline' inventory or as first-class stories suitable for the first issue. I had sensed that finding a 40% Australian content was going to prove something of a headache, so I was delighted to find a couple of established names—Lee Harding and Jack Wodhams, both with several excellent stories. David Rome was another name I recognised, and although his story was clearly a reject from an Australian Man's magazine (then the only market for SF in Australia) with the SF elements rather cynically brushed in, I bought it in order to help meet my quota. There were also a couple of stories by an emerging young writer Damien Broderick, which I thought were immensely promising. They had a sense of darkness and vividness, that marked an unusual talent—just what I was looking for. One of them even featured Ayer's Rock ('The Vault') so that was a definite story for the first issue's Australian quota.

I sent a long appreciative letter to John, giving reasons for both acceptances and rejections. I urged him to solicit more material from the accepted authors.

His next selection was intensely disappointing. It consisted almost entirely of *poetry*! I returned it immediately, with some asperity, pointing out that poetry was most definitely *not* wanted. I wanted new short stories and novelettes *only*.

A subsequent package also contained little of interest—as well as more poetry! About the only thing I found acceptable was another short story by Lee Harding, together with author profiles of Harding and Jack Wodhams, which John had written at my request. However, I now had enough acceptable Australian material for the first two issues, with some borderline filler inventory for later issues as well. I thanked John for his efforts, and gave more guidelines as to the type of stories I was looking for. I also implored him to stop sending me poetry!

But my editorial duties were only the tip of the iceberg. I was also the to become Manager of the new company Graham was formally setting up in England, Ronald E. Graham (Publishers) Pty Ltd, and as the only employee I was responsible for a multitude of mundane but vital matters, including a great deal of legal and contractual prerequisites. Publishing a monthly professional magazine, I soon discovered, was a big undertaking. I had to find a reliable firm of printers willing and able to take on a monthly magazine, and then negotiate a contract with them. I talked to several firms, before selecting the Northumberland Press, in Gateshead (some ten miles from my parental home, where I was still working out of my bedroom.) The Northumberland Press were one of the leading printers of genre novels in the country, and I was immensely satisfied at having secured their services. However, as a new account, I was required to provide my own paper—which meant further investigations and negotiations to secure another supply contract with a paper merchant. I also needed to open a bank account in the company's name. On interviewing my own bank manager I learned that a prerequisite of opening an account was for the Articles of the new company to be sent to the English Registrar of Companies. An entire farrago of legalities had to be waded through. Graham's Australian solicitors were encountering immense legal difficulties in setting up a firm in another country. Delays mounted. I still had to find a national distributor—and investigate and learn the arcane mysteries of the publishing trade, of which I had no experience. I pursued this by contacting and interviewing publisher's reps. Endless travelling, interviews, letters and telephone calls, learning new skills—company management was a far more demanding job than simply being the editor.

And on top of all this, until the new company could be officially created, I was still working full-time in Local Government, as Assistant Registrar at the new and rapidly expanding South East Nortumberland Technical College in Wallsend. As an engaged man I should have been giving all my attention to my fiancée Maureen, and to househunting. I was often working on both jobs from 9 am until midnight, and all through Saturday and Sundays, day and night. Without her sympathetic understanding and support I could not have done it.

One day I was astonished (and dismayed) to receive a letter from

Graham asking me to open immediate negotiations with German publishers Moewig, to acquire the English language rights to the *Perry Rhodan* series of novels in magazine format. I knew nothing about it, until Ron pointed out that it was the fastest-growing character series in Germany, hugely successful, and running into hundreds of novels. He enclosed a couple of sample issues. He was certain that the first publisher to get hold of English language rights was sure to make a fortune. It was a matter of good business, and he was first and foremost a businessman. I was to get on the case immediately.

I was not enthusiastic. The samples were obviously pulp adventures on the line of *Captain Future*. But orders were orders. I asked the Head of languages at my Technical College to translate a sample chapter for me, and wrote to the Managing Director of Moewig, taking the address from one of the magazines. I also wrote to one of my old fan contacts, the Austrian academic Franz Rottensteiner, whom I knew to be an expert on German sf.

Whilst he considered *Perry Rhodan* to be lowest-common-denominator SF, Franz confirmed Ron's analysis—in fact, the series was even bigger than Graham had indicated. I asked him to write an article about it, which I would publish in *Vision* as a contribution towards the '10% European' interest I hoped to include in the magazine—which had led me to secure a story by Stanislaw Lem, via his then UK agent, Peter Roberts.

My College friend handed me a translation, which did little to enthuse me, so I was secretly relieved when I received a letter from Moewig. They were agreeable in principle to selling the English rights, but they were asking what I thought was an exorbitant price (but which probably wasn't, considering that English language rights also embraced the American market.). In forwarding the letter to Ron, I enclosed the sample German translation (which read appallingly) and pointed out that he would have to pay twice for the rights, i.e. plus our translator. Ron was very disappointed—but he agreed the price demanded was far too high, and decreed the idea "wiped." I breathed a sigh of relief. I'd thought the idea was ill-judged.

However, in retrospect, I was wrong and Graham's business instincts were entirely correct. A year later Forry Ackerman and Ace Books in the US stepped in and adopted Graham's original idea themselves. They made a fortune. I'd like to think that in some alternate world another

Ron Graham dropped his plans for *Vision* and English paperbacks, and plunged his entire resources into bringing out *Perry Rhodan*! And I stayed in Local Government and became a Chief Officer!

I was still working all hours, with hardly any free time, which did not materially change when the legalities were finally sorted, and Graham offered me a full-time contract as his salaried employee, guaranteed for two years. This enabled me to quit my job, and to work full-time for the publishing company. I was still working mainly from home, and putting in a 12-hour day, but I was doing something I enjoyed, and could take a break whenever I needed to. I quickly finalised arrangements for a rented office and telephone in Newcastle, bought a typewriter and office furniture, and hired the services of a part-time typist, through an agency. Contracts for printing and paper, and a company bank account and cheque book were also secured.

I was immensely grateful to Ron Graham for that contract, which increased my annual salary by a munificent 50%—to £30 a week! It enabled me to buy a decent house—and to set the date for my wedding (September, 1969). In the late '60s mortgages were strictly controlled to two and one half times one's annual salary (a wife or partner's salary was not taken into account). The mortgage repayments approximately equated to just over one week's pay. It meant that, with some savings, I could now afford a decent semi-detached suburban property (£4,000) instead of a grotty terraced house near to a railway line (£2,500) which was all my old salary would have ran to.

All of Graham's letters were typed by his personal private Secretary, a lady called Cy Hord, who had worked with him for years. She was absolutely wonderful, often writing to me privately to reassure me when, occasionally, Ron would blow his top with me about some tiny detail or other. Cy would explain that Ron was such a perfectionist, that anything not entirely to his liking would occasionally lead to an autocratic tantrum that soon passed. She also acted as an intermediary between us, and kept my confidences. Without her skilled counsel, it might have been difficult to maintain our working relationship as well as we did. As it was, there were hardly any problems whatever. Ron was a man of his word, and allowed me full editorial control. He gave me his full backing from day one. Cy Hord also had an expert knowledge of science fiction, and its writers, since she had for years handled all Ron's "hobbyist" SF collecting, which he conducted on a massive scale. Thanks to her, things worked wonderfully well. Some commentators have speculated that the magazine failed because overseas liaison was impractical. They are wrong: the idea was perfectly feasible, using cablegrams for any urgent consultations.

More packages came from John Bangsund in Australia. One contained a full-length novel—more material that was not required. Not only that, but the mss was severely aged and creased, each chapter ravaged with rusty staples. It was clearly several decades old. I dipped into it, found it almost unreadable, and decided it must have been written in the early 1930s, and was probably a reject from the Doc Sloane *Amazing*. (In retrospect, though I cannot now be sure after more than 40 years, I believe the novel might have been by Phil Collas, and was an unpublished sequel to his October 1935 *Amazing Stories* novelette 'The Inner Domain'. Whatever, if it hadn't been good enough for 1935 *Amazing* it wasn't likely to find favour with me!) This I also returned promptly, with a desperate plea for usable new short material. There were, however, a couple of 'borderline' acceptable stories from new Australian writers Brian Waters, Maurice Whitta, and Robert Bowden, and a rather good 'Aboriginal' story by Eric Harris. I bought them all, hoping for more and better material from them.

Gerard Quinn's first batch of artwork arrived through the mail from Belfast. It included his design for a *Vision of Tomorrow* title logo (which I immediately adapted for my letterhead), as well as interior illustrations for the magazine. He also executed in oils a cover painting (based on Frank Arnold's story) for the first of our book titles *Journey To Tomorrow*, an anthology of reprinted short stories. (This was fated never to be used.)

Actual publication of both the magazine and the books was still on hold whilst I searched desperately for a reliable national distributor, encountering successive disappointments and rebuffs. Distribution of books and magazines was a closed world, utterly secretive and arcane, and difficult to break into—but I was making progress, and actually had a prospective book distributor in the frame as the planned date of the first issue approached—July, 1969. Then suddenly all my plans were turned upside down. They were, in fact "wiped" (Graham's favourite expression when he made an autocratic vetoing decision.)

Ron and his Secretary were flying to England for a week's stay over Easter, before going on to America. He planned to attend SF conventions in both countries, beginning with the BSFA Easter Convention, being held at Oxford. Cy had planned the whole trip with absolute precision.

After a few days in London, Ron hired a car and drove several hundred miles north to Wallsend, on Tyneside, to meet me and my parents—as well as my fiancée Maureen—at my parent's home (27 Cheshire Gardens) It had been arranged that they would stay over and spend the night there, as there were two spare bedrooms. My sister Valerie had been married and left home the previous year, and I had just bought a house not far away (32 Tynedale Avenue). Whilst still largely unfurnished, it did have a bed, and I spent the night there and then rejoined everyone at my parent's home, after breakfast. The next stage of the plan was for me to join Ron and Cy as they drove later that same morning to Oxford for the start of the three-day convention, over the Easter weekend, where Cy had booked us in as overnight guests.

My first meeting with Ron and Cy went very well. Ron was a young-looking 59—he wore glasses and had thinning hair, but was powerfully-built, and looked every inch the part of a successful businessman. Whilst quietly spoken, he was clearly nobody's fool. Cy was a small but dynamic woman, possibly in her early 50s, and with her gravelly voice looked and sounded (in retrospect) rather like one of American TV's "Golden Girls." My fiancée (who had joined us for the day) was then still employed as a secretary at the Technical College I had recently left, but Ron had agreed that once the company had been set up, she should become my Secretary. I had, in fact, only agreed to accept my job on this understanding. Whilst my new salary was enough to meet the mortgage, in setting up and maintaining a home, a wife's salary would also be crucial. Ron kept his promise, and such was his generosity, she became the new company's second employee at twice her then salary. She would have been happy to join me if her old salary had been matched. The raise was an unexpected offer she was pleased to accept, and naturally I had no objection.

Whether the offer was planned or spontaneous I had no idea, but it was typical of Graham's generous nature and facility for making up his mind quickly. I, too, evidently passed muster, and my parents did me proud as welcoming hosts for the visitors, putting themselves and their home at our disposal over two days.

We would take with us some leaflets (which my brother-in-law Joe Armstrong, who worked for a printing company, had printed up for me) together with the illustrations for the first issue, to show them to the assembled fans and authors at the convention—where Ron and I were booked to give a short talk and presentation. As well as promoting the magazine, it would be an opportunity for me to meet and recruit both authors and artists.

On arrival at the Convention Hotel in Oxford, we went straight to our rooms, where I unpacked my cases. I was horrified to discover that in all of the excitement I had left behind all of the *Vision* artwork and related material I needed for my presentation!

I apologised to Ron, who took the news phlegmatically, but I was plunged into self-reproach. My despondency was short-lived, however, because within half an hour a message came through from reception. Could I attend there urgently—there was a party waiting to see me?

I was flabbergasted to find the smiling figures of my Father, Mother and Maureen waiting in reception, as I was handed the missing portfolio of artwork! My father explained that they had discovered that I had left it behind within minutes of our leaving. Knowing its importance to me, they had jumped into his car and followed us all the way down to Oxford!

Having delivered the precious package, my parents and Maureen were all set to drive back to Tyneside, but Ron Graham would have none of it. He insisted that all three of the party should stay for the weekend at Oxford—and at his expense. He nodded to Cy, who disappeared into her room and got busy on the telephone. Within minutes this super-secretary returned to report that she had fixed up their accommodation at a nearby hotel. It was a wonderful gesture by Ron, and typical of his kindness and largesse to those he considered had helped him.

The Convention was a great success, and a hugely enjoyable experience. I was especially delighted to meet Walter Gillings. Ron Graham had failed to keep his promise to write me articles on SF history, so I asked Gillings if he would rewrite and continue his series of fanzine articles, "The Clamorous Dreamers" that had appeared in Mike Rosenblum's *The New Futurian* in the mid fifties. Wally was not enthusiastic—he thought that no one nowadays would be interested. I said that I would continue to badger him until he agreed, so he gave in. His revised memoirs, documenting the history of British science fiction from the early 1930s, became one of *Vision's* most popular features, and Wally became one of my closest professional friends (and later, my partner in our Cosmos Literary Agency until his death in 1979.)

I was pleased also to renew acquaintance with Ted Tubb and Ken Bulmer, two consummate professionals and wonderfully warm personalities, and also Ted Carnell, who was in the same mould—this time as a fellow professional rather than as a fan. On the Saturday night, Ron Graham hosted a room party for professional authors and editors, and I was thrilled to meet many of the great names in the field—in particular, Don Wollheim and James White. I had known in advance that Wollheim was to be there, and betrayed my fannish credentials by asking him to autograph the copy of *Portable Novels of Science* I had brought with me for the purpose! Wollheim told me to was editing a series of *World's Best SF* anthologies, and would be grateful if I sent him copies of *Vision* as it was published, as he had the utmost respect for British SF writers.

Then occurred the one jarring and distressing incident of the entire weekend. As word of the 'Professional's' party in Ron's room spread, there was a stream of knocks on the door as new admissions joined the group to enjoy his largesse, Ron himself answering the door and announcing the new arrivals and their partners. I was standing right next to Ron when he answered one particular knock. Standing outside and confidently hoping for admission, was Birmingham fan Peter Weston.

Peter was the editor of Britain's leading 'sercon' (serious and constructive) SF fanzine, *Speculation*, which he had launched (initially under the name of *Zenith*) in 1964, following a very successful BSFA Convention in Birmingham. I had met him there, together with his other friends of the 'Birmingham Group', Mike Higgs and Rog Peyton, and considered him to be a friend of mine. I had regularly contributed artwork, letters and articles to his fanzine since its launch, and had in fact earmarked Peter as one of my book reviewers for a regular 'Fantasy Review' feature in *Vision*. I had already prepared an advert for his fanzine which was due to appear in our first issue, and hoped that *Speculation*—which had rapidly progressed in leaps and bounds and was now internationally read and attracting many leading authors as contributors and correspondents—would be a useful source of news and publicity for our publishing operation.

As I stood smiling at Peter—in pleased recognition—Ron suddenly exploded into vituperation. Peter was informed that as "an amateur" his presence was decidedly not welcome at this 'Professional' gathering. He was given what can only be described as "the bum's rush" in no uncertain terms, as if he had been an unwelcome Jehovah's Witness or Travelling Brush Salesman. The door was slammed in his dismayed face before I realised what was happening.

I immediately protested to Ron that he was a friend of mine, and not 'just' an amateur. He most definitely warranted admission, but Ron was adamant. He had already decreed that there would be no fanzine review column in *Vision*, and no letter column either. "We don't need amateurs. Forget him!" he snapped. There was nothing I could do. I returned to the throng, with the sick realisation that, to the hapless Peter Weston, it must also have looked as if I was grinning approvingly as Ron had launched into his exclusion tirade.

History repeats, I thought, as I rejoined Don Wollheim. *He* had been amongst a small group famously excluded by Sam Moskowitz and Will Sykora at the First World SF Convention at New York in 1939! I consoled myself with the thought that it hadn't done *him* any harm, and Peter would surely get over it—especially after I apologised and explained things to him the next day—which I did. However, I don't think Peter ever quite believed my subsequent sincere apology. Following the convention he began to run denigrating remarks in *Speculation*, dismissing as worthless the entire works of John Russell Fearn (his credentials being that he had once read *one* novel by him—*1,000 Year Voyage* [1954], which he'd considered to be atrocious).

To be fair to Peter, that novel was not one of Fearn's best. He had, in fact, been contractually obliged to write it whilst looking after his dying mother at home. Mrs. Fearn was a devout Christian Scientist, and would have no doctors attend her. Fearn had to write that novel whilst feeding, washing and bandaging her, keeping vigil and waiting for her inevitable death. Many years later my sister and I similarly administered to our own terminally ill mother, who had expressed the wish to leave hospital; and die at home. We shared the task for just a single week, and it left us shattered. Certainly, I could have barely written my name, much less a 45,000-word SF novel. Fearn, I had been told by a close family friend, had kept his vigil for several *weeks*, during which time he had not only written *1,000 Year Voyage*, but continued to edit the *British SF Magazine* as well. (It is perhaps significant that every single character in the novel dies . . .)

Of course, Peter could not have been expected to know *any* of this, but it seemed to me that by attacking Fearn, for whose work my admiration was well known, by clear innuendo he was attacking my competence to edit a magazine. Whilst "wishing me well," he "feared for the future of the magazine if Fearn was ever reprinted." Although apparently even-handed, I believed (perhaps mistakingly) that his remarks had been deliberately constructed to cause me maximum annoyance and embarrassment. The entire business was in any case a deliberate red herring: I had already told Peter—and others—that the magazine was to contain *new stories only* and any Fearn reprints would be issued *totally separately* from the magazine. I would soon forget all about Peter and his fanzine, however, as I was to have far more pressing things to worry about. Ron's decision to bar Peter was a serious misjudgement, as was his vetoing my plan for a regular fanzine review column.

Meantime, back at the Oxford Convention, I made a point of seeking out Eddie Jones, a well-known genial fan artist who lived in Bootle. He pursued a mundane career, but he was also a talented part-time professional artist, who had made a few forays into magazine and book illustration for *Nebula* and Badger Books—one of his covers had illustrated R. Chetwynd-Hayes' first novel, *The Man From the Bomb* (1959) But with the demise of *Nebula* and the low esteem in which Badger Books were rightly held, he had yet to really make his mark. His biggest commercial success had been a series of Bubble-Gum cards (on the line of *Mars Attacks*) but these were not widely known to be his. I asked Eddie if he would like to illustrate for *Vision*. He seemed reluctant at first—we had not met or corresponded before, and the magazine had yet to be published. But we finally agreed that I would send him a copy of the magazine in due course, and a few assignments, and we would take it from there.

On Sunday morning, after the Convention, Ron and Cy drove back to his hotel in London—he still had several days of his holiday in England left to enjoy before leaving for America—and I returned to Tyneside in my father's car, full of enthusiasm and plans for the magazine—not to mention my forthcoming marriage to Maureen. Ken Bulmer's wife, Pamela, had agreed to write book reviews for *Vision* (as 'Kathryn Buckley') and Ken was to create a series character for me ('Fletcher Cullen') whose adventures would be deliberately light-hearted and comedic. In discussions, I had mentioned to him that nearly all the stories I received (especially by his friend Ted Tubb!) were full of doom and gloom, with characters snapping and snarling at each other. I thought that a few laughs would not go amiss, and Ken agreed to see what he could do for me.

On the following Tuesday afternoon I received a phone call from Ron in London, that knocked me for a loop. I was to cancel any book distribution arrangements, and stop the presses on *Vision* immediately. The magazine was now to be an A-4 sized slick magazine, and to be distributed by Transworld Publications (Corgi Books). Could I arrange to fly to London the next morning and meet him at his hotel? He had arranged a meeting for both of us in the afternoon with Patrick Newman, the Managing Director of Transworld. He then put Cy on the phone as I collected my wits. She had already booked me into a Hotel in Kensington the next day for bed and breakfast. Could I arrange my own flight from Newcastle airport? I said that after working with and learning from her, I could do anything. I'd meet them at their London hotel at noon the following day.

I had never flown to London before, and didn't even know where the Newcastle airport or their hotel in London was, but that was just par for the course. I was learning everything fast. I made the appointment with time to spare, using my wits, the telephone, and taxi-drivers—in that order.

I learned that, unknown to me, immediately on his return to London the previous day, Ron had set up a meeting with Transworld. As previously noted, they were publishers of the *New Writings In SF* paperback series, which—to some degree—I had hoped to emulate, although my plans were actually based on the old Compact *New Worlds*.

Transworld's Managing Director, Patrick Newman, had convinced Ron of the need to scrap his entire paperback proposals. He believed that *Vision of Tomorrow*, as the *only* SF magazine in the country, had tremendous potential—but only as a magazine. As such it should be distributed through newsagent's shops, as well as W.H. Smith and the big chains. It would need to be in the conventional large magazine size, 8.5 X 11 inches, printed on slick paper, with lots of interior illustrations. As for the paperback novels by Fearn, Tubb, and others, these would now appear in a companion reprint magazine, also large size—a revival, in fact, of my own old original idea of a modern version of *Fantastic Story Magazine*—with a featured novel and short stories. Ron had arranged another meeting that afternoon with Newman for the both of us to discuss the proposal further, but it was clear to me he was keen on the idea.

We met Newman in his plush offices in Harlesden, West London, and he was smooth, dynamic and entirely convincing. But I was still more than a little suspicious of the whole set-up. At the back of my mind was the idea that Newman must have perceived a new specialist SF paperback line as a rival to his own operation. But what convinced me to agree was when Newman revealed that Corgi Books had recently diversified into general magazine distribution. They had set up an entirely new magazine division, and had a crack sales force, with direct access into every newsagent's shop, as well as W.H. Smith and other big chains.

That clinched it. I knew that the entire success of the magazine hinged on good distribution. Everything else was peripheral. And I had yet to finalise my own paperback distribution arrangements—all I had was a forthcoming interview with one distributor (whom I had finally uncovered after months of fruitless part-time investigation). That might turn out to be a bust anyway, and could easily be cancelled. Transworld's offer was on the table in front of me now; all I had to do was to pick it up. It seemed a heaven-sent opportunity.

In falling in with the new plans, I pointed out the immense practical difficulties. The paperback version was actually already set in type, and the tons of paper needed for the 25,000-copy print-run already bought and warehoused. Could I make the switch?

I would have to stop the printing, find someone to buy the prepared pulp paper, find and buy a new supply of *slick* paper, commission more artwork, design an entire different interior layout and create individual story headings—as well as persuade the printer (a specialist *book* printer) to alter my existing contract with them and persuade them that they could handle a magazine; I would also have to find advertising for the magazine to offset the undoubted hugely increased production costs.

I was a one-man operation. I was engaged to be married in the autumn. I had just bought an empty house, with two large gardens that had weeds five feet deep front and back, which needed to be completely rewired, decorated, renovated (new doors and window frames) and furnished. It was now April, and the planned publication date for the magazine was July. Could I do possibly do it?

I said I could, but that I would need to concentrate on *Vision* first, before tackling the companion magazine (which at the moment did not even have a title.) And on this basis, all parties shook hands. I left for my hotel, and Ron and Cy returned to theirs, ready to fly to America the following day, whilst I flew back to Newcastle.

That night in my London hotel, I took the opportunity to place a local call to Ted Carnell, and told him of the latest developments. He said that I had made the right decision, and that Patrick Newman was an honourable man, and that—in his own experience—Corgi were a first class outfit. He offered to help me all he could, and to my delight said he would shortly be sending me stories by his clients Philip E. High and Douglas R. Mason (who I learned also wrote as John Rankine) As I chatted to Carnell from my hotel room it suddenly occurred to me that the best way to solve the problem of material for the proposed companion magazine would be to reprint Fearn's Golden Amazon novels there, rather than his other novels we had optioned simply because they were available (though they were perfectly good novels, they weren't as good as the Amazon.) The problem was Mrs. Fearn had still not agreed anything. I described the problem to Carnell. Could he, with his vast experience as an agent, suggest how to break the impasse? He could—and did.

He suggested that I should draft a detailed contract for all 24 of the published Golden Amazon novels, making a substantial non-returnable cash offer on signature to secure an option, and then further payments only as each novel was actually published. That would protect the publisher's interests. If, through circumstances, Graham failed to publish the novels with a given time span, then all rights would revert to Mrs. Fearn. That would protect *her* interests. It was superb advice, and I thanked Ted warmly for it. But he went even further, and actually dictated to me the wording of a few sample key clauses. Again, I was learning fast.

I made notes of our conversation for future action, had a drink at the hotel bar and went to sleep. The next morning I flew back to Newcastle.

I returned to the fray, not without some trepidation. In both magazine layout and preparation, and home decoration and renovation, my experience and knowledge was practically nil. My task wasn't helped by my forthcoming marriage. After standing by me with wonderful understanding during the preceding months, now that the wedding date was drawing nearer, my fiancée suddenly became frantic that I wasn't paying enough attention to either her or our forthcoming nuptials. My mother and my prospective mother-in law were constantly exhorting and nagging me to forget this "science fiction rubbish" and undertake the needed major decorations and alterations to my new house. My 12 hour day became a 16 hour day, as, sleeping alone in my new house, and commuting to my Newcastle Office and my one part-time (3 hours a day) temp typist—Maureen, my wife-and Secretary-to be had yet to resign her job and work her notice—I worked assiduously at both tasks. It would have made a wonderful scenario for *The Likely Lads*, the famous Tyneside-based television sitcom.

Gerard Quinn's cover painting design for the first issue was late in arriving and was a major disappointment. I had requested a space scene taken directly from Bill Temple's story: space-suited man confronting a strange mechanical alien life form on the surface of a desolate alien world. Instead of the beautifully realistic work for which he had made his reputation on the covers of the Nova magazines, it was almost abstract. Modern art, impressionistic—call it what you will—it was totally unsuitable for the cover of a newsstand magazine, and an SF magazine in particular.

The printing deadline was only a few days away, so I did the only thing possible. I sketched a new cover myself, and implored my father (an experienced commercial painter) to execute it for me in oils. (I could draw, and dabble in watercolours, but I had never learned to paint in oils.) My father was an expert painter in all mediums, including oils, but he had never painted an SF scene before. The finished result wasn't at all bad, considering the circumstances and rush in which it was completed. It was a hell of a lot better than Quinn's design. It was professionally painted, and at least showed instantly that *Vision of Tomorrow* was a science fiction magazine. In the magazine it would be credited to 'James'—also my father's Christian name.) Ron Graham, fully aware of all the circumstances, was perfectly happy with the situation, and grateful to my father for stepping into the breech. After he had seen the printed proof, he promptly asked for the original to be sent to him. The cover was duly delivered just within the printer's deadline, and I awaited the first issue.

As a historical footnote, it should perhaps also be recorded that the 25 advance copies of the first issue (which I had ordered for Graham, the authors and promotional purposes) were actually delivered into my hands on the same July afternoon when Neil Armstrong and the crew of *Apollo*

12 were taking off into space for the Moon. After taking delivery of the magazine, I dashed out of my rented Newcastle office in Eldon Square to a television and electrical retailer's shop window around the corner. All the sets in the window were showing the Moon voyage live, and huge crowds had gathered on the pavements.

Clutching the magazine, I pushed through the throng, and heard the immortal words: *"We have lift-off!"*

The two events were transfixed in my mind. Two of my cherished dreams as an SF fan had come true—*and both of them at the same time.* It wasn't the only parallel, either.

The Apollo space programme would eventually fail, and cost a lot of money. And so would *Vision!*

Recalling my euphoria at this first voyage to the moon has reminded me that Les Johnson had added a wonderful postscript to *his* memoir of the British Interplanetary Society, detailed extracts from which are quoted in Chapter 2. It is perhaps apposite to include some of his postscript here:

In later years, I was very pleasantly surprised to receive a letter dated July 16th, 1968, from Messrs. Metro Goldwyn-Mayer Pictures Ltd. to state that Arthur Clarke has asked them to extend to me a cordial invitation to see the picture, *2001: A Space Odyssey* together with a friend, when the picture of which Arthur had written the script was shown at the Abbey Cinema, Liverpool. I was most pleased that Arthur had remembered me after so many years, and so it came to pass that Jimmy Free and myself were able to enjoy the film as Arthur's guests.

I had renewed acquaintance with Colin Askham after the War, having accidentally encountered him one day in Cases Street, Liverpool, near the Headquarters of Messrs. Littlewood's Mail Order Stores. John Moores had taken Askham into the Firm as his Personal Secretary. Although the matter of the transfer of the Society to London had not been entirely forgiven, Colin was later good enough (as a director of Everton Football Club, for some years) to present Norman Weedall and myself with Cup Final tickets, whenever we had the urge to attend Wembley—and on condition that the tickets were for our own personal use . . .

And it was to Askham's bungalow in Formby (then in Lancashire, but now in the Sefton District of the Merseyside County Council) that my wife and myself were invited one Sunday afternoon, July 20th, 1969, in order to witness (or at least to listen to the broadcast) when the Lunar Module, 'The Eagle', landed on the surface of the Moon. Also present was Colin's wife, Eileen Hastie, who had been a pre-war Member of the BIS, and who had taken the Chair during at least one Meeting of the Society during that period.

The television presentation of the Lunar Landing was not due to take place until between midnight and dawn on the Sunday night/Monday morning; accordingly, on arriving home from our visit to the Askhams, I set up the television in the bedroom. When 12.30 a.m. arrived with no sign of action, and with the prospect of a day's work ahead of me (and especially a Monday's work!) I soon fell asleep,

I woke up during the night, and squinting at the alarm clock saw that the time was 3.55 a.m. I decided that Neil Armstrong must have emerged from the Lunar Module by that time, and switched on the set to see at what stage the proceedings had arrived. I was astonished to hear the announcer state that in five minutes Armstrong would emerge from the Lunar Module; so in spite of myself, I was not to be denied. Almost as if by some miracle of thought transference, I had woken up just in time to witness an event that I had not expected would have taken place during my lifetime.

After the initial euphoria of *Vision's* launch coinciding with that of the lunar astronauts had worn off, I was quite disappointed with the printing of the first issue. The typesetting used had been designed to sink into pulp paper. In the event, whilst it was perfectly clean and legible, it lay somewhat light and grey on the slick paper used. But the main problem was that because of the tight time-scale, I had not been given proofs of the magazine. So I was dismayed to see that many of the stories ended near the top of the page—with the inevitable result that there was a lot of blank space below. In a small paperback, this would not have mattered or even been noticeable.

But I had in fact already anticipated this possibility, and had instructed the printer how it could be avoided. The original typesetting had been retained, but instead of each column filling a small paperback page, it was now printed double column across the larger size. It fitted perfectly, and was in fact standard magazine layout. My story headings (all of which I had had to produce quickly myself, using letra-set, because the book printers did not have fancy type-faces) were designed as single page headings, i.e. single column. I imagined that the printer could simply *reposition* the headings in the *centre* of the page, which would have the effect of pushing and displacing the text below downwards, to fill up any empty space at the end of each story. Another method would be to reduce or expand the size of the illustrations within the body of the text. I had been assured by the printer that my instructions would be followed where appropriate. In fact, because of using blocks and leaded type, he had ignored my instructions altogether. It made the magazine—and me—look decidedly amateurish.

I left the printer in no doubt that this must not happen with the second and third issues which were being prepared in the same way. To overcome the problem, I whipped up lots of small 'filler' spot illustrations, some of which I drew myself, and others that were reprinted from old fanzines (by Terry Jeeves, Alan Hunter and Gerard Quinn). I paid the artists for my use, whilst also commissioning some new filler-illos from them for future use.

I considered I had solved the problems of layout and artwork. Eddie Jones was soon to enter the fold, and I had acquired yet another artist. Chris Priest had put me in touch with his friend Dicky Howett (whom I knew from my days as an active fan—we were both fans of *Garth* in the *Daily Mirror*.) Howett was essentially a cartoonist, but he had a clean modern style that I felt could be suitable for certain stories, especially humorous ones, so I gave him several commissions, and was generally happy with the results. The contrite Gerard Quinn explained to me that he had left the SF magazine field years ago, and the exigencies of modern (mainly advertising) work he was doing, had necessitated that he change his style completely. But he promised that his next covers would be executed more in his old style—a promise he kept splendidly. All his subsequent art for me, (including covers) was first-class. But I was still to encounter problems over authors and stories . . .

I had earlier been in friendly correspondence with Chris Priest for several years, and knew that he had recently left his regular job (I think it had been in accountancy) and had taken the plunge to support himself by full-time writing—a fraught and courageous undertaking. He told me that he was writing anything and everything, fiction and non-fiction for any paying markets he could find, and he seemed eager to write stories for me. He had sent me two short stories, 'Breeding Ground' and 'Nothing Like the Sun.'. I wanted him as a regular contributor, so I promptly bought both of them. I considered the latter story to be vastly superior. It was not a conventional adventure story, and had an atmospheric darkly surreal quality that appealed to me immensely. It was exactly the material I wanted for *Vision*. 'Breeding Ground' on the other hand, telling of 'space bugs' which get inside of space suits, seemed conventional by comparison. It was typical of a number of mss I had been getting—and rejecting. It seemed to me that some writers considered that simply because I was on record as liking old-style SF, I was looking for more of the same. *I wasn't*. After an initial flurry, acceptable mss had quickly begun to dry up, and I was rapidly running short of material. I had reluctantly bought a number of conventional stories, but always with the hope of getting better material.

In the case of Sydney J. Bounds, this had worked perfectly. My editorial practice, right from the beginning, was not to sit and wait for mss to come through the mail, but to write to known authors and *ask* them for material. Syd Bounds had replied to my initial enquiry to the effect that he did not have any material on hand—the market for short SF being almost non-existent in Britain—but he did have a short story he had sold to *Nebula* ten years earlier, which had fallen back on his hands. Would I like to see it whilst he worked on new material? The story he sent, 'World To Conquer', was a typical 1950s story, imaginative and colourful, but not especially well written. I was short of material and so accepted it. The prompt payment encouraged Bounds to submit new stories, and he quickly became my favourite and most reliable contributor. Whilst using familiar sf tropes, Bounds had the knack of developing the human interest side of his plots, to make them fresh and interesting. I bought many stories from him. Some of them, such as 'Limbo Rider', were amongst the best stories I ever published. I considered my purchase of the borderline 'World To Conquer' to have been well justified.

In an earlier incarnation, I had been a very active fan in the early sixties, contributing articles—and more especially, illustrations—to many British fanzines, in particular *Xeron*, edited by a young Mike Ashley. I specialised in illustrating fan fiction, and had done illustrations for fiction by aspiring young writers such as Richard Gordon and Brian Stableford (writing as 'Brian Craig'). By a happy coincidence, by 1969 Gordon was a student at Newcastle University (I think he was doing an M.A. in History) and he called in to see me at my temporary rented office in Newcastle. As a student, he was in need of money, and I invited him to write stories for my magazine. I can only dimly recall him from this initial meeting, but he came across as a reserved, dour Scot. Certainly he gave no hint of his later flamboyant baroque writings. I bought his first three stories, two of them steeped in historical tropes. The first was a short routine time travel story about Charles II, 'A Year Ahead', which I bought as a filler to encourage him to produce something more ambitious. He followed this with two novelettes, 'The Phoenix People' and 'All the World's a Stage'. I never published the first short story, but both novelettes were published in due course. I recognised him as a writer of real potential, and would have bought more stories from him had he submitted any. Unfortunately for me he quickly plunged into writing novels, and although he offered me his first novel, a baroque fantasy, I was unable to consider it. Graham had decreed that serials were not to be used until the magazine became more established.

Stableford sent me a good short story, 'Prisoner in the Ice' which I published in the third issue, but to my disappointment he did not follow it up.

Another similar instance was the young writer, Peter Cave. Peter was a close friend (and occasional collaborator) of Priest's, and he sent me two stories at around the same time, 'Prime Order', and 'Lost In Translation'. Both stories were old-fashioned and retreads of well travelled paths in robotics and outer space, but they had a definite *frisson* that marked Cave as a writer with great potential. Again I bought them as filler material, and was duly rewarded when Cave sent me a long novelette, 'Rebel Planet' which reminded me of the great Eric Frank Russell. I had to cut the too-long story somewhat, but Eddie Jones liked the story well enough to award it the cover spot. Alas, Peter Cave thereafter left the magazine field, and achieved considerable success as a novelist!

I accepted 'Breeding Ground' for much the same reasons. Whilst conventional, Priest's story was at least well written, and I bought it as a filler. After paying for the stories, I explained this in a letter soliciting more stories. To my astonishment my letter—which had been intended as friendly and constructive encouragement—provoked a positively anguished reply. Chris had found my comments about 'Breeding Ground' to be positively insulting and deeply wounding, and I had shattered his creative process and confidence, etc, etc, etc. So I should not have been too surprised when he too began to slate my magazine in *Speculation*, reviews which Peter Weston was only too happy to publish.

Although I was never privileged to publish any more stories by Priest in *Vision* after 'Nothing Like the Sun' (though he had written a book review for me in answer to my SOS after his name appeared on the cover of issue No.5 in which 'Sun' was supposed to appear, but had to be postponed until a later issue for lack of space) I take some wry satisfaction from subsequent events.

Chris never did write any more stories like 'Breeding Ground'. Instead, he developed the style he had shown in 'Nothing Like The Sun', *and then went beyond it*. He went, in fact, way beyond the level of anything that I had ever aspired to in my magazine, and developed his own style to such an extent that he soon became recognised and feted as one of the finest and most innovative writers in Britain! Nowadays he has deservedly achieved international success and is feted by the literary establishment. Not bad going for someone whose creative process and confidence had been supposedly shattered by my clumsy remarks in 1969!

I had been given a strong hint that Chris was taking his literary career very seriously indeed when a couple of years later I received a letter from him out of the blue. It informed me that he had just made a bonfire of the scores of letters I had sent him over the years, together with copies of his replies. His letter tersely advised me that he would be greatly obliged if I would do the same with his letters, and any copies of my letters to him which I still had. He asked me to burn the lot of them. Naturally, I could not refuse such a request, and so his letters asking me to sell him my collection of Ace Doubles and loan him my pulp magazines—presumably because they might cause him future embarrassment with the literati if ever published—were safely converted to ashes!

More recently, I was surprised and delighted when again, quite out of the blue, Chris sent me a transcript of his Guest of Honour speech at a national SF convention. In his speech Chris had actually paid warm tribute to me as one of his early mentors in his finding out about SF history. Evidently he had only borrowed my pulp magazines and books *purely to educate himself about the SF field*! His literary achievements were such by then that he could cheerfully admit to our earlier association!

Meanwhile, back in my *Vision* editorship days, and even more serious for my editorial ambitions than the loss of Chris Priest, was the loss of John Bangsund—which threatened to cut off my supply of Australian mss.

It came like a thunderbolt out of the blue, and was most emphatically something that I had neither expected, nor wanted.

I was constantly writing to John, keeping him informed of progress, and the type of stories I needed, and stressing that I urgently needed many more mss than he had been sending if I was to keep up to the hoped-for 40% Australian quota. Because of the monthly schedule and production lead-in times, I was working three issues ahead, and was about to run out of Australian mss.

John responded to my SOS with an imposingly large air parcel. I fell upon it eagerly, and discovered that it *consisted almost entirely of poetry!* I was flabbergasted! He had done this before, and each time I had 'bawled him out' and implored him not to send any more damn poetry! And here was a steaming bundle of it! I returned it with another acerbic letter.

Then I received Eddie Jones' first illustration—an excellent one, reminiscent of Kelly Freas. It illustrated a Lee Harding story I had lined up for my second issue. I settled to reread the story to compare it with Eddie's illustration, and suddenly something clicked. I had read this story years before! I did some swift checking, and soon discovered that the story was an exact copy of 'Echo' a story Lee had published in *New Worlds* several years earlier. It had been presented to me by John—and paid for—as a brand new story. And of course, we used new stories only—*no reprints*. I immediately sent the story back with an angry note. I added that Harding should keep the money—which would be credited to the purchase of his *next* story. I never did hear back from John regarding the two incidents—or, that I can recall, ever again. (Anyone who is interested will find Eddie's illustration for the unused story was used as a filler on page 54 of the second issue of *Vision!*)

Ron Graham wrote to John Bangsund (copying his letter to me) informing him that he had been "wiped"—was being sacked as Australian associate editor. There was to be no appeal, and no discussion. It was a typical Ron Graham executive decision—swift and ruthless.

I did not agree with the sacking, and desperately wanted to retain John (with whom I thought I had been getting on well, apart from his recent (admittedly serious) lapses. I was sure he could explain or redeem himself. As ever in these situations, I expressed these views to Ron's Secretary in confidence. She wrote back to say I had been prudent to do so. I was *never* to question Ron's executive decisions. The matter was closed. But both she and Ron himself would be seeking to restore the flow of Australian material.

By working round the clock, I had prepared issues two and three of *Vision* by the end of April, and now turned my attention to the reprint magazine, which Ron had provisionally entitled *Mind's Eye*. But first, I really needed a holiday.

I discussed matters with my fiancée, and Maureen made what was, to me, to prove a life-changing suggestion: "Why don't we go to Blackpool?" She added that she had enjoyed several holidays there as a small child.

I readily agreed, and promptly booked a week's holiday with my fiancée in Blackpool, selecting a guesthouse at random from the plethora of holiday adverts in the *Daily Mirror*. It was only *after* I had done so, that I realized that Blackpool was also the home town of Mrs. Fearn. Graham's attempt at negotiations through Mrs. Fearn's solicitor were going nowhere. But what if I was to call on Mrs. Fearn personally, and take Maureen with me . . . ?

Once there, I telephoned Mrs. Fearn, and she agreed to meet me the following day. Maureen and I called on her at her home at Princeway, in Blackpool's South Shore district. I also took with me a draft contract for the Amazon series, which I had prepared in accordance with Ted Carnell's suggestions.

Face to face with Mrs. Fearn, my preconceptions of her went out of the window. She was utterly charming—was, in fact, a very close approximation in voice and stature of the modern television character "Mrs. Merton!" Small and petite (I would never have guessed her age at 69) and with a charming Lancashire accent (though she had been born in Yorkshire) she listened as I poured out my story of my trials and tribulations. I explained to her the laws of copyright, publishing and advances and royalties, and assured her of mine (and Graham's) sincere intentions to see that she got a fair deal—not to mention restoring Fearn to print as a tribute to him. We hit things off brilliantly, and she promised to take the contract to her dithering Solicitor, and get things moving. She also insisted that Maureen and I should call on her again whenever we were in Blackpool—and to call as often as possible! (She was in fact to become a dear friend of ours, and, eventually, an adopted "Auntie" to our daughter Claire who was born in 1972.)

On my return after the holiday, I reported the success of our mission to Graham, who was delighted. He was happy to hand over completion of the contract for the Amazon novels to me. I instructed a firm of Solicitors in Newcastle to act for us, and turned my attention back to *Vision*.

More and more I was learning that the best way to make progress in publishing and editing was the personal touch. Eddie Jones wrote to tell me that he had completed all the assignments he had, and had ideas for a new cover design. I sent him another batch of mss and suggested that when he had finished them, he came to see me, bringing his cover design with him. I would meet him in Newcastle (I had secured much more spacious new offices in Newcastle, very near to the Railway Station) and we could spend the whole day together. Then I would take him for the evening and night to my parental home, where we could talk further. After breakfast we could go back to my Newcastle office, from where he could catch a train back to Bootle. *Vision* would pay his expenses. I wanted to discuss with him a proposal whereby he would become *Vision's* Chief Artist.

A week later Maureen and I welcomed him into our Newcastle office. He had brought with him a huge portfolio of artboards, containing his black and white illustrations for all the stories I'd sent him (each one hand lettered, freeing me from the irksome chore of doing these myself) together with not one, but two dynamic spaceship covers, each incorporating a radical new logo design that was more modern and clean looking than our old logo (which Gerard Quinn had actually prepared from my own design).

The artwork was outstanding, and I lost no time in making my offer. To my surprise, Eddie—always an immensely confident individual—came back with an offer of his own. He had already worked out exactly what he wanted—he wanted to become not just Chief Artist, but actual Art *Editor*, and whilst doing the bulk of the illustrations himself, he would farm out remaining assignments to my other artists—in effect, to take charge of all of the illustrations used in each issue.

However, I wanted to retain a degree of artistic involvement myself, so we agreed that he would be designated as "Art Consultant" and that I could obtain some artwork myself—always provided that I "consulted" him, and that the vast bulk of the illustrations would pass through him. We agreed the scale of his remuneration and shook hands on it, then went out to very long lunch.

On arrival at my parent's home—they having agreed to put Eddie up for the night—he presented them with an attractive framed picture of a Japanese girl. It was one of the then-new novelty 'three dimensional' pictures, printed on silk, where the girl would wink at the onlooker, depending on the angle from which she was viewed. I considered that it was a nice gesture on his part, and that I had gained a valuable assistant and ally in my quest to constantly improve the standards of my magazine. I also gave Eddie further mss to illustrate, in particular the first 'Golden Amazon' novel I had selected for the companion magazine, now renamed *Image of Tomorrow*, for which Eddie was also to paint a cover.

Then came another bolt from the blue. Transworld announced that the first issue of *Vision* had been a complete sell-out, and they enclosed a fat cheque—but with the sting in the tail that they were *dropping the magazine completely!* They were, in fact, *disbanding their entire distribution operation!*

I immediately telephoned Pat Newman to protest that we had a contractual understanding with them and that I wasn't prepared to accept the situation. He explained that it had not been his decision, but that of his board. However he invited me to discuss matters in his office.

Once again I flew to London. By now I was not the green fan I had been when Graham had first contacted me more than a year earlier. I pointed out that Graham was a very rich and high-powered businessman and that the breaking of a witnessed verbal contract would be contested. The outcome was that I obtained a compromise: Transworld would continue to distribute the magazine for another six months, but that our agreement could be instantly dissolved if either of us could find another new distributor in the meantime.

I cabled a full report to Ron Graham, who was understandably wroth at Transworld's actions, but he agreed to abide by my compromise, and, as ever, he gave me his full backing—including the go-ahead on *Image of Tomorrow*, though we both agreed this would have to be held in abeyance until the new distributor was secured.

I received a very contrite letter direct from Lee Harding in Australia, offering his apologies for the misunderstanding over 'Echo', and offering me two new mss, one a free of charge replacement for the offending story. I seized on his letter eagerly, and in accepting his second story I asked him to let me have the addresses of Jack Wodhams and Damien Broderick, if he knew them, so that I could use direct touch. I was also looking for new authors, and would be grateful if he could spread the word Down Under that *Vision* was wide open to Australian authors.

Lee Harding thereafter became my staunchest Australian ally. Not only did he give me the addresses I asked for, but he also put me in touch with Frank Bryning and Bertram Chandler, and promised me first look at his new work. Would I be interested in a long novelette, set entirely in Australia, illustrated with photographs he had taken? He warned that it would not be conventional space opera, but rather an exploration of Australia's cultural heritage and traditions, and that I might consider it was only borderline SF. I replied saying that it sounded *exactly* the material I was looking for, and to go ahead and write it. That story would eventually be published as 'The Custodian' in issue # 8. I was so enthusiastic about Lee's stories that I commissioned him to write stories around some of the covers Ron Graham would soon be sending me by the very talented Australian artist Stanley Pitt. Lee was a friend of Stan's and actually saw the paintings before Stan sold them to Graham! I corresponded with many authors in similar ways, always the direct personal touch. Waiting for good stories to emerge via the slush-pile was a complete waste of time.

I felt under constant pressure as a result of the bewildering turn of events—all of them things entirely beyond my control, and none of them connected to the merits—or otherwise—of my editing. I knew that *Vision* itself was improving by leaps and bounds, and would go on doing so. I had learned so much and so fast that the actual *editing* of it was no problem at all to me, but unless I could solve the distribution problem, I knew the enterprise was doomed. And as someone who had given up his career to fight its cause, and taken out a new mortgage and was about to be married, I knew I had to come up with something—and fast.

I was about to make an appointment to see my original distributor—who now told me they could handle magazines as well as books—Transmutation Ltd of Guildford—when I received a telephone call from the New English Library Ltd. Could I come to London for urgent talks—they were interested in taking over distribution of *Vision of Tomorrow*!

This time I took the train to London—an overnight sleeper. The meeting was similar to my first meeting with Transworld. NEL were a very successful paperback firm who were expanding their operation into magazine distribution. They had just set up a new distribution department, and were keen to carry *Vision*. They would book regular back cover advertising, and so would have an extra interest in ensuring that the magazine sold well. They promised me that they could definitely ensure the success of the magazine.

Invited to a tour of their offices, I met Peter Haining, and told him of my conversations with Mrs. Fearn, and how that I'd had no trouble at all in obtaining permissions from her. He looked suitably embarrassed, especially when I remarked that it was funny how some of the stories in the pulp magazines I had once loaned him kept turning up in his anthologies. To my great surprise, I also met Ken Bulmer, who was on his way to an interview with another NEL editor, Laurence James. Ken had sold him a sword and sorcery novel and was in negotiations about a possible series of historical novels. I agreed to meet Ken later on at reception, and we went for a drink and discussed the situation.

I had decided to accept NEL's offer, not least because I thought that with Ken Bulmer being a regular contributor to both *Vision* and their paperback line, they might be able to do us both some good.

I travelled back on the train to Newcastle. A Director at NEL had promised to get in touch with Transworld and make the necessary changeover arrangements, and to confirm our new contract in writing. I thought that, at last, my troubles were finally over. In fact, my problems were only just beginning . . .

It was the last week in August 1969, and *Vision # 2* was due from the printer at the end of the month. This time, I had actually seen the proofs, and by inserting filler illustrations and making last minute adjustments, I knew that the appearance of the magazine would be vastly improved. However, I decided to go and see them personally, not only to give them the new address following our change of distributor, but also to check up on the printing of the magazine.

The Print Director at Northumberland Press, eager to impress me after their botching of the first issue, showed me into the print room, where the magazine had just finished printing. He proudly handed me the completed but as yet unbound signatures. I looked at them with interest, then felt like I had been kicked in the pit of the stomach.

Every alternate page had been printed upside down!

I thrust it under his nose. "Stop the presses!" I roared. "What the hell do you buggers think you're playing at! How many copies of this crap have you printed?" I gritted.

The Print Director went green around the gills. "25,000."

I headed back to Newcastle in a black mood. The Printer had been left in no doubt where he stood. Not only would he have to reprint the entire

25,000 copies, but he would have to buy and pay for the replacement paper himself, and would not receive a penny against the print bill until the copies were reprinted and safely in NEL's warehouse. They had protested, but I was adamant. "Well, we can't possibly have the issue reprinted by the end of the week." Bang went the regular monthly schedule I had worked my balls off to ensure. Still, with the cock-up coinciding with the changeover in distributors, perhaps it was just as well that the issue would be late. It would give them more time to prepare. *What the hell next, I wondered?*

The next day I felt that I had earned a day off, so my fiancée and I went shopping for furniture and fittings to Bainbridges, a big department store in Newcastle. We were due to be married in three weeks and there was still much to be bought for the house. As we looked around, I was astonished to see a large framed print—obviously for sale—that showed a giant orange-red star shedding its light onto the surface of a desolate, alien planet. It was a striking scene, brilliantly painted in the style of the great Chesley Bonestell. But he was not its artist.

An examination of the back of the print showed it to be the work of "David Hardy, Astro-Art." I bought the print for our living room—it matched our red carpet perfectly—and set about tracing the mysterious David Hardy, whom I telephoned later that afternoon. At the end of the call, I had David's agreements to paint covers for *Vision*! He had never painted for any SF magazines before, but he had been a fan for years! I was very pleased to have 'discovered' him for the field. One step back—another step forward!

I was about to take my biggest step of all—I was getting married.

My printer continued to delay, claiming that he was having trouble buying the paper. I washed my hands of the whole business, got married, and flew off on my honeymoon to Jersey, having received his firm promise that the issue would be reprinted and delivered whilst I was away.

But when we returned—the second week in October—it was to discover that the issue, dated September, had still not been delivered. Furious, I cabled Graham and received his permission to sack the printers the moment I could find a new firm to take over. I informed NEL, and was slightly mollified to learn that the delay was not harming anything so far as they were concerned. However, the delay certainly concerned me, because it meant that the cash flow of our company's accounts was all going one way—out. I was now really settling into the editorial chair, and I was able to commission work from my most reliable contributors, whilst continuing to unearth the very occasional gem from the slush-pile—people like K.W. Eaton and Peter Oldale. Oldale's story 'Problem Child' (which I had extensively revised before publishing it in *Vision* No. 9) was snapped up for anthologizing in Richard Davis' *Year's Best Horror Stories*, published on both sides of the Atlantic by Sphere and Daw Books, along with Ted Tubb's classic 'Lucifer'! from No.3. Its appearance there caused Ted's story to win the 1972 Europa Prize, and further international recognition came when it was reprinted (several times) in Switzerland and Germany.

Steadily, I was tracking authors, and would eventually get good material by most of the leading UK professionals—including Dan Morgan, John Brunner, and even long-silent talents like Robert J. Tilley. Since my policy had always been to pay promptly on acceptance—a policy popular with authors and which was beginning to pay off—I was rapidly spending all the money received from the sales of the successful first issue.

Finding a new printer proved easy for me. I looked in the yellow pages for local printers, and my eye came across one particular entry: "Clifford Paul, Printer and Publisher, Clavering Place, Newcastle." I blinked. *Clavering Place was less than 100 yards from my new offices!* Definitely worth a visit, I thought. I telephoned to make an appointment, and was invited to come round immediately once I told them my location. I took a copy of our first issue with me.

Clifford Paul turned out to be a small, fairly elderly man with smiling eyes and a genial manner. He had been in business for years, and was himself the publisher of a very successful *Bride and Home*-type monthly magazine. He showed me a copy. It was beautifully printed; nice crisp dark typeface although it was on slick paper, with many pages in full colour. And it was in the same format as *Vision*!

I had found my new printer!

Clifford Paul was efficiency personified. He agreed to start printing our third issue immediately, and undertook personally to get all the plates and blocks from Northumberland Press to enable him to do so. He also invited me to assemble No. 4 and the following issues, and we agreed a deadline day each month, when the copy would be collected by him from my office. Thereafter every issue was delivered and printed on time.

The system I employed was to have two proof copies of several stories and articles individually printed, in single column, on which I proof-read and marked corrections. I had a given number of lines per page, and a given number of pages. I counted the lines on every story, and then cut out and pasted and fitted up each issue like a jigsaw puzzle, allowing space for illustrations. I had just *two days* to do this with each issue, and I worked until midnight every month, fitting the whole thing together. Where a story overran by just a couple of lines (which by Sod's Law was frequently) I would edit the text in minor ways to reduce the number of lines. The result was that every issue of *Vision* from No.4 onwards had no surplus space whatsoever. The editorial had to be written at the very last minute (since it reflected the contents, and I did not know the finished line-up until the morning the proofs were to be collected.) Another reason for this was that Ron Graham had faithfully promised to write "general" editorials for each issue himself, and I waited in vain for them to arrive. They never did, so I had to write them myself as first drafts in half an hour or so, dictating them to Maureen, who typed them up just before Clifford Paul called at my office at 10 a.m. to collect the proofed dummies. Thoroughly fed up with this, I commissioned my local Vicar to write the editorial of No.6. The Rev. John Clay had told me he had been a film extra in the Korda/Wells classic *Things To Come*, and so was familiar with SF. However, after his piece 'Whither SF?' appeared, Ron Graham was absolutely furious, and instead of commencing to write the editorials himself—as I had hoped—he ordered me to write all editorials myself henceforth!

So efficient was my new printer that it became apparent that he would have our third issue printed at the same time as the second issue was belatedly finally completed and delivered. I had arranged that NEL's sales rep would call to see me on alternate months, whilst I myself would make regular trips to their offices in London to discuss policy and how best to promote the magazine. When the NEL rep saw the advance copy of the third issue, dated November, with its new colour section and eye-catching new cover logo by Eddie Jones he was mightily impressed. He advised me that it would be best for him to start distribution with that issue, since it was much more attractive and dynamic looking than the second issue—an assessment with which I was in complete agreement. The only problem was that 'The Impatient Dreamers' historical series by Wally Gillings was unfolding in chronological sequence, and each episode was numbered 1, 2, 3 . . .

I solved the problem by having Clifford Paul overprint the second issue as 'December' and add an extra couple of pages carrying a note apologising for the fact that due to circumstances beyond our control, the third episode had been printed last month. As deliberate, planned policy, NEL distributed # 3 in November, followed by # 2 in December, and # 4 in January 1970, and the magazine appeared on the dot each month thereafter, until it was discontinued with # 12 in September, 1970.

I thought—and still think—that this was a sensible thing to do, and perfectly clear to anyone seeing the two magazines together. I was also quite proud of my managerial skills in sorting the matter out. I considered it to have been one of the highlights of my brief editorial career. Unfortunately, the event seems to have passed into science fiction history as an example of how the magazine was somehow jinxed because of my editorial incompetence.

We were printing 25,000 copies of each issue—the actual recorded and paid for sales of the sell-out first issue. However, I was disturbed to receive NEL's sales returns—they recorded a massive drop in circulation to around 12,000 copies. Low, but bearable. I began to cut the print run, but with the visible improvement in *Vision's* appearance and content with successive issues—covers by both Eddie Jones and David Hardy, outstanding fiction by E. C. Tubb, Lee Harding, Bob Shaw and Michael Moorcock (both of whom I had met at the 1970 Easter BSFA Convention in London and successfully commissioned to write for me).

Throughout 1970 I was in regular contact with Walter Gillings, the noted editor of Britain's pioneer SF magazines, *Tales of Wonder* and *Fantasy*. Responding to my enquiries, Gillings had searched his archives to discover some old manuscripts still in his possession—stories accepted for both of his earlier magazines, but which had never been used. As 'new' stories they would not breach Graham's 'no reprints' stipulation, and provided they were good enough, I could use them.

He sent me a number of short stories by Norman Lazenby, which, alas, had dated too badly for me to be able to use them. But on being informed by Walter that Lazenby had lived in Gateshead on Tyneside, I consulted the telephone directory and discovered that there was a Lazenby still living in Gateshead. This turned out to be Norman's brother, who passed on my letter to Norman, who now lived in St. Annes, just a few miles from Mrs. Fearn in Blackpool! Norman thereafter became a good friend whom

I would visit on my frequent visits to Blackpool, and he wrote a new story, 'Lalee' which I bought. The Gillings cache also included two novelettes by John Russell Fearn, one each from the inventory of his two magazines: 'The Retreat' and 'The Arbiter', written in 1934 and 1944 respectively.

Both stories required a little editing to make them suitable for publication, but this 1 was well able to do, having made a life-long study of Fearn's work. After purchasing the magazine rights from Carrie Fearn, the author's widow (who was grateful for the unexpected money to supplement her pension), I arranged for their publication in *Vision* The second story was retitled by me as 'Rule of the Brains', as Fearn had used 'The Arbiter' on a different and shorter version of the story, which had later been published in the American *Startling Stories*.

I also retitled the prosaic-sounding 'The Retreat' as 'Into the Unknown', which appeared first, in the April 1970 issue. This proved to be the most popular story I ever ran in *Vision*, winning particular praise from William F. Temple, who used to send me his critique of each issue. Encouraged by its reception, and anxious to help Mrs. Fearn further I implored her to search her Blackpool home for any other unpublished manuscripts Fearn might have left, after his sudden demise in 1960. I was in a position to consider buying anything of a science fictional nature, as there were very few UK professional SF writers producing magazine fiction at that time, and I was constantly on the lookout for suitable material.

When I travelled to Blackpool and called on Mrs. Fearn. I found her visibly distressed. Over tea, she confided to me her dread of entering Fearn's study, because of the poignant memories it evoked. Fearn had died of a heart attack ten years earlier, having just completed a first draft of *Earth Divided*, a new 'Golden Amazon' novel.

He had been engaged on retyping a corrected final version. Finding the manuscript by his typewriter, Mrs. Fearn had completed the typing of the final manuscript, and sent it off to Fearn's Canadian publishers. "I knew that Jack would have wanted me to do this for him," she told me. *Earth Divided* had been accepted, and appeared posthumously in the Toronto *Star Weekly* in 1961. However, the strain of sitting at Fearn's typewriter, reading his final work, coupled with her natural grief at the death of a beloved husband, had had a devastating psychological effect on Mrs. Fearn. In complying with my request to search the study—which had remained locked for ten years—she had obviously reopened old memories and old wounds. She handed me a small pile of manila envelopes, quietly insisting "that was all there was."

Naturally, I thereafter respected her feelings, and the subject of the study and any other manuscripts it may still have contained was never again mentioned between us. In the event, the manuscripts she had retrieved consisted of four novels and one novelette. Unfortunately, I was not able to buy any of the novels for *Vision*. Two of them were detective stories and the remaining two were 'Golden Amazon' novels. They had been written in 1959 for the Toronto *Star Weekly*, but had both been rejected, having been adjudged too technical for the magazine's largely female readership. Rather than revise them at that time, Fearn had simply written more new stories—all of which had been accepted and published.

Forming, as they did, part of the series of novels we planned to use later, I was unable to use either in *Vision*. However, the remaining 20,000-word SF manuscript, 'The Slitherers', *was* entirely suitable. I lost no time in buying this novelette, which (with minimal editing) appeared in what turned out to be the last issue of *Vision* (September 1970). I had no idea at the time that this had been condensed from a 40,000 word novel version, which mss was still in the study—along with many other short stories, novels, plays, and TV scenarios.

Ron Graham was delighted with 'Into the Unknown', for which Eddie Jones did a stunning double-page illustration, and we were both confident that sales would soon pick up. It was surely just a matter of time . . .

Ron cabled me more capital, and plans went ahead for our companion reprint magazine *Image of Tomorrow*, and two complete issues of a brand new fantasy magazine Ron had decided to publish, *Sword and Sorcery*, which in view of my heavy workload, was entirely edited by Ken Bulmer. Ken's magazine was an outstanding effort, and was to have featured a brand new Elric *novel* by Mike Moorcock, a new Conan-style hero series by Ted Tubb ('Malkar'), and even a bizarre new story by Brian Aldiss.

Brian was one of the two British authors I had really wanted, but had failed to attract to *Vision*. He was a regular reader and contributor to *Speculation*, and with the adverse reviews of *Vision* running against me there (and, somewhat to my bewilderment, also now in *Vector* following a change of editorship of the old guard in the BSFA who had been supportive) it was perhaps not surprising that Aldiss decided he would not want to be seen dead in my 'anachronistic' magazine. Upon reading his latest story

'The Saliva Tree'—which I considered to be an absolute masterpiece, and *exactly* the type of story I wanted to publish—I had written him pleading to be favoured with his stories. Alas, he gave me an even bigger "bum's rush" than Graham had given Peter Weston. It was the *only* instance where an established author did not respond positively to my request for fiction. I was upset, and recorded the incident (obliquely) in my editorial in issue No.3, hoping that Brian would see it and change his mind. He didn't—or at least, he never changed his mind!

The second author I had wanted to use was Arthur C. Clarke. Not for his fiction—I realized that I could never have afforded him for that—but I'd hoped that he might write short *non-fiction* articles, which could then be illustrated by David Hardy. William F. Temple had introduced me to him at the Easter 1970 London Convention. Smiling, he apologetically turned down my offer of £20 a thousand words (five times the rate for fiction!), explaining that everything he wrote went through his agent who syndicated it world wide for *hundreds* of pounds per thousand! But he *did* autograph my Sci-Con nametag card, adding his London contact address of 88 Nightingale Road, N2. (I kept that card, and would contact him years later in my capacity as Mike Ashley's agent, and buy anthology reprint rights to some of his best stories—and Brian Aldiss, too!)

In fact, just about every top name was within the pages of *Sword and Sorcery*, including Dan Morgan and his friend John Kippax (John Hynam.) It carried illustrations by Eddie Jones and fellow Tynesider Jim Cawthorn, whom I had recently traced and added to *Vision's* roster of illustrators.

Image of Tomorrow featured Fearn's novel *Conquest of the Amazon*, together with reprint stories by Jack Williamson and Donald Wandrei, and was lavishly illustrated by Eddie Jones, who did a 'Barbarella'-style Golden Amazon cover, complete with kinky boots. All three issues of the magazines were actually typeset and proofed and both magazines were scheduled for release in October.

NEL's sales returns suddenly dipped to only 5,000 copies, so I immediately went to London for a showdown meeting. I had bust a gut to improve the magazine—what had *they* done? They admitted to me that their magazine division—being "new kids on the block"—had failed to persuade W.H. Smith to stock our magazine—*it was actually banned from their entire chain of shops across the country.* Nearly all of our print runs had never even gotten out of their warehouse! The situation was absolutely intolerable, and though Ron would have been prepared to carry on—and had the financial clout to sustain further losses—I was not prepared to preside over a company that was not making profits for my employer, especially Ron Graham, to whom I felt deeply obligated. I recommended that the line be aborted, to which Ron reluctantly agreed.

The magazine had failed, after an agonising and traumatic 18 months of unremitting effort and thousands of pounds poured into it by Ron Graham. His dream—and mine—to help British and Australian writers get published—was now ashes.

It did *not* fail because of its editorial content. It failed, purely and simply, because we had been betrayed and let down by our distributors. *They could not get the magazine out of their warehouse and into the shops.*

However, I had not resigned from my job—far from it. I only recommended the cancellation of our magazines on the understanding with Ron that *we were to revert to a modification of my original plan, and publish science fiction paperbacks.* I still had six months of my contract to run, and I was determined to make the book line successful, and to recover the considerable sums of money that Ron's company had lost. And besides, I had my *own* future to think about. My wife and I both wanted to start a family, and we needed the security of a steady job to do that. I had given up my career for this job, and therefore I had a burning, intense desire to succeed. I was hoping to extend my contract, and make a career in editing. As Ted Tubb had put it in one of his many supportive letters, "Printer's ink gets into your blood."

I threw myself into the task, travelling regularly to all parts of the country, seeking advice from people already in the trade, and taking advantage of all the contacts and friendships I had built up during my *Vision* editorship. Author William F. Temple put me in touch with leading US agent Forrest Ackerman. This enabled me to augment the already-optioned British novels with classic American novels by A.E. van Vogt and Jack Williamson. None of their titles that I optioned had ever appeared in England. Working with former *Vision of Tomorrow* contributor Walter Gillings, I edited with him a series of paperback originals by John Wyndham. These comprised two collections of short stories which had never appeared in book form in either England or America, and two 1930s novels which were long out of print, and had previously only appeared under his 'John Beynon' pen name. Wyndham had died the previous year, and publication under the 'John Wyndham' byline for the first time meant that they would be received by the trade as brand new books, thus assuring them of massive sales.

I showed my proposed programme to one of Britain's most successful publishers, Gordon Landsborough (who had created the phenomenally successful Panther Books and Four Square books amongst many other companies). I had earlier met Gordon at the Sci-Con 1970 SF Convention in London. He was in the audience with his friend George Hay (an author he had 'discovered' during his Hamilton days) and after I had made a short speech, he had introduced himself. I subsequently interviewed him, commissioning his SF publishing memoirs for serialization in *Vision of Tomorrow*.

When I knew the magazine was to be discontinued, the articles were adapted (along with others by John Carnell, Walter Gillings, E. C. Tubb, Ken Bulmer and myself) to form the backbone of a book on British science fiction history, *The Impatient Dreamers*. It was accepted for publication by Frank Dietz for Luna Publications, an American fan Press, but as they dithered and procrastinated, I eventually demanded the mss and tearsheets from *Vision* back. To assist Mike Ashley with his *History of the Science Fiction Magazine* series of books, I let him use selected extracts from it in his third volume (1976), but for various reasons, my book did not appear until 1992, as *Vultures of the Void*. By then it was minus the articles by Gillings, who had sadly died in 1979. Although he had given me his written permission to use them in my book, I felt I should get the approval of his family first. Unfortunately they never answered my letters, so I reluctantly rejigged the book without them, and retitled it.

Gordon Landsborough knew exactly what it took to create a new publishing imprint. He was so impressed with my proposed opening publishing programme of 'Graham SF Classics'—Wyndham, Tubb, Temple, Williamson, Van Vogt, two anthologies edited by myself, to eventually be followed by Fearn's 'Golden Amazon' series—that he offered his services as an unpaid adviser to the line. Using his own contacts in the publishing world, he secured for me a deal with the largest paperback printer in the U.K. (on the same advantageous discounted terms he was receiving for his own company, Dragon Books).

He also introduced me to his friend and contemporary Ralph Stokes, whom he had known during the mushroom days of the early 1950s. A publishing veteran (amongst others, he had launched Kaye Publications) and now a survivor of that turbulent era, Stokes had successfully launched Tandem Books. Tandem agreed to act as UK distributor for the new line of paperbacks. The deal was essentially similar to one that Don Wollheim would create many years later with the New American Library (for 'DAW Books' substitute 'Graham Books'). Contracts and options were prepared and everything was set to go. The plan was to open with the four 'block-buster' John Wyndham titles, which were assured of national distribution by W. H. Smith and other big book chains (thus overcoming the problems which had killed *Vision of Tomorrow*). I cabled to Ron Graham for the funds to have the titles printed (following the delivery of which Tandem had promised immediate reimbursement "on account", so sure were they of the line's sales potential.) I was confident that Ron would back the programme. But to my utter mortification, he was coldly unenthusiastic about the whole thing. He bluntly informed me that he wished to open the line with the Australian novel *Out of the Silence* by Erle Cox. This had originally appeared in the Australian magazine *Argus* in 1919, and had appeared in book form in Australia and England in 1925. It had been out of print in England since 1927, and had last appeared from a small American publisher in 1947. Whilst revered as a legendary 'classic' it was known only to a tiny handful of collectors, and Cox was completely unknown in England. When I told Landsborough of Graham's change of my plan—substituting Erle Cox for John Wyndham—he was horrified. "W.H. Smith will never touch it with a forty foot pole—you've got to establish your credentials with them with someone like Wyndham *first*, or your line will fail." I expressed the point forcibly to Ron Graham, stressing that it was essential to build the new company up by using "big names" before introducing lesser fry like Cox.

I implored him to give me the go-ahead on the original programme, where success was already assured. All it needed was the money to print the four Wyndham titles, after which Tandem's advance would be sufficient to pay the agreed advance to the Wyndham estate. The sum involved was only a fraction of the amount already lost. Thereafter, the line should be self-financing.

Ron replied angrily to the effect that it was *his* money, and he was therefore entitled to publish anything he liked. If he couldn't publish whatever titles *he* wanted, and had to publish only stuff acceptable to *W.H. Smith*, why should he publish *anything*?

Why indeed? After all, Ron likely blamed W.H.Smith as having killed *Vision*.

So it was a perfectly good question, to which I could only think of one answer. I sent him my resignation. The SF pb line was aborted. My career in science fiction book publishing was over before it had started. I felt that I had been hung out to dry.

Ron was very gentlemanly about our parting of the ways. He sent me his Australian 'Ditmar' Award (*Vision* had won the 'Best International Science Fiction Publication' category in 1970) and even offered to find me administrative employment in his company if Maureen and I were prepared to emigrate to Australia!

We weren't, and I decided to try and resume the Local Government career I had been obliged to leave to form the new company. I was lucky enough to quickly find another job, this time with Tynemouth Education Department. It meant a big drop in salary, and of course Maureen also lost her job, though Ron's final act of generosity was to continue to pay her through to the end of the following summer, when the office lease also ran out, It was just as well, as Maureen in fact continued to work out of the office alone, attending to the many unexpected administrative details and problems associated with the winding up, and the last thing we did was to find and engage a shipping company to transport by sea to Ron in Australia all of the many thousands of unsold copies of *Vision of Tomorrow*. Hopefully, by selling them himself through his friend Mervyn Binn's famous SF shop in Australia, he was able in time to get some— maybe all—of his money back.

I had kept in touch with my friend Walter Gillings, and we formed a partnership as Cosmos Literary Agency. (Walter knew only too well the misery I was going through, having suffered the same fate himself on three occasions). I was acutely conscious that Walter had done sterling work in persuading Wyndham's heirs to allow his established name to be used, and had acted as unpaid editorial adviser. So in 1972 I turned all four Wyndham books (and Walter's introductions to them) over to London publishers Hodder and Stoughton. They couldn't believe their luck. They snapped them up immediately, and rushed all four books into print as quickly as they could before any other publisher got wind of them:

Stowaway to Mars, The Secret People, Sleepers of Mars and *Wanderers of Time.* They remained in print for years afterwards, selling thousands upon thousands of copies, and going through reprint after reprint, after reprint.

If only Graham had agreed to back my plan! If only . . . If only I'd had the courage and confidence to borrow the money and publish the books myself! Alas, at the time that thought, strangely, never even occurred to me.

Although Walter later received a small fee for his introductions, I never received a penny—or any editorial credit for having thought of the idea in the first place. Hodder's editor had earlier promised to name me in the books as "series editor" and to consider bringing out my other aborted 'Graham Classics' titles, but since they could simply keep the four 'new' Wyndham books in print indefinitely, they had no further need of me, or books by any other writer.

One learns some hard lessons in the publishing jungle, and I was to learn several more in succeeding years. To rub salt in my wounds, my van Vogt and Williamson selections later appeared successfully from other UK publishers, and both writers became very well established in the UK paperback field.

At this point I feel it is important to mention the contributions to British SF of the late Walter Gillings. Prior to his enforced departure from Nova Publications in 1951 (in order to save money by having one editor [Carnell] instead of two, for which Gillings blamed Frank Cooper as the instigator), he had suffered a double blow from a personal domestic tragedy. Embittered, he all but disappeared from the British SF scene. He did not fully return until 1969, when I invited him back into an almost unrecognizable British SF scene. He became my most loyal ally, helping me unstintingly with my magazine *Vision of Tomorrow.*

He was welcomed with open arms as a regular columnist for various British magazines, and continued to spread the gospel according to science fiction until the very end of his days. His untimely death, on July 19, 1979, was a shock to his many friends and colleagues. First Fandom in America had invited him to the United States, pledging to supplement his fare, and he and I were planning a new fan magazine, *Science Fiction Archives,* aimed at collectors, and planning to reprint his legendary pre-war *Scientifiction* to try and raise money for his trip.

He left the field a poorer place to work in. Many projects were left incomplete, including an earlier incarnation of this book—although a long and thoughtful series covering the history of British SF in the '30s and '40s entitled 'The Impatient Dreamers' did appear in *Vision of Tomorrow* in 1969-70, giving an even more detailed *personal* description of the early British SF history than this volume covers in its opening chapters. Gillings was the founder of so much that makes British SF what it is today, and his efforts are well appreciated by those that knew how much love and affection he put into his work—hopefully this book will go some little way towards telling part of his story, and to keeping his memory alive.

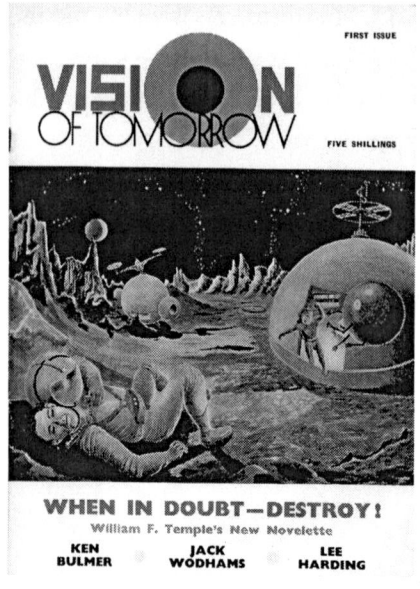

Vision of Tomorrow # 1, July 1960
(James Harbottle).

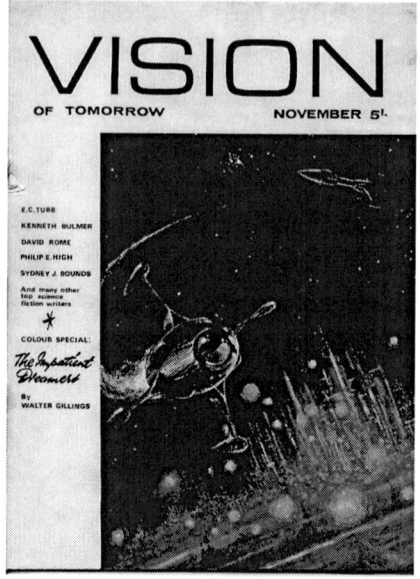

Vision of Tomorrow # 3, November 1969
(Eddie Jones).

Vision of Tomorrow # 7, April, 1970
(David Hardy).

Vision of Tomorrow # 12, September
1970 (Stanley Pitt).

Vision's Australian Personalities and Contributors

1. Ron Graham (Publisher)
2. Lee Harding
3. Stanley Pitt
4. David Rome
5. John Foyster
6. Jack Wodhams
7. Damien Broderick

Photo page; (1) Ronald E. Graham, (2) Lee Harding, (3) Stanley Pitt, (4) David Rome, (5) John Foyster, (6) Jack Wodhams (7) Damien Broderick. *Vision of Tomorrow,* April 1970

CHAPTER 18:
MORE TRAVAILS

In 1973 *New Worlds* ran an extract from one of the chapters of Brian Aldiss' forthcoming History of Science Fiction book: *Billion Year Spree*. This was a typical Aldiss piece, sharply dissecting some of the older SF writers, chiefly Jack Williamson. It was a brilliantly argued and not unsympathetic piece, but made the (to me) cardinal sin of saying that in recent years Williamson had "fallen silent". This was not in fact true—Williamson had produced *several* notable novels after the interval when Brian stated that he had stopped writing, and was in fact actively writing new works. I knew this because ever since buying once-only reprint rights to his short story 'Passage to Saturn' for Graham's aborted magazine *Image of Tomorrow*, I had kept in touch with him and reprinted the story myself in my *Fantasy Booklet* (very much a shoestring reprint operation, but I did manage to publish new stories by Eric Frank Russell and E. C. Tubb). Jack had very kindly thereafter sent me some of his new books.

Brian had also erroneously given Fearn's birthplace as Liverpool instead of Worsley in Manchester (he was obviously mixing him up with Eric Frank Russell). Accordingly I wrote to him respectfully, but firmly pointing out these minor depredations. To my delighted surprise Aldiss quickly sent me an appreciative reply, asking me for details of Williamson's latest novels (of which he'd been unaware) and asking me if I would care to check the proofs of his book, and toothcomb it for any similar little errors, such as dates of first editions of the scores of books he was discussing in the book, plus any biographical details of authors, etc. The only problem was I would have to do this in the next few days, as the book was soon due to be delivered back to his UK and American publishers.

I readily agreed, and was privileged to read Aldiss' masterly dissertation before any one else, other than his editors. There were, inevitably in a work of such massive scope, a few minor errors I was able to catch, for which Brian was appreciative. But Brian explained that he had deliberately *left in* the error about Fearn's birthplace—in order to annoy Eric Frank Russell! Brian kindly sent me a gratis copy of his book when published, which still has pride of place on my extensive reference shelf.

In 1976 Aldiss again showed his generosity by recommending me to Trewin Copplestone as Principal Research Consultant for their planned reference work, *The Visual Encyclopaedia of Science Fiction*. Copplestone had asked Brian to do the job, but he was too busy on his latest novel and had declined, suggesting me. I was delighted to agree, and Copplestone sent me the framework they had already decided on for the book.

It was to be split into some twenty iconic 'thematic' sections (such as 'Spacecraft and Star Drives', 'Galactic Empires', 'Cataclysms and Dooms', etc), in which it was expected that someone would research and describe all of the progenitor stories on that theme, and trace their development to date—and in addition, provide an additional detailed bibliography of other related stories! And there were a further nine essays to be written on 'Fandom and Media'! It was a *massive* task, made even more difficult by the fact that Brian Ash, who had been engaged by Copplestone as the 'editor', was not actually writing *any* of the these essays, apart from a couple of the sub-sections in a small 'lit-crit' section entitled 'Deep Probes'; he had already contacted a few authors who would complete the rest of this more 'literary' section. He had also conceived the idea of 'flowchart' giving a year-by-year and month-by-month chronology of the first appearances of noted magazines, stories and authors, etc.

My brief was to write as many of the 29 unallocated sections (forming the vast majority of the book!) as I could and/or to enlist the help of friends if I couldn't complete it myself. And not only that, but we were expected to supply *hundreds* of book and magazine covers and illustrations as well! What was more, time was of the essence, as the book had been pre-sold to Pan in the UK and Crown in the USA!

A score of noted authors, including such famous names as Aldiss, Ballard, Clarke, Niven and Williamson, would be writing short introductions to each of the thematic sections, *but the actual authors of the pieces that followed would not be credited, in a deliberate attempt to make it look as if the famous authors had actually written the section that followed their introduction!* However, I was assured that Cosmos Literary Agency and its clients would be separately credited as having written the various sections, and that I would be named as Principal Research Consultant.

I was assured by Ash (who I found to be a decent chap, grateful for my help) that payment would be made promptly upon his acceptance of each thematic piece, as it was written. So, like a fool, I accepted the assignment.

The task was quite impossible for one person, so I enlisted the help of my friend and colleague Walter Gillings (with whom I had formed the Cosmos Literary Agency) and also my client Michael Ashley, who was rapidly becoming a noted anthologist and researcher. *Between the three of us*, we *did* have a pretty well encyclopaedic knowledge of the field, and I also had a couple of friends and correspondents who could make useful contributions to certain sections.

Whilst in my youth I had began by reading exclusively British SF of the mushroom period, I had in fact long since 'graduated' to the American field as early as 1957. This followed my discovery—courtesy of Ken Slater's Fantast (Medway) Ltd book and magazine catalogues—of the American pulp magazines, and the fact that Fearn had contributed to them extensively between 1933 and 1948. Ken very kindly retyped for me a checklist of Fearn's many stories, which he extracted from Don Day's landmark *Index to the SF Magazines, 1926-1950*. Hunting these pulps down, I soon discovered the many great old stories by the likes of Edmond Hamilton, Henry Kuttner, Murray Leinster, Theodore Sturgeon and Jack Williamson, etc., and I had became an instant convert to, and collector of, American SF. (I had in fact missed seeing—at the time they were published—any of the many hardcover UK anthologies described earlier in this book.) And so, having promptly taken out a subscription to *Astounding* in 1957, by 1976 I knew a good deal about American as well as British SF. As did both Mike and Walter (whose favourite author was Theodore Sturgeon!).

Walter, Mike, and myself met up in London, and shared out the sections according to our various personal enthusiasms. We decided that between us, we could compile some 21 of the 29 sections—the greater part of the encyclopedia. They would each write their chosen sections, and submit their mss direct to myself. I would then edit or add to it, and submit it to Ash for his 'approval' and 'final edit.' Proofs of the completed section would then be sent to me for final spell-checking, and on my returning them, payment was supposed to be made. All payments would be made to myself, which I would then share proportionately with Walter and Mike.

The effort very nearly killed all three of us, but we managed it. We also turned over much of our vast personal lifetime collections, and provided hundreds of rare magazines and books, together with contributions from three other eminent collectors: John Eggeling, Gerry Webb, and Colin Lester.

The first few agreed payments (for all rights) for the earliest completed sections came through . . . and then stopped. Days, weeks, and even months went by—no payment! I found this acutely embarrassing, as Walter and Mike had done sterling work, trusting me to obtain their just reward, as had a couple of my other friends. When I complained to Ash, he apologized and said he had passed the work to the publisher, and the payment was therefore not his responsibility. When I complained to the publisher, giving a detailed schedule of when each section had been completed and sent, they claimed that a) they had not received them any time soon after the dates I claimed to have sent them, because b) they were so poorly written that Ash had had to extensively rewrite them, and this was taking time and causing the delays. This was a monstrous lie—the mss of Gillings, in particular (Walter was a professional journalist) were quite brilliant, and I knew they would have required no alterations whatsoever—and especially not by Ash, whose knowledge of the older pulps and rare books upon which Walter was a preeminent authority, was practically non-existent. Furthermore, Ash had *already* sent me proofs as each section was completed by him, and I could see for myself that no substantive changes had been made to any of our mss; his editing being mainly confined to the 'Additional input' bibliographies. I pointed this out to the publisher in no uncertain terms, sending photocopies of my original mss and the finished proof to ram home my point.

Still no payment. I then learned that the book was actually on the point of publication because I was receiving frantic phone calls from Janet Sacks, an editor who had been called in at a late stage to handle the myriad vital illustrations, asking me for information to go into the captions, etc. After a while I refused to help her further on a matter of principle, believing that in doing so I would force the publisher into coughing up the payments due to Ashley and Gillings, as well as myself.

Exhausted, furious and embarrassed, I eventually instructed my solicitor to take out an injunction on their using my unpaid for Cosmos Literary Agency material, since until they bought it, it was still my copyright. For good measure, I sent a copy of the correspondence to Pan Books.

The publisher then paid up in full. The book was published, and went into at least four different editions with four different publishers, two in paperback by Pan and Crown, and two in hardcover by Triune Books and the BCA. My name as Principal Research Consultant was removed—and that of Mike Ashley substituted. My name was listed, but only as a "Researcher" just above that of George Hay, who had written a single tiny piece on the Origins of Dianetics. My US fan friend Michael Banks who had collaborated with me on one section was not listed at all.

When I phoned Mike to ask how come he was listed as Principal Researcher, he admitted that he had been giving information to Sacks and her assistants all along, they having telephoned him direct after my refusal to co-operate.

Ironical? I think so.

The actual credits on who wrote what in *The Visual Encyclopedia of Science Fiction* have never been published. I give them now:

01   Program: Brian Ash, edited and revised by Mike Ashley & Philip Harbottle

02   Thematics

02.01 Spacecraft and Star Drives: Walter Gillings & Philip Harbottle

02.02 Exploration and Colonies: Mike Ashley

02.03 Biologies and Environments: Philip Harbottle

02.04 Warfare and Weaponry: Walter Gillings & Philip Harbottle

02.05 Galactic Empires: Philip Harbottle

02.06 Future and Alternative Histories: Mike Ashley

02.07 Utopias and Nightmares: Walter Gillings

02.08 Cataclysms and Dooms: Philip Harbottle

02.09 Lost and Parallel Worlds: Walter Gillings & Mike Ashley

02.10 Time and Nth Dimensions: Mike Ashley

02.11 Technologies and Artefacts: Philip Harbottle & Michael Banks

02.12 Cities and Cultures: James Goddard

02.13 Robots and Androids: Mike Ashley

02.14 Computers and Cybernetics: Mike Ashley & Philip Harbottle

02.15 Mutants and Symbiotes: Philip Harbottle

02.16 Telepathy, Psionics and ESP: Mike Ashley

02.17 Sex and Taboos: James Goddard

02.18 Religion and Myths: Mike Ashley & Philip Harbottle

02.19 Inner Space: James Goddard

A 20th section, Supermen, Pantropy and Genetics was commissioned, and written by Philip Harbottle. However the section was dropped and a butchered version was annexed to Mutants and Symbiotes without consulting me.

03   Deep Probes

03.01 Interface: Brian Ash & Edmund Cooper

03.02 Science Fiction as Literature: George Turner

02.03 Recurrent Concepts: L. Sprague de Camp & Brian Ash

04   Fandom and Media

04.01 Fandom: Colin Lester

04.02 Science Fiction Art: Jon Gustafson

04.03 Science Fiction in the Cinema: Philip Strick

04.04 Science Fiction on Television: Mike Ashley

04.05 Science Fiction Magazines: Colin Lester

04.06 Books and Anthologies: Mike Ashley

04.07 Juveniles, Comics and Strips: John Eggeling & Philip Harbottle

04.08 Commentators and Courses: ?? (Alas, I did not record this at the time)

04.09 Fringe Cults

04.09.1 The Fortean Influence: Walter Gillings & Mike Ashley

04.09.2 Shaver and the Gods on Earth: Walter Gillings & Mike Ashley

04.09.3 Origins of Dianetics: George Hay

The illustrations for the book were chosen from those initially selected and made available by Mike Ashley, John Eggeling, Walter Gillings, Philip Harbottle, Colin Lester and Gerry Webb.

Despite its commercial success, the book did not garner any critical kudos, and was panned on the grounds that it was difficult—if not impossible—to actually *use* as a reference book.

But at least one person *was* able to make good use of it. In 1983 an Italian, Sandro Perameno, published a large and very handsome hardcover anthology with Editrice Nord, entitled *I Mutanti*. In his introduction, Sandro made very good use indeed of my essay on the development of mutants in science fiction. He 'lifted' whole swathes of it, working it into 'his' introduction. He made even better use of several of the old SF magazine stories I had identified as notable 'mutant' stories, by reprinting them in his book, including 'Between the Darkness and the Daylight' by Algis Budrys, 'After the Atom' by John Russell Fearn, 'Way of the Gods' by Henry Kuttner, 'The 100th Generation' by Nat Schachner, and 'Prodigy' by Theodore Sturgeon. The book was spotted by my Italian agent and friend Antonio Bellomi, and he ensured that I got paid for the use of Fearn's story, which was at least some compensation for the literary theft involved. And since Copplestone had taken all copyrights in the essay, I didn't have any redress anyway. The jacket of the book advertised three other similar anthologies by Sandro, *Robotica, Storie Dello Spazio Interno*, and *Storie Dello Spazio Esterno*, and I would bet a pound to a penny that some of Mike Ashley's splendid thematic essays were similarly plundered.

Billion Year Spree by Brian W. Aldiss (Your Company). Weidenfeld & Nicholson, 1973

"Sword in the Snow" by E.C. Tubb (Philip Harbottle after Edd Cartier). Harbottle, 1973

Eternal Rediffusion by Leslie J. Johnson and Eric Frank Russell (Astronomoval plates). Harbottle, 1973

Passage to Saturn by Jack Williamson (Hans Wesso). Harbottle, 1973

The Visual Encyclopaedia of Science Fiction (Tim White). Pan, 1977

Page from *The Visual Encyclopaedia of Science Fiction* (Mutants and Symbiotes). Pan, 1977

Page from *The Visual Encyclopaedia of Science Fiction* (Religion and Myths). Pan, 1977

I Mutanti edited by Sandro Pergameno (Michael Whelan). Editrice Nord, 1983

CHAPTER 19:
VARGO STATTEN RETURNS

Vision of Tomorrow was to have other legacies. Both Eddie Jones and David Hardy had gone on to have glittering careers as SF cover artists. Many of Eddie's covers were sold direct to Europe, and some of them adorned the Italian books of Fearn and also E. C. Tubb (of which more shortly). Michael Coney, Lee Harding and Damien Broderick became internationally known novelists. All five would have done so without *Vision* having its brief existence, but I like to think it helped a little. Of course, Ken Bulmer, William F. Temple and E. C. Tubb were famous before and after *Vision*—but Ken's experience as editor of the aborted *Sword and Sorcery* may have helped him to become the successor editor to John Carnell's *New Writings In SF* series, when the latter died in 1972.

After resigning with Graham, I had gone to see Mrs. Fearn in order to explain how things had gone wrong. She graciously thanked me for my efforts in restoring the Amazon series to print, and asked me to become her literary agent. This would have profound repercussions and legacies for myself.

Ron Graham's time-limited option on the 'Golden Amazon' novels eventually lapsed, and thanks to John Carnell's reversion clause, all rights reverted to Mrs. Fearn. In 1973 I myself self-published *Conquest of the Amazon*, the 7th novel in the saga (following directly on the last title in the World's Work series), in an attractive chapbook edition, illustrated by Eddie Jones—purely to act as a showcase for the series.

My strategy was successful, and I was particularly pleased to sell *Conquest of the* Amazon to a new English paperback publisher, Futura Books in London, then being run by SF enthusiast Anthony Cheetham.

Their Orbit Books edition appeared in 1976, with a nice illustrative cover by Chris Achilleos. Cheetham had also commissioned me to edit a first collection of short stories by Edward E. Smith when he learned of their existence from me when I visited him to finalise the Fearn contract. One of his rival publishers was having a big success with Smith's novels, and he wanted to get in on the act. In my naivety I did not insist on a written contract, and the promised one percent royalty as my editorial fee for having provided the story selection he published as *The Best of E. E. 'Doc' Smith* never materialized. Nor was I credited as its editor on the published book. I received a £25 flat fee and a complementary copy of the Futura paperback, but was not told it had also appeared in hardcover from Dobson, and had to buy my own copy. And I never learned that it had later appeared as an American paperback from Jove Books until many years later . . .

My hoped-for reprinting of other titles in the 'Golden Amazon' series did not materialise, following the departure of Cheetham and the appointment of a new SF editor with his own personal agenda (ever the bane of authors and agents!).

Meanwhile, I had been unaware that across the Channel back in 1973, the leading French comics publisher, Aredit, launched a reprint of the old 1950's Fleuve Noir 'Anticipation' series—but as adult graphic novels in paperback. 'Vargo Statten' returned with a vengeance. The Aredit editions were full-length books, absolutely faithful to the original French text, some of them running over 200 pages, or published in two parts. They were illustrated novels. They reached a new generation of French and European readers, the 1970s counterparts of the same readership of the 1950s. Italian publishers were aware of the books, but contented themselves merely with reprinting their covers to place on other regular novels.

Then in the late 1970s, there was a sudden renewed interest by Italian publishers in the old stories of adventure SF, probably generated by the success of the film *Star Wars*. Editors and publishers began a desperate search to trace the copyright owner of the well-remembered 'Vargo Statten' novels, many of which had appeared in Italy during the late 1950s, and they were eventually successful in contacting me.

The first to do so was Antonio Bellomi of Milan, a freelance SF author and editor. During a stay in England in the late 1960s, and following a visit to the White Horse in London, he had struck up a friendship with noted author Arthur Lay, (who wrote SF as 'Arthur Sellings') and his wife. During a stay at their Worthing home before returning to Italy, he had read and been intrigued by Arthur's copy of one of my books on Fearn, *The Multi-Man*. Remembering this in 1976, he had set about tracing me, and had eventually discovered my letter in a 1956 issue of *Authentic Science Fiction*. His letter to that address was forwarded to me by my parents. I responded enthusiastically, and he came to see me on his next visit to England.

I was more than happy to agree to his becoming Fearn's agent in his country, with he himself having the pick of any stories and novels. The first book he published was *Cosmic Exodus* (Il Picchio, March 1977) under the ' Vargo Statten' byline, since this was still remembered in Italy. To my great delight, the book had a cover by Eddie Jones (recycled from a German paperback, where Eddie's covers were now appearing regularly).

I continued to visit Mrs. Fearn on numerous occasions throughout the 1970s, first with Maureen and then later with our daughter Claire during the summer holidays. To my delight, as Antonio Bellomi became an editorial consultant to several more Italian publishers, I was able to supplement Mrs. Fearn's meagre state pension by having several of his Vargo Statten and other SF paperbacks translated. I also succeeded in selling a number of Fearn's SF novels in Germany myself.

In the decade following *Star Wars*, close on fifty Fearn stories and novels appeared in Italy, eleven of them in hardcover. Most remarkable of all was an omnibus 'Vargo Statten' volume of nearly 1,000 pages published by Libra Editrice of Bologna, Italy, in their 'Classic' series. The volume carried an impressive 100 pages of bibliographical analysis and critical appraisal of 'Statten's' career by three leading Italian critics: Antonio Bellomi, Luigi Cozzi, and publisher Ugo Malaguti. The four novels reprinted in the volume were meticulously translated by a leading Italian author, Roberta Rambelli. It was part of a series featuring the best work of such authors as van Vogt, Williamson, Simak, Clarke, Sheckley, Asimov, and Wyndham.

Interspersed with occasional anthology appearances in England and America, the regular European royalty payments from Fearn reprints helped ease Mrs. Fearn's financial worries, although the main benefits to her were on the social side. She always insisted that I gave her the payments personally, in cash, at her home in Princeway, in Blackpool's South Shore district, so that I would have to go to see her!

I was happy to comply with her request, because my frequent visits to Blackpool also enabled me to meet many of Fearn's surviving personal friends who still lived in the town, or at nearby Lytham St. Annes. In this way, I learned a great deal about Fearn's life and work, even discovering new pseudonyms, all grist for the mill for my later researches and writings. In particular, I became great friends with St. Annes-based Tyneside-born author Norman Lazenby and his wife Kathy. Norman had corresponded with Fearn during the war and afterwards, until 1953, during which period his own career had paralleled Fearn's to a remarkable degree. Norman was a mine of information on the 'mushroom' publishers and their dubious practices.

They were happy days. Antonio Bellomi continued to be successful in arranging for the reprinting in Italian of many of the Vargo Statten and Volsted Gridban novels (also as 'Statten') and numerous short SF stories, which he ran as fillers in the Italian edition of *Perry Rhodan* magazine, which he edited.

The original *Fantastic Adventures* 'prototype' Amazon surfaced again in 1978, when I sold permission for the noted anthologist Michel Parry to include the third novelette, 'The Golden Amazon Returns' in his fun pb anthology, *Superheroes* (Sphere Books, 1978). (The story was later reprinted in a new shorter edition of the book, expurgated for younger readers, and issued by Granada in 1984.)

When the vogue for adventure SF eventually began to wane in Italy, the enterprising Bellomi became editor of Garden Editore, a publishing house that specialized in crime and detective stories, which were ever-popular. Edgar Wallace was by then out of copyright in Italy, and Bellomi scented an opportunity to release all his many dozens of titles, some of which had never appeared in Italy. He recruited my services as a bookfinder for the harder to find titles. The Wallace titles were successful, and Bellomi expanded his lists to include detective collections that featured a lead novel and additional short stories by diverse writers, including 'classical' authors such as Mark Twain and G. K. Chesterton, as well as oldtimers such as Gaston Leroux and William Le Queux. He also featured detective novels by John Russell Fearn, and published several of his John Slate 'Black Maria' and Hugo Blayn 'Dr. Carruthers' novels, along with pulp short stories from *Thrilling Mystery* and Gerald G. Swan magazines. They were instantly popular, and so I seized the opportunity to arrange for first-ever book publication of some of Fearn's Toronto *Star Weekly* mysteries, such as *Within That Room*, and also some fine and hitherto unpublished novels, most notably *The Man Who Was Not*. Such was Fearn's popularity, that Bellomi also launched him into a Western series, translating his Scion novel *Skeleton Pass*, and following it with two hitherto unpublished westerns, *Dynamite's Daughter* and *Massacre Trail*. Mushroom period detective thrillers from Sydney J. Bounds (*Two Times Murder*) and Norman Lazenby (*Yellow Cargo* and *Death in the Stars*) also sold readily. This was extremely satisfying for me, and not just financially. I felt I was repaying my personal debt to Bounds and Lazenby for the support and friendship they have given me since *Vision of Tomorrow* had brought us together. And it showed me that, once removed from the unjust opprobrium of the mushroom period, both they and Fearn were being internationally recognized as first-rate storytellers. The run of detective sales only came to an end in 1984 when Bellomi disagreed with the publishers over their policy of reprinting already published novels without further payment to writers, and resigned.

In January 1982, I had received a disturbing letter from Norman, informing me of the recent death of Mrs. Fearn in hospital, following a long illness. He enclosed a cutting from the 'In Memoriam' section of his local paper, which had fortunately been spotted by his wife. "I should imagine a lot of bits and pieces of Fearn's literary life are already being discarded at Princeway and thrown in various dustbins—a pity," he wrote, " . . . perhaps someone has already written you?"

In fact, no one *had* written, and within seconds of reading the letter, I realised that urgent action was needed to prevent Norman's sombre reflections from becoming reality. The newspaper cutting gave the telephone number of the funeral director, which I quickly rang. He in turn gave me the telephone number of the executor, Harry Masterman. Seconds later, I was through to a surprised Harry, who told me he had been literally going out of the door when I rang. Another second or two later and I would have missed him entirely—with disastrous consequences! He told me that he had actually been setting out on his way to supervise the Council workmen engaged in the removal of ruined household effects at Mrs. Fearn's home. Whilst Carrie had been terminally ill in hospital, the house water tank had burst. The words 'Council workmen' and 'removal' sent a chill up my spine. Desperately, I implored him to cancel this until the following afternoon, to give me the time to travel to Blackpool "to salvage Fearn's books and any papers and manuscripts there might be." Fortunately my name was known to the executor, I'd been named as a beneficiary in Carrie's will—she had bequeathed me the Fearn copyrights, and her solicitor had been due to contact me 'in due course' (the same solicitor who bungled the earlier negotiations).

To my intense relief, he agreed to postpone the workmen's depredations until after my arrival. However, I would have to get there no later than eleven a.m. the next morning. I promised him that I would, and rang off.

Easier said than done. Lacking my own transport, I turned for help to my best friend at work, Kevin Lee, who had only recently passed his driving test. We hired a car, in which he drove me to Blackpool, both of us taking a day's leave from work. Getting there for 11 am meant driving at top speed and setting out at 7.30 am.

During the journey, I dazedly ruminated that had Norman's wife not happened to glance at the 'In Memoriam' section of her local paper, and had her husband not written to me the same day, I would never have found out about Mrs. Fearn's death until it was much too late. And had I hesitated even momentarily and telephoned the executor just a few seconds later, he would have closed the front door and not heard the telephone ringing. Predestination? Other-worldly intervention? Fearn could have written a wonderful fantasy about it!

Later that morning, I was received at the Fearn home by the executor and his wife. I learned that his wife, Ethel, had been an old friend of Mrs. Fearn's—had, in fact, been a lodger in her home, prior to her own marriage. Mrs. Fearn had bequeathed her the house and its contents in her Will (written prior to her having met me—but my bequest had been added as a codicil in 1972, as a special gift, following the birth of my daughter—something I had not known at the time). Naturally, the Mastermans had been anxious to have the workmen start on clearing the house, in order to repair the severe water damage caused by the burst tank. I thanked them profusely for their cooperation in delaying this work.

Fearn's own large personal bookcase (containing signed copies of most of his books) had been situated in the small downstairs living room, which had been inundated by the burst water tank in the bathroom above. Although the furniture had been ruined, the bookcase and its priceless contents, situated atop a sideboard, had been miraculously untouched by the flood!

I was then escorted to Fearn's upstairs study. Situated on the same floor as the bathroom, and some distance along the corridor, this room was also untouched by the flood. Tingling with expectancy, tempered with deferential awe, I entered the room. And stopped dead!

The room was a positive Aladdin's Cave of manuscripts, books, plays, letters and canisters containing all of Fearn's legendary self-made films!

Many exciting literary discoveries were made, with several unpublished novels, neatly bound in manila folders. On the floor were several tied black plastic sacks. I made to open them, but I was told not to bother. "We've already packed them ready to throw out," I was told. "They're only old letterheads and bills from Mrs. Fearn's first husband's firm—*Billy Worth's Holiday Tours*." So I never opened the bags, and they were destroyed later that afternoon.

What neither I—nor the executor—realized then, was that they contained vast amounts of Fearn's mss carbon copies, which he had written since his marriage. To save paper, he had used the backs of the now disbanded firm's old letterheads and documents. Heaven only knows what might have been lost. However, I did not worry about this at the time—I was too elated with the large amount of mss that *had* been saved.

My elation at these discoveries was tempered with a great sadness. Her devotion to her husband's memory had deprived Mrs. Fearn of the considerable sums I would have paid back in 1970 for the many new SF manuscripts I found, and which, with a more prolonged and diligent search in 1970, she would have found, too. And there were many other kinds of saleable manuscripts which 1 would have been able to agent for her during the twelve years I had represented her. But money had played no part in her thoughts and memories of a husband cruelly taken from her after only four years of marriage.

There was so much stuff, that I was only able to take a small part of it back with me, even after loading the boot and back seat of the car (where Kevin was patiently waiting!). A telephone call to Norman Lazenby at nearby St. Annes saved the situation. He kindly agreed to call round in his own car and collect the rest of the material, and store it in his own home, for collection by me at a later date.

I wish here to express my sincere thanks to the late Norman Lazenby and his wife Kathy, and the sympathetic Mastermans (who later discovered several *other* manuscripts in the bedroom and promptly forwarded them to me). And not forgetting my old friend, Kevin Lee, without whose driving I could not have arrived in time to prevent the destruction of Fearn's papers. Between us, we saved a valuable literary heritage from destruction. How it happened can best be described by the title of one of Fearn's *Thrilling Wonder* stories—'The Multillionth Chance'!

Needless to say, all of the eight completed and unpublished novels (SF, western and detective) I found that day have since been published, along with several short stories. The only major items remaining unpublished were numerous three-act comedy plays for the small theatrical trouple (the 'Good Companions') that Fearn and his wife ran, performing his plays for local Churches and Charity organizations. And one day I may try novelizing them . . .

The success of Fearn's detective and western novels in Italy, had, alas, come too late to benefit Mrs. Fearn. But at least the proceeds of these Italian later sales were able to benefit my daughter Claire, eventually helping to send her to University—which would be entirely in accordance with Mrs. Fearn's wishes. On learning of Claire's birth in 1972, she had added the special codicil to her Will bequeathing all Fearn's copyrights to me. Childless herself, she became very fond of my daughter, who came to know her as "Auntie" Carrie.

Following the sad but merciful death of Mrs. Fearn in 1982 (she had lately been suffering from Alzheimer's) all rights in the Amazon and Fearn's other works had passed to myself. Soon afterwards, as the copyright owner, I granted a request from artist and writer David Lloyd to licence his doing a comic strip adaptation of *The Golden Amazon.*

David produced a 7 page 'pilot' strip, which appeared in the fourth issue of a new British adult comic magazine, *Warrior.* His adaptation, which was excellent, stressed the dark, amoral side of the Amazon, in which she operated as a law unto herself in a post-war environment. Lloyd had been attracted to the character because there was a strong affinity between the early Amazon and the character of "V" which Lloyd was already drawing for *Warrior.* However, the runaway success of his first strip, *V for Vendetta* (written by the illustrious Alan Moore), prevented Lloyd from continuing with his Amazon adaptation. *V For Vendetta* was later expanded and published to acclaim in America, and was recently made into a major film.

I like to fantasize that in an alternate universe this might have happened to the Golden Amazon!

The late Ron Turner has long been recognized as one of Britain's most individual and stylish science fiction comic strip artists. For more than three decades, he produced SF adventure strips characterized by clean lined architecture, sleek spacecraft and strange alien life forms and landscapes.

But by the early 1980s, he had became disenchanted with the UK comic scene, and prepared for retirement.

But in 1987 Turner fans would have been delighted by a feature article that appeared in *Speakeasy* magazine, the newspaper of the comics field. Written by myself and my friend and colleague John Lawrence, this revealed that new Ron Turner comics were to be released by Martin Lock's Harrier comics. *Nick Hazard* #1 was to be the first of these productions, to be followed by *SF Adventure Classics* #1 featuring an adaptation of E. C. Tubb's short story 'Kalgan the Golden'. These instant classics were to be drawn by Turner in collaboration with myself as scripter and John Lawrence as editor.

The *Speakeasy* article quoted extensively from an earlier interview conducted by John and myself. Turner spoke for the first time about his long and distinguished career in British comics as a premiere SF artist.

Ron Turner was justifiably famous for his sleek and futuristic machines: "I've never found visualisation too much of a problem. Once the function of a machine has been determined it's simply a matter of applying this to some practical design, bearing in mind that the final design should appear fairly stylish."

Ron Turner's penchant for science fiction and his facility for the rendition of futuristic machinery had earlier made him a natural choice for such strips as *The Daleks* on the back page of *TV21* in the late 1960s. This had the added bonus of full colour. "Obviously," he explained, "colour provides an extra dimension and results can be far more satisfying and rewarding, but at the same time they can introduce problems of their own to overcome, and become time consuming. From that point of view black and white is a comparitvely simple process, and where a tight deadline is concerned I would certainly prefer to work in black and white, or even half tone as a happy medium."

Working on *The Daleks* led to assignments on strips featuring the Gerry

Anderson characters, and although this denied Turner the chance to create a plethora of new machines the assignments had other compensations. "I did quite enjoy the *Thunderbirds* and *Stingray* projects and, in fact, due to my involvement with these strips, I was fortunate in being invited down to Bray Studios to watch the making of a *Thunderbirds* episode. It was fascinating to note that a whole day was taken up in completing a small sequence showing one of the craft swooping low over a volcanic island. Drawing is one thing, filming, quite another. But, in spite of the fact that much of the hardware was pre-designed so to speak, I found there was still room for inventive thinking."

In 1984, Ron Turner had dropped out of the British newsstand comic scene to reappear in a set of three comic booklets published by "JRF Enterprises", a small press I had created with John Lawrence.

These comics contained the first *Nick Hazard* adventure, 'Mission To Vorga', adapted by me from a 1940 pulp SF story by John Russell Fearn ('Special Agent to Venus') and then further developed by both John and Ron Turner.

John Lawrence explained to *Speakeasy* how the self published *Nick Hazard* comic came about. "A few years ago I decided that Ron Turner deserved some recognition for all his marvellous work, and I wrote an article of appreciation which appeared in the comic fanzine *Golden Fun*, published by Alan Clarke.

"Phil came across it quite by chance and immediately contacted me explaining that he was also a great fan of Turner, but his interest stemmed from a different source; the marvellous covers that Ron had produced in the 1950s for Scion's 'Vargo Statten' SF paperbacks. Phil also explained that as literary executor to the Fearn estate he now held copyright on all the JRF material. In recent years Ron hadn't been getting the type of quality SF material that he could really do justice to, and Phil and I quickly agreed that it would be tremendous if we could involve him in illustrating some of Fearn's best stories."

Turner's association with the Scion paperbacks by Fearn written under the pen names of 'Vargo Statten' and 'Volsted Gridban' has already been well documented in this book and elsewhere. Turner explained his working method on his many Scion covers.

"In choosing the cover scene I would have been given the manuscript to read and then select an episode which I considered best encapsulated the essence of the story. In the early stages of working with Scion, I was required to produce a few roughs for consideration and selection, but as the work progressed this idea was dispensed with and the finished artwork was left to my discretion. I think I had about four days to complete each cover, some but not all, lettered by myself. The going rate was about £15 then, with perhaps an extra five for the lettering. The subsequent flow of work from Scion resulted from the first cover I produced for them— *Operation Venus*—which I thought would be only a one off commission, but in fact proved to be the first of many. Regarding Fearn, the only time I can remember his making contact was when he wrote to congratulate me for the cover I produced for his novel, *The Genial Dinosaur*."

Our admiration of the work of John Russell Fearn and Ron Turner led to a collaboration involving all four of us, even though Fearn's contribution was posthumous. " 'Mission To Vorga', our first *Nick Hazard* adventure," John Lawrence told *Speakeasy*, "appeared in our own self-published, three part mini-series, *JRF Presents*. We were really feeling our way with this one and we made several changes before we were finally satisfied with the result. But to progress, we had to get across to the US market and that's when we contacted Harrier to see if they were interested in publishing further work of this type."

Martin Lock of Harrier comics was not only interested publishing *Nick Hazard*, but all other science fiction titles produced by Fearn/Turner Enterprises. "Alternating with *Nick Hazard* will be *SF Adventure Classics*," I told *Speakeasy*, "adaptations of outstanding SF magazine stories, beginning with E. C. Tubb's 'Kalgan the Golden'. Turner's art matches the saga-like quality of the story. Very few changes were needed to adapt it to the comics medium, and Tubb was so pleased with the result he's given us permission to adapt other stories. Since he's arguably the best writer of adventure science fiction in the country, it's a rich lode. And since Turner also illustrated many of Tubb's earliest novels in the 1950s, it gives me quite a kick to be the catalyst in reunite these two great talents.

"One of John Russell Fearn's most flamboyant characters is "The Golden Amazon", who will also be joining the Harrier line-up . . . The new Ron Turner version of the Amazon, whilst being faithful to the original, is set many years on in her career, when Fearn was moving towards the outer planets in the solar system, then to the stars. I'm scripting from *Conquest of the Amazon*, wherein the Amazon—previously a loner and somewhat of a man-hater—is made to team up with a new character, Abna, a descendent of Atlantis who is just as intelligent and strong as she is. We're planning an initial three issue mini-series to introduce the Amazon."

Ron Turner had worked for many publishers over the years but he found these new Fearn-inspired commissions offered the ideal working pattern, and an appreciation of his very individual art style. "Most editors these days seem to require four or five pages of art per week," Turner commented, "and after many years in the business, working to relentless deadlines can and does take its toll. From that point of view I find the present work for Harrier quite congenial, and the easing of pressure is certainly welcome. Plus the fact that the scripts are of a much higher standard than some of those inflicted on me in the past by the larger publishing companies."

In the course of his career Ron Turner had worked on a great variety of strips, some more enjoyable than others. "I think possibly producing the Vargo Statten covers gave me the most pleasure," he remembered, "as they allowed full rein to my imagination and the development of my creative and artistic qualities, somewhat rusty after five years of war. *Rick Random* would come a close second. I think. *Stark*, the Football strip I drew for D. C. Thompson a few years back, would head my list of least liked series. Being neither a sports, nor keep fit fanatic, the subject bores me, a fact probably reflected in the artwork."

Sadly, this ambitious publishing programme was not to be fully realized. *Nick Hazard* # 1 duly appeared, featuring a longer adventure entitled "Invaders From Time," which I had very freely adapted from a 1938 Fearn story 'Lords of 9018', together with Tubb's 'Kalgan the Golden' story, in two very attractive and fully professional looking Harrier comic books. But whilst *The Golden Amazon* was still in production, we discovered that the house of Harrier Comics had been built on shifting financial sand. We were not being paid a penny in royalties, which was pretty devastating, as we had been paying Ron Turner upfront for his artwork. We immediately ended our association with Harrier Comics, which promptly disappeared soon afterwards.

Apart from *The Golden Amazon*, Turner had also completed a second *Nick Hazard* adventure, *Planet of Doom*, which I had freely adapted from Fearn's Vargo Statten novel *A Time Appointed*, plus another E. C. Tubb story, 'Sword in the Snow'.

Our adaptation of *Conquest of the Amazon*, brilliantly drawn by

Turner, was eventually published in 1990 by Alan Whitworth, publisher of *The Comic Journal*, a UK semi-prozine for comics enthusiasts. It was issued in a spiral-bound A5 format chapbook edition, signed by Turner and myself, making it something of a collector's item. Both this and the remaining *Nick Hazard* story would eventually appear some years later in a paperback 'special' from New York small press Gryphon Books, but their reproduction standards did not do full justice to Turner's exquisite artwork.

Despite the collapse of the comics, Ron Turner did not end his association with us. Instead, it entered an entirely new phase. Turner had appointed John as his official agent, whilst, sensing retirement from my job in local government on the horizon, I once again began to aspire to realizing my old dream of becoming a science fiction book editor and literary agent.

But these aspirations remained dreams, and I had no idea how to accomplish them—until the forces of serendipity and the legacy of the Vultures of the Void took a hand.

I had been reading the adventures of *Garth,* the famous UK *Daily Mirror* newspaper strip illustrated by Steve Dowling and John Allard since the 1940s, and later by Frank Bellamy and Martin Asbury, and such was my enthusiasm for it I had somehow managed to assemble a *complete* clippings collection, comprising every single daily strip from its beginning in 1943.

In 1992, I wrote to the strips editor of the *Daily Mirror* suggesting how the stories of my favourite SF strip cartoon might be improved by its current writers paying more attention to the precepts laid down in the heyday of Dowling and Allard, when the stories had been written by 'Don' Freeman and Peter O'Donnell.

I had no idea then who the strips editor was, but he turned out to be none other than John Allard himself—a lucky break for me! Allard wrote back saying that he agreed with me, and invited me to see if I could do better than the current writers myself.

The fantastic array of past stories by superb writers made his proposal extremely daunting. But they were also inspirational. I had a complete collection of them, which I had read and reread, and so had a feeling for the character. But I also had a complete collection of the works of Fearn. What if I was to combine my two enthusiasms?

Swiftly I conceived *Twin Souls*, a new *Garth* story entirely of my own devising, but which incorporated little snippets and plot elements and ideas from a wide variety of disparate Fearn stories, including 'The Golden Amazon Returns' (1941), and the Vargo Statten novels *2,000 Years On* (1950) and *Cataclysm* (1951). Drawing on my own misspent youth when I had drawn my own *Dan Dare* and Fearn-inspired comic scripts, I wrote a scenario which also detailed how I envisaged the actual picture scene in each panel, storyboard style. Allard liked the story, but in accepting it, he explained that such detailed storyboarding was not in fact necessary, and that some verbiage and detail would need to be trimmed. He very kindly rewrote the story himself in the manner that a daily strip—and a general public rather than SF buff readership—required

Allard arranged to meet me shortly thereafter, making an overnight stay on Tyneside on his journey to Scotland for a holiday. He confided to me that he was urgently looking for a reliable writer for the strip before his own impending retirement. Time was of the essence. If I couldn't respond quickly, he'd be obliged to look elsewhere.

I was financing my daughter through University, and was steadily falling into debt. At that time my full-time job involved increasing amounts of unpaid overtime, and I had little spare time. So I turned for help to Syd Bounds.

When *Vision of Tomorrow* had closed in 1970, I had several unpublished Bounds stories in my inventory, and Syd agreed to my becoming his agent. In 1986 I sold his short horror story 'The Circus' to US television series *Tales From the Darkside* for adaptation by George Romero, and Syd was delighted: "I've never received so much money!" We had become friends, and had kept in close touch.

Bounds knew little or nothing about *Garth*, but I sent him references. Ever the pro, Syd drafted out several superb story synopses in record time. I duly submitted them—and won the commission.

The first two stories selected, *Warlord* (1993) and *Champions* (1994), were first conceived and drafted by Syd, then revised and submitted by me. They in turn were edited again by Allard—although he had by then retired from the *Mirror*, he had a year's contract to continue as Garth's script editor. We split our share of the cash on these collaborative stories 50/50, which I shared with Syd, who was content to remain anonymous. It was a wonderful gesture that cleared my debt and enabled my daughter to complete her B.A. Degree. Later in 1994, when my overtime situation eased, I was able to create new stories myself, and sold to the new strips editor Ken Layson another two strip serials, *Twilight World* (1994), again inspired by Fearn short stories—'The Unbroken Chain' (1946) and 'The Arbiter' (1947), and *Devil Woman* (1995) inspired by Fearn's 'The Multillionth Chance' (1946) and his Vargo Statten novel *Nebula X* (1950). Syd and I had then collaborated on a parallel worlds story about Garth and Sherlock Holmes—which Allard had agreed was excellent when I'd sent it to him as a courtesy, and which Ken Layson also accepted. But before it could be paid for, my luck ran out. With Allard's tight editorial control gone, artist Martin Asbury staged a 'coup' and insisted on both writing and drawing the strip himself. Ken Layson was under pressure (this was in the wake of the Robert Maxwell scandal) and agreed. Not a good move, as it turned out. The strip folded a year later, after a more than 50-year unbroken run (a record for a UK newspaper strip).

But by then I had received enough money to clear all my debts and to enable my daughter to stay on at University and study for her M.A.

Ever alert to any possibility of promoting Fearn's work, in 1986 I had managed to sell reprint rights to the book edition of *Conquest of the Amazon* (along with some Fearn Scion westerns) to Trojan Books, a mass-market 'instant remainder' publisher. Trojan was the brainchild of one of the sons of the Pemberton family, whose various imprints had flourished during the post-war boom (another mushroom legacy!). Their edition, a reprint of the Orbit book, used a recycled cover from the 1983 UK reprint edition of Sharon Green's *Jalav, Amazon Warrior: The Crystals of Mida*, and so unfortunately did not illustrate Fearn's story. However, the Trojan edition had a large print run and excellent distribution, and so served my purpose at that time, in keeping the Amazon in circulation.

Throughout this entire twenty year period, despite my hopes being alternately raised and then dashed, my faith in the Golden Amazon as a viable literary property never wavered. From all his many characters, the Golden Amazon was the personal favourite of both Fearn and his wife, and before she had died, I had given my word to Mrs. Fearn that I would use my best endeavours to restore the entire saga to print. It was a promise I was determined to keep.

Time passed. The Amazon still lived on in the fading memories of book collectors, but even most of them were unaware that Fearn had published so many additional Amazon novels in magazine form. And only a handful of my personal friends and family knew that before her death Mrs. Fearn had entrusted to my safekeeping the only surviving single mss copy of *Duel With Colossus*, an unpublished Amazon novel that, had it been published at the time, would have been # 21 in the sequence. And that after her death I had discovered a *second* unpublished Amazon mss in Fearn's effects, entitled *Lords of Creation*.

I therefore decided to repeat my earlier action of publishing another chapbook edition, once again choosing the next Amazon novel that had not so far appeared in book form. Maurice Flanagan of Zardoz Books agreed to act as publisher, and so we published a nicely produced chapbook edition of the eighth novel, *Lord of Atlantis* (Zeon Books, 1991) with a new colour cover and a back cover illustration by Ron Turner. I also wrote an introduction giving the first detailed history and chronology of the Amazon series, and revealed the existence of the two unpublished Amazon novels. My hope was that some other publisher might pick up on this.

Esodo Cosmico (Cosmic Exodus) by
Vargo Statten (Eddie Jones).
Il Pucchio, 1977.

Travers les Ages (Across the Ages) by
Vargo Statten (unidentified).
Aredit, 1978

Warrior # 4 (Steve Dillon). Quality
Communications, 1978

The Best of E.E. 'Doc' Smith by E.E.
Smith (Karel Thole). Futura, 1975.

The Golden Amazon by John Russell
Fearn and Philip Harbottle (Ron Turner).
Whitworth, 1990.

Nick Hazard # 1: Invaders From Time
by John Russell Fearn and Philip
Harbottle (Ron Turner). Harrier, 1988

Kalgan the Golden by E.C. Tubb
and Philip Harbottle (Ron Turner).
Harrier, 1988.

Montage of *Garth* stories written
by Philip Harbottle and drawn by
Martin Asbury. *Daily Mirror*, 1993-5.

CHAPTER 20:
VULTURES OF THE VOID

The following year the first book on exclusively British post-war science fiction publishing, *Vultures of the Void* (Borgo Press, 1992) was published in America, as by Philip Harbottle and Stephen Holland.

I had first prepared the book that was to become *Vultures of the Void* towards the end of 1970, when it was then entitled *The Impatient Dreamers*. It was in fact an edited version of the various articles by editors Walter Gillings and John Carnell that had recently appeared under that title in my magazine *Vision of Tomorrow*, chronicling British SF history up to 1946, plus unpublished chapters by myself and others, taking the story on a further ten years (the end of the postwar SF 'boom' period).

The book had been commissioned by American fan publisher Frank Dietz, who published the printed monthly, *Luna*, a very professional-looking news magazine, and a precursor to *Locus*. I had been in correspondence about *Vision*, and had met Frank at the 1970 World SF Convention at Heidelberg in Germany.

It was accepted for his Luna Books imprint, but when Frank failed to issue it after a decent interval, I asked for the return of the mss. It languished in a drawer until I volunteered extracts from it to appear in 1975 in the third volume of Mike Ashley's *History of the Science Fiction Magazine* series for New English Library. Mike wrote that it deserved to be published as a book, but there was no publisher interest, and the mss went back into the drawer for several years. That is, until I was contacted by Steve Holland, a schoolboy who wanted my help in writing an article on science fiction for his school magazine.

On learning of the existence of the unpublished book, Holland asked if he could see it. He found it fascinating, and asked me why on Earth I hadn't published it as a book. I confessed I had more or less given up on it, and that the now battered mss—much of which was still in the form of tearsheets from *Vision*—wasn't really in a fit state to be circulated to prospective *professional* publishers. Holland told me he was about to leave school, and had just acquired a new electric typewriter. He offered to retype and edit it for me, and suggested how it might be expanded to include a bibliography of the paperback books and magazines discussed (he offered to do some research at the British Library for any titles then missing from my collection).

The resultant revised and enlarged book, by now retitled *Vultures of the Void*, and concentrating mainly on the decade following the Second World War, was sent first to Howard Baker and then Batsford in the UK, who both rejected it. Sent to America, it was accepted first time out by Robert Reginald at the Borgo Press. Reginald and his editor Daryl Mallett proposed splitting it into two volumes: *Vultures of the Void* by myself, and *British Science Fiction Paperbacks and Magazines 1949-1956* by myself and Holland. I agreed, but as an acknowledgement of his assistance in retyping and helping edit *Vultures* (without which it might never have appeared at that particular time) I told Borgo that Holland's name should also go on the first book. *Vultures* was eventually published in 1992, but the annotated bibliography (which I had extensively rewritten and updated at proof stage after having completed my collection in the interim) did not follow until 1994.

Whilst publication from Borgo was frustratingly delayed, stretching well over a year, Holland suggested that we might collaborate on *another* book, *The Mushroom Jungle*, to deal with *all* the popular fiction genre titles published during the postwar 'boom' decade. He would undertake the research needed to assemble it, mainly at the British Library. I gave him a good deal of information about genre publishing that I hadn't used in *Vultures* (which had deliberately concentrated on SF) to help get him started. I did not share Holland's enthusiasm for *all* genre fiction of the mushroom period—and in particular gangster fiction, which I detested—but in return for the 'start' I had given him, I was to be the agent for his book when completed.

The book being proposed was *not* to be a written 'history' that would in any way impinge on *Vultures* territory, but instead was to be simply a complete *checklist of titles* with publisher and date noted (on pretty much the same lines as *Whitaker's Cumulative Book Lists*, to which I had referred Holland to get him started) and set out alphabetically by author, plus brief biographical details on prominent authors and their pseudonyms to add interest. The energetic Holland made good progress on the book, actually sending me a near complete draft version within a few months. It was essentially an impressive (and extremely useful) checklist.

I heard nothing more for some time, until I was surprised to receive a letter from Holland saying that he had sent the completed book himself to an American University Press who had "accepted" it. At which point our "collaborations" promptly ceased.

So when some time later UK publisher Zeon Books rang to tell me they were about to publish *The Mushroom Jungle*, and did I have any objection to it, I naturally assumed it was the *same book*. I gave the publisher my blessing, and told him that I had seen the draft some time ago and entirely approved of it! The fact that Holland did not contact me himself failed to sound any warning bells.

What I did not know was that he had also written another book entirely, using the same title, which was a detailed 'history' of *all* postwar British genre publishing in the late forties and early fifties. His new version of *The Mushroom Jungle* (Zeon, 1993) covered exactly the same ground as *Vultures* and in much the same way, but had widened the focus to include gangster novels and westerns, etc.

However, whilst offering admirable new coverage of western and gangster fiction (for those interested) and some details of the publishing firms, this book did not *add* anything of significance regarding *science fiction* history (most of it having been simply taken from *Vultures of the Void*, along with great swathes of Gordon Landsborough's copyrighted memoirs on the mushroom publishers),

When Reginald learned of the book and its contents, he was understandably furious—and I wasn't exactly thrilled myself. Borgo at first threatened to slap an injunction on the UK publisher, but when I told them of my conversation with him and how we had been at cross-purposes, he gave him the benefit of the doubt and eventually settled for handling the offending book's US distribution rights.

It had been my hope that when published, the Borgo titles would help other researchers and collectors to produce their own books that would *add* to its revelations of British science fiction history. My hope had not been realized—nor would it be for a long time afterwards.

Borgo had rejected my urgings to include plenty of cover illustrations, claiming they were not needed in a reference work, and would indeed lower its tone and value to scholars. I had finally twisted their arm to include a few black and white Tuner Scion covers in *Vultures,* but that was as far as they would go, However, the Zeon book contained *lots* of covers—many in full colour. Holland's book was reviewed in the UK national press, and he was invited to contribute to TV and radio programmes dealing with postwar publishing—and never looked back.

The Borgo titles (despite good reviews in *Locus* and a slightly grudging lukewarm one in the highbrow *Interzone*) had sold slowly, and after Borgo stopped promoting them and distributed *The Mushroom Jungle* instead, they more or less sank without trace.

The 1991 Zeon small press edition of *Lord of Atlantis*, with which I'd hoped to attract publisher interest in the entire 'Golden Amazon' series, eventually bore fruit.

The publisher turned out to be Gary Lovisi, who lived in Brooklyn, New York.

I had first known Gary through correspondence, when I became a contributor to his magazine *Paperback Parade* in 1991, and had met him when he came to London in October of that year to attend the first UK Vintage Paperback and Pulp Fair organized by bookseller Maurice Flanagan (Zardoz Books, and the publisher of the Zeon imprint). Gary and I struck up an immediate rapport, based on our mutual love of the better old pulp fiction. Over the next few years we kept in touch by correspondence, and I continued to write articles for his magazine on Fearn, E. C. Tubb, and vintage UK paperbacks generally.

Late in 1994, following my article in *Paperback Parade* # 33 detailing Fearn's 'Martian' quartet of novels—the Clay Drew series published by Hamiltons in 1950, pastiching Burroughs' John Carter—Gary asked me if he could reprint these four books in his fledgling Gryphon Books imprint. I readily agreed terms, which included my commissioning new artwork and illustrative colour covers by Ron Turner.

I had promised my daughter Claire a holiday in the U.S.A. the following summer if she was successful in gaining her M.A. in her University examinations—which she duly did, with honours. So, in the sizzlingly hot summer of 1995, we flew to New York for a short holiday. Naturally I had mentioned the holiday to Gary, and was immensely pleased when he agreed to take a day off work to spend with us, and invited us to visit him at his Brooklyn home.

At long last, the forces of Serendipity were at work to redress the disappointments and lost opportunities of the previous two decades!

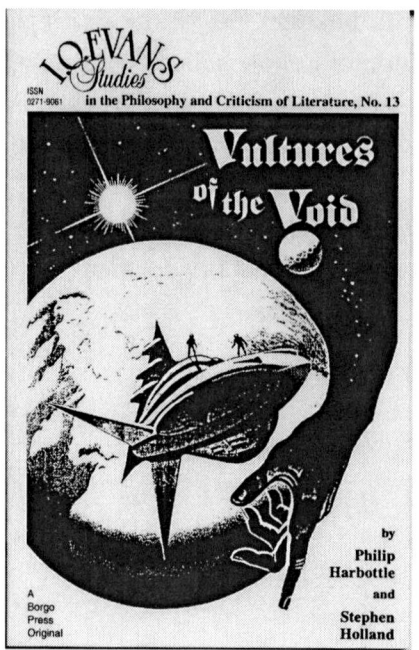

Vultures of the Void by Philip Harbottle
(Ron Turner). Borgo, 1992

*The History of the Science Fiction
Magazine Part 3* edited by Michael
Ashley (R. Layzen). NEL, 1976

*British Science Fiction paperbacks and
Magazines: 1949-1956* by Harbottle and
Holland. Borgo, 1994

Lord of Atlantis by John Russell Fearn
(Ron Turner). Zeon. 1991

Emperor of Mars by John Russell Fearn
(Ron Turner). Gryphon, 1995

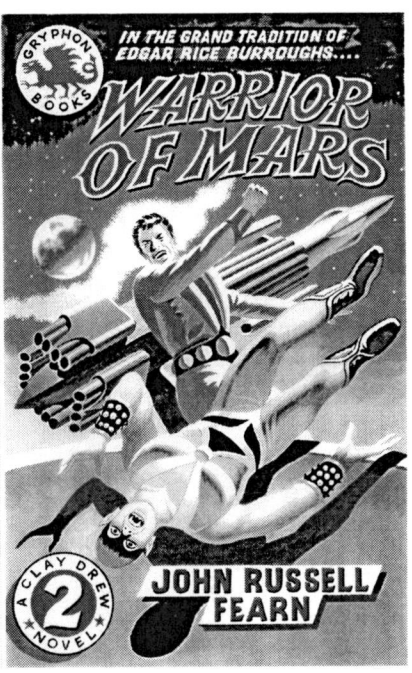

Warrior of Mars by John Russell Fearn
(Ron Turner). Gryphon, 1995

Red Men of Mars by John Russell Fearn
(Ron Turner). Gryphon, 1995

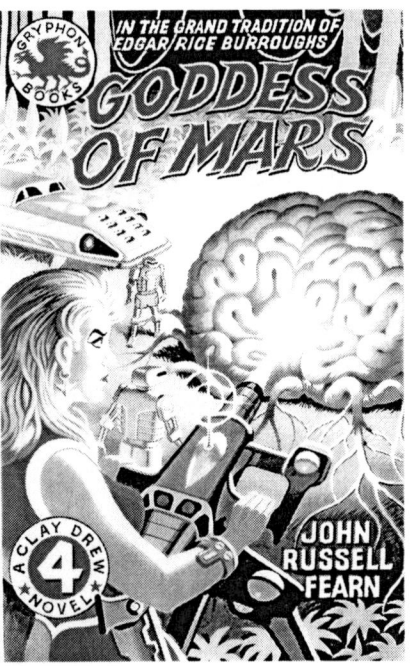

Goddess of Mars by John Russell Fearn
(Ron Turner). Gryphon, 1995

CHAPTER 21:
LEGACIES

When Claire and I flew into New York, Gary had pulled out the stops to get all four of Fearn's 'Emperor of Mars' novels ready in time to present me with complimentary copies. We had arranged to meet the following day, and I was immensely impressed, not only with the books, but with his enthusiasm and enterprise. We got on so well that by the time Claire and I flew home at the end of the week, Gary and I had verbally agreed contracts for an entire *series* of vintage British novels—which became the *Gryphon Science Fiction Rediscovery* series—for which I would provide the books and an introduction, along with new Ron Turner covers. As well as more Fearn titles, there would be new and reprint material by E. C. Tubb, whom I also now represented.

Included in our first batch of contracts was a 'trial balloon' reprinting of *The Golden Amazon*. Gary's 1996 edition constituted its first-ever American edition, and within three months of its publication Gary asked me to ready my introduction for the next book, *The Golden Amazon Returns.*

I was delighted to do so, and mindful of previous reversals of fortune respecting the Amazon series, my private hope was that we might continue and extend the series to include at least one 'new' Amazon novel (# 9. *Triangle of Power*) before my inevitable bad luck took over (as I fully expected it would). At the time I was perfectly ready to settle for that, and I never for a moment dared hope that Gary's books would be successful enough to lead to the publication of the *entire series*.

It was not until I found myself writing the introduction to the *fourth* novel, *The Amazon's Diamond Quest* in July 1997, that I suddenly realized that the possibility actually existed for *all 26 novels* to eventually see publication. That was an exciting moment!

Slowly, steadily, the parade of Amazon titles continued, interspaced by many other titles by Fearn, Tubb, and others that Gary and I wanted to see in print. They included much material published in book form for the very first time, most notably the early pulp novels of Jack Williamson, beginning with *The Fortress of Utopia*, and Don Wilcox's legendary *The Whispering Gorilla*. Even the graphic novel version of the Amazon was incorporated into the ongoing *Science Fiction Rediscovery* Series.

For me, one of the greatest thrills was the opportunity to work closely with the legendary British artist Ron Turner. Working again with my mutual friend John Lawrence, we commissioned Ron to paint exciting new illustrative covers for each book. There is no doubt that his dynamic artwork contributed in no small way to the success of the series, one of his finest covers illustrating Jack Williamson's *The Ruler of Fate and Xandulu* (1999).

My first personal milestone was reached with Gryphon's publication of *Triangle of Power* in 1999. This was the first-ever book publication of the ninth novel, and thereafter all titles in the series would be world first editions. Tragically, it also carried the last new cover to be painted by Ron Turner, who had died the previous December, aged 76. Those who believe in coincidence and gropers for the rabbit foot may find some sinister supernatural significance in this, having regard to what I have written above regarding my original aspirations to settle for a run of nine titles.

The Amazon series was continuing to do well, so there was no question of our not continuing with it. But Gary was naturally worried about the cover art.

Fortunately, it was still possible for me to supply him with new Turner paintings. From the time we had first worked together on the Amazon graphic novel, I had given Ron a large number of *personal commissions* to both recreate covers and to paint new ones for many of my favourite Fearn novels. So Ron had painted a more than sufficient number of unpublished SF covers for me to use on the remaining books.

In June 2005—just ten years after we shook hands at his home in Brooklyn—Gary published *Earth Divided*, Fearn's last Golden Amazon novel, # 26 in this extraordinary series. And the series *was* truly extraordinary.

The Amazon's adventures had begun on Earth, in the midst of the wartime London Blitz. They had extended into an imaginary future, in which the Amazon had adventured on all nine planets in the solar system, from Mercury to Pluto. She had acquired a daughter, Viona, then a husband, (Sic! See *The Amethyst City*), visited the atomic microcosm and macrocosm, and explored the Milky Way and the entire limits of the universe—and beyond!

There is no other series quite like it in all of science fiction history. Its creation by Fearn was an historic achievement—and no less an historic achievement is the fact that Gary Lovisi, with only the slender resources of a Small Press, had succeeded in publishing it, where the big publishing houses had all failed.

Following Gary's pioneering efforts and example of what could be achieved by a Small Press, George Vanderburgh's Battered Silicon Press in Canada announced their intention to eventually republish all of the Amazon novels in three hardcover omnibus volumes. His superbly produced three-volume set appeared between 2004 and 2008, along with two other omnibus collections of Fearn's best science fiction and detective novels, and the first edition of Fearn's unpublished mss, *Land's End—Labrador* (2005), with introductions by myself and Canadian scholar and anthologist John Robert Colombo, who had been instrumental in its publication. Later all these other novels would be separately reprinted in the UK, with *Land's End—Labrador* being retitled as *The Atlantic Tunnel* (2009).

After the first few books in the series, each new Amazon novel followed on chronologically from the previous one, ending on a cliffhanger. Thus it was that Fearn's last novel, *Earth Divided*, still in his typewriter when he died, had ended on a tantalisingly inconclusive note, leaving the Amazon saga incomplete.

For more than 40-odd years, ever since I first read the novel in the pages of the Toronto *Star Weekly*, I had wondered and worried what had next happened to the Amazon, and whether her adventures would ever be continued by other hands. There was precedent with many other great fictional characters, such as Sherlock Holmes and Doc Savage—and for me, the Amazon was in the same league.

But who could write that continuation? Especially when some of the biggest names in science fiction—as represented by the mighty Scott

Meredith Literary Agency—had all failed when invited to do so by the Toronto *Star Weekly* in the early 1960s.

Ideally, it would have to be someone who had read all the stories, and who loved the character and understood what had made the Amazon tick. I knew of no living authors who met the profile, except, perhaps . . .

Myself!

My life-long interest and study of Fearn's work had particularly intensified in recent years when, as his literary executor, I decided to retype into my computer scores of his novels and stories to take advantage of the internet as a medium for offering them to publishers, especially in the US. This created new opportunities for their reprinting, or, as in the case of his later Golden Amazon novels, first book-publication. And as I retyped and edited his stories, it gave me a detailed insight into Fearn's style and methods of story construction.

Beginning in 2000, in my capacity as a literary agent, I had succeeded in reselling reprint rights to London publishers Robert Hale for every one of Fearn's many paperback westerns (along with those of E. C. Tubb, Syd Bounds, Tony Glynn and John Glasby). Hale subsequently issued the first-ever hardcover editions of Fearn's westerns, and also first-published a couple of hitherto unpublished western novels, which I had revised and edited from Fearn's original mss.

But when, after some two-dozen titles, the supply of Fearn western novels to reprint ran out, I had hit on the idea of trying to write my own western novels, based upon a number of Fearn's western *short stories*. In this I was essentially emulating Fearn's own technique, which he had employed with some of his early science fiction pulp magazine short stories, when he later turned them into paperback novels.

As copyright holder—by virtue of Mrs. Fearn's Will—I was entitled to do this. So, by taking a couple of his disparate western short stories, and then revising them to incorporate the same characters, and expanding them to novel length, I found I could produce a pretty good pastiche— certainly good enough for Hale to publish. And since all these collaborative novels were later reprinted in paperback by Ulverscroft, they must have had something going for them . . .

So I decided to see if I could reprise my western technique to create a new 'Golden Amazon' science fiction story in the same way! I took two totally unconnected Fearn short SF stories, 'Chameleon Planet' (1940) and

'Destroyer From the Past' (1942)—neither of them an Amazon story—and then completely revised and expanded them with new material of my own to short novel length, replacing their original characters with the Cosmic Crusaders. The result was *Chameleon Planet* book # 27, which Lovisi accepted and published in 2006. This resolved all the loose ends, and ended on a 'clean finish', paving the way for sequels.

I then invited other writers—clients of my Cosmos Literary Agency—to accept the challenge of continuing the saga. I avoided the earlier error of the Toronto *Star Weekly* by providing writers with a sample novel and a detailed dossier. Brian Ball and Ted Tubb expressed interest, but the first to step forward and actually deliver the goods with not one, but four new novels, was John Glasby. And they were terrific, and faithful to the character, requiring only the slightest editing by me to make them perfect. If any man was born to continue the Golden Amazon, that man was John Glasby, whose career has uncannily parallelled Fearn's own. Writing with all Fearn's trademark fast-action verve and imagination, he was also able to add to it his own strengths, honed over a long literary career.

The first two Amazon novels by Glasby, *Seetee Sun* (# 28) and *The Crimson Peril* (# 29) were published by Gryphon in 2007, and *The Sun Movers* in 2010. *Primordial World* was delayed whilst Lovisi's small press struggled to overcome the present recession. It is scheduled for later this year, but sadly, John Glasby won't see it, having died in June, 2011.

New generations of readers and collectors will surely come to appreciate the extraordinary *SF Rediscovery* series of books, all of them destined to become collectors' items, and featuring colourful Ron Turner covers.

Since the line mainly featured the novels of both Fearn and Tubb, it provided a great opportunity for Turner to return to his first love, and the reuniting of Turner with the novels of these writers (along with such other pulp greats as Jack Williamson) showed that he'd lost none of his old painting skills.

Shortly before his death he had also returned to painting his favourite colour strip, *The Daleks*, from a new script especially written for him by John Lawrence, with the work published by Marvel Comics for their *Doctor Who* magazine.

Ron Turner's last years were happy ones, when he was again producing work he really enjoyed. He died in 1998, but his artwork has continued to appear into the 21st century. As previously stated, throughout the 1980s,

I had privately commissioned Ron to paint covers for the remainder of Fearn's SF novels that he had not illustrated first time around. At the back of my mind, I never lost faith in the belief that I would eventually find publishers willing to republish Fearn's novels—and when that happened, I wanted them to feature a Ron Turner cover! My belief was well founded, and so many wonderful Turner covers have appeared posthumously, not just from Gryphon, and most notably on the *Fantasy Adventures* series of books, published by Wildside Press.

The latest exciting new development has been the revival in the UK of Ron Turner's SF comic strips in a stunning colour format, published in Rod Barzilay's full colour magazine *Spaceship Away*. The magazine had been created as a tribute to Hampson's *Dan Dare*, Barzilay having been licensed to continue Dare's adventures in their original Hampsonian tradition. But as well as new Dan Dare strips, the magazine featured other classic SF strips, such as *Journey Into Space*.

At this point I hand over to my colleague John Lawrence:

> At the start of 2009, Rod Barzilay was actively looking at other strip possibilities for *Spaceship Away*. Ron Turner's *Rick Random* was considered but the copyright fee was a stumbling block. Then Rod came across a copy of *Nick Hazard* #1 and got in in touch with me, suggesting John Ridgway might colour the work for reprinting in his magazine. I suggested that he should start from the beginning with the original *Nick Hazard* story from *JRF Presents* and I sent examples to artist John Ridgway. John coloured them, using the latest cutting edge computer techniques, and the impressive results prompted Rod to agree to run the 'Mission to Vorga' story.
>
> So began our ongoing association where John Ridgway reformats the strip into four page episodes, and I approve or suggest other frames, amend dialogue and text to suit, and John then takes on the task of beautifully colouring the work and relettering the frames. His treatment is superb and one of which I'm sure would have had the approval of Ron Turner himself.
>
> Ron Turner remains one of Britain's most unique comic strip artists, although his work in recent years has sadly been less evident. But with the revival of *Nick Hazard* in *Spaceship Away* and the vast amount of unpublished strips still available, there's no reason why he shouldn't regain his popularity in a stunning new full colour format for a whole new generation of readers.

Back in 1995 I had been contacted by a young American E. C. Tubb and Dumarest fan, then still at High School in Ohio: Sean Wallace. He was about to publish a fanzine bibliography of E. C. Tubb, and he'd sent me a draft copy, inviting any comments. I have to admit I was not impressed: it was basically just an incomplete checklist. My view was that the proposed work should offer some critical insights and attempt to put Tubb's work in historical context.

As a fan and sometime professional since the 1950s, and a friend of Tubb's I had all the extra knowledge of his work Sean lacked because I had read and owned copies of Tubb's entire US *and UK* output—something that had been denied to him in America. At that time I had no pc, and no internet knowledge. Sean on the other hand, was very computer literate, and was studying business and marketing at his school, and so had all the essential knowledge *I* lacked! The idea of a partnership quickly took shape. I would write and compile a complete book on Tubb, with a critical annotated biblio, and biographical details. The problem was that I was still in full-time employment, and did not really have the time to write a structured book. Sean's solution was to invite me to do it piecemeal, little sections at a time in no particular order, which he would edit and translate into his pc, and typeset and "package" it ready for publication, using his computer skills. More particularly, he offered to surf the internet to discover all of Tubb's world-wide translations, which would form an important part of the book (my own complete Tubb collection and knowledge was limited to English and US appearances only). The resultant jointly-produced book was *The Tall Adventurer.* I found a sympathetic UK specialist publisher in the redoubtable Roger Robinson of Beccon Publications, and we jointly published the book in a small print run. It was a critical and financial success, covering costs with a small profit.

On graduating, Sean first went into the supermarket retail business, but hankered to get into publishing. He offered to set up an imprint, using POD technology, if I would supply the books and covers. I was seeking an outlet for all the many John Russell Fearn properties I owned, and also for Ted Tubb's unpublished inventory, which I had took possession of on becoming his agent (Ted was so impressed with our book, that he left his agent—who was semi-retired anyway—and signed with me). I had formerly published some semi-pro titles under my imprint Cosmos Books, and I had registered Cosmos Literary Agency as my business name. I took early retirement from my Council job, and Sean and I launched 'Cosmos Books', a POD operation. Our first titles were a paperback magazine, *Fantasy Annual*, followed by three novels, *Manton's World* by Fearn (a Toronto *Star Weekly* tabloid novel in book form for first time) and two new Tubb sword and sorcery novels, *Death-God's Doom*, and *The Sleeping City*. We printed 200 copies upfront, which we were able to sell fairly quickly through specialist dealers, book fairs, and word of mouth.

Fantasy Annual was essentially a vehicle for encouraging some of the veteran British writers, many disaffected from the old Carnell Agency, who had fallen silent, having had no encouragement to submit anything from modern editors. I roused them out of retirement, and commissioned new stories. For the new works I encouraged supernatural, weird and "offtrail" SF—hence our choice of the all-embracing *"Fantasy" Annual* as a title.

In the nature of things, mainly to help the limited budget, I used a few selective reprints, together with resurrected old 'lost' unpublished stories by Fearn and others which finally saw print, together with brand new commissioned stories. Amongst my writers were the likes of E. C. Tubb, Syd Bounds, E. R. James, and Eric C. Williams. I also used a few new stories from newer generation writers whom I knew—such as Andrew Darlington and the well-known supernatural novelist Stephen Laws, who did a nice short for me as a special favour—his wife Melanie used to be a good friend and colleague of mine when we had both worked for Blyth Council.

These quite professional-looking publications attracted the attention of the established American POD publisher John Betancourt (Wildside Press). He was looking to expand his operation. He offered to take over my proposed programme (books by my agency clients, Fearn, Tubb, Syd Bounds, Phil High, Brian Ball, Ernest Dudley (crime) and the magazine, if I transferred the imprint to him. He would also hire Sean Wallace full time to edit and oversee the imprint. I then licensed the name Cosmos Books to him, in 2000, and he began publishing our magazine *Fantasy Annual* from issue 4, and lots of titles by my clients.

If the magazine proved successful, we hoped to eventually be able to move to all new material for the magazine, which we achieved with *Fantasy Annual # 5*. By this time, Sean and I were increasingly 'going for' authors and material, so we managed to get new stories from the likes of Dan Morgan, Barry Bayley and David Redd. Unfortunately this bumper (and costliest to date) issue fell victim to some mysterious delay with Wildside's production schedules, and since we'd paid for all the stories on acceptance this represented something of a disaster. As Sean was becoming increasingly busy as general editor of Cosmos (and also Prime Books, his own imprint) we decided to terminate *Fantasy Annual*. The delayed issue eventually appeared, but by then we had already gone our separate ways.

I was still committed to commissioning new stories from the older authors (many of whom were now my clients) and so, having by now acquired a personal computer, I created my own magazine, *Fantasy Adventures*, carrying on the same tradition—but this time, with only one editor and backer. Budget considerations meant that only one third of the 60,000 words contents were new stories, but I still managed to obtain some fine material, most notably two new Dumarest stories by Tubb, which I managed to coax out of him. The rest of each issue was made up with a reprint of one of Fearn's better novels from the 1950s, each issue featuring new covers by famed ex-Scion artist Ron Turner.

My editorial policy throughout consisted of three main strands: to bring to light fine stories that had been accepted for other markets, but for one reason or another had never appeared at the time; to reprise classic stories too long out of print; and to actively solicit brand new stories that might otherwise never have been written. This latter strand eventually became the most important.

Gradually, as the magazine became established, in addition to works by Bounds, Fearn, High and Tubb, new stories by other veteran UK writers, including Brian Ball, John Glasby and Tony Glynn were added, all of whom wrote excellent new stories especially for *Fantasy Adventures*. One highlight was the posthumous first publication of 'Something in the Air' by Gordon Landsborough, a novelette I had actually commissioned from Gordon for *Vision* in 1970. It was a beautifully written and subtle satire, its central character being a science fiction editor working for an uncaring publisher (based on Gordon himself and his days at Hamilton's editing *Authentic*). I was also proud to have been favoured with new stories by rising star Eric Brown, and the noted Italian author and editor Antonio Bellomi.

As with most POD ventures, sales were disappointing, and the magazine itself never made any money (at least for me)—but I was able to resell the Fearn novels appearing in it to my UK publisher, which more than recouped my editorial outlay. I had hoped to continue in this vein, soliciting more new stories from Eric Brown and other younger British writers, but it was not to be.

In 2006, first Philip E. High, and then Sydney J. Bounds died. Both men were born storytellers who loved to write, and although they knew they were dying from cancer, they continued to write for me as long as they were able. Their final stories were truly inspirational, remarkably good, and completely free from any trace of bitterness or self-pity. After their deaths I was left holding numerous unpublished stories by them in my inventory, an inventory that was already large because of my being favoured with new material by all of the other still-living authors mentioned above. The inventory had grown because for some time my publisher had found it increasingly difficult to issue my magazine on a regular basis, because of other commitments as his business expanded exponentially. This placed me in an embarrassing position, because all of my unpublished stories had been contributed by their authors on my promise that they *would* be published. That they should remain in limbo for an indefinite period of time was completely against all of my editorial principles, so I decided that it was better to terminate the magazine.

But I felt that I owed it to the memory of Bounds and High—and their families, friends and fans—that their final stories should see print. I was grateful therefore for the suggestion of Wildside's award-winning editor Sean Wallace (my former editorial colleague on *Fantasy Annual*) that they would publish a giant-sized special issue of *Fantasy Adventures* to enable me to clear my inventory of new stories by still active writers, and to present a generous helping of unpublished stories by Bounds and High, including their very last works.

Sean kept his promise and a bumper final issue # 13 appeared in 2008.

Once no longer involved with the magazine and Wildside, I found that I had more time to devote to agenting, and I was successful in selling more and more novels in the UK. Not just reprints or revisions, but also new works, by Brian Ball, Syd Bounds, Ernest Dudley, John Russell Fearn, John Glasby, Tony Glynn, Gordon Landsborough and Ted Tubb—westerns, science fiction, and detective thrillers, together with overseas translations of Fearn and Tubb throughout Europe, particularly in Italy once again.

Today I am busier than ever, and the Legacy of the mushroom publishers—the Vultures of the Void—is clear: whilst an awful lot of rubbish was produced that deserves the opprobrium and obscurity that has befallen it, a large amount of excellent material produced at the same time was unfairly tarred with same brush. This better material, if edited and re-presented by a dedicated agent, is capable of pleasing modern publishers and entertaining modern readers. Enough time has passed for new generations of publishers and readers to have no knowledge of the dubious origins of this material, and to simply accept it for what it is: honest craftsmanship written by professional natural storytellers who, in the words of Ted Tubb, wrote that type of entertaining fiction because they liked reading it themselves!

In 2006 I was again contacted by Antonio Bellomi and Ugo Malaguti, and asked to make available vintage Scion material by both Fearn and E. C. Tubb, beginning with Fearn's *To The Ultimate* (the famous 'Mathematica' stories) and Tubb's *City of No Return*. Both quickly appeared in handsome hardcover translations, and more followed. As this is being proofed, in July 2011, the third 500-page hardcover omnibus of Tubb's 'Dumarest' novels has appeared in Italy under Malaguti's Elara Books imprint, and more titles by Fearn and Tubb are contracted to follow.

In 2009, another Italian publisher, Della Vigna (Luigi Petruzzelli), featured translations of stories by Fearn and Tubb in his anthologies and his edition of Tubb's novel *The Possessed* (with a Ron Turner cover) won the 2009 Premio Italia Award (an 'Italian Hugo') for the Best International SF Novel published in Italy.

From the vantage point of the present day, we can now see a remarkable genealogy of some of Fearn's 1950 paperbacks. For example:

1941   *Marvel Stories*. 'Last Secret Weapon', by 'Polton Cross' [American magazine version].

1950   Scion, England. *The G-Bomb*, by 'Vargo Statten' [novelization of above story].

1952   Fleuve Noir, France. *La Bombe 'G'*, by 'Vargo Statten' [French translation].

1960   Utopia, Germany. *Pulverfass Ende*, by 'Vargo Statten' [German translation].

1974   Aredit, France. *La Bombe 'G'*, by 'Vargo Statten' [French graphic novel].

1979   Libra, Italy. *Notte Sul Mondo*, by 'Vargo Statten' [Italian translation, hardcover].

1988   Garden, Italy. *Notte Sul Mondo*, by 'Vargo Statten' [Italian reprint, paperback].

2010   Ulverscroft, Leicester, *The G-Bomb* by John Russell Fearn [paperback]

2011   Borgo Books, USA. *The G-Bomb* (as Fearn) [paperback]

The same story has carried through nine incarnations over nearly seventy years, and if that is not proof of 'established writing', what is?

In retrospect, it can be seen that the critic's assessment that none of the authors had established themselves was wrong. Not that the statement was unjust at the time it was written: the books were either reprinted abroad, or long after his remarks were made.

Since 1996, *more than a hundred and thirty* of Fearn's novels have been re-issued (some of them several times) including a *'Best of'* collection and some posthumous first editions. In 2010 alone, quite astonishingly, no less than a *dozen* of his Scion SF novels, edited by myself, were reprinted in England by Ulverscroft: *A Thing of the Past*, *The Black Terror* (aka *Cataclysm*), *Endless Day* (aka *Space Warp*), *The G-Bomb*, *Glimpse* (aka *Across the Ages*), *The Gold of Ajada*, *The Lie Destroyer*, *The Miracle Man* (aka *Decreation*), *The Multi-Man*, *Prisoner of Time* (aka *Time Bridge*), *The Red Insects*, *Return to Akada* (aka *Anjani the Mighty*)!

More Scion titles preceded them and 2011 led off with *The Silent World* (aka *The Dyno-Depressant*), followed by new collections of Fearn's short SF and crime stories. More remarkably, a contract has been agreed for Fearn's 1954 'Vargo Statten' novelization of the iconic film *Creature From the Black Lagoon*. It will be reprinted by DreamHaven Books in the USA, with the approval of Universal International Pictures. I've also been privileged to arrange the reprinting of scores of works by Brian Ball, Syd Bounds, John Burke, John Glasby, Tony Glynn, Philip E. High, Gordon Landsborough, Norman Lazenby, E. C. Tubb, and crime writers Gerald Verner and Ernest Dudley (including new posthumous 'Dr. Morelle' stories, some of which I adapted from Dudley's BBC radio scripts). It has also been gratifying to renew contact with Robert Reginald, whose Borgo Books imprint will feature my clients in the USA.

Whilst this book was being finalised, E. C. Tubb died on 15 September 2010, only a few weeks short of his 91st birthday, and just before he could be told that his new dystopian novel *To Dream Again* had been accepted by Ulverscroft for publication in 2011. Orion Books have accepted his final, and possibly his most outstanding novel, *Fires of Satan*.

I've loved the man and his work for over 50 years, and will sorely miss him. Ted's literary talent was matched by his generous nature. In 1970 we travelled together to the World Convention at Heidelberg in Germany, where he was Guest of Honour. On arrival I learned the airline had lost my suitcase, and my publisher had failed to arrange and pay for my hotel room. I was stranded with little money, without any toiletries, and only the clothes I was wearing. Ted immediately gave me a loan and offered to let me share his room and facilities with him. How many eminent authors would have done that?

Ted became my friend and mentor, eventually asking me to become his agent, and we rejoiced together as scores of his books were reprinted. I was thrilled to work with him on new books, including a truly wonderful final Dumarest, *Child of Earth*, which he wrote for me—and his fans—despite failing health.

Tragically, he died without knowing that the major UK SF publisher, Orion Books, was set to give his *entire* SF backlist electronic immortality (along with Philip E. High and J.R. Fearn). Nor will he see a French language tribute collection, *Dimension*, edited and translated by Richard D. Nolane, together with his first French translation of *Child of Earth*.

Hopefully, with this book, and my past and continuing sales of these pioneer writers, I may finally have succeeded in putting the record straight.

I married a young Wallsend girl called Maureen Doyle on 27 September, 1969, and made her my Secretary for *Vision of Tomorrow*. The magazine died young. Maureen herself died suddenly on 21st October, 2009, from a massive pulmonary embolism, fatally exacerbated as a result of her old childhood asthma, which had never entirely left her; she was just 61. Her death was, and still is, a tragic loss to myself and family members, including our young grand daughter, Eleanor Rose King. (Rose was also the middle name of Fearn's mother). Sadly, Maureen did not live to see the birth of our grandson, Arthur Philip King in 2010.

But had she not agreed to marry me and to work with me on the magazine, *Vision of Tomorrow* would most emphatically never have existed. And had we not holidayed in Blackpool at her suggestion, and met John Russell Fearn's widow, I would never have become a literary agent.

Artist Ron Turner's career might well have ended in 1984. Fearn's work would very likely never have been reprinted, along with hundreds of books by his contemporaries who became my clients, reprints of whom are still currently ongoing. This gives me considerable satisfaction, and a recent highlight has been the sale of the film rights to one of Syd Bounds' short stories ('The Animators', 1975) to a leading British movie company, Qwerty Films. The film is set to be made in 2011, directed by Ruairi Robinson, with a screenplay by long-time Bounds fan Clive Dawson . . .

Maureen therefore deserves to have her own footnote in British SF history, and so to her, and to all of those 1950's authors, editors and artists (most of whom are also sadly now dead) whose thoughts and works have now influenced several generations and shaped my own childhood dreams—this book is affectionately dedicated.

Fortress of Utopia by Jack Williamson
(Ron Turner). Gryphon, 1991

Chameleon Planet by Fearn and
Harbottle (Ron Turner). Gryphon, 2006

Photo: L to R: Sydney J. Bounds, John
Birchby, Philip Harbottle,
E.C. Tubb, 2002

Fantasy Annual # 1 edited by Harbottle
and Wallace (Ron Turner).
Cosmos Books. 1997.

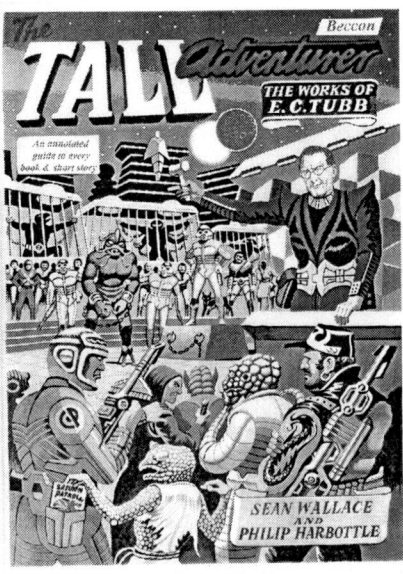

Death God's Doom by E.C. Tubb (Ron Turner). Cosmos, 1999

The Tall Adventurer by Sean Wallace and Philip Harbottle (Ron Turner). Beccon, 1998

Fantasy Adventures # 6 (Ron Turner). Cosmos Books, 2003.

Philip and Maureen Harbottle, wedding day, 27 September 1969

INDEX

A

D

H

S

ABOUT THE AUTHOR

Born there in 1941, and still living in Wallsend, on Tyneside, England, Phil has always been interested in science fiction. As soon as he was able to read, he was devouring the *Daily Mirror*'s full page of comic strips. Captivated by the fantasy and SF adventures of *Garth*, he began clipping and saving the strips—a habit he maintained until he eventually had a complete collection of every single *Garth* daily strip, published over more than five decades.

His interest in science fiction books and researching their history led to his editing a monthly magazine *Vision of Tomorrow* in 1969, the same year in which he was married, and to contributing to many reference books and encyclopaedias, notably *The Visual Encyclopaedia of Science Fiction* (1977).

In the 1980s, he returned to his first love, comic strips, to create the space hero Nick Hazard as a vehicle for noted SF artist Ron Turner. This experience stood him in good stead when, in 1992, he was invited by *Daily Mirror* strips editor John Allard to write the daily serial scripts for *Garth*. The lucrative assignment enabled him to help his only daughter through University.

His two-book sequence, *Vultures of the Void* (1992) and *British Science Fiction Paperbacks and Magazines* (1949-56) (Borgo, 1993) is regarded as the definitive work on post-war British science fiction. He is the heir and administrator of the literary estate of John Russell Fearn, the noted British pulp writer on whose life and work he has written extensively, and posthumously collaborated on new novels and short story collections.

In 1998, following publication of his non-fiction study of the prolific SF writer E. C. Tubb, *The Tall Adventurer* (co-written with Sean Wallace) he took early retirement from his senior administrative job in Local Government, in order to concentrate on his lifelong interest in science fiction.

In recent years he has edited more than a score of science fiction anthologies, notably the *Fantasy Adventures* series. He has published over a dozen novels, mostly hardcover Westerns for Robert Hale, all of which have been reprinted in paperback. His SF novel, *Chameleon Planet* (2006) is a continuation of J. R. Fearn's "Golden Anazon" series. As well as pursuing his own writing, he acts as a literary agent specializing in SF, detective and Westerns, and his clients include many of the most prolific British genre writers.

Now a widower and grandfather, he has no plans to retire any time soon.

Lightning Source UK Ltd.
Milton Keynes UK
UKOW04f2334271114

242264UK00001B/89/P